The 1970s

A Decade of Contemporary British Fiction

Titles in *The Decades Series*

The 1970s: A Decade of Contemporary British Fiction, edited by Nick Hubble, John McLeod and Philip Tew

The 1980s: A Decade of Contemporary British Fiction, edited by Emily Horton, Philip Tew and Leigh Wilson

The 1990s: A Decade of Contemporary British Fiction, edited by Nick Hubble, Philip Tew and Leigh Wilson

The 2000s: A Decade of Contemporary British Fiction, edited by Nick Bentley, Nick Hubble and Leigh Wilson

The 1970s

A Decade of Contemporary British Fiction

Edited by

Nick Hubble, John McLeod and Philip Tew

Bloomsbury Academic
An imprint of Bloomsbury Publishing Plc

B L O O M S B U R Y
LONDON • OXFORD • NEW YORK • NEW DELHI • SYDNEY

Bloomsbury Academic
An imprint of Bloomsbury Publishing Plc

50 Bedford Square
London
WC1B 3DP
UK

1385 Broadway
New York
NY 10018
USA

www.bloomsbury.com

Bloomsbury is a registered trade mark of Bloomsbury Publishing Plc

First published 2014
Reprinted by Bloomsbury Academic 2016
First published in paperback 2017

© Nick Hubble, John McLeod, Philip Tew and Contributors, 2014, 2017

All rights reserved. No part of this publication may be reproduced or transmitted in any form or by any means, electronic or mechanical, including photocopying, recording, or any information storage or retrieval system, without prior permission in writing from the publishers.

No responsibility for loss caused to any individual or organization acting on or refraining from action as a result of the material in this publication can be accepted by Bloomsbury Academic or the editors.

British Library Cataloguing-in-Publication Data
A catalogue record for this book is available from the British Library.

ISBN: HB: 978-1-4411-3391-5
PB: 978-1-3500-0350-7
ePub: 978-1-4411-5671-6
ePDF: 978-1-6235-6385-1

Library of Congress Cataloging-in-Publication Data
A catalog record for this book is available from the Library of Congress.

Series: The Decades Series

Cover design: Eleanor Rose

Typeset by Integra Software Services Pvt. Ltd.

Contents

Series Editors' Preface	vii
Acknowledgements	x
Contributors	xi

Introduction: Britain in the 1970s – Controversies and Cultures
   Nick Hubble, John McLeod and Philip Tew   1

1 Selective Traditions: Refreshing the Literary History of the Seventies
   Mark P. Williams   15

2 The Ordinariness of the Extraordinary Break-Up of Britain
   Nick Hubble   43

3 1970s Feminist Fiction
   Sonya Andermahr   69

4 Black British Culture and Fiction in the 1970s
   John McLeod   93

5 'This Time It's Personal': Reliving and Rewriting History in 1970s Fiction
   Sam Goodman   117

6 Turbulent Times: Conflicts, Ideology and the Experimental British Novel, 1969–1979
   Philip Tew   145

7 Fiction, Representation and the Contemporary British Novel: A Story of the American Reception of British Novels of the 1970s
   Doryjane Birrer   181

8 Melancholy Interest: J. G. Farrell's *Troubles* and the Politics of Perspective
   Tamás Bényei   215

Timeline of Works	242
Timeline of National Events	246
Timeline of International Events	249
Biographies of Writers	251
Index	262

Series Editors' Preface

Nick Hubble, Philip Tew and Leigh Wilson

Contemporary British fiction published from 1970 to the present has expanded into a major area of academic study in the last twenty years and attracts a seemingly ever-increasing global scholarship. However, the very speed of the growth of research in this field has perhaps precluded any really nuanced analysis of its key defining terms and has restricted consideration of its chronological development. This series addresses such issues in an informative and structured manner through a set of extended contributions that combine wide-reaching survey work with in-depth research-led analysis. Naturally, many older British academics assume at least some personal knowledge in charting the field of the contemporary, but increasingly many of these coordinates represent the distant past of pre-birth or childhood not only for students, both undergraduate and postgraduate, but also for younger academics. Given that most people's memories of their first five to ten years are vague and localized, an academic born in the early to mid-1980s will only have real first-hand knowledge of less than half these forty years, while a member of the current generation of undergraduates, born in the mid-1990s, will have no adult experience of the period at all. The rather self-evident nature of this chronological, experiential reality disguises the rather complex challenges it poses to any assessment of the contemporary. Therefore, the aim of these volumes, which include timelines and biographical information on the writers covered, is to provide the contextual framework that is now necessary for the study of the British fiction of these four decades.

Each of the volumes in this Decades Series emerged from a series of workshops hosted by the Brunel Centre for Contemporary Writing (BCCW) located in the School of Arts at Brunel University, London, UK. These events assembled specially invited teams of leading internationally recognized scholars in the field, together with emergent younger figures, in order that they might together examine critically the periodization of contemporary British fiction by dividing it into its four constituent decades: the 1970s symposium was held on 12 March 2010; the 1980s on 7 July 2010; the 1990s on 3 December 2010; and the 2000s on 1 April 2011. During these workshops, draft papers were offered and discussions ensued, with the aim of exchanging ideas and ensuring both continuity and also fruitful interaction (including productive dissonances) between what would become chapters of volumes that would hopefully exceed the sum of their parts.

The division of the series by decade could be charged with being both too obvious and therefore rather too contentious. In the latter camp, no doubt, would be Ferdinand Mount, who in a 2006 article for the *London Review of Books* concerned primarily with the 1950s, 'The Doctrine of Unripe Time', complained 'When did decaditis first strike? When did people begin to think that slicing the past up into periods of ten years was a useful thing to do?' However, he does admit still that such characterization has long been associated with aesthetic production and its relationship to a larger sense of the times. As Frank Kermode so influentially argued in *The Sense of an Ending: Studies in the Theory of Fiction*, published in 1967 just before the period covered by this series began, divisions of time, like novels, are ways of making meaning. And clearly both can also shape our comprehension of an ideological *and* aesthetic period that seem to co-exist, but are perhaps not necessarily coterminous in their dominant inflections. The scholars involved in our symposia discussed the potential arbitrariness of all periodizations, but nevertheless acknowledged the importance of such divisions, their experiential resonances and symbolic possibilities. They analysed the decades in question in terms of not only leading figures, the cultural zeitgeist and socio-historical perspectives, but also in the context of the changing configuration of Britishness within larger, shifting global processes. The volume participants also reconsidered the effects and meaning of headline events and cultural shifts such as the miners' strike of 1984–85, the collapse of communism, Blairism and cool Britannia, 9/11 and 7/7, to name only a very few. Perhaps ironically to prove the point about the possibilities inherent in such an approach, in his *LRB* article Mount concedes that 'For the historian [...] if the 1950s are famous for anything, it is for being dull', adding a comment on the 'shiny barbarism of the new affluence'. Hence, even for Mount, a decade may still possess certain unifying qualities, those shaping and shaped by its overriding cultural mood.

After the symposia had taken place at Brunel, the individuals dispersed and wrote up their papers into full-length chapters (generally 10,000–12,000 words), revised in the light of other papers, the workshop discussions and subsequent further research. These chapters form the core of the book series, which, therefore, may be seen as the result of a collaborative research project bringing together twenty-four academics from Britain, Europe and North America.

Each volume shares a common structure. Following the introduction, the first chapter of each volume addresses the 'Literary History of the Decade' by offering an overview of the key writers, themes, issues and debates, including such factors as emergent literary practices, deaths, prizes, controversies, key developments, movements and best-sellers. The next two chapters are themed around topics that have been specially chosen for each decade, and which also relate to themes of the preceding and succeeding decades, enabling detailed readings of key texts to emerge in full historical and theoretical context. The tone and context having been set in this way, the remaining chapters fill out a complex but comprehensible picture of each decade. A 'Postcolonial Voices' chapter addresses the ongoing legacy of Britain's Empire and the rise of globalization, which is arguably the most significant long-term influence on contemporary British writing. 'Historical Representations' is concerned not just with historical novels but the construction of the past in general, and thus the later volumes will be considering constructions of the earlier decades so that a complex multilayered account of the historicity of the contemporary will emerge over the series. The chapter on 'Experimental Writing' highlights the interaction between the socio-cultural contexts, established in earlier chapters, and aesthetic concerns. The 'International Contexts' chapters allow the chosen international academics allocated them to write about the key international aspects of the British fiction of the particular decade they are focusing on. This might variously concern how the fiction relates to international ideological, aesthetic and other relevant movements and/or how the fiction influenced international fiction and/or international reader reception. Each decade is different, but common threads may emerge.

In the future it is hoped to expand the Decades Series by adding to the first four planned volumes others that extend the period of 'Contemporary British Fiction': both by covering subsequent decades as they complete their course and also by featuring precursory decades, extending the focus of study backwards in time to cover the British fiction of the modern and post-war periods.

Works cited

Kermode, Frank. *The Sense of an Ending: Studies in the Theory of Fiction*. Oxford: Oxford University Press, 1967.
Mount, Ferdinand. 'The Doctrine of Unripe Time.' *London Review of Books* 28 (22). 16 November 2006, 28-30; http://www.lrb.co.uk/v28/n22/ferdinand-mount/the-doctrine-of-unripe-time.np

Acknowledgements

We would like to thank all our contributors for their expertise, patience and generosity when responding to our queries and guidance as this book was gradually taking shape. We have enjoyed excellent support throughout from the editorial team at Bloomsbury, especially David Avital and Mark Richardson, who have been instrumental in bringing this book to fruition.

We gratefully acknowledge the support of the Brunel University Research and Knowledge Transfer Committee for providing the funding which enabled the Brunel Centre for Contemporary Writing to host the 'Contemporary British Fiction Decades Seminar Series' during 2010 and 2011, which has led to the publication of the volumes in this book series. Without the support of the administrative and catering staff at Brunel, these events could not have taken place. We would also like to thank all the academics and postgraduate students who attended and contributed to the discussions at these events.

We would also like to mention the staff at Brunel University Library, the British Library, the National Library of Wales, the University of Leeds Brotherton Library and other research libraries who have provided support to the contributors to this volume.

Contributors

Sonya Andermahr is Reader in English at the University of Northampton, UK. She has written widely on contemporary British and American women's writing. Her publications include *Jeanette Winterson* (2009), *Jeanette Winterson: A Contemporary Critical Guide* (2007) and, with Terry Lovell and Carol Wolkowitz, *A Glossary of Feminist Theory* (2000). Her current research interest lies in female trauma narratives, with a particular focus on narratives of maternal loss in contemporary women's writing. She has recently co-edited (with Silvia Pellicer-Ortín) a volume entitled *Trauma Narratives and Herstory* (2013) and (with Lawrence Phillips) *Angela Carter: New Critical Readings* (2012).

Tamás Bényei is Professor of English Literature at the Department of British Studies, University of Debrecen. His main research fields are post-1945 British fiction, (post)colonial fiction and crime fiction. He is the author of seven books (one of them in English: *Acts of Attention: Figure and Narrative in Postwar British Fiction*) and has published book chapters and journal articles in Hungary, Britain, the USA and other countries on writers like Rudyard Kipling, Anthony Powell, Iris Murdoch, Jorge Luis Borges, Kurt Vonnegut and contemporary British authors like Jeanette Winterson, Graham Swift, Martin Amis, Peter Ackroyd, J. G. Ballard and Angela Carter. He has translated into Hungarian the works of writers including Angela Carter and Anthony Burgess.

Doryjane Birrer is Associate Professor of English at the College of Charleston in South Carolina, where she teaches contemporary British literature and literary and cultural theory. Her research involves the interactions among literature, theory and academic culture, and she has published on McEwan, Byatt, Rushdie and teaching novelists of the 1980s in this context. Her work on hybrid conceptions of humanism and postmodernism post-9/11 appeared in the *Journal of Narrative Theory*. She also presented her more recent thinking on desire, affect and academic utopianism as invited respondent to Fredric Jameson's 2009 Utopian Studies keynote address, 'Marxism and Utopia Today'.

Sam Goodman is Lecturer in Linguistics at Bournemouth University, UK. His research to date has focused mainly on popular fiction of the post-Second World War period and has analysed the representation of anxieties over British identity, space and power in the fiction of Graham Greene, Ian Fleming and John le Carré. He also has interests in both critical theory and medical humanities and is the editor of *Violence & the Limits of Representation* (2013) with Graham Matthews, and of *Medicine, Health & the Arts: Approaches to the Medical Humanities* (2013) with Victoria Bates and Alan Bleakley.

Nick Hubble is Head of English at Brunel University, London, UK. He is the author of *Mass-Observation and Everyday Life: Culture, History, Theory* (2006; second edition 2010) and the co-author of *Ageing, Narrative and Identity* (2013). He is the co-editor of *The Science Fiction Handbook* (2013) and special issues of the journals *EnterText*, *Literary London* and *New Formations*. He has published journal articles or book chapters on writers including Pat Barker, Ford Madox Ford, B. S. Johnson, Naomi Mitchison, George Orwell, Christopher Priest, John Sommerfield and Edward Upward.

John McLeod is Professor of Postcolonial and Diaspora Literatures at the School of English, University of Leeds, UK. His published work includes *Postcolonial London: Rewriting the Metropolis* (2004), *Beginning Postcolonialism*, second edition (2010) and *J. G. Farrell* (2007). He has published over 30 essays on British, postcolonial and diasporic writing, and has co-edited special issues of the journals *Kunapipi* and *Moving Worlds*.

Philip Tew is Professor in English (Post-1900 Literature) and Deputy Head for Research of the School of Arts at Brunel University, a fellow of the Royal Society of Arts, and a member of the Royal Society of Literature. Among his main publications are *B. S. Johnson: A Critical Reading* (2001), *The Contemporary British Novel* (2004; rev. second ed. 2007), *Jim Crace* (2006) and co-edited with Glyn White, *Re-reading B. S. Johnson* (2007). Tew is the founding Director of both the Modern & Contemporary Fiction Studies Network and the B. S. Johnson Society; he is also currently Director of the Brunel Centre for Contemporary Writing. Recent books have included *New Versions of Pastoral* (2009) co-edited with David James; *Zadie Smith* (2010); a multi-authored policy report on ageing, *Coming of Age* (2011); *Ageing, Narrative and Identity* (2013) co-authored with Nick Hubble; *Well Done God! Selected Prose and Drama of B. S. Johnson* (2013) co-edited with Jonathan Coe and Julia Jordan; and the edited collection, *Zadie Smith: The First Decade & Beyond* (2013).

Mark P. Williams has taught literature at Victoria University of Wellington in New Zealand and at the University of East Anglia in the UK. He has also worked as a New Zealand Parliamentary reporter for Scoop Independent Media and as international editor for the Scoop Review of Books (http://books.scoop.co.nz). His primary research interests lie in contemporary literature and politics, specializing in the relationship between science fiction and fantasy and the avant-garde. In 2008 he co-organized 'The New World Entropy: A Conference on Michael Moorcock' and he has been a contributor to various journals, including *The Literary London Journal, The Irish Journal of Gothic and Horror Studies* and *Critical Engagements: Journal of the UK Network for Modern Fiction Studies* (UKNMFS) and *Alluvium: Journal of 21st Century Writing*. Forthcoming publications include chapters in *The 1990s: A Decade of Contemporary Fiction*, in *London in Contemporary British Fiction: The City Beyond the City* and in *China Miéville: Critical Essays*.

Introduction: Britain in the 1970s – Controversies and Cultures

Nick Hubble, John McLeod and Philip Tew

The 1970s in Britain were marked by controversy, a period associated by many with decline in general and industrial unrest in particular. The British Empire was in full retreat. Already by the end of the 1960s, decolonization had arrived in much of sub-Saharan Africa and the Caribbean, on the heels of the South Asian colonies' partition and independence in the late 1940s. Britain's position and image as a major international military and economic unit underwent considerable recalibration, especially after the Suez Crisis of 1956. The 1970s were also a period when the British homeland suffered a series of bombings ranging from those by the Angry Brigade in the early 1970s, IRA attacks including seven deaths in Aldershot in 1972 and 21 in the Birmingham pub bombings in 1974, to the death of Airey Neave in 1979 from a bomb placed by the INLA on his car and which exploded as he left the carpark of the Palace of Westminster. The populist view of the 1970s is still shaped by images of wild-cat strikes and picket-line confrontations, strikers and trades unions challenging legitimate authority. After an almost unprecedented period of nearly full employment from 1945 until the 1960s, unemployment rose to 1 million in the spring of 1975, amounting to 5% of the workforce. Inflation soared. However, despite such headlines, most ordinary families in 1970s Britain were better off than ever, and many Britons finally had the opportunity to buy homes once the Bank of England relaxed its lending rules. Nevertheless, as Andy Beckett writes, it has long been regarded that 'since the Second World War, by common consent for decades now, the worst of times came between the election of Edward Heath in 1970 and the election of Margaret Thatcher in 1979' (1).

As Beckett indicates, there were global problems such as 'world recession and the oil crisis' (2), exacerbated by a divided and conflicted society. However, he problematizes such a simplistic, unvariegated view with a reminder that 'Unemployment in the seventies, taken at that time to be a great symptom of political failure, and notorious as such ever since, was actually low by modern standards, even during the long economic boom of the Blair years' (3). In fact, at the time, Heath's 1970 general election victory over Labour with a majority of 31 seats was regarded as surprising, despite his party polling 13,145,123 votes as opposed to Labour's 12,208,758. That night Harold Wilson found his family staying in Chequers after leaving Downing Street, having made no plans for alternative accommodation. This unexpected transition generated problems. Heath eased controls on bank credit in 1971 (lobbied for by the City of London), which created a short-lived economic boom concentrated mainly on property, which collapsed with the worldwide economic slump and rise in oil prices. In 1972, Heath offered a pay award to the miners after two strikes brought power shortages. In 1973, Britain under his stewardship voted to join the European Community. Heath's focus on changing the law on industrial relations to limit strikes brought further conflict with the trades unions, and joining the European Union created a long-standing schism in his own party, with a sense of betrayal for many. After another miners' strike against his incomes policy, his Conservative government called and lost the snap February 1974 general election, a year that saw 16% retail price inflation. Ironically, the Conservatives' headline slogan was 'Who Governs Britain?' Heath's defeat would reshape the view of a range of Conservative MPs who in 1975 toppled him as party leader. He was succeeded by Margaret Thatcher who as part of the Tory hard right had vilified Heath's supposedly conciliatory politics. After a price inflation of 24.20% in 1975 and 16.5% in 1976, the IMF effectively intervened in the British economy, instituting a form of monetarism under Labour. A sense of crisis prevailed. By 1976, as Kathleen Burk and Alec Cairncross point out in *Goodbye, Great Britain: The 1976 IMF Crisis* (1992), many considered that the economy was out of control, in part because of the balance of payment deficit (xiii). By 1975, the Public Sector Borrowing Requirement (PSBR) was £9 billion, 9% of GDP, and in the view of many, a symptom of Britain's hyperinflation. They ignored the fact, as Burk and Cairncross note, that 'there were large Budget deficits all over the world' (xv), and the role that distrust of government politics by influential figures such as economists played in helping to undermine the economy. By 1978, Labour's Chancellor of the Exchequer, Denis Healey, had imposed tight controls on public spending, including on education and health, leading to a wave of strikes (the so-called winter of discontent), which in turn led to Labour's defeat in the 1979 General Election. Opposed to consensus and resolutely doctrinaire, Thatcher was at the end of the 1970s – according to public opinion polls – the most unpopular prime minster ever (at least since polling began).

As such, in its own terms, without the shadow of the later Thatcher, the 1970s remain difficult to assess. For instance, as Beckett indicates, since 1950, in terms of the Measure of Domestic Progress, the best year was 'rather astonishingly, 1976 – the year of the IMF crisis, of Wilson's undignified resignation, of the disillusioned fury of the Sex Pistols and British punk rock' (4). There was an undoubted growing affluence and set of aspirations among ordinary people that Thatcher was to harness politically and extend, but this was combined with the myth of the previous decade's decline that she propounded through insistent propaganda, which was accepted by many, including whole swathes of the population who did not even support her. As Philip Tew writes in *The Contemporary British Novel* (2007): 'there were conscious attempts to limit union power from the early 1970s even though wage rates were not so high proportionately as those in Europe and there was a decline of workers' earnings and pay rises in the UK economy after the 1976 financial crisis' (44). One underlying trend of the 1970s was the reassertion of capitalist dynamics in the re-emergence of an apparently 'natural' order of middle-class authority and freedom, of which Thatcherism was a part, from what Tew describes as an earlier 'crisis of middle-class identity and privilege' (44).

So, were the domestic political fortunes of Britain in the 1970s intricately entangled with its declining fortunes as a once-colonial power? The 'minimal impact' thesis – that post-war Britain hardly registered decolonization at home, politically and culturally – seems less secure in the seventies, not least because of the political, social and cultural shifts which were becoming discernible by 1979. However, images and attitudes of British greatness and the supremacy of Britannia initially proved far more durable, which resulted in a peculiar tension, indeed lag, between British culture and political realities in the seventies, with the country only very gradually confronting changed conditions which were already impacting directly in social and political life. As Bill Schwarz has mooted, the recirculation of images of Second World War heroism and victory in the post-war decades possibly 'worked to screen other historical realities' (7), specifically the wider public consciousness of British imperial decline. No wonder, perhaps, that in the seventies some of the most popular television series concerned wartime endeavours rather than colonial conflicts. Dominic Sandbrook records that Thames Television's 26-part series *The World at War*, narrated by Laurence Olivier, dominated the television schedules of 1973–1974, while BBC's drama *Colditz* 'concluded in April 1974 with audiences of almost 19 million people' (316). Displaced from public consciousness, screened off by the vainglorious recall of wartime military triumph, full consciousness of Empire's end was anxiously suspended in the decade. This legacy arguably continues into the present: writing in 2004, Paul Gilroy has connected the fraternal nationalism concocted by the popular football supporters' chant 'two world wars and one World Cup', with its dream that 'the nations which triumphed in 1918 and 1945 live on somewhere unseen, but palpable' (119), to a postcolonial melancholia which refuses to admit the ongoing transformative presence of a significant black British community. As regards the persistence of race thinking, the seventies are perhaps closer to today than one might expect.

Indeed, the most visible reality of the impact at home of decolonization abroad by the 1970s was the firm establishment of distinct black British diasporic communities that were coming to be understood at large as permanent rather than temporary, with the coming of age of a distinct group of black Britons: namely, the British-born, who knew little of their parents' birthplaces of Jamaica, Pakistan and Nigeria, for example, but a great deal about the increasingly racist country of their birth where they could expect little sympathy and respect from the police, judiciary and many of their fellow Britons. Such a significant cultural and demographic shift required facing up to by groups and individuals on all sides, but in actuality most British institutions responded with increasing hostility to this new, increasingly youthful constituency of Britons, almost as if in denial of the developing social changes everyone faced. It is worth remembering that the 1970s are bracketed by two subsequently definitional incidents in postwar British history: Enoch Powell's 'Rivers of Blood' speech in Birmingham in April 1968 and the Brixton Riots of April 1981. Between these two dates, at the levels of state and street, Britain increasingly came to regard its growing black communities in terms of criminality, amplifying assumptions that black cultures were a threat to British law and order. Powell's speech, which received support from across the class spectrum in Britain despite it ruining his political ambitions in the Conservative Party, focused insidiously on the increasing numbers of black British children as marking the extent to which white Britons would soon be strangers in their own country. It pivoted on an image of a scared female pensioner besieged at home and followed down the street by 'wide-grinning piccaninnies' who chant 'racialist' at her fearful back. By the seventies, the migrant and British-born children denigrated by Powell were approaching adulthood, only to find themselves living in an environment defined by the kinds of prejudicial thinking that marked Powell's speech, marginalized and criminalized on the grounds of race at the very threshold of their adulthood, with opportunities denied to them. These conditions would shape the increasingly incendiary presence of race in British life, which grew ominously during the seventies.

The violence that broke out at the 1976 Notting Hill Carnival, during which 450 people were injured, evidenced the hostility of the police towards black British youth during the decade as well as the increasing militancy and defiance of black Britons unprepared to accept the unequal conditions under which their parents had laboured since settling in the UK. As that year's Carnival evidenced, a chief perpetrator of racial oppression was Britain's police. Sandbrook comments that in 1972 'there were just 58 black and Asian police officers in England and Wales out of a total of more than 110,000' (578). During the seventies the use of the controversial 'sus' laws, based on the 1824 vagrancy act, became a key mechanism in racial harassment by the police, which served to raise the temperature on Britain's streets, creating, in Salman Rushdie's stark phrase from 1982, a 'New Empire within Britain' which did not arrive overnight: it was indebted to the shifting vocabularies of racism and discrimination which, during the crucial phase of the seventies, targeted black Britons as a new criminal underclass, a racialized enemy within. It involved the coming together of residual colonial-crafted categories of British superiority with a new pernicious mode of racism, legitimated by the words and actions of the state, which enabled racist ways of thinking to function casually as common currency in the seventies, from TV shows such as London Weekend Television's *Mind Your Language* (1977–1979), with its animated opening sequence full of the most excruciating racial and national clichés, to the comments of Home Counties cab drivers. The writer Yasmin Alibhai-Brown, a Ugandan migrant caught up in the expulsion of Uganda's Indian-descended populations in 1972, will never forget arriving at her father's funeral at a Surrey cemetery for Muslims in the early 1970s: 'When I paid the cabbie, he looked at me, took the money and threw it at my face: "Fuck off, Paki, we don't want you here"' (233).

Despite the darkening horizon of race relations in 1970s Britain, it was possible to discern the beginnings of a different envisioning of the country's collectivity, more multicultural than monoracial. While immigration controls were tightened in 1971, restricting the number of new arrivals from the Commonwealth, in 1976 the Race Relations Act legislated against discrimination and established the Commission for Racial Equality. Even if this commitment to challenging discrimination did not often manifest itself in everyday life throughout the country, one area in which anti-racist sentiment could be discerned was in the realm of popular music. Towards the end of the decade, especially, black and white Britons began to blend musical influences from Britain, America and the Caribbean, and form bands which were racially diverse – such as influential ones like The Specials, The Selecter and The Beat, several of which were associated with the 2-Tone record label created by The Specials' Jerry Dammers. Meanwhile, in the late seventies, the Rock Against Racism

(RAR) movement gathered momentum, often conjoined to the activities of a number of left-wing radical groups which, alarmed by the increasing volubility of the National Front, came together under the banner of the Anti-Nazi League (ANL). Andy Beckett argues that, despite such initiatives, 'the seventies did not fundamentally change the political position of non-white Britons' (453). While this is in many ways true, the more forceful challenge to institutionalized racism in the next decade could not have taken the shape it did without the embryonic political and cultural shifts of the seventies, however small they might seem retrospectively.

Another significant consequence, long suspended, of decolonization which exploded in the seventies – with horrific literalness – concerned the matter of Northern Ireland. Created as part of the partitioning of Ireland at the end of the Irish War of Independence in 1921, the British province had suffered a longstanding conflict between its Unionist Protestant majority and Catholic Nationalists who objected to their discriminatory treatment, while postcolonial Ireland's constitutional commitment to uniting Ireland, as well as its withdrawal from the Commonwealth in 1949, meant that relations with the UK were never free from residual colonial-derived tensions. During the 1970s, the vexed fortunes of Northern Ireland moved centre-stage in British politics as violence became the major modus operandi in both governing the province and challenging its place in the Union of the United Kingdom. The paramilitary activities of the Provisional Irish Republican Army (IRA) were matched by those of the Ulster Volunteers Force, while the British Army, which had been deployed in 1969 to restore order, and the Royal Ulster Constabulary (RUC) had very little sympathy with the Nationalists and often preferred assault to diplomacy in maintaining law and order. In January 1972, during a march by the Northern Ireland Civil Rights Association, 26 unarmed protesters were shot by members of the First Battalion of the Parachute Regiment. This grim event, known as 'Bloody Sunday', opened a new chapter in the province's conflicts, in both Northern Ireland and the rest of Britain. In the face of increasing paramilitary activity, successive British governments sought to deal with the situation, but with little effect. The introduction of internment in 1971 did little to defuse an escalating situation, and in the wake of Bloody Sunday the Parliament of Northern Ireland at Stormont was dissolved and replaced by direct rule from Westminster. Plans in 1974 for a power-sharing Executive, which initially had support from the main political forces in Northern Ireland and which included a Council of Ireland where those north and south of the border could deal with key issues, quickly disintegrated when alarmed Unionists, in particular the Ulster Defence

Association (UDA), effectively shut down Belfast through a series of strikes and by erecting barricades. Meanwhile, on the British mainland, in 1973 the IRA began a campaign of terrorist bombing on a scale hitherto never witnessed. In 1974 alone, this resulted in the killing of civilians in pub bombings in Guildford and Birmingham, and off-duty British soldiers in a coach on the M62 motorway (in all three the total dead was 38, with 285 injured). In later years, the mainland campaign would claim the journalist and television presenter Ross McWhirter in 1975 and the Conservative politician Airey Neave in 1979 (killed by the Irish National Liberation Army).

The Irish situation was, at root, a struggle over the future of the Union, even if most mainland Britons seemed indifferent to what was unfolding only a short distance away, despite attempts on both sides of the divide to make the crisis a general rather than provincial one. It would extend into the eighties and claim many more lives. But pressure on the Union also emerged from other sources during the seventies, most notably the so-called Celtic Fringe of Scotland and Wales, so that in hindsight it would seem that the decade prompted the start of what came to be known, after the title of Tom Nairn's influential pro-devolution book of 1977, as the 'break-up of Britain'. The discovery of North Sea Oil fuelled not just the economic dreams of the depleted Treasury's staff, who espied financial Armageddon at every turn in the 1970s, but also those of Scottish Nationalists, whose increasing success in a number of elections suddenly made the issue of Scottish devolution a very pressing one. Welsh devolution was also on the agenda, fuelled in part by the winding-down of heavy industries such as mining which hit the country especially hard, often disproportionately when compared to the rest of the United Kingdom. In 1974 the historian R. R. Davies published an essay titled 'Colonial Wales' which provocatively suggested that 'Wales displays at various stages most of the well-recognised features of a colonial society' (3). Surveying the terrain of the collapsing 'Anglo-British state', as he termed it, Nairn sounded the 'slow-motion landslide' (56) of this pseudo-absolutist imperial structure and proposed that the new Celtic nationalisms were a consequence of Britain's inevitable decline from colonial authority. Britain would not survive for long. Inevitably, the fortunes of central government in Westminster could not be insulated from these competing pressures within a breaking Britain, not least because James Callaghan's fragile Labour government of the late 1970s depended more and more on the support of Scottish Nationalists and Irish Unionists. When Callaghan sought to pursue the matter of devolution for Scotland in 1979, the referendum failed to gain the necessary support north of the border (which was 40% of the entire electorate, not simply of those who had voted). The government consequently lost the parliamentary support of the Scottish National Party, prompting a vote of 'no confidence' that forced a general election in May 1979, won by the Conservative Party leader, Margaret Thatcher.

Ultimately, the political wranglings over devolution which signalled the end of the Labour government in 1979 led not so much to the break-up of Britain, although this process is still ongoing, but to the breakdown of a distinct phase in post-war British politics; ostensibly the post-war consensus of welfare-capitalism with its Keynesian commitment to full employment, a strong state and meaningful partnerships with the trades unions. With Callaghan's government pursuing an increasingly monetarist agenda in the wake of the 1976 IMF crisis, and in the light of the desertion of support for the unions by their traditional devotees who craved security and affluence, tired of autocracy and discontentment, the centre of gravity in British politics at the end of the seventies took a distinct shift to the right. While the alleged break-up of Britain is still to be settled – as Tom Nairn notes in the 2003 edition of his book, the neo-liberal and globalized agendas that were established post-1979 have presented new challenges for anti-Union nationalisms – during the seventies the combination of national decline, economic crisis, civil unrest and cultural anomie often led to an especially apocalyptic rendering of the nation's present and future.

Michael Gardiner has argued that '[t]he late 1970s to early 1980s moment was a deeply troubling one for "British culture", located as it was 'between decolonisation and devolution' (137). Where did this leave England? Bereft of its imperial presence, eschewed by the other members of the United Kingdom and home to a rapidly evolving multicultural citizenry, England in the seventies was compelled, just like the other nations, to pursue an unstoppable process of redefinition, even if the evidence of this was more latent than overt and would be articulated more self-consciously at the century's end. In its literary culture, a new generation of writers shaped a novelistic milieu of moral and political breakdown – one thinks of the concrete wildernesses of Ian McEwan and J. G. Ballard, the emotional savagery of Martin Amis's characters – in which England emerged bereft of its conventional compass points, subject to the increasing deculturing influence of Americana and hollowed within by the disenchantment with the one-time certainties of moral order or economic affluence. If the Britain of the fifties had 'never had it so good', the England of the seventies appeared simply to have 'had it', with terminal demise seeming the only option.

Yet the approaching disintegration that many saw or simply accepted was apocalyptic in the creative sense, in that the end of one order heralded the start of the new. Angela Carter's fantastical *The Passion of New Eve* (1977) ends with its transgendered hero/ine Eve/lyn poised between the ruins of the old patriarchal order and ready to set sail for a fertile post-gendered future; indeed, it is worth noting that the political and cultural gains made by the Women's Movement in the 1970s suggest something of the opportunities presented by a patrician nation-state perceived in decline. In retrospect, we might re-read the 1970s as presenting the inevitability and irreversibility of a vital (and still-unfinished) process of national and cultural redefinition that shuddered violently into being. The results, both recalcitrant and revisionary as the proceeding essays in this book testify, made for a decade which – in literary terms at least, but in other cultural forms too – is much more exciting, varied and unsettled than prevailing clichés of the period often suggest.

Mark P. Williams's introductory chapter to this volume approaches the diverse literary history of the decade by examining the four above-mentioned writers, Amis, Ballard, Carter and McEwan, who are all now considered canonical to the contemporary period from 1970 onwards, in relation to a range of their contemporaries including B. S. Johnson, Richard Allen, Ramsey Campbell, M. John Harrison and Michael Moorcock. By surveying the various interactions in the seventies between literary fiction, pulp fiction, SF, fantasy and horror traditions and experimental work, Williams reveals a network of cultural production that transcends both canon and genre to demonstrate the ongoing valencies of the decade. In this, he draws on Raymond Williams's concept of selective tradition, a process by which the communication and comparison between past, common and new meanings generates cultural and societal change. The implication is that, even in the second decade of the twenty-first century, we are still living with various competing possibilities that first emerged in the 1970s and have not yet been resolved fully.

As discussed above, one such set of possibilities is represented by the idea of the potential 'break-up of Britain', as identified by Nairn in 1977. In the second chapter below, Nick Hubble extends Nairn's thesis that the collapse of the post-war consensus was becoming manifested in territorial disintegration by arguing that the break-up was also psychological. Drawing on the question asked by the narrator of Doris Lessing's quietly apocalyptic *The Memoirs of a Survivor* (1974), 'Could one perhaps describe that period as "the ordinariness of the extraordinary?"' (19), Hubble locates this psychological fragmentation at the level of everyday life and considers it as the manifestation of a series of existential and ontological choices thrown up by the prospect of the collapse of the British state, which could be sensed at many levels during the decade. He represents this through close contextual readings of novels by Lessing, William McIlvanney, Jennifer Johnston, Christopher Priest, and especially Raymond Williams. Aside from representing a Welsh perspective, comparable to its Irish and Scottish counterparts as represented by McIlvanney and Johnston, Williams's fiction can be directly related to his extensive body of social and cultural criticism and thus provides a very clear insight into the 'structure of feeling' that animated the decade. In returning to Raymond Williams, the most important critic and theorist of the period, the chapters of Hubble and Mark P. Williams complicate the canonical accounts that have started to form around the 1970s and reveal that its concerns, far from being confined to the past, may very well represent our future.

A similar possibility is raised by Sonya Andermahr in her chapter '1970s Feminist Fiction', which she argues was more materialist and class-oriented than US feminism, and more pragmatic than French feminism. She shows how the Women's Liberation Movement fed directly into women's writing through consciousness-raising groups, writing workshops, conferences, reading groups, magazines and publishing houses; and so led to a generational shift in which the work of older feminists such as Lessing, whose *The Golden Notebook* (1962) had been hugely influential on a generation, was developed by women writers, such as Carter and Fay Weldon, who were no longer isolated, exceptional figures, but part of a politically organized sisterhood. In particular, a large group of women writers emerged, including Emma Tennant, Sara Maitland, Zoë Fairbairns and Michelene Wandor, through working collaboratively in collectives, and went on to pave the way for the next generation of women writers in the 1980s which included Jeanette Winterson and Pat Barker. Andermahr further illustrates the range and scope of feminist literary production across the decade by including detailed case studies of Eva Figes's *Days* (1974), Michèle Roberts's *A Piece of the Night* (1978), and Zoë Fairbairns's *Benefits* (1979).

John McLeod, in his chapter 'Black British Culture and Fiction in the 1970s', also addresses the publication of women's visions of 1970s Britain, making a point of contrasting this output with the predominantly male-oriented work of previous decades. However, he also shows it to be a much busier decade in terms of its postcolonial and diasporic literary output than is often admitted. For McLeod, the 1970s was when Sam Selvon completed the second part of his important Moses Trilogy with the publication of *Moses Ascending* (1975), E. R. Braithwaite published his probing memoir of black British life *Reluctant Neighbours* (1972), Shiva Naipaul offered a cool survey of migrant Britain's unfolding in his essays and journalism (such as 'Living in Earls Court', 1973), Buchi Emecheta articulated working-class urban life for black women in *In the*

Ditch (1972) and *Second-Class Citizen* (1974), and Beryl Gilroy's ground-breaking book *Black Teacher* (1976) appeared. By calling particular attention both to the frequent turn to documentary modes of writing and to the emergence of black women's writing, McLeod challenges any sense of the 1970s as a minor decade or allegedly less interesting period when measured against other post-war decades, and considers how the important cultural work of the time emerged from and responded to the complex social milieu of the decade.

As Sam Goodman demonstrates in his chapter on the production of historical representations in the 1970s, '"This Time It's Personal": Reliving and Rewriting History in 1970s Fiction', whilst the slow disintegration of the British Empire, which had become unavoidably apparent by the beginning of the decade, and the diminution of the glories of the Second World War lent themselves to a preoccupation with structure and status, the underlying issue was one of struggle and difference in British identity. He examines the circumstance of Britain in the 1970s and argues that the division inherent in identity is not only a crucial concern, but an acutely historical one. Having never wholly recovered from the War, the nation had never forgotten it either, so that it had become enshrined in the collective social memory of Britain, casting a shadow over much of public and social life. Analysing a selection of fiction by authors such as Martin Amis, David Lodge, Malcolm Bradbury and Frederick Forsyth, Goodman illustrates how the literature of the 1970s indicates a split in the contemporary historical consciousness of the nation revolving around the continual search for a secure identity. In this context, he argues that the Second World War retained its relevance even as it was endlessly rewritten.

Philip Tew relates this historical identity crisis, alongside other 1970s insecurities, as one of the motives for the pursuit of an authentic sense of being that motivated the more existentially inspired experimental British writing of the decade. Tew argues that the tone of the decade's experimental writing was set by the publication of John Fowles's *The French Lieutenant's Woman* in 1969, which made explicit its formal challenges to tradition and utilized its neo-Victorian narrative to examine contemporary ideas of feminism, sexuality and the contingency of fate. In a series of readings of works by Ballard, Lessing, Priest, Christine Brooke-Rose, B. S. Johnson, Rayner Heppenstall, John Berger, Alan Burns, Ann Quin and Paul Abelmann, Tew demonstrates how the experimental search for inner truth across the decade also represented a determined move towards the politicization of traditional aesthetics.

Doryjane Birrer's chapter on the American reception of the British fiction of the decade provides an interesting contrast to Tew's account by highlighting the sense to which American critics, and British critics writing for American audiences, reading more traditional novels, such as Margaret Drabble's *The Ice Age* (1977), identified the failures of English – and it was the English they focused on – writers to respond fully to an English crisis of national identity. However, over the course of the decade, the shift to anti-realist approaches in British writing became more apparent to American critics and reanimated literary debate.

Finally, in the last chapter, Tamás Bényei examines the work of J. G. Farrell from a continental European perspective. Arguing that Farrell's Empire trilogy (*Troubles, The Siege of Krishnapur, The Singapore Grip*) brought about a manifold shift in the mode of historical fiction, Bényei demonstrates how this shift was also self-reflexive in that it first examines the possible relationship between modernism and historical experience, thereby also taking stock of the possible modes of transmuting historical experience into aesthetic forms, and, in a broader sense, politics into aesthetics. Second, by surveying and interrogating the politics that are inscribed in various kinds of aesthetics, it performs an essentially postmodernist self-reflexive turn in historical fiction, a turn that is one of the most important gestures towards a genuinely postmodernist historical fiction, one that is acutely aware of the political stakes in transforming any kind of (historical) experience into meaningful narrative and imagistic units. In particular, Bényei reads *Troubles* (1970) as a taking stock and critique of the possibilities and dead-ends of modernist renderings of history and historical experience; a set of concerns that remain central to British writers in the second decade of the twenty-first century, such as Will Self and Zadie Smith.

Overall, therefore, *The 1970s: A Decade of Contemporary British Fiction* seeks to enhance our understanding of the decade by revealing it to have been marked by the opening-up, within a relatively insular post-war British culture and society, of a wide range of contested possibilities, which continue to frame British experience to this day. While the book addresses the writers that have become regarded as central to the period, such as Martin Amis, J. G. Ballard, Angela Carter and Ian McEwan, it also highlights the contribution of others such as Buchi Emecheta, J. G. Farrell, Doris Lessing, Christopher Priest and Raymond Williams, to name only a few of those addressed, without necessarily seeking to establish any form of expanded or alternative canon. Rather, our intention as editors and contributors is to reanimate the literary and cultural debates of the decade itself, and so, like the writers of the 1970s, politicize aesthetics and thus reinvigorate a sense of possibility and cultural agency.

Works cited

Alibhai-Brown, Yasmin. *The Settler's Cookbook: A Memoir of Love, Migration and Food.* London: Portobello, 2009.

Beckett, Andy. *When the Lights Went Out: What Really Happened to Britain in the Seventies.* London: Faber, 2009.

Browning, Richard. 'Historic Inflation Calculator: how the value of money has changed since 1900.' This is Money.co.uk website. Undated. http://www.thisismoney.co.uk/money/bills/article-1633409/Historic-inflation-calculator-value-money-changed-1900.html

Burk, Kathleen and Alec Cairncross. *Goodbye, Great Britain: The 1976 IMF Crisis.* New Haven and London: Yale UP, 1992.

Carter, Angela. *The Passion of New Eve.* London: Victor Gollancz, 1977.

Davies, R. R. 'Colonial Wales'. *Past and Present.* 65, 1974: 3–23.

Gardiner, Michael. *The Return of England in English Literature.* Basingstoke: Palgrave Macmillan, 2012.

Gilroy, Paul. *After Empire: Melancholia or Convivial Culture?* Abingdon: Routledge, 2004.

Kimber, Richard. *UK General Elections Since 1832.* Political Science Resources Webpage. Last Modified: 27 Nov.2012. http://www.politicsresources.net/area/uk/edates.htm. N.Pag.

Nairn, Tom. *The Break-Up of Britain: Crisis and Neo-Nationalism.* Third edition. Victoria: Common Ground, 2003.

Rushdie, Salman. 'The New Empire Within Britain', in *Imaginary Homelands: Essays and Criticism 1981–1991.* London: Granta, 1991. 129–138.

Sandbrook, Dominic. *Seasons in the Sun: The Battle for Britain, 1974–1979.* London: Allen Lane, 2012.

Schwarz, Bill. 'Introduction: End of Empire and the English Novel', in *End of Empire and the English Novel Since 1945.* Ed by Rachel Gilmour and Bill Schwarz. Manchester: Manchester University Press, 2011. 1–37.

Tew, Philip. *The Contemporary British Novel.* Second Edition. London: Continuum, 2007.

1

Selective Traditions: Refreshing the Literary History of the Seventies

Mark P. Williams

Constructing the 1970s as a literary decade

This chapter will focus upon a selection of writers, both major and minor, comparing multiple genres and fictional modes – realist, experimental, science fiction, fantasy and horror – and discuss how they relate to one another and where they have since been situated in respect to the 1970s. In it, I will consider common themes that recur across various literary modes and argue for the importance of interaction across traditions in ways that will foreshadow the networks of cultural exchange discussed by other contributors to this anthology and its companion volumes on the 1980s and 1990s. Throughout, I will ask three linked questions: what were the major concerns of writers of the period; how did they interpret the cultural present of the seventies in terms of its relationship with the sixties and earlier decades; and, through a consideration of responses to these first two questions ask a third, what do the 1970s mean to us now?

The thrust of this chapter draws on Raymond Williams's concept of selective tradition which is articulated in *The Long Revolution* (1961), where Williams explains his conception of tradition in terms of communication as a central part of social action:

> Since our way of seeing things is literally our way of living, the process of communication is in fact the process of community: the sharing of common meanings, and thence common activities and purposes; the offering, reception and comparison of new meanings, leading to the tensions and achievements of growth and change. (38–39)

Tradition is not just the communication of the past to the present, but it is also the intervention of present communities in the enunciation of historical tradition; writers have diverse conscious and non-conscious influences, and may choose to seek out lesser-known forms, creating new lineages which come to be understood as traditions only after their enunciation of a connection. Williams's idea implies the presence of active choice by historical subjects making their own traditions from the plenitude of possibilities offered by history. 'Selective tradition', like Harold Bloom's anxiety of influence, is an attempt to explicate the complex relationship of present aesthetic forms to past ones in terms of representing historical subjects with agency. Such subjects can act within communities where people share common meanings and in the light of these individuals interpret personal meanings. This approach conveys a sense of the literatures of the present emerging from those of the past by the forces of historical, literary and artistic production pressing on the consciousness of individuals and communities in the present; but also of historical traditions as contingent upon present communities continuing to select them and regard them as important. In this sense, in traditions, the present comes before the past and *re-founds* the significance of historical traditions towards the future. Selective tradition is radically democratic, Williams explains, because it enunciates the intersections of individual and community interests and engagements with history, and this corresponds to the lived experience of culture:

> We need to distinguish three levels of culture, even in its most general definition. There is the lived culture of a particular time and place, only fully accessible to those living in that time and place. There is the recorded culture, of every kind, from art to the most everyday facts: the culture of a period. There is also, as the factor connecting lived culture and period cultures, the culture of the selective tradition. (49)

Selective tradition is the conception of contemporaneity from within: each historical period processually re-founds and recreates its own past to determine the meanings of its 'present'. Accordingly, all historical subjects are constantly selecting and re-selecting tradition, even academics and scholars. It is necessary to remember that 'institutions which are formally concerned with keeping the tradition alive (in particular the institutions of education and scholarship) are committed to the tradition as a whole' (52), not to any particular expression, and should therefore be treated cautiously as resources rather than regulators: it is always the present that makes the tradition and retrospectively determines the meaning of the past, not the past which determines the meaning of the future. From this perspective there remains a radical possibility for the development of demotic selective traditions, and for a deeper understanding of the literary production of the decade by examining it as a succession of interventions by present individuals and communities on the plane of the historical. As an important aspect of my forging a selective tradition of 1970s as a period in literary history, then, this chapter will implicitly interrogate periodicity by refashioning the ways in which the seventies can be regarded.

Contemporary scholarship already presents us with versions of the seventies in terms of selective tradition, and some useful work has appeared which seeks to debunk its predominant myths. Bart Moore-Gilbert's *The Arts in the 1970s* (1994) strongly resists the notion that the seventies was a period of cultural closure, less dynamic than the now-mythic 1960s. Laurel Forster and Sue Harper's edited collection *British Culture and Society in the 1970s: The Lost Decade* (2010) suggests that the seventies is ripe for rediscovery through its contributors' focus on the radical cultural energies of the decade – such as Gillian Whiteley's interesting and illuminating discussion of the Welfare State International, 'a nomadic collective of artists, musicians, poets, performers and engineers' (35) and their relationship with Burnley in Lancashire and the Mid Pennine Association for the Arts (MPA); Rochelle Simmons's discussion of John Berger's radical aesthetic which explains Berger's Booker-winning experimental novel *G.* (1972) in terms of a 'revolutionary Marxist modernist aesthetic, at a time when Britain was dominated by a Marxist realist tradition' (16); and, in particular, Laurel Forster's article 'Printing Liberation: The Women's Movement and Magazines in the 1970s'. Recent popular fictional reassessments of the 1970s range from the science fiction-inflected television series *Life on Mars* (2006–2007) to the modernist crime histories of David Peace's *Red Riding Quartet* (1999–2002). The rich potential for stories relevant to our present moment found by the creators of these works contributes to our activity of redrawing the literary history of the 1970s. Such scholarly, televisual and literary endeavours, along with Andy Beckett's recent historical retrospective *When the Lights Went Out: What Really Happened to Britain in the Seventies* (2009), have made important inroads into the oft-neglected nuances of the seventies and suggest compelling reasons also for rewriting the literary history of that diverse and intriguing decade. This latter task is one of the modest aims of this essay. Therefore, the present chapter contends with the co-ordinates of preceding selective traditions from the 1970s by offering a renewed survey of the variety of literary forms produced, disseminated and consumed during the period in terms of their contemporaneity.

The idea of a literature of the seventies takes us into a realm of radical uncertainty. Previous surveys of the literature of the post-war era have cast the seventies as something of a spectral period. To illuminate the reasons why the 1970s might require reconstruction, consider first Randall Stevenson's *A Reader's Guide to the Twentieth-Century Novel in Britain* (1993). Stevenson's chapter concerning the 1970s is entitled 'Crossroads: The Sixties to the Eighties'. The title, a reference to David Lodge's essay 'The Novelist at the Crossroads' (1971), makes the seventies into a liminal decade, a boundary establishing the distance between the sixties and the eighties as periods of primary significance. As a title, 'Crossroads: The Sixties to the Eighties' is emblematic of all attempts to write literary history: periodicity requires the drawing up of boundaries and distinctions, and the abstraction of moments. It suggests that both the sixties and the eighties can be said to define *eras* which distinguish them from other decades, while, consequently, the seventies can be subsumed as either 'the long sixties', which would incorporate 1970–1976 and the shift from concerns about anarchic activist liberation politics to ones about labour union politics; or as part of 'the long eighties' that circumscribes 1975–1979 and the emergence of Margaret Thatcher and the impact of her politics. Stevenson's chapter tends towards the former. He uses the novels of the early part of the 1970s as reflections upon the end of the sixties, describing Fay Weldon's *Down Among the Women* (1971) as 'reflecting a new firmness and determination in women's attitudes by the end of the 1960s' (83) which can be discerned in later texts. Although the distinctiveness of Weldon's text is evoked, its place in time, and its context within a specific tradition, such as the evolution of feminism in the 1970s, is shifted away. The 1970s is evoked as a chaotic zone, one which acts primarily as guarantor of the particularity of the 1960s and the 1980s as coherent wholes which carry specific cultural freight.

The recurring features which Stevenson claims for the seventies are recapitulation and revelation. He locates 1970s texts in relation either to their recapitulation of modernism or to their attempt to write a narrative of ending for the 1960s; we might say that Stevenson reads the seventies as having only historical and future characteristics but no contemporaneity. He selects B. S. Johnson's *House Mother Normal* (1971) and *Christie Malry's Own Double-Entry* (1973), and John Berger's Booker-winning novel *G.*, as exemplary reviews and reassessments of the heritage of modernism and the 1960s' politics of liberation. In so doing, his view of the seventies is inflected by critical debates voiced during the decade itself. Malcolm Bradbury wrote in *Possibilities: Essays on the State of the Novel* (1973) that 'the historicist is these days in all of us; one of the most familiar and fashionable accounts of life now is that history issues formal imperatives, closing man in a world of contradictions with limited options or demanding from him a particular type or act of belief' (26). Writing about the later sixties in general, he observed that the times can be characterized by an impression that it is 'all-important for an artist to be technically up-to-date' in order that their work can engage fully with the artistic and political ideas of their specific time and place (258). He proposed that '[B. S.] Johnson's hole in the page or his novel in a box to be shuffled' had a clear ethical dimension, as they 'are aimed at the reinforcement of truth' (179). Technical proficiency in fiction-making adds to the liberating potential of those fictions under the ideological regime of modernity for Bradbury; hence, although he was a writer of comic realism during the decade, in his 1970s criticism he agitated in favour of an experimental fiction indebted to modernism.

In his survey *Contemporary Novelists: British Fiction Since 1970* (2005), Peter Childs observes of Bradbury's landmark anthology *The Novel Today* (1977) that when it was reissued in 1990, Bradbury made relatively few revisions. These were mostly confined to the introduction: where the 1977 introduction is lengthy, concerned with 'form and experiment, with the ways in which the modern novel has refracted as well as constructed contemporary reality', speculating on the nature of the crisis in the novel, the later version is 'half the length of the earlier prefatory chapter, as though there were only half as much to say' (15). Childs questions Bradbury's apparent decision to avoid periodizing the novel since the 1970s (most of the contributions remain the same as the 1977 version) and suggests that perhaps for Bradbury the idea of 'the novel' appeared to be in danger of being devalued by changes in the commercial status of literature in what David Lodge terms an 'aesthetic supermarket' of increasingly commodified forms (qtd. in Childs 17).

Among the commentators Bradbury chose to retain as representative of critical thought on the novel between the 1977 version and the 1990 reissue are Michel Butor's essay 'The Novel as Research' (1968–1970) and B. S. Johnson's 'Introduction to *Aren't You Rather Young to be Writing Your Memoirs?*' (1973). Both essays adopt a modernist stance, warning against the maintenance of already defunct modes in the face of cultural change and urging literary innovation. Butor's essay takes a wide scope and a large scale, addressing itself to the question of narrative in general in its social forms, arguing that 'the best possible place to study how reality appears to us, or might appear' is the space of the novel and the 'laboratory of narrative' (in Bradbury *Novel Today* 46–47). He calls for an understanding of the principles of novelistic fiction based on the grounds, familiar from Shklovsky, that forms and style are intimately linked to perception of the life-world and that 'new forms will reveal new things in reality, new connections'; the 'search for new novelistic forms with a greater power of integration thus plays a triple role in relation to our consciousness of reality: unmasking, exploration, and adaptation' so that formal invention is not in opposition to realism but constitutes a path towards 'a greater realism' (47–48). His conclusion is that the concept of the novel as such must ultimately be transformed, 'within a transformation of the very notion of literature', in order to comprehend its 'essential role within the workings of society […] as a systematic experiment' (50). Johnson's essay is more overtly pessimistic in tone at times about the status of the novel and written fiction in general. Beginning with a discussion of Joyce's opening of the first cinema in Dublin in 1909, he writes of 'the old territory of the novelist increasingly taken over by other media' (in Bradbury *Novel Today* 166). His thesis is stark and confrontational: 'The novelist cannot legitimately or successfully embody present-day reality in exhausted forms'; the solution is 'inventing, borrowing, stealing or cobbling from other media'; forms which can convey a sense of 'an ever-changing reality, their own reality and not Dickens's reality or Hardy's reality or even James Joyce's reality' (170). Interestingly, Johnson's essay is also a militant expression of the attempt to control and manipulate readers' perception from the level of the sentence to the technical functions of the book as object: 'to the extent that a reader can impose his own imagination on my words, then that piece of writing is a failure [….] If he wants to impose his imagination, let him write his own books' (181).

These utterances contained a sense of urgency and impending crisis which demanded that the present generation of writers and readers find ways of developing a new set of techniques in response to a changing world, that is, to contemporaneity. In turning now to some of the key novels and novelists of the seventies, we may indeed discover a range of new literary techniques which engaged the experimental legacies of modernism but also drew upon a range of emergent popular cultural forms – science fiction and spy novels, horror and the grotesque, fantasy and pulp – in order to capture the new realities of the decade and the social and cultural issues which preoccupied it. The impact of such forms, and the indebtedness of 1970s literary writing to 'popular' forms of fiction-making, have yet to be properly considered. In constellating texts across a range of generic fictional forms, conventionally high and popular, a more complex and dense vision of the decade emerges – one in which the literary legacies of modernism and the alleged liberatory cultural politics of the 1960s are by no means uniformly welcomed.

Ending the sixties

The early 1970s was marked by the conclusion of an epic series of texts defining the post-war period from an upper-class bohemian perspective: Anthony Powell's 12-volume sequence *A Dance to the Music of Time* (1951–1975). In his critical survey of the novels of the 1970s, Allan Massie identifies this sequence as a significant literary watershed. He writes that 'Powell's achievement, unmatched by any contemporary, and indeed unique in the English novel since Henry James, was to render social reality convincing, in a rich expressive prose' through the use of 'factual detail, the accumulation of which makes every page ring true to life, scenes of social, army and business life all being presented with fidelity to common experience' while also imbuing it with 'the golden light of timeless myth' (10). The sequence, then, represents the high point in the novel as the literature of the time for Massie, one with a clear set of aesthetic values and firm expectations about how it should function: it should be realist in its attention to detail and reality, but committed to elevating the mundane by investing it with a mythic quality; simultaneously it should be concerned with 'the human condition' while demonstrating an awareness of the limitations of any art form in expressing universal qualities. Yet the emerging writing of the seventies pointed in a contrary direction, away from the confirmation of values and towards their critique; questioning 'common experience' by exploring gendered identities and multiple worlds; presenting the human condition with the threat of apocalypse and a sense of an ending.

A number of writers came to prominence in the seventies with narratives reviewing the values and ideas of the previous decade and constructing narratives with a profound sense of the end of the sixties in their hearts. Martin Amis's first three novels – *The Rachel Papers* (1973), *Dead Babies* (1975) and *Success* (1978) – were all provocative comic texts which acted as commentaries on the end of the 1960s as an era representing specific cultural values. Michael Moorcock had, by this time, been satirizing the sixties counter-culture from within, and with both fondness and vitriol, since around 1965 with the creation of Jerry Cornelius, while Angela Carter's early novels – *Shadow Dance* (1966), *The Magic Toyshop* (1967) and *Several Perceptions* (1968) – which Marc O'Day calls her 'Bristol Trilogy' (24–59), took a deliberately skewed approach to suburban bohemia, showing up the exploitations still present, sometimes viciously, in its overtly liberal milieu. Campus fictions such as Malcolm Bradbury's *The History Man* (1975) and David Lodge's *Changing Places* (1975) lampooned the higher educated end of bohemia's interaction with central culture through characters such as Bradbury's radical sociologist and swinger Howard Kirk. Amis's fictions therefore emerged into a general reassessment of the 1960s which characterized much-early seventies, literary writing.

The Rachel Papers won the Somerset Maugham prize for best first novel by an author under 35. In this novel and in its successors *Dead Babies* and *Success*, Amis explored the vexed territories of male neuroses, decadence and sexual obsession in the sixties' wake. Nick Rennison summarizes these texts effectively as 'dark morality tales in which Amis never allows readers the comfort of knowing for certain where the moral centre lies' (8). Amis creates a host of male characters whose exploitations and manipulation of those around them make them predominantly unsympathetic and occasionally odious; they constitute caricatured attacks on specific values. He adds to this effect by emphasizing their degree of cultural privilege and making them comically unpleasant physically: Charles Highway in *The Rachel Papers* makes a point of allowing his teeth to turn yellow while his toenails rot and even fall off. Studying to get into Oxford to read English, he uses literature with strained knowingness to impress Rachel, with varying success. In *Dead Babies* we meet Keith Whitehead, described as 'an almost preposterously unattractive young man [,] practically, for instance, a dwarf', whose hair is a 'sparse straw mat atop a squashed and petulant mask of acne'; his body consists of a 'dour, bulgy little torso and repulsively truncated limbs' leaving a 'numb, cadaverous texture of the whole' (16). Whitehead's feet are also grotesquely afflicted, similar to those of Charles Highway. Meanwhile, the symbolically named Andy Adorno – the product of social workers and care homes – is obnoxious, misogynistic and abusive towards women, and a violent bully towards those men he perceives as weaker. His cynicism towards the sixties' counter-culture is thinly veiled. In a chapter headed 'Wars and Shit' Andy argues that '[i]t's only for a few years that we ever thought [man] might not be [violent] and he was still having fuckin wars and shit, Vietnam and that', explaining that violence constitutes 'felt selfhood, realized livingness'(179). Amis uses the allusion to the intellectual left to ventriloquize justifications for violence more typically found in pulp novels of a reactionary bent and as a critical commentary on the end of the sixties and the values of liberationary politics. Unlike the work of certain of his contemporaries, such passages leave the impression that Amis's apocalyptic construction of the 1960s was from a standpoint that was already implicitly distanced.

In Angela Carter's *Love* (1971) the violent relationship between Annabel and the brothers Lee and Buzz in the novel is also deliberately stylized in its description and uses some of the same points of literary reference as Amis, such as Jonathan Swift. But where Amis encourages distance, Carter's writing suggests an intimacy with her characters and their social settings in her dystopian envisioning of post-sixties liberalism:

> Buzz padded after Lee into the adjoining kitchen and, grasping him from behind, pressed his fingertips against the base of Lee's throat until Lee went limp.
> 'I don't like her', said Buzz and released him.
> When Lee could speak, he said: 'Try that unarmed combat stuff on me again and I'll smash you against the fucking wall'.
> 'Bad...' said Buzz effortfully... 'vibes...'
> Lee shrugged and broke eggs into a pan of hot fat.
> 'But I don't like her!' wailed Buzz childishly. He wound the cloak round himself to hide. 'And you're knocking her off, aren't you; you're screwing her all night'.
> Lee menaced him briefly with the breadknife and he fell back, whimpering, for knives, his favourite weapon, impressed him horribly when turned against him. He crouched on the floor like a dog to eat his food in the tent of the black cape and Annabel still sat where they had left her, in the dark. (5)

Buzz pads like a dog and, for all his attempts to be sophisticated and soldier-like, threatening his brother with 'unarmed combat' skills, falls more easily into animalistic patterns of aggression and territoriality. He endlessly photographs Annabel and Lee in bed together and forms a collection of the photographs. These are literally fetishistic in both sexual and anthropological senses: the camera becomes a tool for creating a fantastic world which reflects the world symbolically rather than mimetically to Buzz. Annabel, Lee and Buzz all perform what they each think it is to be adult and normal, manipulating one another and those around them with their behaviour, but none of them seems to move beyond this meticulous secondary world of their own desires.

Carter partially normalizes outlandish behaviour in *Love* by focalizing the narrative through Annabel in a way Amis does not in either *The Rachel Papers* or *Dead Babies* which each maintain their ironic distance even in their scatological, Swiftian representation of bodily dysfunction and sex. Carter clearly has as much sympathy with the troubled masculinities of Buzz and Lee as she does with the scarred femininity of Annabel, who returns needily to the brothers even when brutalized. Contrastingly, Amis's writing uses stylization to create separation from the activities of his central characters and the cultural pretensions that they entertain. This is clearest towards the conclusion of *The Rachel Papers* where Charles Highway finds his Oxford entrance exam interview completely unlike his expectations of it: his examiner asks if he even *likes* literature, prompting the reader to consider the comparison between Highway's treatment of the literature he purports to love and his use of literature to woo Rachel. The novel makes the actual events secondary to a preoccupation with style.

Style in *The Rachel Papers* takes the form of an excess of machismo (which has marked the reception of these novels as well as the characters). Each central figure seems to vary between seeming Rabelaisian to their own eyes and appearing simply crass in the eyes of other characters, and the reader's. Most of the male characters are emotionally limited and view women at a distance in terms of trite sexual or maternal roles. Amis offers a vision of seventies' manhood, left crippled and lost by the shifts of the 1960s and helpless in the face of continuing change. All three of his early novels are characterized by men masking personal inadequacy in aggressive hyper-masculine rhetoric, making women, consciously in some instances, into their Other, the repository of negative association, while simultaneously using male–female relationships as emotional crutches. The texts' dialogue is often indicative of this and of the critical presentation of an embattled, aggressive masculinity, as in this moment from *Dead Babies*:

> 'Quentin and Andy say Lucy's really something. She's really... quite a nympho'.
> [...]
>
> 'Bob Henderson and all that lot have fucked her', said Giles. 'Yes, I suppose she does fuck quite a lot of people. Cy Harling and all that lot have fucked her'.
>
> Whitehead, who had hardly fucked anyone, hadn't fucked her, and it was his dream to do so this very weekend. (21)

Amis clearly felt that little had changed in certain important respects regarding men's behaviour and attitudes between 1975 and 1978; in an early passage from *Success* (1978) where Gregory Riding is discussing his girlfriend, the dialogue reprises and parodies the exchange from the earlier novel: 'Everyone at Kane's has fucked her. Everyone at Torka's has fucked her. Everyone everywhere has fucked her. Everywhere we go people have fucked her' (9). The sixties counter-culture may seem to have set long-established gender roles and relations on the move, but Amis's early work shows a series of recalcitrant males seeking to maintain their authority through bleak displays of crass, priapic chauvinism, keen to embrace the hedonistic sexual liberalism of the 1960s but *not* its politics of sexual liberation.

It is easy to see why Amis's seventies writing is sometimes described in terms of its adolescence: but in fact Amis is suggesting that adolescence is the general and defining characteristic of the young British male in the 1970s. In so doing,

Amis seems to partly concur with Angela Carter, but because of his novels' focalization they do not capture quite the same sense of the interrelationships of class and gender as does Carter's. Peter Childs has suggested that Amis is 'a writer who contrives a plot in which the reader is not expected to sympathise with the character but to appreciate the aims of the author' (36), a judgement which makes Amis's fictions similar in intentionality to those of B. S. Johnson. This characteristic, perhaps unknowingly and unwillingly, places Amis's novels in a similar position with respect to the upper-middle-class milieu to that demonstrated in the narratorial outlook of popular pulp novelists of the period towards the working-class world: a perspective of ambiguous instruction. Richard Allen's prefaces suggest a moral, political or ethical position on working-class life underpinning his narratives, but their presentation as sensationalist enjoyment places both the intention and function of the 'lesson' in doubt. Similarly, Amis's presentation of his early antiheroes appears to offer ethical positions, but through the interplay of self-satire, comic distance and the grotesque he places this in doubt. The effect of both is to situate the reader in an uncertain relationship with the characters, constantly reassessing to what degree and why they might identify with those characters, but it also begs the question of the extent to which the reader is intended to sympathize with the apparent intention of the author.

Science fiction, pulp fiction: New Worlds and new forms

J. G. Ballard's literary style developed within the context of *New Worlds SF* magazine. Under Michael Moorcock's editorship from 1964 to 1971, followed by a period until 1979 as associate editor, *New Worlds* embraced concepts from the cutting edge of scientific theory alongside equally groundbreaking theories of psychology, art and philosophy to create a genuinely new innovation in literary aesthetics which became known as the 'New Wave' of science fiction. Moorcock linked the idea of entropy as liberty to his own fantasy sequences where the lives of his many fictional heroes consciously reflected one another. His main characters performed parallel actions and occupied similar narrative functions in the formal sense; they also interacted in adventures where it was revealed to them that they were alternative versions of each other in an overarching 'multiverse' of many confluent universes. Moorcock's multiverse is defined and structured by an eternal conflict between Law and Chaos, for which the Order and Entropy of *New Worlds* are alternate names. Through *New Worlds*, Moorcock added the swinging-sixties' superhero Jerry Cornelius to his multiverse, a character who went with the flow of either Chaos or Law, Order or Entropy, depending on circumstances. Jerry operated as a freeform satire on the contemporary world of the 1960s, but his critical function was soon extended and deepened as Moorcock not only continued his adventures, winning the Guardian Prize for *The Condition of Muzak* (1979), but also allowing other science fiction authors from the pages of *New Worlds* to write their own Jerry Cornelius adventures, among them Norman Spinrad and M. John Harrison.

Moorcock used his editorship to encourage *New Worlds* to take up from where he felt the older SF magazines had left off, namely those regions generally regarded as the mutual reserves of the literature of style and the literature of ideas, and attempted to unify the philosophically inclined side of speculative fiction with the escapist interests that actually got wider audiences reading such ambitious fictions. Michael Butterworth, formerly of *New Worlds*, now of Savoy Books, recalls that 'Moorcock always said that the appeal he wanted *New Worlds* to have was to factory workers in the North' (qtd in Mitchell 64); this is an ambition based on a specific view of working-class intellectual development and mass literacy itself informed by Moorcock's encounters with like-minded authors through his own political and cultural activities (he elaborates on his view of genre and experiment in an interview with Colin Greenland (1991)). Moorcock's ideal for his intended audience was that they would form a fluid continuum from fans of adventure through to surrealists; some writing escapism, others deconstructing it.

When Ballard's condensed fictions were published as *The Atrocity Exhibition* (1970), they sat alongside Moorcock's Cornelius stories as texts which commented on their cultural moment using a blend of avant-garde and pop-cultural references to connect multiple discourses. These techniques were mobilized to engage with the immediate surroundings of a changing Britain. Ballard expanded his vision in the post-experimental works *Crash* (1973) and *High Rise* (1975): the post-war social mobility symbolized by the car, and the class mobility symbolized by the vertical housing thrown up over the wreckage of pre-war culture and buildings, created pathological mind-states that propel the men and women who live in and use them to uncover obsessive and violent drives. In the more famous passages from *Crash*, Ballard makes the presence of these drives specifically psychosexual by using the conventions of pornographic writing within an avant-garde framework:

> In the rear-view mirror I could still see Vaughan and the girl, their bodies lit by the car behind, reflected in the black trunk of the Lincoln and a hundred points of the interior trim. In the chromium ashtray I saw the girl's left breast and erect

nipple. In the vinyl window gutter I saw deformed sections of Vaughan's thighs and her abdomen forming a bizarre anatomical junction. Vaughan lifted the young woman astride him, his penis entering her vagina again. In a triptych of images reflected in the speedometer, the clock and the revolution counter, the sexual act between Vaughan and this young woman took place in the hooded grottoes of these luminescent dials, moderated by the surging needle of the speedometer. (143)

The juxtapositions between sexuality and technology have become notorious for causing controversy, and there is ambivalence within the writing of *Crash* that suggests Ballard is aware that an avant-garde intent remains viable only so long as it plays with its own limitations. Equally notable is the apocalyptic tone of the main characters' relationship. Vaughan is self-conscious of his doomed narrative trajectory, constantly acting out obsessions with collision and celebrity in a way which implicitly links fame with the death drive. The avant-garde prose technique is echoed by the fortunes of the characters: the critique offered by the obsessive textual language deliberately risks travelling too close to Vaughan's own obsession and self-destruction. Ballard's approach is similar to B. S. Johnson's use of exhaustion in his experimental work: both bring the liberatory aspect of experiment into proximity with experiment conceived as the expression of disillusion; the result is a powerful blend in both cases.

The year 1970 was a watershed for the publication of pulp fiction thanks to the many popular texts published by the New English Library. Its 'youth exploitation' novels acquired a cult following among disaffected schoolboys across Britain. These would, in conjunction with punk music, have a decisive effect on the development of the aesthetics of several notable underground novelists of the 1980s and 1990s, such as Stewart Home, Steven Wells and Tony White. The most important author from the period was the prolific James Moffat, better known as Richard Allen, author of *Skinheads* (1970). *Skinheads* was the first in a sequence of youth-centred texts concerned with violent youth subcultures which Allen would expand and generate spin-offs from; these include *Suedehead* (1971), *Skinhead Escapes* (1972), *Skinhead Girls* (1972), *Knuckle Girls* (1977), *Punk Rock* (1977) and *Mod Rule* (1980). It should be clear from these titles that Allen operated a deliberate policy of updating his novels in response to changes in seventies' subcultural fashion. In *British Low Culture: From Safari Suits to Sexploitation* (1998), Leon Hunt analyses Allen's texts in terms of their overdetermined use of authorial position. Writing through authorial intrusions, Allen and others literalize the metaphor of the author's god-like status in a way that makes the texts seem parodies of the realist novel. Pulp authors become 'protean, excessive presences' within their own books, consciously working to position their characters and readers, in a way which makes them politically propagandist and self-conscious about the social status of their fictions and the symbolic exchanges they enter into as fantasies of subcultural violence (77–79). In the work of Johnson, Amis and Allen, a proprietary authorial attitude towards characterization and style signals an attempt to locate the historical moment as the end of an era and the beginning of something new. This aspect of Allen's texts has been extensively employed, subverted and parodied in the 1990s avant-garde work of Stewart Home in particular, while the more mainstream contemporary novelist John King uses a style derived self-consciously from Richard Allen in his novel *Skinheads* (2008) as a way of exploring the place of working-class culture in contemporary Britain compared with that of the 1970s through pulp genres.

The impact of pulp genres and science fiction on so-called literary fiction marks some of the decade's most significant writing, and indeed much of the output of the seventies deemed 'literary' today needs to be read with an awareness of its popular cultural moorings. For example, by 1972 Angela Carter had moved on from her 1960s interest in provincial bohemia and turned to the canvasses of pulp fantasy and science fiction with her own distinctive surrealist inflection. Her 1970s writings draw upon established traditions in science fiction and fantasy, as well as upon the innovations in speculative fiction of the radical writers associated with the 'New Wave', particularly Michael Moorcock and *New Worlds SF* magazine which brought to SF an emphasis on the unity of concept and style every bit as experimental as the work of Johnson. This new emphasis on 'speculative fiction', to differentiate it from stricter definitions of 'science fiction', was a style with which Carter had much sympathy. In attempting to imagine new ways of engaging with the existence of social injustice, Carter created her own version of 'speculative fictions' which encouraged the re-reading of historically canonical texts in terms of the conflicting ideologies interacting within and around them. In this, she referred back to the same canon of anarchic figures, surrealists and experimenters – including in the roster 'the blue-eyed dements of the novels of John Cowper Powys's (*Nothing Sacred* 73) and the 'demonic aspect' of Englishness found in Mervyn Peake (76) – as can be found in the marginalia of the *New Worlds* writers and the continuities and ruptures of the counter-culture.

Carter's writing from this time can best be read as demythologizing the sixties, exploring alternative cultural currents along the way. *The Passion of*

New Eve (1977) is concerned with apocalyptic cults and desert landscapes, and for this reason invokes the spectre of Charles Manson's infamous 'Family' based in California in the late 1960s. The novel is filled with cult followers and followings, from Evelyn/Eve and his/her worship of a female Hollywood icon whom he/she eventually discovers to be a travesty, through to the millennialism of Mother and, of course, the sadism of 'Zero the poet' (82). In this novel, there is an intersection with the vision of America as it appears in J. G. Ballard's *The Atrocity Exhibition*, while the Hollywood worship resembles his dissections and fetishizations from *Crash* (Zero also prefigures Ballard's President Manson from *Hello America* (1981)). Zero's regime amidst his followers is particularly brutal and degrading: 'to illustrate the humility he demanded of his wives, he would smear his own excrement and that of the dog upon their breasts' (85). The extremes of debasement that Zero expects of his followers seem to come directly from the annals of tabloid reportage surrounding the Manson Family as exemplified in the infamous, if rarified, 1970s text on the subject. Richard Allen's *Satan's Slaves* (1970) speculates at considerable length about the possible ritualistic behaviour attributed to Charles Manson, perpetuating the legends of his 'hypnotic' eyes and 'charismatic' character. The language of several of the passages describing the activities of subcultural groups in *New Eve* certainly parodies the kind of discourse in Allen's novel: Carter's description of Zero amidst the harem of his followers above is a version of the wild speculations in which Allen's text on Manson indulges. In a passage entitled 'Night Scene' Allen imagines the Master selecting a victim: his 'eyes piercing the gloom like a demented deity [...] an obscenity about to perform his bestial act', then, '[l]ike a fiend, he mounts her – taking her, savaging her willing flesh, yelling filth as he feels the acid rip through his mind' (35). The scene concludes with the confirmation that '[t]he above is conjecture' while insisting that it is 'not far short of the terrible scenes they enacted in their desert commune' (36) and goes on to detail over and over how these things are the inevitable result of allowing the hippie subculture to continue. Carter's apocalyptic writing moves contrary to Allen's overt intent. Allen's text sought out subcultures and youth cultures as fodder for sensationalism; his constructions of subcultures are reactionary and vitriolically normative. Carter takes a far more ambivalent and progressive approach. She allows the possibility of redemptive qualities to emerge from the most estranged of subcultural fields but is also clearly suspicious of certain subcultural characteristics and echoes the same contemporary concerns with the various manifestations of cultural 'crisis' which the sixties is considered to reflect.

The conflict between an aesthetic of liberation and an aesthetic of disillusionment is a feature which occurs in Carter's work throughout the seventies. Her picaresque novel *The Infernal Desire Machines of Dr Hoffman* (1972) demonstrates a degree of connection to her contemporaries in science fiction and fantasy as well as genre fiction of a more apocalyptic bent. In the essay 'New New World Dreams' (1994), Roz Kaveney locates Carter's interests explicitly with *New Worlds* magazine and the work of Moorcock and Ballard, and she writes that Carter was one of few who 'did not regard their genre roots as an embarrassing past folly'; rather 'when she praised Moorcock's *Mother London*, it was as much as anything else the sheer fecundity of Moorcock that she admired, a fecundity which included his potboiling but often excellent fantasy trilogies as much as the more careful work for which he won awards' (173–174). Carter's sensibility is eclectic, spanning multiple generic traditions, and elements of this can be perceived in the various roles occupied by Desiderio, the central character of *Dr Hoffman*. Desiderio is sent to stop Dr Hoffman from destroying normal life with a cavalcade of illusions and expressions of untrammelled desire pulled from the collective and individual unconscious. He is a civil servant elevated by the power of imagination into a glamorous superspy; his mission is given to him by the Minister of Determination (by 'M') to kill the mad-scientist Doctor who is threatening to destroy his home state. His status is that of 'the most secret of agents' (40), and his name means 'the desired one' (54) who is constantly being seduced by and sleeping with attractive women. Hoffman's former teacher, a Professor turned peep-show vendor, even asks Desiderio whether or not he is 'licensed to kill' (94), adding a layer of comparison with Cold War spy adventures such as James Bond narratives to the frame of reference. Carter playfully suggests that the action-adventure mode of spy fiction popular in the 1960s dooms itself to being an inadequate representation of the tensions which permeate seventies' society – tensions created out of the warring worlds of gender, sexuality and desire, so artfully rendered in her fantastic fictions of the 1970s.

Indeed, the spy fiction which came into its own in the seventies concerned small acts and overwhelming paranoia. John Le Carré's *Tinker, Tailor, Soldier, Spy* (1974) was one such spy novel which, considered alongside the paranoiac panoramas of J. G. Ballard, Ramsey Campbell and Ian McEwan, builds towards a picture of the decade as a distinctive era. Le Carré's Britain in *Tinker, Tailor* is one caught between massive ideological power blocks, within which it must whisper diplomatically, as if to avoid rousing either. The very quietness and persistent mannered conversation of George Smiley, worrying his way slowly to the identity of the double-agent in the novel, stands for a construction of Britain's sense of identity at the time. One former MI5 man even hides by taking on a minor job at a public school, as if he is consciously taking refuge in an earlier, more secure, and less precariously negotiated sense of Britishness. Smiley's meditative conversations convey by hints the violence which saturates the novel's background, creating a tension in the worldview of the fiction which goes far beyond narrative necessity; it presents itself as the state of Cold War Britain, not just of the spy fraternity, a cool restraint constructed to make bearable a vertiginous abyss of unpredictability and disruption, present everywhere but never overtly acknowledged.

Allan Massie writes of Le Carré that whereas earlier spy adventure novelists 'characteristically portrayed the murky world of secret politics as an interruption in the decent and ordinary lives of their heroes, Le Carré makes it an image sufficient in itself' (42); for the characters there can be no untainted world beyond, as they are 'so formed and corrupted by their experiences in the secret world that they are incapable of conceiving any decent way of life as a practical impossibility' (42). This point can be extended further: Le Carré implies that the possibility of a decent alternative world has always been a delusion and the circumstances of the secret world, perversely, make visible an inherent deception within the transactions of everyday life. For Le Carré's characters, like those found in the work of Carter, Ballard and – as we shall see – early McEwan, the secret world with its violence and treachery constitutes the kernel of truth within the overweening deceit of the peaceful, mundane world at large. It is horror which lurks at the heart of the 1970s.

The nasty bits: Horror and the 1970s

In the mid-seventies Ian McEwan published his first collections of short stories, *First Love, Last Rites* (1975) and *In Between the Sheets* (1978), followed by the short novel *The Cement Garden* (1978); these texts would set McEwan's reputation as a literary writer whose work contains 'nasty bits', and they have since been considered as juvenilia based on an aesthetic of shock; Adam Mars-Jones, for example, describes them as containing 'an element of artificial perversity' (26). McEwan's early fictions are often concerned with violent ruptures of suburban normalcy, and are characterized by indeterminacy and radical irresolution. Incest, child abuse and murder occur within mundane suburban environments as integral parts of a landscape of separation and demarcation which describes the suburban geography and the emotional states of his characters. Events are described in matter-of-fact tones and no sense of closure or moral accounting is applied to the events, making them radically disconcerting as well as significant as commentaries on their historical period.

In his essay 'On Sex and Horror' (1993), John Nicholson contextualizes McEwan's early work against a tradition of British Cold War horror fiction. Nicholson traces a history of horror texts of both pulp and literary pedigree which share a concern with the appearance within suburban environments of inexplicable and explicitly sexualized violence throughout the 1970s and on into the 1980s. He describes this as a symptom of two simultaneous events. On one hand, English sensibilities were confronted by imported American horror fictions in the form of both novels and films set in suburbia, such as William Peter Blatty's *The Exorcist* (1973) and Stephen King's *Carrie* (1974), where sexuality is overtly linked to the disruption of home and society in a way that was both visual and visceral (and arguably therefore primarily cinematic). On the other hand, there was the persistent possibility of destruction on a hitherto unimaginable scale which characterized the threat of the Cold War. This latter was manifest as the proliferation of post-apocalyptic scenarios, originally derived from 1960s science fiction narratives, within a more general cultural mood.

Horror is certainly important to the sensibility of the seventies. Nicholson argues that it provides an emotional framework for receiving the threats that science fiction of the sixties was primarily concerned with intellectualizing: normality under tension, conscious of its fragility. McEwan's fictions seem to fit quite smoothly into this schema. Nicholson traces a tradition of apocalyptic horror through Iain Banks's debut novel *The Wasp Factory* (1984), via 1980s splatterpunks and on into the extreme horrors of 1990s avant-garde fictions which take horror techniques to grotesque and avant-garde excesses, which he compares to McEwan's early seventies aesthetic (249–276). Such avant-garde horror fictions include Creation Books publications *Red Hedz* (1990) and *Red Stains* (1991), which self-consciously render the unconscious in terms of the visceral. They are concerned with shock and excess to particular social purposes: their bleakness and omission of moral or spiritual resolution is a function of this. McEwan's 1970s fictions, although more realist, partake in the same use of explicit sex and violence as a mediation on the unconscious of modernity; in his suburbs there are 'No bug eyed monsters, no supernatural forces, simply the unnatural [...] The unnatural creatures are children' (Nicholson 262). McEwan's children imitate the activities of adults and his adults become child-like, a theme he returns to in a less horrific and more emotional manner in *The Child in Time* (1987). These inversions unsettle the familiarity of his suburbs, while their lack of resolution in socialized terms implicitly questions the authenticity of the social values of normalcy, suggesting that normalcy only conceals the exploitation which is made explicit in the stories of *First Love, Last Rites*. In 'Conversations with a Cupboard Man', for example, we meet a man who has been infantilized throughout his childhood and adolescence by his obsessive mother, who later rejects and abandons him to flounder in the world; while in 'Butterflies' the paedophilic narrator approaches everything around him with a childlike acceptance that becomes all the more disturbing when his predatory nature is revealed. Innocence and exploitation mirror one another in McEwan's early fictions, as sexual abuse is clothed as an imitation of adulthood, so that adulthood emerges as an edifice of exploitative relationships maintained by adults who are themselves childlike. All imitate a construct called 'adulthood' that seems increasingly inauthentic, ultimately only a simulacra.

For these reasons, McEwan's early fictions bear comparison with the work of Liverpudlian horror writer Ramsey Campbell, who uses the simulacra of ordinary life as a recurring theme within his 1970s short stories. Campbell wrote prolifically and with a distinctive style, but his work has been eclipsed by the emergence of Clive Barker's *Books of Blood* (1984) and subsequent stardom based on the swift adaptation of his stories *The Hellbound Heart* (1986, 1988) and *Cabal* (1988) into varyingly successful horror films *Hellraiser* (1987) and *Nightbreed* (1990). This means that the development of Campbell's fiction has not been linked to certain major figures in the horror tradition, which was fast becoming more interested in the visceral, nor has his fiction been explored as fully in its own right. But there are clear thematic connections between his fictions and those of McEwan; although Campbell uses supernatural elements which McEwan avoids, the attitudes of their texts towards metaphysical horror both favour irresolvable menace as an integral part of post-war suburban British life. Campbell's early stories from the 1960s were derivations from Lovecraft, but his style quickly moved away from this as he developed his own fictional English provincial town of Brichester, suburban Liverpool and other English settings, into distinctive and idiosyncratic spaces. From around 1969, with stories such as 'The Scar', Campbell's fictions acquired their particular character. 'The Scar' depicts a man duplicated by unknown forces hidden within a deserted suburban house; he seems to alter his personality from family man to wife-beater and bully, before revealing that he is a simulacra, and taking his whole family to be similarly duplicated. 'The Brood' (1976) concerns a man watching his neighbours in an ordinary street discovering that a strange brood of moth-like creatures has occupied the house opposite and is preying on the neighbourhood.

He investigates only to fall inside the house and damage his spine, landing, helpless, beside the alien cocoons in the cellar. The last sentence of the story is: 'They were round, still, practically featureless as yet, hardly even alive' (188). The alien grows within ordinary Englishness and ultimately replaces it with a sinister and silently destructive simulation. In 'The Voice of the Beach' a very Ballardian event occurs in a small seaside town with a deserted village which can be seen growing in the shifting patterns of the sand, something which will one day grow to be the same size as the world. The lead character writes: 'The beach as a subconscious, my notes say: the horizon as the imagination [...] the debris as memories, half-buried, half-comprehensible' (224). This image is Surrealist in its application of symbolic sense to a landscape, but, like Ballard's similar scenes in texts such as *The Atrocity Exhibition*, it defies explication. The story ends with the narrator waiting for the beach to claim him, to make him into itself.

In McEwan's stories, it is the real or 'adult' world in its non-supernatural form that creates similar grotesque and meaningless simulacra. In 'Butterflies', the story ends with the juvenile killer of a little girl speculating with a strange distance on the events and choices that led him to lure her murderously to the canal with the promise of seeing butterflies. The banality of the last lines as he goes to meet her parents creates symbolic patterns out of small details of story, yet these patterns deny the reader any ability to either escape from or find meaning in the events:

> 'See you tomorrow, then ... '
>
> 'Yes, tomorrow'. We would go out drinking together when we were older, and I would learn to like beer. I stood up and began to walk slowly back the way I had come. I knew I would not be joining any football games. The opportunities are rare, like butterflies. You stretch your hand out and they are gone. I went along the street where they had been playing. It was deserted now and the stone I had stopped with my foot was still in the middle of the road. I picked it up and put it in my pocket, and then walked on to keep my appointment. (*First Love, Last Rites* 88)

The reader has returned to the story's beginning but is left also in a morally unsettling hinterland: the world is both banal and symbolic, but the one does not explain or lend moral meaning to the other. The narrator's appointment is to tell the parents that he was the last person to see their daughter and, presumably, to deny the murder. Here is the true horror of the story, and, McEwan seems to be suggesting, perhaps the horror of the seventies as a whole: the moral force of certitude in values is left suspended, in tension, over the abyss.

Fantasy in the 1970s

Much seventies fantasy fiction was marked by an aesthetic determinism where the construction of the fantasy world is of greater importance than events within that world or the development of individual characters. This is derived in part from Tolkien's construction of fantasy primarily in terms of the 'sub-creation' (23) of a 'secondary world' (37) in opposition to the primary world of reality, the Judeo-Christian notion of 'creation'. The 1970s saw the expansion of this principle from the book to the tabletop with the advent of Role Play Games and the creation by Gary Gygax and Dave Arneson of *Dungeons & Dragons* (1974). Games such as this proceed from the idea that the worlds created by fantasy writers are so complete in themselves that they can be backgrounds against which to play out scenarios for groups of individual fans. Martin Hackety describes the experience as 'like being a character in a book, while the book is still being written' (11). These table-top games, in turn, produced variants and alternative gaming systems, all of which prompted spin-off novels (notably in the case of *The Dragonlance Chronicles* (1984 onwards) by Margaret Weis and Tracy Hickman, the first two trilogies were based directly on actual games of Dragonlance played by Hickman). This widening market also led to the creation of new textual form, the 'fighting fantasy' or 'choose-your-own-adventure' narrative, originating with Steve Jackson and Ian Livingston's *The Warlock of Firetop Mountain* (1981). These interactive texts are marked by a distinctive approach to character and narration: the reader identifies with the character and the role of the narrator/controller/Dungeon-master, who is predominantly malign, encouraging the reader in a hermeneutics of suspicion to 'survive' the story. Such fictions present a view of fantasy as a genre which is wholly codified and where imagination is reduced to the playing of predetermined roles in a process of symbolic exchange dictated from above.

Two of the most popular individual fantasy fictions of the seventies were both beast fables. Richard Bach's *Johnathan Livingston Seagull* (1970) and Richard Adams's *Watership Down* (1972) were reprinted and widely disseminated during the period. In *Johnathan Livingston Seagull*, Bach makes an explicit comparison between flight and art, where Johnathan resists conformity to the everyday world of the other gulls to learn the greatest secrets of flight. The text operates in a visionary tradition, emphasizing the spiritual dimension of the central metaphor: through his quest for higher things Johnathan finds himself in a community of gulls for whom 'the most important thing in living was to reach out and touch perfection in that which they most loved to do, and that was fly' (53). Bach's novel was an international bestseller. Adams's text was located in an Arcadian British tradition, concerned with rabbits struggling to find a countryside home which would be free from the threats of oppression and modernity, not dissimilar from Tolkien's Shire. The popularity of *Watership Down* prompted a famous comment from Michael Moorcock in an essay on heroic fantasy where he wrote provocatively, '[i]f the bulk of American sf could be said to be written by robots, about robots, for robots, then the bulk of English fantasy seems to be written by rabbits, about rabbits and for rabbits' (138). Moorcock diagnosed the sentiment of talking-animal fantasy as the natural reverse-side of the adolescent obsession with titillation and violence which he saw dominating the popular pulp fantasy of the period, such as the *Gor* novels of John Norman (John Lange). Norman's *Gor* novels began as some of the most popular fantasy of the early seventies but found themselves shunted from publisher to publisher as a result of personal and political concerns, presumably caused by Norman's espousal of 'sexual utopia' in the texts, as Mark Berry explains:

> In summary, Norman believed that equality between the sexes is impossible as we are genetically programmed to be very different, and women trying to gain equality with men are being tricked by social conditioning and are doomed to a life of misery. On his planet of Gor, women find true physical and mental fulfilment as 'kaijira', slaves to a master race of muscle-bound warriors. (27)

The demise of Norman's popularity was the result of the inevitable clash with second-wave feminism, together with the use of fantasy as a means of deconstructing sexist ideas characteristic of writers such as Carter and Moorcock, as well as the spread of sexual equality into popular discourse generally during the decade.

It is worth noting that more recent radical re-readings of Norman's *Gor* novels have allowed a more progressive interpretation of their gender politics. Similarly, to the precedent of Carter's appropriation of Sade for feminism in *The Sadeian Woman* (1979), Trotskyist cultural theorist and poet Ben Watson argues that the sexual role-play of 'John Norman's multivolume epic of sexual materialism' constitutes a fictional space where 'social relations are transparent, the sexual charge of domination and submission evident and titilating' (95), and he suggests that 'the intricacies the author unravels in the masochistic ecstasy of his slave girls indicate[s] an unconscious longing for the feminine subject position' on Norman's part (97). Watson's critique is very much in step with the innovative perspectives of the seventies' counter-culture, inverting and subverting fantasy through its formalist tendency.

The impact of counter-culture can be discovered throughout the 1970s. Richard Neville's *Play Power* (1971) combined his anecdotes and thoughts on the revolutionary potential of the counterculture during the 1960s and his own history as publisher of *Oz*. Alan Burns's *The Angry Brigade: A Documentary Novel* (1973) attempted to grasp the threads of violent radicalism in the UK, and explain them to a wider audience using the voices of those involved. Burns employs what he terms 'the method of "collective autobiography", telling the story in the words of the participants, but without "naming names"' based on interviews with four women and two men associated with the 'three groups in London, and at the time of writing (Spring 1973) at least two outside' (2) who constituted the active networks of the Angry Brigade. Another small counter-cultural depth-charge, mixing fantasy, satire and anti-establishment polemic, was launched when the text of prison notebooks written by Brian Barritt was smuggled out of an HM Prison between 1966 and 1969 and published as *Whisper: A Time Script* (1971) with an afterword by Timothy and Rosemary Leary. The text is grotesque and fantastic, interspersed with illustrations and all heavily influenced by the work of William S. Burroughs whose significance for the British counter-culture and post-New Worlds speculative fiction continued long after the 1960s. Its nearest companion text is probably the prison notebook of American 'Yippie' Jerry Rubin, published as *We Are Everywhere* (1971), but in its attention to mundanity, Swiftian imagery and interior migration, it enunciates a more ambivalent and possibly more widespread dissatisfaction than Rubin's polemical text. Similarly, a later counter-cultural charge was launched by the publication of *The Savoy Book* (1978) edited by David Britton and Michael Butterworth, both former contributors to *New Worlds* who went on to continue the counter-cultural tradition in provocative, transgressive directions throughout the 1980s and 1990s. *The Savoy Book* collected eccentric, decadent artwork and prose with surrealist poetry. It is notable now for its publication of Harlan Ellison's 'Eggsucker', a prequel to his post-nuclear story 'A Boy and His Dog', and M. John Harrison's enigmatic and evocative narrative of illness and inner-city séances, 'The Incalling'. Writers associated with *New Worlds* were already using fantasy's extreme formalism to create anti-fantasy fictions which would come to inform later writers, of whom the most influential was M. John Harrison.

Harrison's subversion of the form of fantasy begins in earnest with the publication of the baroque and meditative novel *The Pastel City* (1971):

> Some seventeen notable empires rose in the middle period of Earth. These were the Afternoon Cultures. All but one are unimportant to this narrative, and there is little need to speak of them save to say that none of them lasted for less than

a millennium, none for more than ten; that each extracted such secrets and obtained such comforts as its nature (and the nature of the Universe) enabled it to find; and that each fell back from the Universe in confusion, dwindled and died. (25)

Harrison's subsequent Viriconium sequence stands as a clear attempt to reverse some of the views of fantasy as a primarily commodity-oriented form limited to particular manifestations and reproducing stereotyped masculinities and femininities. The fantasy of the Viriconium novel is surrealist in inflection. Both the terrain of subjectivity and of the city itself are defined fluidly: Viriconium is always changing whilst always seeming to be the same city; its inhabitants exist in existential uncertainty, always on the edge of radical subversions of their socially determined roles. David Punter writes in *The Literature of Terror* (1996) that Harrison's work was a development of ambiguous Gothic heritage of 'half-lights, ambiguities and figures moving in a dusk of their own devising' (170). Since his 'baroque period' (Britton and Butterworth qtd in Mitchell 77) Harrison's career has been defined by repeated traversing of marginal and central cultural spaces. His work can be seen as part of an important wider movement to reassess the meaning of the fantastic in the 1970s, following on from the radical innovations of the 1960s 'New Wave' and also an attempt to open up new spaces in genre literatures.

In the 1970s, then, the innovations of counter-cultural and feminist critiques inspired an anti-fantasy which comes to define later developments of genre fantasy traditions selectively rewritten to meet the needs of the present. Without our cognisance of these counter-cultural endeavours and their legacies, our sense of the seventies would be incomplete.

This chapter has attempted to demonstrate the diversity of ways that the various interlaced traditions of 1970s literature each contributed distinctively to an overarching structure of feeling that we may now term 'the seventies'. The very real thematic intersections which these traditions stage build towards a rich and complex picture of the decade as a dynamic whole, full of ebbs and flows, with unexpected undercurrents – and one can read this dynamism across a range of texts, from the work of Angela Carter and Martin Amis to that of J. G. Ballard, Ian McEwan and M. John Harrison. We can use this knowledge, as I hope to have done above, to construct a new selective tradition of the literature of the seventies that meets the complex demands of our own cultural moment of contemporaneity, specifically how we now constitute the seventies as a period in recent literary history.

Works cited

Allen, Richard. *Satan's Slaves*. Hove: CodeX, 1998 [1970].
Amis, Martin. *The Rachel Papers*. London: Penguin, 1984 [1973].
———. *Dead Babies*. London: Jonathan Cape, 1975.
———. *Success*. London: Vintage, 2004 [1978].
Bach, R. *Johnathan Livingston Seagull*. London: Pan Books, 1972.
Ballard, J. G. *Crash*. London: Vintage, 1995 [1973].
———. *The Atrocity Exhibition*. London: Flamingo, 2001 [1970].
Barritt, Brian and Ball, David. *Whisper: A Time Script*. London: Whisper Promotions, 1971.
Beckett, Andy. *When the Lights Went Out: What Really Happened to Britain in the Seventies*. London: Faber and Faber, 2009.
Berry, Mark. 'Blood and Gor' from *Pulp Mania#1*. Bristol: Holt Cherry, 2000. 27-33.
Bradbury, Malcolm. *Possibilities: Essays on the State of the Novel*. Oxford: Oxford University Press, 1971.
———. *The Novel Today: Contemporary Writers on Modern Fiction*. London: Fontana, 1977 [1990].
———. *The History Man*. London: Arrow, 1979 [1975].
Britton, David and Butterworth, Michael, eds. *The Savoy Book*. Manchester: Savoy, 1978.
Burns, Alan. *The Angry Brigade: A Documentary Novel*. London: Allison & Busby, 1973.
Butor, Michel. 'The Novel as Research', in *The Novel Today: Contemporary Writers on Modern Fiction*. Ed. by Malcolm Bradbury. London: Fontana, 1990 [1977]. 45-50.
Campbell, Ramsey. 'The Brood' (1976), in *Alone with the Horrors: The Great Short Fiction of Ramsey Campbell, 1961-1991*. Illus. J. K. Potter. London: Headline, 1994. 79-88.
———. 'The Scar' (1967), in *Alone with the Horrors: The Great Short Fiction of Ramsey Campbell, 1961-1991*. Illus. J. K. Potter. London: Headline, 1994. 35-50.
———. 'The Voice of the Beach' (1977), in *Alone with the Horrors: The Great Short Fiction of Ramsey Campbell, 1961-1991*. Illus. J. K. Potter. London: Headline, 1994. 221-50.
Carter, Angela. *The Sadeian Woman: An Exercise in Cultural History*. London: Virago Press Ltd, 1979.
———. *The Infernal Desire Machines of Dr Hoffman*. London: Penguin, 1982 [1972].
———. *The Passion of New Eve*. London: Virago, 1982 [1977].
———. *Love*. London: Virago, 1997 [1971].
———. *Nothing Sacred: Selected Writings*. London: Virago, 2000 [1982].
Childs, Peter. *Contemporary Novelists: British Fiction since 1970*. Basingstoke: Palgrave Macmillan, 2005.
Forster, Laurel. 'Printing Liberation: The Women's Movement and Magazines in the 1970s', in *British Culture and Society in the 1970s: The Lost Decade*. Ed. by L. Foster and S. Harper. Newcastle: Cambridge Scholars Publishing, 2010. 92-106.

Greenland, Colin. *Michael Moorcock: Death Is No Obstacle*. Manchester: Savoy, 1991.
Hackety, Martin. *Fantasy Wargaming: Games, Magic and Monsters*. Wellingborough: Patrick Stephens Ltd., 1990.
Harrison, M. John. *The Pastel City*. London: Panther, 1971.
Hunt, Leon. *British Low Culture: From Safari Suits to Sexploitation*. London and New York: Routledge, 1998.
Johnson, B. S. *Albert Angelo*. London: Constable, 1964.
———. *House Mother Normal*. London: Collins, 1971.
———. 'Introduction to *Aren't You Rather Young to Be Writing Your Memoirs?*', in *The Novel Today: Contemporary Writers on Modern Fiction*. Ed. by M. Bradbury. London: Fontana, 1977 [1990]. 165–83.
Kaveney, Roz. 'New New World Dreams', in *Flesh and the Mirror: Essays on the Art of Angela Carter*. Ed. by L. Sage. London: Virago, 1994. 171–88.
Le Carré, John. *Tinker, Tailor, Soldier, Spy*. London: Pan Books, 1975 [1974].
Mars-Jones, Adam. *Venus Envy*. London: Chatto & Windus, 1990.
Massie, Allan. *The Novel Today: A Critical Guide to the British Novel 1970–1989*. London and New York: Longman/British Council, 1990.
McEwan, Ian. *First Love, Last Rites*. London: Vintage, 2006 [1975].
———. *The Cement Garden*. London: Vintage, 2006 [1978].
Mitchell, David M. *A Serious Life*. Manchester: Savoy, 2005.
Moorcock, Michael. 'Epic Pooh', in *Wizardry and Wild Romance*. Texas: MonkeyBrain Books, 2003 [1977, revised 1985]. 123–40.
Moore-Gilbert, Bart. *The Arts in the 1970s: Cultural Closure?* London and New York: Routledge, 1994.
Neville, Richard. *Play Power*. London: Paladin, 1971.
Nicholson, John. 'On Sex and Horror', in *Gothic Horror: A Reader's Guide from Poe to King and Beyond*. Ed. by C. Bloom. Basingstoke: Macmillan, 1998. 249–76.
Norman, John. *Assassin of Gor*. London: W. H. Allen and Co., 1973.
O'Day, Marc. "'Mutability Is Having a Field Day': The Sixties Aura of Angela Carter's Bristol Trilogy", in *Flesh and the Mirror: Essays on the Art of Angela Carter*. Ed. by L. Sage. London: Virago, 1994. 24–59.
Punter, David. *The Literature of Terror: The Modern Gothic*. London and New York: Longman, 1996.
Rennison, Nick. *Contemporary British Novelists*. London and New York: Routledge, 2005.
Rubin, Jerry. *We Are Everywhere*. Harper and Row: New York, Evanston, San Francisco, London, 1971.
Simmons, Rochelle. 'John Berger's Revolutionary Narratives', in *British Culture and Society in the 1970s: The Lost Decade*. Ed. by L. Foster and S. Harper. Newcastle: Cambridge Scholars Publishing, 2010. 14–23.
Stevenson, Randall. *A Reader's Guide to the Twentieth-Century Novel in Britain*. London: Harvester Wheatsheaf, 1993.

Sutherland, John. *Bestsellers: Popular Fiction of the 1970s*. London, Boston and Henley: Routledge and Kegan Paul, 1981.

Tolkien, J. R. R. 'On Fairy-Stories' (1947) in *Tree and Leaf*. London: HarperCollins, 2001 [1964]. 3–81.

Watson, Ben. *Art, Class and Cleavage: A Quantulumcunque Concerning Materialist Esthetix*. London: Quartet, 1998.

Weis, Margaret and Hickman, Tracy. *Dragonlance Chronicles*. London: Penguin, 1988.

Whiteley, Gillian. '"New Age" Radicalism and the Social Imagination', in *British Culture and Society in the 1970s: The Lost Decade*. Ed. by L. Foster and S. Harper. Newcastle: Cambridge Scholars Publishing, 2010. 35–50.

Williams, Raymond. *The Long Revolution*. London: Chatto and Windus, 1961.

2

The Ordinariness of the Extraordinary Break-Up of Britain

Nick Hubble

In the 1973 film adaptation of Michael Moorcock's *The Final Programme* (1969), the actor Jon Finch, in the role of Jerry Cornelius, snarls: 'The Third World War has been going on for years but everybody is too busy watching the bleeding adverts to notice'. This neatly captures the fact that the seventies were characterized as much by a consumer culture disseminated through iconic advertisements on the newly arrived colour television service, as they were by social and political concerns. Forty years later, the decade still provides an endless armchair fare of flares, frisbees and space hoppers for nostalgia television even as its class-based politics appear increasingly alien to present-day Britain. Nevertheless, these apparently opposed tendencies towards consumerism and class war were linked as part of an ongoing post-war process described by the leading socialist public intellectual of the period, Raymond Williams: 'Many British working-class people welcomed American culture, or the Americanised character of British commercial television, as an alternative to a British "public" version which, from a subordinate position, they already knew too well' (*Television* 132-133). Williams points out that while this commercial television was apparently free-floating and accessible, in contradistinction to class-based forms of British culture, it was also very much controlled and planned by American corporations. More significantly, however, he linked the spread of this form of cultural consumption to the wider historical development across the twentieth century of a simultaneously 'mobile and home-centred way of living: a form of *mobile privatisation*' (26). By the 1970s, the broadly suburban practice of nuclear-family units living commuter-based lifestyles had become demographically and culturally dominant, at least in terms of public representations of the nation. As Williams notes, it was broadcasting in general and centralized television programming (throughout the decade there were only three channels) in particular that supplied the ideological cohesion of a national consciousness to what, considered objectively, was a fractured and contradictory state of affairs arising from the accelerated breakdown of settled communities and mass dispersal of populations over the preceding decades.

In *Towards 2000* (1983), written after the opening years of the Conservative government led by Margaret Thatcher, which had initiated a ruthless process of disassembling the post-war British Industrial Welfare State and trebled the number of unemployed people in the country, Williams returned to the rise to dominance of commuting lifestyles and considered how they had enabled such an unthinkable transformation to occur so rapidly and with so little (effective) social dissent. Implicitly, he argues that by establishing this 'mobile privatisation' as the dominant way of life, the capitalist social order had implanted a 'deep assent to capitalism' that functioned in a way that was all too easy to comprehend:

> All the decisive pressures of a capitalist social order are exerted at a very short range and in the very short term. There is a job that has to be kept, a debt that has to be repaid, a family that has to be supported. Many will fail in these accepted obligations after all their best efforts. Some will default on them. But still an effective majority, whatever they may do in other parts of their minds or in other areas of their lives, will stick in these binding relations, because they have no practical alternative. (254)

Crucially, though, what he also demonstrates earlier in the book is that because 'mobile privatisation' is a mode of living that develops in response to an international market in commodities and cultures, it has direct consequences for how national identity is constructed. For that international market to operate, national economies had to be fully permeable and therefore British companies had to be able to compete or else 'go bankrupt; get out of the way of the leaner and fitter; join the real world' (190). The upshot of such a global economic system is that nations are no longer nations in the nineteenth-century sense of the term. What had been Britain was no longer 'a whole lived order but a willed and selective superstructure' merely sufficient to maintain the necessary level of social and economic order for the international market to function (191). Instead of the old Britain there was now the United Kingdom: '"the Yookay", no longer a society but a market sector' (191).

Viewed retrospectively from 'the Yookay' of the twenty-first century, in which 'mobile privatisation' has become further ingrained and expanded by the rise of another generation of communication technologies, the various political attempts made in the 1970s to preserve Britain by creating a stable relationship between state, employers and unions, whether within or without of the 'Common Market', as the European Union was then known, appear not just farcical, given what happened in the following decade, but simply pointless and irrelevant. As Andy Beckett observes at the beginning of his history, *When the Lights Went Out: What Really Happened to Britain in the Seventies* (2009), today the seventies are only ever invoked politically as a failure of mythological proportions: a decade blighted by the 'British disease', largely defined by reference to ideological resistance to capitalism and industrial strikes to further workers' power, which had to be burnt out at the roots. However, this chapter will argue that there were significant political successes during the period and that these motivated, and were reflected on by, some of the most compelling fiction of the decade. The positive developments that emerged from the process identified by Williams of Britain ceasing to be a meaningful nation state were best summed up at the time by Tom Nairn's uncompromising political and historical study *The Break-Up of Britain* (1977).

Nairn's argument began by stating that although Britain was the product of aggressive military expansion of the English state from the time of Norman feudalism onwards into Wales, Scotland and Ireland, these conquests, except in the case of Catholic Ireland, 'had been followed or accompanied by episodes of assimilation and voluntary integration – and until the 1960s it looked as if the latter tendencies had triumphed' (12). However, despite these appearances, the post-war loss of the wider Empire, upon whose interrelationships the State was structurally dependant, meant that, in fact, the writing was on the wall:

> There is no doubt that the old British state is going down. But, so far at least, it has been a slow foundering rather than the *Titanic*-type disaster so often predicted. And in the 1970s it has begun to assume a form which practically no one saw [...] the break-down began to occur in the form of territorial disintegration rather than as the long-awaited social revolution. (13-14)

This was not the version of Britain's decline that was being presented in the media at the time, in which a focus on economic emergencies and militant trade unionism did indeed tend to imply imminent social revolution. Of course, written after the 1973 report in favour of establishing a Scottish Parliament by the Royal Commission on Scottish Devolution, at a time when the Scottish National Party, who had won over 30% of the Scottish vote at the October 1974 General Election, seemed to hold the balance of power in Parliament, Nairn's argument was not without logic. However, by the mid-1980s, after the yes vote in the Scottish referendum of 1979, despite registering 52%, had failed to pass the somewhat arbitrary required hurdle of 40% of the total electorate in favour (and the Welsh had rejected devolution), a combination of Thatcherite counter-revolution and the British Naval campaign in the Falklands had generated an Imperial British fervour unseen for decades. At this point, Nairn's analysis appeared somewhat wide of the mark. Yet, viewed again from the twenty-first century in which Scotland, Wales and Northern Ireland all enjoy popular self-government, Nairn's arguments appear uncannily prescient and the Thatcherite jingoism an historical blip, an aberration. On this evidence, it is reasonable to suggest that Nairn managed to tap into a deeper undercurrent of social change beneath the surface level of 1970s public opinion.

This idea that something might be going on beyond official recognition was a feature of the time as indicated, for example, by Doris Lessing's *The Memoirs of a Survivor* (1974):

> One of the things we now know was true for everybody, but which each of us privately thought was evidence of a stubbornly-preserved originality of mind, was that we apprehended what was going on in ways that were not official. Not respectable. Newscasts and newspapers and pronouncements were what we were used to, what we by no means despised: without them we would have become despondent, anxious, for of course one must have the stamp of the official, particularly in a time when nothing is going according to expectation. But the truth was that every one of us became aware at some point that it was not from official sources we were getting the facts which were building up into a very different picture from the publicised one. Sequences of words were crystallising events into a picture, almost a story: *And then this happened, and so-and-so said*... but more and more often these were words dropped during a casual conversation, and perhaps even by one self. 'Yes, of course!' one would think. 'That's it. I've known that for some time. It's just that I haven't actually heard it put like that, I hadn't grasped it...' (8)

In this passage, personal experience is privileged over the public record even as bourgeois individualism – 'originality of mind' – is undermined by a collective coming to consciousness. There is a particular politics of everyday life at work here in which the resistant everyday component of everyday life – the almost subconscious animal physicality of human existence – is being raised to the surface in order to contest the repetitive everydayness of everyday life. Lessing's narrator finds this process extraordinary:

> Could one perhaps describe that period as 'the ordinariness of the extraordinary?' Well, the reader should have no difficulty here: these words are a description of the times we have lived through. (A description of all life? – probably, but it is not much help to think so.) (19)

There is a realization here that the very claim to say what is ordinary necessarily includes the admission that one can stand outside the ordinary to make that judgement. In other words we are all extraordinary but fear usually prevents us from admitting it. However, once this extraordinariness is admitted it has the effect of marginalizing all forms of public authority; not in an obvious political sense – the idea of conventional class struggle does not feature in Lessing's novel – but simply by erasing their relevance:

> Attitudes towards authority, towards Them and They, were increasingly contradictory, and we all believed that we were living in a peculiarly anarchistic community. Of course not. [...] the use of the word 'it' is always a sign of crisis, of public anxiety. There is a gulf between: 'Why the hell do they have to be so incompetent!' and 'God things are awful!' just as 'Things are awful' is a different matter again from 'It is starting here too,' or 'have you heard any more about it?' (8–9)

'It', argues Lessing, is a matter for everyone, not just the authorities, because 'it' has already grown beyond the scope of the authorities. As she elaborates further into the novel: 'perhaps, indeed, "it" is the secret theme of all literature and history'; 'it' is a word for 'man's inadequacy' and 'above all a consciousness of something ending' (130). This conceptual analysis can usefully be employed to think about the wider implications of the break-up of Britain. Although Lessing's novel is set in an unnamed city, the fact that the narrator talks at one point about escaping to North Wales, where she has enjoyed holidays in the past, situates us squarely in a Britain that is rapidly disintegrating into a tribal nomadic barbarianism. The tower block in which the narrator lives undergoes a transformation that is quite as extreme as anything found in the work of J. G. Ballard. This irreversible decline is interwoven with both the narrator's descriptions of a series of transcendental experiences she undergoes in which she passes through the wall of her flat and an account of the development through puberty of a girl, Emily, who (along with her sentient pet dog, Hugo) is entrusted to her mysteriously. The cumulative effect is extremely unsettling as Emily's typically early teenage oscillation between childhood and adulthood – in which, torn between the street life of her peer group and her loyalty to her dog and the narrator, she experiments with smoking, drinking and sex – is contrasted with the increasingly psycho-sexual scenes that take place behind the wall. On one level, the ostensible concern is about society's indifference to teenage sex: 'no one really cared much that young women of thirteen, fourteen, had sexual relations. We had returned to an earlier time of man's condition' (85). But it quickly becomes clear that Lessing is not arguing in favour of protecting civilization as we know it, but condemning it utterly. The accelerated decay she presents serves both to highlight the endemic structural flaws of the old repeating patterns of patriarchy and hierarchy (112, 115–116) and to put them into reverse, as in the disturbing scene where Emily is regressed in Lacanian terms through the mirror stage and out of the symbolic realm entirely. In the parallel universe through the wall, the narrator and Hugo watch in horror as Emily in a scarlet evening dress 'of blatant vulgarity' sits before a mirror 'her lips open for fantasy kisses':

> Into the room came the large tall woman, Emily's mother, and her appearance at once diminished Emily, made her smaller, so that she began to dwindle from the moment the mother stood there. Emily faced her and, as she shrank in size acted out her provocative sex, writhing and letting her tongue protrude from her mouth. The mother gazed, horrified full of dislike, while her daughter got smaller and smaller, was a tiny scarlet doll, with its pouting bosom, its bottom outlined from waist to knees. The little doll twisted and postured, and then vanished in a flash of red smoke, like a morality tale of the flesh and the devil. (158–159)

However, in this morality tale, it is society which is being cleansed from the flesh rather than sexuality. The next time the protagonists pass through the wall, at the end of the novel, it is out of the story and into the multiplicity of possibilities held by the pure realm of the Imaginary.

One way of understanding Lessing's subsequent *Canopus in Argos* series, which is considered to be a major factor in her award of the Nobel Prize for Literature in 2007, would be as an exploration of this realm of the imaginary. For example, the second volume in that sequence, *The Marriages Between Zones Three, Four and Five*, written at the end of the decade and published in 1980, contrasts the utopian matriarchal Zone Three with the militaristic patriarchal Zone Four. However, it is not a simplistic fable; in fact the highlighting of the obvious inadequacies of Zone Four does not serve as an end in itself but as a means of critiquing the complacency of Zone Three. Lessing's point is that overcoming patriarchy is not the end point of a successful transformation of society but merely the necessary first step. The first volume in the series, *Re: Colonised Planet 5: Shikasta* (1979), occupies an intermediary position between *Memoirs of a Survivor* and *The Marriages Between Zones Three, Four and Five*. Whereas the former situates a realm of the Imaginary parallel to, but outside of a thinly disguised but nonetheless recognizable depiction of contemporary Britain, *Shikasta* relocates a version of Britain wholly within a realm of the Imaginary. The planet Shikasta is, in effect, Earth located within six concentric numbered zones with various defining characteristics – such as Zones Three and Four discussed above – and subject to the influence of no less than three galactic empires. The main narrator of the novel is Johor, an emissary of one of the empires, Canopus, who, having visited Shikasta during pre-historical periods, returns during the late twentieth century. These framing devices serve to estrange Britain and enable the reader to view it outside its contemporary ideological constructions as simply 'a small island that had, because of its warlike and acquisitive qualities, overrun and dominated a good part of the globe, but had recently been driven back again' (75). In contradistinction to a patriarchal symbolic order, Johor rejects individualism – '[t]o identify ourselves with individuals – this is the very essence of the Degenerative Disease' (38) – and writes from an holistic perspective, which finds the very idea of Western 'politics' to be inherently false:

> Nearly all political people were incapable of thinking in terms of interaction, of cross-influences, of the various sects and 'parties' forming *together* a whole, wholes – let alone of groups of nations making up a whole. No, in entering the state of mind where 'politics' was ruler, it was always to enter a crippling partiality, a condition of being blinded by the 'correctness' of a certain viewpoint. And when one of these sects or 'parties' got power, they nearly always behaved as if their viewpoint could be the only right one. (76–77)

The narrative goes on to suggest, in a chilling expansion of George Orwell's critique of the effects of totalitarianism on middle-class intellectuals in *Nineteen Eighty-Four* (1949), that perhaps the dominant characteristic of all inhabitants of the planet now is the capacity 'to hold, and act on – even forcibly and violently – opinions and sets of mind that a short time later – years, a month, even a few minutes – they might utterly repudiate' (79). It is interesting to note that Lessing's indictment of a system in which 'people were taught to live for their own advancement and the acquisition of goods' (89) just predates the rise to dominance of explicitly neoliberal social and economic doctrines in the West that was marked by the election of Margaret Thatcher in Britain and Ronald Reagan in the US. Rather, she indicates the extent to which this narrow self-serving individualism was already embedded in post-war Western society and enabled precisely by the debilitating effects of an ongoing 'Twentieth Century War' that originated in Western quarrels over colonial spoils and was characterized not so much by the intensive phases – the First and Second World Wars – as the continual fighting in different parts of the globe that is promoted by the armament industries and Western government agencies (see 84–90). Furthermore, Lessing describes the colonial conquest and expansion that preceded and set the conditions for this permanent condition of war as being enabled by the feudal history of the West, which bequeathed a rigidly divided class system and the belief that extreme material inequality is an acceptable norm.

In relating the contemporary social crisis to feudalism, Lessing's analysis is very similar to that of Nairn's although not so historically specific to the 'uniqueness' of Britain, which he sums up as its being the location of 'the first national capitalist class which emancipated itself from city or city-state mercantilism and created the foundations of industrialization' (15). While the British national state that emerged following the revolutions of 1640 and 1688 was not a direct continuation of feudalism, it did maintain the model of rule from above by large landowners:

> The conquering social class of the mid-17th century civil wars was an agrarian élite: landlordism in a new form, and with a new economic foundation, but emphatically not the urban bourgeoisie which later became the protagonist of modern European development. Although no longer feudal, and allied increasingly closely to the urban middle class, this class remained a patrician élite and concentrated political power entirely in its own lands. In a way quite distinct from later 'ruling classes' it constituted the actual personnel and machinery of the English state. (25)

As Nairn goes on to discuss, this political settlement consisting of a 'patrician hegemony' over a 'clearly demarcated order of classes' guaranteeing 'the effective social subordination of the lower classes' (32) was to remain structurally dominant ever after. Such structures contributed to the limitations of post-war politics targeted by Lessing and they were directly responsible for the particular divide in Britain between the political classes and everyday life that she identifies as 'an unreality at the very heart of their every-day decision-making, thinking, functioning' (*Memoirs* 79–80). While the Second World War saw a rapid democratization and radicalization of British society, the failure to abolish keystones of the pre-existing ruling order such as the public schools, the House of Lords and even the Monarchy itself, meant that the potential for long-reaching structural change was not realized. As Anthony Howard noted, 'Far from introducing a "social revolution" the overwhelming Labour victory of 1945 brought about the greatest restoration of traditional social values since 1660' (qtd in Marwick 80). However, the democratization of social and cultural agency that occurred during the war years remained a powerful force within British everyday life and provided the grounds for challenges to be made to the cultural dominance of the patrician elite, such as that made in the work of

Raymond Williams in books and essays including 'Culture is Ordinary' (1958). Nairn regarded this type of vigorous contestation of the meaning of Britain at the level of everyday life as one of the key factors contributing to its impending break-up. He grouped Williams together with E. P. Thompson and Raphael Samuel as part of a broad intellectual movement constellated around the general concept of 'history from below' and went so far as to call for this to be extended into a full-blown English cultural nationalism (303–304).

As part of a robust rebuttal of the suggestion that he himself might be involved in any movement which could be described as nationalist, Thompson pointed out that Williams was an 'unlikely "English nationalist"' (1978: iii). Indeed, by the time that *The Break-Up of Britain* was published, Williams, who was of course Welsh, was heavily involved with Plaid Cymru and in the process of writing a series of essays and papers on topics such as 'Welsh Culture' (1975), 'The Social Significance of 1926' (1977), 'The Welsh Industrial Novel' (1979) and 'The Importance of Community' (1989) – the latter originating with a lecture given to the Plaid Cymru Summer School at Llandudno on 13 July 1977. If this seemed a surprising trajectory for the author of seminal works of British cultural analysis such as *Culture and Society* (1958) and *The Long Revolution* (1961) to be following, it was to some extent presaged by his novels, which beginning with his first, *Border Country* (1960), had always been concerned with the relationship between Welsh and English values. In the series of interviews which Williams conducted with members of the editorial collective of the journal *New Left Review* in 1978 and 1979, which form the content of *Politics and Letters* (1979), he spoke about how he had originally taken inspiration from the Welsh working-class fiction of the interwar period such as Lewis Jones's *Cwmardy* (1937) and *We Live* (1939), and Jack Jones's *Rhondda Roundabout* (1934). However, he notes that there was a consequence to the actual writers excluding themselves from the working-class communities they depicted in order to preserve the homogeneity of that community:

> The result was the separated novel about the working-class community, which became a kind of regional form – the enclosed class as a regional zone of experience. It was very characteristic of all these novels that they were retrospective – a recapturing of an early experience from another social world. The early versions of *Border Country* were continuous with these kinds of writing. But I was dissatisfied with that form, initially without quite knowing why. Then I gradually realized that with the degree of change after 1945 the problem was to find a fictional form that would allow the description both of the internally seen working-class community and of a movement of people, still feeling their family and political connections, out of it. (272)

The form he settled on in order to 'establish the difference between the two worlds and explore the problem of rejoining them' (273) adapted the generational strategy of some earlier novels such as Jack Jones's *Black Parade* (1935) and combined this with his own predilection for divided protagonists to tell the story of Harry Price, who like Williams's father is a railway signalman, and his son Mathew, who like Williams himself, goes to Cambridge and thus experiences both a working-class community and the wider world beyond it. As his interviewers point out, and to which judgement he agrees, the novel is partially flawed in that the integrated moral vision of the father figure, secure in his community, still appears the strongest force in the novel even though Williams's expressed intent was actually to show its limitations. In this respect, the novel can still too easily be classed as the kind of regional novel that Williams was trying to transcend, although it successfully escapes what had become the dominant mode of signifying Welshness in fiction at that time: a verbally exuberant presentation of garrulous eccentrics in the manner of Dylan Thomas. However, following *Second Generation* (1964), which features Welsh families relocated to Oxford to work in the car factories, Williams did find a way of writing about Wales that went beyond representing it as merely a subordinate region of a larger Britain in the third of this loose trilogy of novels, *The Fight for Manod* (1979), which took over a decade to write.

This novel brings Mathew Price from *Border Country*, now a leading industrial historian, together with two of the characters from *Second Generation*, the young radical sociologist Peter Owen and the former lecturer Robert Lane, who is now a government advisor. Lane employs Price and Owen to investigate the social consequences of a proposal to build along a valley in mid-Wales a new kind of post-industrial, post-electronic edge city: 'a city of a hundred, a hundred-and-twenty thousand people, but a city of small towns, a city of villages almost. A city settling into its country' (13). The two uncover a complicated web of land speculation aiming to profit from the development and this, in turn, reveals the generational differences between them. While Peter's aim is to trace out fully and expose publicly the vested interests at work behind the scheme in order to get it halted, Mathew takes a more nuanced view. As Fred Inglis describes in his 1995 biography of Williams, the novel is one element of an argument being conducted with a younger generation of leftwing critics and intellectuals such as the *New Left Review* editorial collective and Terry Eagleton, who had accused Williams of '"socialist humanism", "romantic populism", social-democratic tendencies and other corruptions of the day' (249). Williams's perspective was that uncompromising opposition to the current order missed the point that Britain was not just on the verge of breaking up but was already past the point of no return, which had certain consequences as voiced by Robert Lane in *The Fight for Manod*:

> 'The whole of public policy,' he said, emphatically, 'is an attempt to reconstitute a culture, a social system, an economic order, that have in fact reached their end, reached their limits of viability. And then I sit here and look at this double inevitability: that this imperial, exporting, divided order is ending, and that all its residual social forces, all its political formations, will fight to the end to reconstruct it, to re-establish it, moving deeper all the time through crisis after crisis in an impossible attempt to regain a familiar world. So then a double inevitability: that they will fail, and that they will try nothing else'. (181)

As Inglis implies, the point for Williams was not to denounce these repeated failures but to break out of the pattern once and for all by opening up, in Mathew's words, 'some new possibility' (187), which is represented in the novel by the idea of the new city. However, despite Inglis's praising of the novel – and noting of its publication in the Soviet Union with a print run of 100,000 – he somewhat undermines its effectiveness by describing it as passive (256).

Tony Pinkney comes closer to catching the work's power when he refers to Lane's description of the British State quoted above as evidence that *The Fight for Manod* is 'written under the sign of apocalypse' (76). He continues:

> It is as if, within the careful sociological detailing of Welsh rural depopulation, some uncanny shift of generic gears takes place in *The Fight for Manod*, so that we are in a world that is both realistic and science-fictional at once; for the most suggestive generic parallel here seems to be recent fictions of nuclear apocalypse. (77)

Pinkney develops this analysis through an extended reading, which also encompasses the gothic aspects of the novel including allusions to witchcraft, its affinities to Ibsen's *The Master Builder* (1892) and its relationship to modernist and postmodernist space, before concluding with the suggestion that the genre elements of the novel serve as 'a sombre warning of what awaits this devastated valley if its future is after all blocked' (90). While this is perhaps too didactic an interpretation of Williams's purpose, it does suggest how the novel's temporal schema might allow a future for Wales to exist within the constricting narratives that have dominated so much of its past. This interplay between the past and the future is encapsulated perfectly in a sequence early in the novel during which Mathew segues from a childhood memory of looking across the valleys with their green near sides and blackened far sides and so 'seeing the history of his country in the shapes of the land' (36) to a vision of what is to come:

> He could close his eyes and then open them in the city in the valley. the grey cluster of works at St Dyfrog. At Llanerch and Manod, at Bronydd and Fforest, and Parc-y-Meirch and the Cwm, terraces of houses, central white towers. Circles of white light at the road intersections. The traffic, the sound, of a hundred thousand people. (37)

Mathew's capacity to sense two 'realities' co-existing simultaneously is comparable to that displayed by the protagonists of Christopher Priest's *A Dream of Wessex* (1977), which is discussed later on in this chapter. What this capacity reflects is a relationship similar to the one identified by Fredric Jameson between the genre of science fiction, itself, and that of the historical novel from which it developed: 'SF [is] a form which [...] registers some nascent sense of the future [...] in the space on which a sense of the past had once been inscribed' (285–286). It is this generic force at work in *The Fight for Manod* that provides it with a valency exceeding its apparent passivity when viewed from the perspective of realist representation.

Pinkney also detects science fiction elements in Williams's other, quite different, novel of the 1970s, *The Volunteers* (1978). One way of approaching this work is by first briefly returning to Lessing's *Shikasta*. In a long 70-page section of 'case studies' and 'illustrations' that depicts the decay of British and Western society at a personal level, she includes the description of a workers' leader, who after coming from a poor working-class background and spending five years in the army during the war becomes a trade unionist fighting for a 'decent living wage' (121), but this struggle is gradually subverted by the Age of Affluence in which there seems no limit to what would become possible for the workers even to the point of gaining revenge for the poverty of earlier generations. He finds such consumerism ideologically subversive in terms of solidarity and becomes disturbed by the attitude of younger unionists and even his own children, who seem to care for nothing but 'their own good pleasure, their possessions, their comfort' (122) and allows his own position to become compromised with perks even as he comes to comprehend how the workers' movements have become utterly subverted:

> They were not victors, he and his kind, not in any way, they were the defeated still, for they had become like their 'betters.' He, his kind, had been taken captive by everything they ought to hate, and *had* hated but had forgotten to hate. They *had* looked, earlier in their history, into the faces of their oppressors, who bullied and bluffed – and tricked; and had felt themselves superior, because they were honest, and stood on the truth. And now they, too, bluffed and bullied and

> tricked – just like everyone else of course. Who did not? Who did not lie and steal and filch, and take what he could grab? And so why should they be any different? (123–124)

It is easy to see how Lessing's account of working-class politics losing its way in post-war Britain could collapse into a right-wing critique of union power and, as discussed further below, critics such as Bart Moore-Gilbert have accused her of an inherent cultural conservatism. However, what the above example highlights more than anything else are the difficulties that faced writers in the 1970s, especially those on the political left, who wanted to address the failure of the Labour Party and the trade union movement to break free from the doomed cycle, identified by Williams in the excerpt from *The Fight for Manod* quoted above, of attempts to 'reconstitute a culture, a social system, an economic order, that have in fact reached their end'. The approach adopted to these issues by Williams, himself, in *The Volunteers* was to make them the direct focus of the novel.

The Volunteers is set in the then near-future of the late 1980s and begins with the shooting of a government minister, which appears to be a reprisal for the army's shooting of a striking worker at a South Wales colliery depot some months earlier. The connections are investigated by a hard-boiled reporter from media corporation Insatel, Lewis Redfern, who is a disillusioned former political activist: 'It's great to belong to a young radical generation, until you have to watch them grow up' (68). His findings soon cause him to focus on Mark Evans, an older figure on the left who had once written an influential book, *The Limits of Representative Democracy*, before becoming absorbed into the compromises of being a junior minister in the Labour government of the 1970s, only to lose his seat in the 1983 election (accurately predicted by Williams) and become Director of the American-funded Community Politics Trust 'supporting social projects and experiments in scores of cities and towns' (69). The plot is complex but it is the relationship between the two men that becomes important as the older man's willingness to accept and come to terms with his own generation's failures and compromises helps release Lewis from being trapped within his own cynicism. This narrative resolution stems directly from Williams's critical and theoretical work, which becomes incorporated into the warp and weft of the novel as the ongoing investigation does not so much reveal who is responsible for the individual crime as uncover the social conditions which result in people behaving in apparently divided and duplicitous ways:

> The whole point about living in a society like this is that people get so confused by what our theoreticians call the immanent structural contradictions, that they don't have to change, dramatically, in old soul-saving or soul-selling ways.

> Radically divergent potentials continue to inhabit them, Their ordinary active condition is profoundly divided. Often they don't change at all but simply live with the other half, as the limits and pressures allow. (107)

By illustrating that these divergent potentials exist and therefore underpin the possibility of existential choice, Williams demonstrates the persistence of agency and the capacity of people to choose what kind of society they want to live in. As Pinkney observes, 'The question in the long run is not epistemological – who dunnit? – but ontological: which *world* are you in, Insatel's or the Welsh workers'?' (103). During the 1970s, Williams made this ontological choice as reflected by the following statement in *Politics and Letters*: 'I want the Welsh people – still a radical and cultured people – to defeat, override or bypass bourgeois England' (296).

Like Williams, but perhaps even more so, William McIlvanney is open to the criticism that his work becomes dominated by a moral vision that is overwhelmingly masculine but, also like Williams, he generates a sense of deliberative, existential agency. In *Docherty* (1975), the story of a miner set in the opening decades of the twentieth century, we follow the protagonist, Tam Docherty, on his path to self-realization through a succession of stages such as the following:

> [...] perhaps he wasn't a Catholic. He felt cold without the word. It had happed his thoughts as long as he could remember. Whatever misery, anger, bitterness, despair had come to him, it had still been vaguely containable in the folds of that loose word, to be thawed to a sort of comfort. Even now he wasn't sure that the word didn't belong to him. He merely suspected that it night not, as if the deciding of it wasn't up to him. He could not make the intellectual choice. He could only sense that he somehow had to be himself, whatever that might be, and it might not be Catholic. What he felt profoundly was the uncertainty of himself, simply that he had to meet life without protection. (41)

This sense of Docherty as a living force is enhanced, as Douglas Gifford observes, by McIlvanney's 'ability to make character emerge from background as inevitable product' (866), which is compatible with the achievement of Lewis Grassic Gibbon in *Sunset Song* (1932). Indeed, Gifford also suggests that the novel represents a link between the work of pre-war Scottish authors such as Gibbon and later ones such as Iain Banks. In this context, Cairns Craig argues in *The Modern Scottish Novel* (1999) that *Docherty* is a kind of alternative history which privileges the possibility of a socialist history for Scotland over the failure of the General Strike in 1926: 'The sign of socialist solidarity in expectation of a new history is asserted by the novel in refusal of the actual events through which the country has lived in the intervening period' (124).

If this history never quite re-emerged, despite the phenomenon of 'Red Clydeside' in the 1970s, McIlvanney found a means of interacting with the actually existing modern Scotland by writing the crime novel *Laidlaw* (1978), in which the eponymous detective hero brings a distinctively philosophical approach to the streets of Glasgow. For example, the novel revolves around what would conventionally be described as a horrific sexually driven murder but Laidlaw points out that the true horror of this kind of crime is that it is 'the tax we pay for the unreality we choose to live in. It's a fear of ourselves' (72). The effect of this approach is not to displace the violence endemic to a hierarchical society on to a scapegoat murderer but to rehumanize the apparent aberration and so place the blame back squarely on society. In so doing, McIlvanney attempts to overcome the fearful divided self so prevalent in Scottish culture – most famously in Robert Louis Stevenson's *The Strange Case of Dr Jekyll and Mr Hyde* (1886) – and advance the possibility of Scotland as a modern, open, sexually liberated society. McIlvanney's novels contributed to the subsequent overcoming of this fear, and the related fear that he identified in the run-up to the 1979 Devolution Referendum (see Craig 74), and helped catalyse the fulfilment of the promise of the modern Scotland that was to come in the subsequent decades.

It might be objected that Jennifer Johnston is an Irish writer and not therefore eligible to be discussed in a book concerning contemporary British fiction. However, she has lived near Derry in Northern Ireland since the late 1970s and her work illustrates some of the possibilities raised by the historical break-up of Britain; a process which began with the formation of the Irish state in 1922. *Shadows on Our Skin* (1977) was her first novel to deal directly with the contemporary situation in Northern Ireland. The novel revolves around a working-class Catholic family living in the backstreets of Derry and focuses on schoolboy Joe and his friendship with Kathleen, a Protestant schoolteacher, who is run out of the city at the book's end by his brother. In *Fiction and the Northern Ireland Troubles since 1969* (2003), Elmer Kennedy-Andrews argues that 'the novel's pessimism lies in its failure to imagine any alternative agency of social change to nationalist paramilitary chaos' (228). However, *Shadows on Our Skin* does at least imply an imaginary alternative expressed in the inscription on a book that the departing Kathleen gives to Joe on the last page of the novel:

Kathleen Doherty is my name,
Ireland is my nation,
Wicklow is my dwelling place,
And heaven my destination. (214)

Kathleen, like Johnston herself, is a Protestant who grew up in the Republic and, therefore, she lays claim to a different sense of Ireland than that advanced by the nationalist paramilitaries. Although Johnston never explicitly maps out the details of this alternative Ireland, it is not purely an absence. Earlier in the novel, in a scene where Kathleen and Joe go for a walk, she talks of growing up in County Wicklow: '"On a clear day you can see Wales from the top of the hill behind the village. Quite clear. Big blue mountains." She spoke with pride' (95). The fact of Wales – crucially, not England – being visible from Ireland suggests the possibility of a different way of thinking about the collective identity of the British Isles as opposed to the divisive legacy of the historical British state. A similar effect is achieved by a passage in J. G. Farrell's *Troubles* (1970) describing the orientation of the Majestic Hotel:

> It was into the Irish Sea (and not into Ireland) that the most magnificent flight of steps led, and they were in the middle of the crescent whose curving arms spread out to embrace the distant coast of Wales across the vast expanse of windswept water. (67)

Although the tone here is ironic, Farrell's absurdist charting of the decline and fall of the British Imperial presence in Ireland also registers a sense of lost possibilities. In an interview given in the 1980s, Johnston voiced similar possibilities in the form of a more direct counterfactual proposition:

> The effect that World War I had – the massacre of a whole generation of young men – embittered a large number of people who remained. In Ireland, it was the beginnings of the troubles we are now in [...] I think that had the [1916] uprising not happened, come 1918, we would have had Home Rule. There would have been no problems with the North because the British wouldn't have allowed there to be problems, and we would have moved on from there in some cumbersome but logical way to becoming a Republic. (qtd in Kennedy-Andrews 239)

This idea can be detected as underpinning the novel she wrote after *Shadows on Our Skin*, *The Old Jest* (1979). Beginning with Nancy Gulliver's 18th birthday, we follow her over the course of the next eight days as she sets out 'to become a person' (10). Ostensibly, Nancy is caught between the conflicting values of the Anglo-Irish big house, of which she is the daughter, and the enigmatic figure hiding on the local beach, who she thinks at first might be her missing father but is actually a revolutionary, despite also coming from an Anglo-Irish background. However, rather than being represented as an absolute clash of values, these competing traditions are realigned in shared opposition to the materialism represented by a local property dealer intent on buying the house and its lands in order to build suburban villas. While walking across the fields with the prospective son-in-law of the property dealer, Nancy, who has just announced her two main aims as being to lose her virginity and join the Republicans, metaphorically tramples over this bland future:

> 'We are probably at this moment striding,' she strode for a moment, 'across someone's precious rosebed, trampling the pink and yellow hybrid teas into the earth. Getting thorns into our legs. Or ...' she let go of him and began to run, 'running through the dining room, where some startled maid is laying the table for dinner, polishing up the glasses with the corner of her apron. Oops, sorry!' She stopped dead in front of Harry. 'Close your eyes like a good chap, Madam has been discovered in her bath. Only a sponge to protect herself'. She climbed over the gate and out on to the road. (110)

As Kennedy-Andrews notes, '*The Old Jest* projects a discourse of anti-colonial Nationalism supported by existentialist notions of choice and "commitment", and the evocation of a civilised, aristocratic ideal derived from colonial influence and symbolised by the disappearing big house' (243). In part, it is the vitality embodied by Nancy that provides this perhaps unexpected combination of values with the transformative power to portray a genuine alternative vision of a fully independent Ireland. However, the fact that the novel's protagonist is a young woman also allows Johnston to escape some of the symbolic baggage that Williams and McIlvanney remain encumbered by despite their best efforts. While characters such as Mathew Price, Lewis Redfern, Tam Docherty and Jack Laidlaw all embody to varying degrees the contradictions inherent in relating the past to the present, Johnston apportions this role in *The Old Jest* to Major Barry, the revolutionary on the beach, and so is able to represent a decisive break from the past through the portrayal of Nancy's coming of age. In this respect, Johnston foreshadows the fiction that was to appear in subsequent decades across the Celtic countries of the British Isles setting out the possibilities of new identities and new gender and group relations within the context of emergent devolved national identities. While such work could be marginalized from an English perspective in the 1980s and 1990s, the revival of devolution as a political project following the election of the Labour Party in 1997 has rendered such condescension no longer possible.

What now appears problematic is the way that novels written about England by English writers since the 1970s have been taken as expressing British values. For example, such iconic 'British' novels as Martin Amis's *Money* (1984) and Ian McEwan's *Saturday* (2005) are principally concerned with the gradual disintegration of an English class system directly descended from the patrician hegemony enshrined in 1688. In retrospect, Nairn was clearly right to call for a specific examination of English culture as English at the end of the 1970s, even if this annoyed self-proclaimed internationalists such as Thompson. Such an approach would have helped avoid the subsequent tendency to view the 1970s as dominated by accounts of impending disaster for *Britain*, as exemplified by Bart Moore-Gilbert's essay 'Apocalypse now?: the novel in the 1970s' (1994):

> The novel was deeply implicated in the sense of social and cultural crisis characteristic of the 1970s, most obviously because so many novelists expressed the condition of contemporary Britain in apocalyptic terms [...] Industrial confrontation, class warfare, terrorism, regional tensions, conflict between the races and genders – all are staples of the decade's fiction, giving the impression of a society on the verge of disintegration, or even civil war. In many cases the brink has already been crossed, producing social chaos and some kind of totalitarian backlash. (152)

While it is true that all these ingredients may be found in the English fiction of the decade, they do not necessarily support Moore-Gilbert's interpretation. As it happens, one of the key texts he takes for analysis is Lessing's *The Memoirs of a Survivor*, which he cites as an example of both how the 'decline of linguistic purity and competence alike were seen by many as ominous for the future of literature' (156) and how 'profound disillusion with contemporary political institutions led a number of important writers towards a metaphysical or mystical explanation of the contemporary malaise' (159). The net effect is to imply a certain cultural conservatism to Lessing, which is compounded by his claim that her protagonists are 'intensely vulnerable to the power of the dominant ideology' (160). Furthermore, even her feminism is apparently limited by her tendency not to see patriarchy as institutional and her presentation of the suffering of her female protagonists 'as an existential condition rather than a consequence of gender subordination' (161). Yet, as we have seen, one of the key factors in enabling the emergent national identity expressed by Welsh, Scottish and Northern Irish fictions was a notion of choice drawn from existentialism that suggested the possibility of choosing alternative options to those apparently available. It is difficult not to see the tendency of English critics to deny these possibilities for England, itself, as ideological.

Finally, Moore-Gilbert raises the problem of Lessing's 'chiliastic' Sufi-inspired plots which see the individual saved at the expense of humanity: 'The extreme determinism of such ideas appears to preclude any real possibility of social renewal in Lessing's fiction, though it is just possible that this may be a deliberate provocation to the reader to organize and act before it is too late' (159–160). However, while some of the texts he discusses, such as Malcolm Bradbury's *The History Man* (1975), might uphold values that could plausibly be described as those of individualism and 'liberal humanism', Lessing's work explicitly rejects individualism as we have seen. This saving clause at the end of Moore-Gilbert's sentence is obviously provoked by a suspicion that something else is going on in the novel but its failure to acknowledge Lessing's radical position is symptomatic of the limited scope of a certain kind of theory-based literary criticism, in vogue in the mid-1990s, which functioned by gauging texts against a checklist of binary oppositions and cannot account for anything structured according to different rules. The capacity for social renewal, in such apparently 'apocalyptic' fiction as Lessing's lies, as Fredric Jameson argues, precisely in its refusal to represent social renewal:

> its deepest vocation is over and over again to demonstrate and to dramatize our incapacity to imagine the future, to body forth, through apparently full representations which prove on closer inspection to be structurally and constitutively impoverished, the atrophy in our time of what Marcuse has called the *utopian imagination*, the imagination of otherness and radical difference; to succeed by failure, and to serve as unwitting and even unwilling vehicles for a meditation, which setting forth for the unknown, finds itself irrevocably mired in the all-too-familiar, and thereby becomes unexpectedly transformed into a contemplation of our own absolute limits. (288–289)

For example, in *The Memoirs of a Survivor*, Lessing exposes the limits of conventional utopian thought in order to force her readership to think harder about the different possibilities of inter-subjective existence. She is particularly ruthless in her dismissal of the impoverishment of the human condition implicit within the notions of hippy-like alternative lifestyles emerging in that decade:

> In some parts of the city whole suburbs had reverted. Miles of people, all growing their potatoes and onions and carrots and cabbages and setting guard on them day and night, raising chickens and ducks, making their sewage into compost, buying or selling water, using empty rooms or an empty house to breed rabbits or even a pig – people no longer in neat little families, but huddled together in groups or clans whose structure evolved under the pressure of necessity. At night such an area withdrew itself into a dangerous obscurity, where no one dared go [...] Even in the daytime [...] such an expedition was like a foray into enemy territory or into the past of the human race. (91)

Arguably, the social experience of the 1970s served to demonstrate the limits of the post-war British political settlement and the Welfare State as a whole precisely through realizing, rather than marking the failure of, the utopian aspirations that underpinned those decades. For example, Andy Beckett refers to the publication of Bernard D. Nossiter's *Britain: A Future that Works* (1978) and its list of indicators of national well-being: 'increasing life expectancy, growing meat consumption, more universities, shrinking poverty, cleaner air, the return of fish to the Thames, the oil riches in the North Sea'. Nossiter concluded: 'Britons... appear to be the first citizens of the post-industrial age... [They] are choosing leisure over goods' (qtd in Beckett 416). Indeed, in the second half of the decade, during the years when Jim Callaghan was the Prime Minister, Britain was 'probably more equal than it had ever been before – and certainly more equal than it ever was since':

> The Gini coefficient, a common measure of income inequality, reached its lowest levels for British households in 1977. The proportion of individual Britons below the poverty line did the same in 1978. Social mobility, measured as the likelihood of someone becoming a different class from their parents, also peaked in the Callaghan era. (Beckett 409–410)

This condition of equality represented the fruits of a social revolution that had gathered pace since the Second World War and utterly altered Britain in a way that would have seemed unimaginable following the failure of the General Strike in 1926. Yet the culmination of this utopian transformation of the prospects of the working class, the millennial 'Winter of Discontent' of 1978–1979, the biggest British labour stoppage since the General Strike, was also precisely the moment that revealed the limits of that utopian impulse. Beckett describes the situation in Hull as 'a kind of peasants' revolt' (488) in which shop stewards from the Transport and General Workers' Union took control over national road freight distribution. Looking back 30 years later, one of those involved reflects that 'in many ways and on many occasions, I've regretted it. But it was so effective. We stopped everything. The employers, they were so humiliated. Humiliated!' (qtd in Beckett 489). This period of 'the world turned inside out' (ibid.) exposed enduring class divisions and the complete bankruptcy of the post-war consensus. It also demonstrated the relative impotency of mass industrial action in the modern state, as within ten years the power of the unions was broken and Thatcherite neoliberalism had become generally accepted by the English public.

One English novel that predicted this potential of the post-war British utopian impulse to break down either into its constituent nations or a condition uncannily prescient of the Thatcherism of the 1980s is Christopher Priest's *A Dream of Wessex* (1977). The novel begins:

> The Tartan Army had planted a bomb at Heathrow, and Julia Stretton, who had gone the long way round past the airport to avoid the usual congestion on the approach road to the M3, had been delayed for two hours by police and army checkpoints. (1)

Julia Stretton's desperation to escape the terrorism, police road blocks and traffic congestion which characterize the disintegrating Britain of the 1970s, motivates her participation in a scientific experiment which gathers both the conscious and unconscious wishes of its members for the collective projection of a viable future. This future is formed by the 'collectivization of industry and agriculture [and] absorption into the soviet bloc' following the collapse of the monarchy and 'the destruction of the British union' (139–140). The utopian vision of a sunny island Wessex 150 years in the future, attracting tourists, is disrupted when Julia's former boyfriend, Paul Mason, joins the project. Paul's character is summed up in a scene where he attempts to rape Julia; he is a manipulative man seeking power over others. His effect on the project is made apparent to the readers in the way that the landscape of the future changes to an industrial one including an oil refinery. However, the participants simply adapt to the changes and remain unaware that things were ever different until Julia and her current lover, David Harkman, try and relocate a spot where they made love to the position of the refinery:

> "Do you remember? When we last met … what did we do?"
> "We went on the heath and talked."
> "Yes, and we made love. There was a storm coming, but while we were there it was warm and dry. Do you remember that?"
> "Yes, David."
> "And so do I. I remember loving you out there, on the heath." He pointed suddenly. "Just there, where the refinery is!"
>
> […]
>
> "It was there, David … but somewhere behind us."
> "Are you sure?"
> "I think so … ."
> The refinery was there, it had always been there.
> "And I think so too. I'm not sure, though. I know that the refinery has been here for years, that when Dorchester was rebuilt it was an oil-port, and that the economy of Wessex depends on the wells here. But do you remember the tourists?"
> "What? Here in Dorchester?" She laughed.
> David said: "I was amused too, when I remembered them."
> "There have been one or two," she said. "They visit all parts of Britain."
> "Britain?" David said. "Or England?" (155–156)

Here, David's last question politicizes the act of remembering that is taking place by articulating what is at stake when history becomes obscured by ideology. Paul wants the participants of the future projection to project themselves forward further into a future where

> Britain had *again* become a constitutional monarchy, when Britain *again* was a unified state, when the world was *again* a keenly competitive place, when the balance of power was *again* between Soviet Russia and the U.S.A., when there were *again* the seemingly insurmountable problems that gave life a challenge and a purpose, when technology and science *again* had a vital role to play in the world's development. (160)

However, David and Julia realize that this is really a ploy to return to the original point of departure; Britain in the 1970s. Only this time, it would be a reinvigorated Britain and not the disintegrating state described at the beginning of the novel. Most of the participants in the experiment do indeed go back to 1977 but David and Julia manage to rejoin the original projection of a utopian English future. Therefore, as I have argued elsewhere, from the perspective of the novel, 'rather than David and Julia's escape being a wish-fulfilment fantasy, it is "reality" that is shown to be the wish-fulfilment fantasy' on the part of a clearly sociopathic character (Hubble 43). In this manner, Priest reinvigorates the utopian imagination precisely by both avoiding a narrative predicated on a teleological notion of progress and emphasizing the provisional and mutable nature of history.

However, unlike the work of Williams, McIlvanney and Johnston, *A Dream of Wessex* reveals a national consciousness that remains divided about, rather than moving towards a unified sense of, the future. While Priest imagines the possibility of a specifically English future, he does not simply contrast it with a British past. At the novel's end, Paul remains in some future 'reality' of his own. While this future is rejected on moral grounds as being characterized by monomania and insecurity, Priest does not deny it the same ontological possibilities as the other alternatives he outlines. The net effect was a prescient demonstration that post-war Britain could break down in two ways. History dictated that rather than into utopian possibility, it was to be the ontological possibilities represented by Paul that prevailed as the basis for the Thatcherite 'reality' of the 1980s.

Read in retrospect, therefore, the world that Paul Mason inhabits is familiar to readers not only from dystopian novels but also from their experience of living within the neoliberal system of 'mobile privatisation' in the particular market sector called 'the Yookay', whose emergence in the 1970s and consolidation in the 1980s was described by Williams, as we have seen at the beginning of this chapter. In 'The Importance of Community', the text of his 1977 lecture to the Plaid Cymru Summer School, Williams argues that if this state of affairs is not challenged then 'politics will be only the capitalist interplay of interests, and that would be the end of politics in any sense that would have been understandable by me when I first started looking at political life' (118–119). In a situation where socialist intellectual politics was becoming effectively limited to negation and abstraction, Williams called for a move beyond these politics by 'carrying the kind of affirmatives of community through these negotiations into a different kind of politics' (118). This was what he was attempting to do in both *The Fight for Manod* and *The Volunteers* by depicting protagonists who had become buried in the tortuous manoeuvrings of leftwing politics cautiously reconnecting with an integrated politics of people and place. The desired result would not stem from an extension of the organic community but from a collective determination to overcome the systematic obstacles placed by the modern global economy in the way of establishing meaningful social relations across a nation; the necessary precursor for living a fully social life at any level of organization more complex than a village. This process, as described by Williams, can also be seen in the Scottish and Northern Irish fiction of the period, as represented in this chapter by works by McIlvanney and Johnston:

> The moment when we move from a *merely retrospective* nationalist politics to a *truly prospective* politics, we begin that affirmative thinking which some of the most developed and intelligent left politics in certain other centres of Europe has truly lost. For however sophisticated, however militant that politics may be, it has lost something at its heart which is recognised again and again by those who are inside it: the sense of what any of this liberation is for, the sense of what the struggle would be able to attain, the sense of what that human life would be, other than merely Utopian rhetoric, which is the object of all the preoccupied conflict and struggle and argument. That sense has been so truly lost in so many of those areas, especially through the complications of the modern history of socialism, that what is now being contributed, I think still very incompletely, but what is being contributed and almost alone is being contributed from the new nationalist movements, is a reconnection inside the struggle, including the negations, but also the sense of an objective which has the possibility of affirmation. (118)

The move to reject simple utopian rhetoric in pursuit of a sense of what life could actually be is also evident in the novels of Lessing and Priest examined here but while these estrange and negate the English component of 1970s Britain in order to indicate the existence of other possible ways of living, they lack the option of affirming an existing alternative. In particular, it is the sense of an achievable objective – defining a Welshness, Scottishness or Irishness separate from the decaying British Imperial State – that gives the fictions of Williams, McIlvanney and Johnston an ontological plausibility that is retrospectively strengthened by the subsequent success of political devolution. In other words, the identities represented in these novels have become more representative of lives in these nations today than the alternatives they contested. What seemed extraordinary in abstract terms turned out to be ordinary and, while the question of Englishness still remains to be determined, the break-up of the apparently monolithic British State had been set inexorably in motion by the end of the decade.

Works cited

Beckett, Andy. *When the Lights Went Out: What Really Happened to Britain in the Seventies*. London: Faber and Faber, 2009.
Craig, Cairns. *The Modern Scottish Novel: Narrative and the National Imagination*. Edinburgh: Edinburgh UP, 1999.
Farrell, J. G. *Troubles*. London: Phoenix, 1993 [1970].
Gifford, Douglas. 'Scottish Fiction since 1945 I: Continuity, Despair and Change', in *Scottish Literature*. Ed. by Gifford, Sarah Dunning and Alan MacGillivray. Edinburgh: Edinburgh UP, 2002. 834–98.
Hubble, Nick. 'Priest's Repetitive Strain', in *Christopher Priest: The Interaction*. Ed. by Andrew M. Butler. Cambridge: Science Fiction Foundation, 2005. 35–51.
Inglis, Fred. *Raymond Williams*. London: Routledge, 1995.
Jameson, Fredric. *Archaeologies of the Future: The Desire Called Utopia and Other Science Fictions*. London: Verso, 2005.
Johnston, Jennifer. *The Old Jest*. London: Fontana, 1980 [1979].
———. *Shadows on Our Skin*. London: Headline, 2002 [1977].
Kennedy-Andrews, Elmer. *Fiction and the Northern Ireland Troubles since 1969: (De-)Constructing the North*. Dublin: Four Courts, 2003.
Lessing, Doris. *Shikasta*. New York: Knopf, 1979.
———. *The Marriages between Zones Three, Four, and Five*. London: Granada, 1981 [1980].
———. *The Memoirs of a Survivor*. London: Harper Perennial, 2007 [1974].
Marwick, Arthur. *British Society since 1945: The Penguin Social History of Britain*. Harmondsworth, Penguin, 2003.
McIlvanney, William. *Laidlaw*. London: Sceptre, 1992 [1978].
———. *Docherty*. London: Sceptre, 1987 [1975].
Moore-Gilbert, Bart. 'Apocalypse Now?: The Novel in the 70s', in *The Arts in the1970s: Cultural Closure?* Ed. by Moore-Gilbert. London: Routledge, 1994. 152–75.

Nairn, Tom. *The Break-Up of Britain: Crisis and Neo-Nationalism* [1977]. 2nd edition. London: Verso, 1981.
Pinkney, Tony. *Raymond Williams*. Bridgend: Seren Books, 1991.
Priest, Christopher. *A Dream of Wessex*. London: Sphere, 1987 [1977].
Thompson, E. P. *The Poverty of Theory*. London: Merlin, 1978.
Williams, Raymond. *Politics and Letters: Interviews with New Left Review*. London: NLB, 1979.
———. *The Volunteers*. London: The Hogarth P, 1985 [1978].
———. *Towards 2000*. Harmondsworth: Penguin, 1985 [1983].
———. *Border Country*. London: The Hogarth P, 1988 [1960].
———. *Second Generation*. London: The Hogarth P, 1988 [1964].
———. *The Fight for Manod*. London: The Hogarth P, 1988 [1979].
———. 'The Importance of Community', in *Resources of Hope*. London: Verso, 1989. 111–19.
———. *Television: Technology and Cultural Form*. London: Routledge, 1990 [1975].

3

1970s Feminist Fiction

Sonya Andermahr

Introduction

The 1970s is a period that is remembered in Britain as a byword for social and cultural crisis, characterized by territorial disintegration abroad, economic mismanagement and decline at home, and political embarrassment for the Right and Left alike, as the country faced a series of debilitating strikes, shortages and crises. However, some saw it as a chance for a new beginning; for feminists the 1970s offered an opportunity to change society for the better. Looking back on the 1970s, Marsha Rowe, the first editor of *Spare Rib*, founded in 1972, stated: 'We made our own world' (Daly 1). In the course of this chapter, I explore the world of 1970s British feminist fiction which, while not as well-known and widespread as US feminist literature, was nevertheless dynamic and iconoclastic. There was a close and dialectical relation between politics, theory and literature: the Women's Liberation Movement fed directly into women's writing through consciousness-raising groups, writing workshops, conferences, reading groups, magazines and publishing houses. In fact, the 1970s saw the creation of a new feminist counter-public sphere, arguably something that had not been experienced in Britain in such a radical way since the time of the suffragettes. While the decade saw a continuation of the radical work of 1960s writers such as Doris Lessing, it also gave rise to a new sense of collective endeavour and of writing as part of a larger, shared political project in which women writers saw themselves not as isolated, exceptional figures, but as part of sisterhood 'writing for their lives'. Major British writers, in particular Angela Carter and Fay Weldon, established their writing careers in the period. In addition, a large group of women writers emerged, including Emma Tennant, Sara Maitland, Zoë Fairbairns and Michèle Roberts, who paved the way for the next generation of women writers in the 1980s which included Jeanette Winterson, Rose Tremain and Pat Barker. This chapter explores their work in the context of the social changes and movements which in many ways inspired it. I start with a consideration of key political and cultural events, most notably the women's liberation movement, and the establishment of feminist publishing in the UK. Next, I consider the development of UK feminist criticism and theory in relation to Rita Felski's notion of the feminist counter-public sphere. The main body of the chapter examines the characteristics of the feminist text as it developed in concert with the feminist second wave in the 1960s and 1970s. I discuss some of the primary texts of the period, commenting on the emergence of particular writers, genres and styles of writing, identifying key themes, and providing close readings of three exemplary 1970s feminist texts. Finally, I draw some conclusions about the feminist writing produced in the decade. My approach is motivated by the belief that the texts produced cannot be meaningfully understood as a series of individual contributions even when the writer concerned is relatively divorced from political concerns. My contention is that all writing has a relation to social and cultural contexts and is produced out of and in dialogue with that wider context.

Political and cultural contexts

The 1970s coincides with the flowering of British second-wave feminism, which represented a thoroughgoing challenge to the widespread discrimination faced by women in employment, tax and social security laws, in family law, and in social convention and expectation. Angela Carter, writing about the summer of 1968, stated that 'I can date to that time [...] my own questioning of the nature of my reality as a *woman*' ('Notes' 70). The Women's Liberation Movement (WLM) lasted a decade from 1968 to 1978 and cut across the seventies, highlighting in one way how artificial and arbitrary are the boundaries imposed by the notion of the 'decade'. The movement was built around networks of local women's groups, which met to offer advice and support to women, a forum for discussion and debate about women's lives, and analysis of women's social roles and relationships, known as 'consciousness-raising'. It is important, however, not to present an overly monolithic account of the feminist counter-public sphere. As Selina Todd comments, '"The Women's Liberation Movement" is a deceptively coherent term, covering a diverse range of localised activity and a proliferation of political and social movements' (62). One of the earliest networks of women's groups was the Women's Liberation Workshop formed in London and Bristol in 1969, which published its own newsletter, *Shrew*. An early edition of *Shrew* reported on the first National Women's Liberation conference, which took place at Ruskin College, Oxford, on 27–28 February and 1 March 1970 with the aim of examining and challenging the causes of women's inequality. Among its organizers and participants were some of the feminist intellectuals and activists, such as Juliet Mitchell, Sheila Rowbotham and Sally Alexander, who shaped British feminist studies in the 1970s. As a result of the conference, four basic WLM demands were agreed: equal pay for equal work; equal educational and job opportunities; free contraception and abortion on demand; and free 24-hour nurseries. Direct action was an important part of feminist activism of the decade, which witnessed a number of high-profile events. Foremost amongst these was the demonstration in November 1970 against the Miss World Competition at the Albert Hall in London, which was inspired by similar events in the US. Demonstrators carried placards with eye-catching, witty slogans such as 'Miss-fortune demands equal pay for women' and 'We're not beautiful, we're not ugly, we're angry' (British Library 'Dreamers' 1). Among the Miss World demonstrators were many feminist writers and activists including Lynne Segal, Sheila Rowbotham, Susie Orbach and Fay Weldon. Weldon had been invited to be in the audience for Miss World and was put in the 'pro' section by organizers, but remembers, 'I suddenly felt total revulsion and walked from one section to another. I was a mother, married with two young children, and had a job, I was seen as a woman who was perfectly happy ... when you could see it was actually terrible' (Cadwalladr 4).

On 6 March 1971, four thousand people marched through London on the First International Women's Day March where a petition with the movement's demands was handed to the prime minister. In 1974, the Women's Aid Federation was formed to provide support and refuge to women and children experiencing domestic violence. Among the feminist campaigns for improving women's social and economic status, was the Wages for Housework Campaign, which demanded a government wage for any woman who looked after children at home, to give her financial independence from her husband (Dalla Costa and James 24–25). A controversial proposal, it divided feminists, some of whom campaigned against it on the grounds that it would confirm women in their subservient roles. In mainstream politics, the Labour government made a commitment to introduce Child Benefit, a payment for mothers in acknowledgement of the work they did. However, the government's decision in 1976 to pay the benefit to the main breadwinner rather than to the woman led to a public outcry from the women's movement and numerous other groups on the Left and Right of the political spectrum. Eventually, the government capitulated and Child Benefit, paid directly to mothers, was introduced in 1977. By the end of the decade, many WLM demands had been met in a series of laws, which introduced greater equality for women: the Equal Pay Act of 1970 granted equal wages for men and women doing the same work; the Sex Discrimination Act, which outlawed sexual discrimination in the workplace was passed in 1975; and the Domestic Violence Act of 1976 enabled women to obtain a court order to exclude violent partners. Accounts of the period foreground the energy generated by the movement; according to Sue Crockford, an activist and film-maker: 'It was an amazing buzz. I think it was one of those rare times in your own history when you know you're there at an occasion that's historically important' (Women in London 1).

Alongside such events and campaigns, an unprecedented development in feminist publishing extended the influence and impact of the WLM. Over the course of a few years, a number of independent feminist publishing houses were established: Virago Press in 1973, Onlywomen Press in 1974, and the Women's Press in 1978. Britain's first feminist academic journal, *Feminist Review*, was launched in 1979. By the end of the decade, 'feminism' had become a broad cultural politics, which included independent publishing houses and academic journals. As Zoë Fairbairns states, 'New opportunities were opening for women all the time, and there was a thriving feminist culture in the worlds of writing, art, publishing, music and dance as well as politics […] It was an exciting time to be a young and activist woman' ('1984' 3). Indeed, according to the feminist critic Rita Felski, 'The women's movement has offered one of the most dynamic examples of a counter-ideology in recent years to have generated an oppositional public arena for the articulation of women's needs in critical opposition to the values of a male-defined society' (166). Her concept of the feminist counter-public sphere, derived from the theories of Jürgen Habermas, incorporates cultural and ideological interventions as well as explicitly political practices:

> [T]he feminist public sphere also constitutes a discursive arena which disseminates its arguments outward through such public channels of communication as books, journals, the mass media, and the education system. This gradual expansion of feminist values from their roots in the women's movement throughout society as a whole is a necessary corollary of feminism's claim to embody a catalyst of social and cultural change. (167)

A prominent example of the dissemination of feminist discourse at the time is the magazine *Spare Rib*. Launched by Rosie Boycott and Marsha Rowe in 1972 and initially edited by Rowe, it aimed to provide an alternative to traditional women's magazines, challenge conventional images of femininity and explore the ideas of the emerging women's movement. The magazine's first issue sold out, after which it sold approximately 20,000 copies monthly; notably, the newsagent W. H. Smith refused to stock it (Todd 61). Despite its relatively modest sales, as Rowe states, 'it had a powerful effect and each copy was read by lots of women' (Daly 1). According to Selina Todd:

> The significance of *Spare Rib* was that it suggested that women's pleasure was an area that feminism should engage with; it offered women a space to explore the potentialities of the relationship between the feminine fantasy embodied in the fashion model, and the reality of women's lives: work, family, sex, bodies. (77)

In its attempt to appeal to a wide range of readers, not simply self-defined feminists, the magazine drew on heterogeneous viewpoints and produced multiple, often contradictory, messages as a result. Rather than a providing a single theorization of women's oppression, the magazine offered a public and collective sounding board for women dissatisfied with existing gender relations and looking for alternative forms of social and personal life. As Rowe states, 'I found my voice by writing *Spare Rib* and a lot of women were doing the same thing' (Daly 3). Its constantly articulated themes of sexual inequality, the social construction of female identity, and the sexual objectification of women were also issues being explored in 1970s feminist fiction.

Feminist theoretical discourse also proliferated in the 1970s. Key works include Germaine Greer's *The Female Eunuch* (1970), which became an international 'bestseller' and catapulted its author to media notoriety; Eva Figes's *Patriarchal Attitudes* (1970); Marina Warner's *Alone of All Her Sex* (1976); the 1977 reissue of Virginia Woolf's *A Room of One's Own* (1929); Susie Orbach's *Fat Is a Feminist Issue* (1978); and Amrit Wilson's *Finding a Voice* (1978), the first published work of Black feminist criticism in the UK. Women's writing and women's studies courses also emerged in the decade in the adult and higher education sectors although the first full-fledged academic women's studies course was not introduced into the UK until 1980 when the MA in Women's Studies was established at the University of Kent, Canterbury. In addition, a number of US academics, including Elaine Showalter, wrote influential studies of the strong tradition of British feminist writing from the nineteenth century onwards. Many of these texts have created a lasting legacy but the most striking feature of the list as a whole is the preponderance of Marxist, Marxian and/or socialist feminist perspectives, especially in the first half of the decade; in particular, the work of feminist historian Sheila Rowbotham and that of feminist sociologists Ann Oakley, Lynne Segal and Elizabeth Wilson stands out as significant. In my deliberate exclusion from the list of the majority of North American theory and criticism, the very materialist basis of British feminism in the period may be seen, suggesting that it was much less willing than US feminism to repudiate Marxism as an explanatory theory. Indeed, it could be argued that UK feminism was motivated by the attempt to reinvent Marxian socialism in the light of radical feminist insights about women's position in patriarchy, a claim that is also compatible with fiction of the time as we shall see.

In this respect, the Marxist Feminist Literary Collective is indicative of the British feminist counter-sphere in the decade. It began as an informal network of women students and teachers in adult and higher education, which met in London from 1975 to 1977. It comprised a reading group, which focussed on classic Marxist texts and new French theories (which were distributed in translation). The Collective is best known for their collaborative essay, 'Women's Writing: *Jane Eyre, Shirley, Villette, Aurora Leigh*' (1978), which has become a key and much anthologized document in socialist-feminist literary criticism. Originally written for the Sociology of Literature Conference at the University of Essex in 1977, it was delivered polyphonically in a line of 9 women across the lecture room. The Collective represented an attempt to move beyond the 'images of women' criticism that dominated 1970s feminist theory, especially in the US, which they subject to a Marxist-feminist critique. Appropriating the work of Pierre Macherey, the Collective attends to the 'not-said' of the text as much as to what is explicitly represented and ideologically permitted, and reads the contradictions of the text as symptomatic of the inscription of gender difference:

> Any rigorous Machereyan analysis must account for the ideology of gender as it is written into or out of texts by either sex. Women writers, moreover, in response to their cultural exclusion, have developed a relatively autonomous, clandestine tradition of their own. (170)

The fact that they argue for the specificity of women's writing demonstrates their debt to gynocentric works such as Ellen Moers's *Literary Women* (1978) and Elaine Showalter's *A Literature of their Own* (1977). The Collective applies a Lacanian analysis to Charlotte Brontë's novel *Jane Eyre* (1847), which previously had been read in terms of bourgeois class mobility or as feminist triumph, and concludes that the novel is both more and less radical than these readings suggest:

> *Jane Eyre* does not attempt to rupture the dominant kinship structures. The ending of the novel affirms those very structures. The feminism of the novel resides in its 'not-said', its attempt to inscribe women as sexual subjects within this system. (174)

While working at a more self-consciously theoretical level than magazines such as *Spare Rib*, the Collective was engaged in similar questions about the relationship between the personal and the political, the relationship between gender and class, and the suitability of adapting 'male' theories to female subjects. Like magazine publishing, academic feminist criticism in the 1970s was part of a feminist counter-public sphere which sought to analyse and contest patriarchal attitudes and assumptions.

Defining the feminist text

The 1970s is perhaps the first period in history in which women wrote books as part of a collective, if diverse, feminist enterprise. As Rita Felski acknowledges, the feminist counter-public sphere comprised a critical mass of oppositional voices that allowed for the co-presence of multiple, even contradictory, discourses. But how did 1970s feminist fiction compare to the tradition of women's writing in Britain developed since the late eighteenth century? In *Beyond Feminist Aesthetics* (1989), Rita Felski argues that

> [t]he defining feature of the feminist text is a recognition and rejection of the ideological basis of the traditional script of heterosexual romance characterized by female passivity, dependence, and subordination, and an attempt to develop an alternative narrative and symbolic framework within which female identity can be located. (129)

In other words, feminist fictions eschew the plot and trajectory previously followed by the majority of women's texts and texts about women. They offer a decisive break with the marriage plot and an alternative to the two resolutions offered in the woman's novel of the preceding two centuries – namely, marriage or, not infrequently, death – even though opportunities for women in the immediate post-war years were seen as scarcely less limited than fictional ones with the alternatives being marriage and self-denial or spinsterhood and social stigma. Felski associates this literary shift with the social changes that began to happen from the 1960s onwards:

> As ideologies of female identity have changed, so too has the nature of women's plots. Thus the last twenty years have seen the emergence of a distinctive new narrative structure for women, tracing a process of *separation* as the essential condition for any path to self-knowledge. (124)

Significantly, the integration of women into patriarchal kinship structures is replaced by separation. Whereas earlier, especially modernist, women's novels may have called into question the marriage plot and undertaken a degree of psychological separation, it is only in the decades since the 1960s that this has been articulated so insistently in terms of a discourse of women's rights and an explicit exploration of alternatives to the status quo. As a result, feminist texts are frequently characterized by open-endedness, suggesting that they both evade traditional closure and gesture towards 'utopian' alternatives 'beyond the page'.

In terms of modes, one might expect social realism to dominate the years when WLM was prominent. In fact, the feminist novel takes a wide variety of forms in the 1970s including the Bildungsroman, the novel of self-discovery, the novel of ideas (utopia/dystopia), social(ist) realism, (post)modernist experimentalism and comic metafiction and fantasy. There is a marked emphasis on confessional modes, 'psychoanalytical' approaches, and a political patchwork of voices. Literary confessionalism is clearly congruent with the feminist practice of consciousness-raising. According to Patricia Waugh:

> Consciousness-raising, confessional writing, and the quest to find new forms in which to explore women's experience, were practiced in conjunction with a Marxist-feminist analysis of economic oppression and an existential critique of liberal exclusion and separation of the public and private. Confession was part of an attempt to forge, for the very first time, the political solidarity of a woman-centred culture organized to subvert the patriarchal structures (political and economic) of the liberal state. (200)

The self-discovery narrative becomes a key, if not dominant, mode of the period as a means of exploring the relationship between 'subjectivity' and the objective conditions of women's lives. It differs from the Bildungsroman in that it does not necessarily involve a move out into the social world but represents a kind of psychological and mythic journey of self-discovery. The genre is often accused of formal and ideological conservatism, and of bourgeois individualism but, as Felski argues, forcibly challenging the post-structuralist equation of radical form and content, this would be to misunderstand its function in the context of feminism:

> The feminist self-discovery narrative is not interested in the issue of the fictionality of literary representation as such, but seeks to negate the cultural authority of one version of women's experience in order to put alternative versions in its place. While rejecting the atomized individualism of the bourgeois literary tradition, it proceeds from the assumption that autonomous selfhood is not an outmoded fiction but still a pressing political concern. (151)

As Felski suggests, women writers of the 1970s did not feel the need to celebrate the postmodern dissolution of identity in the way that some men did. As Waugh observes, just as the WLM got underway, the postmodern critique of representation, identity and grand narratives challenged its very basis in the collectivity of women and female authorship, thus complicating the optimism of early confessional modes (198). However, it would be wrong to characterize 1970s feminist writers as predominately realists averse to experimentation and indifferent to questions of 'fictionality'. Indeed, as my research suggests, there is a surprising amount of formal experimentalism in 1970s fiction, both by more mainstream, literary writers such as Figes, Weldon, Carter and Tennant whose work is formally innovative using modernist and postmodernist techniques to deconstruct myths of the feminine; and by writers such as Michèle Roberts and Sara Maitland who emerged from feminist writers' groups and also experiment with form and voice.

In fact, rather than categorizing feminist fiction in terms of whether it is either 'social-political' or 'psychological-personal' in nature and making value judgements on this basis, Felski argues that feminist fiction works to collapse binaries and dualisms that characterize Leftist as well as bourgeois thinking:

> The importance of subjectivity, identity, and narrative in feminist fiction in turn raises a number of more general questions about the politics of literature and the insufficiency of sterile dichotomies – of realism versus experimentalism, identity versus negativity, tradition versus modernity – which have long structured oppositional thinking about cultural practices and in which the second term is unconditionally privileged over the first. The example of feminist literature suggests that the cultural needs of subordinate groups cannot be adequately grasped by continuing to think in terms of such antithetical dualisms. (152)

Felski's view of literature as serving or meeting the *needs* of women as a subordinate group might be regarded as overly functionalist here. The complex relationship between form, content, authorship and audience reception cannot be adequately or fully grasped by the notion of needs. But as she suggests, in the simultaneously social and experimental practice of consciousness-raising, all aspects of women's lives, cutting across the personal and political, were subject to discussion, exploration and analysis in texts of the period.

A decade of women's writing: Some key texts

There was already an established group of women writers by 1970, published by mainstream presses, which included Muriel Spark, Doris Lessing, Margaret Drabble and Iris Murdoch – to whose work Waugh gives the name 'Cautious Feminism' (192). Muriel Spark's novels from the early 1970s – *The Driver's Seat*

(1970), *Not to Disturb* (1971), and *The Hothouse by the East River* (1973) – treat a number of themes including the impediments to female authorship, the illusions of romantic love, and the relationship between power and myth. Iris Murdoch's *A Fairly Honourable Defeat* (1970) and *The Black Prince* (1973) use a range of metafictional devices and exploit several genres – thriller, romance and comedy – to explore the nature of deception and the relationship between truth, art and love. Doris Lessing's *The Summer before the Dark* (1973) is in many ways an exemplary feminist Bildungsroman, in which female self-discovery is depicted as a process of confrontation with the social world. The protagonist, Kate Brown, abandons her middle-class life as housewife, gets a job and has an extramarital affair, before moving to London to consider the feminine stereotypes that have governed her life. In *The Memoirs of a Survivor* (1974), Lessing uses the dystopian genre to depict a post-nuclear future in which sociobiological ideas about sex and gender come to the fore. These writers represent the first generation of post-war women writers, which is characterized by self-reflection on the problem of the woman writer. Collectively, they undertake an interrogation of grand narratives to show how they are lacking from a woman's point of view. Waugh argues that Lessing's use of the self-reflexive personal mode is one of the ways that 'women writers have tried to expand and explore a semiotic feminine subjectivity without abandoning the category of "women's experience" and the concept of an authorial voice' (204), and sees this mode being utilized by feminist writers throughout the period and up to the present day.

Secondly, there was a group of distinctly feminist writers emerging in the late 1960s and early 1970s, including Angela Carter, Fay Weldon and Eva Figes. Weldon's early novel, *Down among the Women* (1971), presents a feminist critique of the situation of women, especially the domestic drudgery of their roles as wives and mothers. In her later *Female Friends* (1975), Weldon explores the rivalries and antagonisms among women, depicting divisions between married and unmarried women, mothers and child-free women. Angela Carter's surrealist fantasy *The Infernal Desire Machines of Doctor Hoffman* (1972) explores the rival claims of (masculine) fascistic reason and (feminine) irrational desire, deconstructing both and arguing for the need to reconnect desire and affect. According to Waugh, Carter ultimately resists a thoroughgoing postmodernism and retains a commitment to the experience of the body (195). *The Passion of New Eve* (1977), according to Carter's own account in 'Notes from the Frontline', represents an 'anti-mythic' text, which she calls, in line with the times and with tongue only partly in cheek, a 'feminist tract about the social creation of femininity' (71). This summary, whether ironic or not, could stand as an apt description of many 1970s feminist texts. In parodic style, the novel exploits the distinction between biological sex and culturally constructed gender that it is the premise of post-Beauvoir second-wave feminism. Significantly, it attacks myths of femininity promulgated by feminism itself as much as by patriarchy.

Thirdly, there was a younger generation of feminist writers who emerged after 1975: Emma Tennant, Michèle Roberts, Zoë Fairbairns and, just outside the decade, Anna Wilson. Tennant's *Hotel de Dream* (1976) is a comic fantasy in which femininity represents the repressed unconscious of the patriarchal order. *The Bad Sister* (1978) takes the form of a Gothic fantasy, examining the meanings of sister and sisterhood, and showing them to be sites of conflict and contradiction. Waugh identifies both these generations with a phase of explicitly 'writing as a woman', which involves a 'quest to reconcile the collective and the personal voice' (192), and explores the meaning of the slogan 'the personal is the political'. She sees the dominant themes of the feminist middle period of post-war writing as 'identity, experience and female authorship' (197). While 'commentators often argue for sharp distinctions between a pre-1968 and a post-1978 generation of women writers, with the latter far more alert to the instabilities of the very category woman' (197), notions of feminine identity are interrogated by women writers in the whole period.

In terms of my fourth group, black women writers in the 1970s, one name stands out – Buchi Emecheta, who had a substantial number of UK publications following emigration from her native Nigeria. Emecheta's *In the Ditch* (1972) and *Second-Class Citizen* (1974) are autobiographical novels which foreground the destructive effects of racism and colonialism while exploring her experience as a female migrant bringing up several children in an alien and hostile country. Her novel *The Joys of Motherhood* (1979) records the impact on female selfhood of the loss of the mother. Unlike in many white feminist texts, the mother is not rejected or reviled; on the contrary, the loss of the mother makes it difficult for the protagonist to form a sense of female identity. *A Question of Silence* (1974) by the South African Bessie Head should also be mentioned, along with a notable publication by the Indian writer Ruth Prawer Jhabvala, *Heat and Dust* (1975), which was made into a successful film in the 1980s. One of the few mainstream texts produced by a non-white writer in the period, it explores the sexual status of women across cultures and through time, providing a pessimistic assessment of the fate of women in a world determined by patriarchal structures. There was a distinct lack of black British feminist texts in the decade; much more activity occurred in the US with writers such as Alice Walker, Toni Cade Bambara and Gloria Naylor coming to prominence. Black and Asian women's writing did not appear to reach a critical mass in the UK until 1980s, partly under the impetus of GLC funding for Arts and writers' groups and partly because of the groundswell of black feminism. As John McLeod argues in this volume, the 1970s was a distinctly pessimistic period in terms of black literary representation.

The same can be said of explicitly lesbian writing; there is no equivalent of US writers like Lisa Alther or of the comic lesbian novel at this time in the UK. (Britain would have to wait until 1985 and Jeanette Winterson for that.) Anna Wilson's *Cactus* (1980), published by the radical feminist Onlywomen Press just outside the period, is a wholly original novel, distinct from other feminist texts of the period. It represents an exploration of changing constructions of lesbian identity across two historical periods, following the concerns of two lesbian couples: Eleanor and Bea, an isolated couple living in the 1940s and 1950s, and Dee and Ann, who are part of the 1970s lesbian feminist movement. While the former relationship breaks down in the face of social obstacles, the latter benefits from the support of a collective movement. In many ways, it exemplifies US lesbian-feminist Adrienne Rich's concept of 'lesbian continuum', combining a critique of compulsory heterosexuality with representation of the bonds between women. It is a poignant, poetically crafted text, which combines feminist politics with psychological subtlety and depth.

While Waugh identifies the postmodern engagement with difference and performance as characterizing feminist fiction from the 1980s onwards, as self-reflexive uncertainty replaces the earlier faith in forms of confessional writing, she identifies an ongoing resistance to monolithic identity in women's writing whether this is imposed from outside by patriarchy or from within by feminist ideology itself. Indeed, much of the more mainstream feminist fiction of the seventies by Weldon, Carter and Tennant is characterized by the adoption of positions critical of, if not antithetical to, those of the dominant feminist politics of the time.

Key themes in 1970s feminist fiction

The major themes treated in 1970s feminist fiction may thus be summarized as follows: women's unequal position within patriarchy; female selfhood and identity; reproduction and motherhood; women's community; body politics; mother-daughter relations; (hetero)sexuality and lesbianism; women's work; and the woman writer. While class emerges as an issue to some extent, 'race' is relatively absent as a topic for fictional treatment. According to Paulina

Palmer, the themes treated in feminist fiction are largely radical feminist rather than socialist feminist in character (3). Given the previously discussed preponderance of socialist-feminist theory in the UK feminist public sphere, this is a very interesting point. The issues of identity, motherhood and sexuality rather than work, class and economic relations are uppermost in fiction of the period. There are exceptions such as Zoë Fairbairns's *Benefits* (1979) as I discuss below. However, rather than presenting 1970s fiction according to such typologies, I would argue that many of the psychological and psychoanalytic fictions of British feminist writers are informed by socialist and Marxian perspectives. The women writers involved in the group that produced *Tales I Tell My Mother* (1978), including Michèle Roberts, Zoë Fairbairns, Sara Maitland and Michelene Wandor, all come from a socialist background and integrate class issues to a much greater extent than comparable US fictions.

A key aim of the fiction was to explore 'woman's consciousness in a man's world' as Sheila Rowbotham's 1973 work put it or, as construed by French feminists, woman's place in the phallocentric Symbolic Order. The work of Kristeva and Cixous, as my discussion of the Marxist-Feminist Literary Collective showed, was being read in new translations and fed into the writers' and readers' groups of the period (a groundbreaking collection of writings, *New French Feminisms* was published in English translation in 1981, edited by Elaine Marks and Isabelle de Courtivron). The central theme of Eva Figes's *Days* (1974) is woman's marginal position in a male-dominated world and as such it coincides with the work of the French feminist writers and critics who were elaborating their theories of écriture féminine, the semiotic, and women's time in the mid-1970s. The novel's nameless narrator reconstructs her life and explores her relationship to her mother, grandmother, daughter and to men. *Days* depicts in a minimalist, modernist style the cycle of betrayal and repression that characterizes patriarchal family life and in particular mother–daughter relations. The novel charts the cyclical narrative of female oppression and collusion as a version of 'herstory'. Only women enter the narrative frame, which represents the space of the marginal and the repressed. Both the life lived and the style in which it is represented is spare. As the novel begins, the nameless narrator is lying paralysed in a hospital bed. Neither we, nor apparently she, knows who she is or why she is there:

> In this room there is not much for me to know. It is small, rectangular. In the days I have already spent here I have noted everything there is. I doubt whether there is anything left which I have not taken into account. And since I have

> nothing to occupy my mind, since I lie here incapable, I have also measured the walls and detected minor flaws: a long hair-crack in the ceiling and, round the lightswitch, a dark penumbra no doubt caused by the many hands which have rubbed against the wall whilst turning the light on and off. (8)

The room is at once her world, her prison and, indeed, a metaphorical coffin. Gradually, the narrator becomes accustomed to her surroundings and she begins to reconstruct the history of betrayal, disillusion and marginalization that has brought her to this point. It emerges that this history is a highly gendered one in which her mother, her grandmother and possibly her own daughter are trapped. From the textual fragments, we ascertain that as a child her mother was abandoned by her father; her mother had a breakdown, was hospitalized just as she now is, but refused ever to acknowledge or come to terms with her desertion. The narrator is forced to care for her brother and put her own needs second. On her mother's return, she takes on her care. In the meantime, her brother grows up, graduates, gets a well-paid job and moves away to start his own family. The narrator remains at home locked in a cycle of repression and silence. She is courted by a young doctor and is even encouraged by her mother to accept him on the basis that beggars can't be choosers, but defeated by circumstances, she lets the relationship peter out. Although she gets a secretarial job, she discovers that she is pregnant and returns to her mother's home to bring the baby up whereupon her mother takes control, reproducing her own mothering. The narrator goes back to work but by the time she returns home her daughter is asleep in bed. Her sense of desperation and the painful exchanges between mother and daughter are vividly depicted as is the irony of her response to the fiancé's assertion that she has her own life to lead: 'He was quite wrong about it: I never had my own life to lead. It has always belonged to other people' (79–80).

The narrator's story is a representative one of how a young girl becomes a woman and, in de Beauvoir's terms, 'the second sex' (351–390). The novel explores women's collusion with male abuses of power, with the ways in which women compound their own oppression by upholding traditional notions of male privilege. As Palmer states, the narrator's adult paralysis is a consequence of the 'immobilizing effect to which the destructive aspects of the mother-daughter bond can give rise' (118). As the novel progresses, the narrator's identity begins to merge with that of her mother in a cyclical, repetitive narrative exemplifying the notion of women's time theorized by Julia Kristeva in her 1979 essay of that name. In the following extract, the voices of mother and daughter across the generations are interspersed and represented in the first and third person simultaneously in a radical form of female dialogism:

> She (I) came into the room and kissed me (her) on the cheek, bending down over the bed. Her face felt fresh and cool from the winter evening outside. (Her warm face felt dry, almost desiccated to my touch.) How are you, mother? I felt my age: looking at her. She was looking youthful, her face flushed from the cold air, and smart, in the dark blue coat I had bought several weeks ago. (I always wanted to look nice.) And she was breathing hard as though she had been running, down the long corridors and up the stairs. Whew, she said, I'm puffed. I was afraid I'd be late. (I pulled up the chair and sat down to get my breath back. Now I saw that she was looking dreadful [...]). (Figes 96)

Perhaps surprisingly, given the consistent bleakness of tone, the novel concludes on a note of ambivalent hope with the narrator finally getting out of bed and moving to the chair on the other side of the room, but the reader is left unsure whether she will be able to resolve her maternal ambivalence, find a measure of autonomy and begin her life again.

Days represents a bleak, and radical feminist-inspired, assessment of women's symbolic placement. It is an extraordinary text that is influenced by the existentialist nihilism of both Kafka and Beckett to depict the alienation of woman within the phallocentric symbolic order. Continuing the anti-realist tradition of European modernism, it demonstrates Figes's commitment to modernist experiment and anti-realism in its foregrounding of stream of consciousness, metafictional techniques and epistemological uncertainty. Indeed, to some extent, the novel challenges Felski's view of feminist literature as privileging the confessional mode; *Days* represents an anti-confessional text, in the narrator's inability or refusal to illuminate her situation.

A common assumption about feminist fiction in the 1970s is that women writers did not write as mothers and eschew motherhood for literary creation. As Palmer points out, the figure of the mother was vilified in 1960s cultural discourse, especially by radical psychology, as the symbolic representation of repressive bourgeois society, a model feminists inherited in the 1970s (113). As part of that counter-culture, it was unexceptional for feminists to blame the mother who was seen as a tool of patriarchy by a succession of angry daughters. In this respect, the negative representation of motherhood seen in *Days* is characteristic of fiction of the period. Arguably, it took the best part of the decade to work through that maternal ambivalence to a more generous representation of the mother. The shift to a more positive representation in which matrilineage enables rather than constrains women's creativity occurs towards the end of the period and in the 1980s, although as may be seen in *Oranges Are Not the Only Fruit*, the monstrous mother is still a powerful motif in the mid-80s.

Nevertheless, some feminist writers may be seen to explore the contradictions and ambivalence of mothering from the perspective of the mother herself, and some writers make this a central theme. For example, the work of Michèle Roberts, influenced by French feminisms, explored the subversive possibilities of the pre-oedipal bond, positing the maternal as a form of resistance to patriarchy regardless of the biological act (Roberts herself is not a mother, incidentally). Roberts's first published novel, *A Piece of the Night* (1978), was one of the first to be published by the newly established Women's Press in 1978. It is dedicated to the women writers group that Roberts was a part of in the 1970s, including Wandor, Fairbairns, Maitland and Valerie Miner. All these writers contributed to the collection *Tales I Tell My Mother* and went on to explore aspects of women's movement informed by the feminist methodology of consciousness-raising, albeit in very different ways. While Fairbairns chose a social realist novel of ideas in *Benefits*, Roberts writes a psychoanalytically inflected, poetic text to explore female identity and collectivity.

A Piece of the Night is noteworthy not least for its ambitious attempt to encompass psychological and political themes and to unite socialist and radical feminist interests. The novel explores psychic processes, the semiotic realm and mother-daughter relations as well as depicting feminist collectivity, alternatives to heterosexuality, and attempts to reorganize family life. It charts the protagonist Julie's attempt to bring her daughter up in a women's household, her lesbian relationship with another woman, and her return home to look after her sick mother. The novel explores the mother-daughter relationship and motherhood as an institution along the lines of the US feminist Adrienne Rich. As Palmer comments, the novel highlights the 1970s debates about motherhood and the polarized attitudes that existed (95). It contrasts the attitudes of two generations of women: Julie, the daughter, sees feminism as a supportive and positive force in women's lives, while her mother Claire sees it as a threat to everything her generation values:

— Feminism's about mothers, Julie says despairingly: it's about backing them up.
— You could have fooled me, Claire says with great bitterness: as far as I can see, you hate everything that I believe in. (Roberts 91)

The novel is stylistically innovative and ambitious, at times approximating a Cixousian écriture féminine, the identification of femininity with an experimental, fluid form of writing as in Figes's *Days*. It is full of references to contemporary feminist theory and is clearly setting out to work through these artistically. It is also an apprentice work, which is arguably sometimes weighed down by its theoretical precepts as, for example, in the description of Julie performing a version of desirable femininity, which exemplifies John Berger's influential 1972 analysis of the way which 'men act and women appear' (45):

> Julie is never for a second free of the consciousness of what she looks like. She moves along the streets holding out to male passers-by photographs of herself taken from the most flattering angle, she spends hours despairingly contemplating her face and body in the mirror; her work suffers, she does not see other people but sees them seeing her. She does not know what it is to live inside her own skin, to look out from her body and forget it sometimes. Her body bombards her from every advertising poster and hoarding; long, lean, supple, golden, it simply *is*: passive, therefore enticing. She is a travesty of her body. She is laid out on a marble slab, chopped up and sold to the male public. She does not know where she resides when she looks at the sections of body spread out in front of her: head, tits, legs, cunt, bum. (Roberts 68)

Here, the use of free indirect discourse presents Julie as subject and object simultaneously. Julie's process of consciousness-raising leads her to reject traditional constructions of the feminine and to explore marginal and repressed identities of madwoman, whore and lesbian, which lead to conflict with her mother. In an allusion to theories of the monstrous feminine such as Cixous's 1976 essay 'The Laugh of the Medusa', and the motif of the 'madwoman in the attic' theorized in Gilbert and Gubar's 1979 critical study, Roberts represents the monstrous images of femininity that Julie appropriates and performs:

> Nobody dares to name me woman, for I am dangerous and powerful. I can make others go mad too, just by desiring them. I cause storms and migraines, I turn milk sour, I am both the ruined harvest and the shameful blood that sickens cattle. I am the witch whom you call your crazy daughter. You tell me I am mad; I tell myself that, every time I weep, my face blotched red, every time I scream to touch the silk of your breast and lay my head there. (108)

In the course of the novel Julie brings her daughter Bertha up in a lesbian feminist household and discovers the challenges and value of women's community. Roberts does not seek to idealize women's community; rather, she portrays both the difficulties faced, such as financial insecurity, and the benefits of mutual support. As Palmer comments, the novel is premised on the lesbian feminist theory that 'patriarchal culture is built upon the disruption of attachments between both mothers and daughters, and women in general' (117). Significantly, *A Piece of the Night* ends with a scene of feminist consciousness-raising, which reaffirms the value of women's community:

> Tell me about your past, Julie begins to urge other women, and they to urge her. The women sit in circles talking. They are passing telegrams along battle-lines, telling each other stories that will not put them to sleep, recognizing allies under the disguise of femininity, no longer smuggling ammunition over back garden walls, no longer corpses in the church and mouths of men. (186)

Julie accepts that she will have to work with Ben in the struggle over the care of their daughter Bertha just as she will have to negotiate a place for her mother, friends and lovers in her life. The novel is important in giving motherhood a symbolic place within feminism while providing a critique of the institution within patriarchy. In the earlier *Days* this isn't achieved; the daughter-narrator remains alienated from her own mother and the mothering role.

Feminists utilized literature as a way of voicing and working through contradictions and paradoxes in women's lives. One reason that issues of female identity feature more prominently than those of 'work', even in the fiction of socialist British writers, is that the novel arguably lends itself better to the treatment of individual psychology than broad social and political themes. Waugh argues that the political rights discourse of feminism was not easily compatible with the fictional articulation of 'human' needs such as love and affection (197). Even in the seventies therefore, feminist fiction is dominated by questions of identity rather than politics – 'who am I?' rather than 'what is to be done?' Nevertheless, the 1970s is characterized by the symbolic attempt to overcome this dichotomy; one particularly interesting example of this attempt is Zoë Fairbairns's *Benefits*, which explores the difficult relationship between work and motherhood, and dramatizes contemporary debates concerning paying mothers for the work they do. *Benefits* was published in 1979 in the new Virago fiction series and dedicated to the same women writers' group of which Roberts was part. In writing the novel, Fairbairns

> set out to make fiction of sexual politics, to explore and dramatize sexual politics – of course it is no coincidence that a feminist press should choose to publish it, because those were the issues that interested them too. ('1984', 8)

Unlike *Days* and *A Piece of the Night*, *Benefits* is a realist 'novel of ideas', a key genre in feminist fiction. Ideologically engaged, and committed to women's activism, it works out a specific political issue: what would happen to you, me and the woman next door if women were paid to be mothers? As previously discussed, The Wages for Housework campaign was based on the theory that as women's work is outside the capitalist economy it cannot be afforded a value, therefore it should be brought into the capitalist system and seen as productive labour. In a lecture to commemorate George Orwell's *Nineteen Eighty-Four* (1949), which *Benefits* reworks, Fairbairns describes how the motivation to write her own novel came out of her enthusiastic yet ambivalent response to this political issue:

> It was a controversial campaign, even within the women's movement. Some feminists supported it, believing as I did that financial independence was a necessary precondition for equality; but others took the view that if you pay women to stay at home to look after children it will confirm them in that role and then they will never get away. Oddly enough, I found that argument as convincing as the other one. In the Wages for Housework debate, I was on both sides. Being on both sides is not a very comfortable position to be in ideologically, but it is the perfect posture from which to write a novel. ('1984', 3)

In her fictional working out of the issue, human emotions are shown to complicate the straightforward application of theory, which comes up against the problem of women's work as a 'labour of love'; it cannot be easily quantified. However, as the women's movement insisted, housework is not outside the capitalist and patriarchal system; it props it up and, as in Figes's *Days*, Fairbairns explores domesticity as a form of female alienation. She fictionalizes the debate from both sides, ultimately showing the deleterious effects of paying women for their domestic labour. The text reflects the socialist feminist critique of both Marxism as gender-blind and radical feminism as eliding divisions between women. Like Orwell before her, Fairbairns presents a realistic representation of a dystopian social world, in her case depicting the lived experiences of the women's liberation movement. The following extract could indeed have come from her lecture, so journalistic is it in tone and presentation:

> Women active in what was then known as the women's liberation movement have other reasons for remembering that summer. One of the major demands of that movement was for a woman's right to abortion on demand. It seemed axiomatic that women could not advance without full control of their fertility [...] And throughout that summer, a Select Committee of MPs, under pressure from organized anti-feminists, was considering ways of making abortions even more difficult to obtain, particularly for those women who sought them merely because they did not wish to be pregnant. The women's liberationists' response to these efforts was to commit themselves, this gleaming summer, to vigorous grassroots campaigning [...] (*Benefits* 5)

Fairbairns has been criticized on aesthetic grounds (see Palmer), yet the novel skilfully weaves political ideology and character development just as Orwell did in *Nineteen Eighty-Four*. The novel adopts a patchwork approach, following the different characters as they negotiate contradictions of family life, class and work over several decades. In an Orwellian vein, it also presents a fore-warning of the deleterious consequences of women ceding control of their fertility and decision-making to men or of pursuing an agenda of promoting motherhood as the exemplary feminist issue:

> All mothers, regardless of race, marital state or domestic competence would be eligible for the weekly payment, so long as they stayed at home and looked after children under 16. In calling the payment simply Benefit, no risk was run of confusing it with other benefits, for these were all abolished. They were unnecessary. The explosion of job opportunities that would result from the economic upturn and women leaving work, would ensure that no man need be unemployed; Benefit mothers would not need social security or income supplements; and, as for sickness and old age, people who wished to be insured could make private arrangements. Motherhood, on the other hand, was not a misfortune to be insured against; it was a national service to be paid for. (56)

As the author herself comments, her dystopian vision proved remarkably accurate in some respects, most notably its prediction of 1980s Thatcherite family values and the 'Back to Basics' campaign of the 1990s – but not in others. While women's double burden and relative maternal poverty remain a feature of the twenty-first century, the idea that women could or should be removed entirely from the workplace seems a distant if not fantastic one. As Fairbairns notes, rather the opposite has happened with 'staying at home' seen as not really pulling your weight despite the hardship of childcare ('1984', 7). Of the three novels considered in detail here, Fairbairns's text is the one that now seems the most dated largely because, in its realist register and topical material, it is the one most tied to its historical moment of production. It does, however, succeed in fulfilling the function ascribed by Felski to feminist literature of addressing a collective readership and speaking vividly and immediately to the desires and contradictions in women's lives.

Conclusion

In her essay on post-war women's writing, Patricia Waugh persuasively argues 'a case for underlying continuities in British women's fiction' since even before the emergence of the women's liberation movement in the late 1960s, insisting that it is wrong to divorce the fiction of the late 1960s and 1970s from what came before and afterwards (191). With this point in mind, I would argue that 1970s feminist fiction exhibits both continuities and discontinuities with previous and following decades. It treats similar themes of gender inequality, the problematization of female identity, and the critique of marriage and motherhood, seen historically in women's writing. It also utilizes a similar variety of modes and styles as writing before and since the decade: social realism, (post)modernist experiment and fantasy. Where I would argue it did differ significantly was in the production of this work as 'feminist fiction' as a result of the emergence of women's publishing houses, women's writing groups and the feminist counter-public sphere as a whole. There was a growth in collaborative work, publishing opportunities and in feminist reading communities. Moreover, in the fiction of the 1970s, there was a bold and explicit assertion of previously taboo topics such as lesbianism, the crisis in gender relations, and the feminist disruption of patriarchy. In this respect, 1970s feminist fiction was less tentative than that of the 1960s, and less fragmented than the 1980s. There was, in addition, a new focus on women's activism and movement, relations among women and 'sisterhood', and on consciousness-raising as a transformative tool. What is also significant is that there were fewer texts by black feminists and lesbian feminists than in the US at the time, or in the 1980s in the UK. While there is perhaps no absolute break between the 1960s and the1970s, or the 1970s and the 1980s, both society and feminist fiction were transformed across the period, and new generations of women writers emerged in the succeeding decades including Pat Barker, Rose Tremain and Maggie Gee (Granta Best Young British Novelists 1983); Jeanette Winterson and A. L. Kennedy (Granta list 1993); and Sarah Waters, Monica Ali and Zadie Smith (Granta list 2003). In my assessment of the 1970s as one of the most politically and aesthetically radical periods of women's writing to be seen in any decade or indeed century, I would concur with the feminist critic Gayle Greene who states: 'Feminist fiction is the most revolutionary movement in contemporary fiction – revolutionary both in that it is formally innovative and in that it helped make a social revolution' (2).

Works cited

Berger, John. *Ways of Seeing*. London: Penguin, 1972.
Brannigan, John. *Orwell to the Present: Literature in England, 1945–2000*. Basingstoke: Palgrave Macmillan, 2003.

British Library Website. 'Learning: Dreamers and Dissenters'. (http:www.bl.uk/learning/histcitizen/21cc/counterculture/liberation/shrew/shrew.html) Accessed 24 February 2010.

Cadwalladr, Carole. 'It's Been a Long Journey and We're Not there Yet'. *Observer*, Sunday 7 December 2008. (http://www.guardian.co.uk/lifeandstyle/2008/dec/07/women-equality-rights-feminism) Accessed 24 February 2010.

Carter, Angela. *The Infernal Desire Machines of Doctor Hoffman*. London: Rupert Hart-Davis, 1972.

———. *The Passion of New Eve*. London: Gollanz, 1977.

———. 'Notes from the Frontline', in *On Gender and Writing*. Ed. by Michelene Wandor. London: Pandora Press, 1983. 69–77.

Cixous, Hélène. 'The Laugh of the Medusa', *Signs* 1: 4 1976: 876–93.

Daly, Claire. '"Breaking Out of the Mould", Interview with Marsha Rowe'. *The F Word: Contemporary UK Feminism*. 31 January 2008. (http://www.thefword.org.uk/features/2008/01/marsha_rowe) Accessed 24 February 2010.

de Beauvoir, Simone. *The Second Sex*. Trans. and ed. by H. M. Parshley. London: Vintage, 1997 [1953].

Emecheta, Buchi. *In the Ditch*. London: Heinemann, 1972.

———. *Second-Class Citizen*. London: Fontana, 1977 [1974].

———. *The Joys of Motherhood*. London: Heinemann, 1979.

Fairbairns, Zoë. *Benefits*. London: Virago, 1979.

———. '84 Came and Went'. 2000. (http://www.zoefairbairns.co.uk.1984.htm) Accessed 10 March 2010.

———, Sara Maitland, Valerie Miner, Michele Roberts and Michelene Wandour. *Tales I Tell My Mother: A Collection of Feminist Short Stories*. London: Journeyman, 1978.

Felski, Rita. *Beyond Feminist Aesthetics: Feminist Literature and Social Change*. London: Hutchinson Radius, 1989.

Figes, Eva. *Patriarchal Attitudes: Women in Society*. London: Faber, 1970.

———. *Days*. London: Faber and Faber, 1974.

Gilbert, Sandra M. and Susan Gubar. *The Madwoman in the Attic: The Woman Writer and the Nineteenth-Century Literary Imagination*. New Haven: Yale UP, 1979.

Greene, Gayle. *Changing the Story: Feminist Fiction and the Tradition*. Indianapolis: Indiana UP, 1991.

Greer, Germaine. *The Female Eunuch*. London: MacGibbon & Kee, 1970.

Head, Bessie. *A Question of Power*. London: Heinemann, 1974.

Jhabvala, Ruth Prawer. *Heat and Dust*. London: J. Murray, 1975.

Kristeva, Julia. 'Women's Time'. *Signs* 7:1, 1981 [1979]: 77–92.

Lessing, Doris. *The Summer before the Dark*. London: Cape, 1973.

———. *The Memoirs of a Survivor*. London: Octagon Press: 1974.

Maria, Dalla Costa and Selma James. *The Power of Women and the Subversion of the Community*. Bristol: Falling Wall Press, 1973.

Marxist-Feminist Literary Collective. 'Women Writing: *Jane Eyre, Shirley, Villette, Aurora Leigh*'. *Ideology and Consciousness*, 3, 1978: 30–5.
Millett, Kate. *Sexual Politics*. London: Virago, 1977 [1970].
Mitchell, Juliet. *Woman's Estate*. Harmondsworth: Penguin, 1971.
——. and Ann Oakley, eds. *The Rights and Wrongs of Women*. Harmondsworth: Penguin, 1976.
Moers, Ellen. *Literary Women*. London: The Women's Press, 1978.
Murdoch, Iris. *A Fairly Honourable Defeat*. London: Chatto & Windus, 1970.
——. *The Black Prince*. London: Chatto & Windus, 1973.
Oakley, Ann. *Housewife*. London: Allen Lane, 1974.
Orbach, Susie. *Fat Is a Feminist Issue*. London: Hamlyn, 1984.
Palmer, Paulina. *Contemporary Women's Fiction: Narrative Practice and Feminist Theory*. New York and London: Harvester Wheatsheaf, 1989.
Rice, Philip and Patricia Waugh, eds. *Literary Theory: A Reader*. London: Edward Arnold, 1992.
Rich, Adrienne. *Of Woman Born: Motherhood as Experience and Institution*. New York: W. W. Norton, 1976.
——.'Compulsory Heterosexuality and Lesbian Existence', in *The Lesbian and Gay Studies Reader*. Ed. by Henry Abelove, Michele Aina Barale, and David M. Halperin. London & New York: Routledge, 1993. 227–54.
Roberts, Michèle. *A Piece of the Night*. London: Women's Press, 1978.
Rowbotham, Sheila. *Women, Resistance and Revolution*. London: Allen Lane, 1972.
——. *Hidden from History*. London: Pluto Press, 1973.
——. *Woman's Consciousness, Man's World*. London: Penguin, 1973.
Segal, Lynne, Sheila Rowbotham and Hilary Wainwright. *Beyond the Fragments*. Newcastle upon Tyne: Newcastle Socialist Centre, 1979.
Showalter, Elaine. *A Literature of Their Own: From Charlotte Brontë to Doris Lessing*. London: Virago, 1977.
Spark, Muriel. *The Driver's Seat*. London: Macmillan, 1970.
——. *Not to Disturb*. London: Macmillan, 1971.
——. *The Hothouse by the East River*. London: Macmillan, 1973.
Stubbs, Patricia. *Women and Fiction: Feminism and the Novel 1880–1920*. Brighton: Harvester Wheatsheaf, 1979.
Tennant, Emma. *Hotel de Dream*. London: Gollanz, 1976.
——. *The Bad Sister*. London: Gollanz, 1978.
Todd, Selina. 'Models and Menstruation: *Spare Rib* Magazine, Feminism, Femininity and Pleasure'. *Studies in Social and Political Thought*. 1, (1999): 60–78. (www.sussex.ac.uk/cspt/documents/issue1-5) Accessed 10 March 2010.
Warner, Marina. *Alone of All Her Sex: The Myth and Cult of the Virgin Mary*. London: Weidenfeld & Nicholson, 1976.

Waugh, Patricia. 'The Woman Writer and the Continuities of Feminism', in *A Concise Companion to Contemporary British Fiction*. Ed by James F. English, Oxford: Wiley-Blackwell. 2006, 188–208.

Weldon, Fay. *Down among the Women*. London: Heinemann, 1971.

———. *Female Friends*. London: Heineman, 1975.

Wilson, Amrit. *Finding a Voice*. London: Virago, 1978.

Wilson, Anna. *Cactus*. London: Onlywomen Press, 1980.

Wilson, Elizabeth. *Only Halfway to Paradise: Women in Postwar Britain, 1945–1968*. London: Tavistock, 1980.

———. *Women and the Welfare State*. London: Tavistock, 1977.

Women in London. 'Ms Understood: Women's Liberation in 70s Britain – Women's Library' – 8th October to 31st March 2010. (www.womeninlondon.org.uk/2009/09/event-women-library/). Accessed 24 February 2010.

Woolf, Virginia. *A Room of One's Own*. London: Grafton, 1977 [1929].

4

Black British Culture and Fiction in the 1970s

John McLeod

Black British writing in the shade

If many popular accounts of the decade are to be believed, there was no black British 1970s. Howard Sounes's entertaining cultural retrospective, *Seventies: The Sights, Sounds and Ideas of a Brilliant Decade* (2006), casts a transatlantic eye across the art of David Hockney, David Bowie and the advent of glam rock, the impact of the films of Steven Spielberg and Francis Ford Coppola, the anger of punk, the novels of Iris Murdoch and the comedy of Monty Python, but has nothing to say about the emergence of two-tone bands and ska in Britain's increasingly multicultural cities, the films of Horace Ové or the poetry of Linton Kwesi Johnson. While Andy Beckett's *When the Lights Went Out* (2009) recalls the infamous Grunwick strike called in 1977 predominantly by British Asian workers, this incident is enveloped within his wider portrayal of Britain's political tensions, particularly between trade unions and government, with only the occasional nod made to the increasing significance of race in British political culture at the time (such as the 1976 Race Relations Act and attempts by government to restrict immigration). And hardly any attention is given to the growth of black political culture at this time as signalled by the establishment and popularity of the publication *Race Today*, which first appeared in 1969 and was published from 1973 by the influential *Race Today* Collective; or protests against police intimidation such as the 1970 march against the police's harassment of the patrons of Notting Hill's Mangrove Restaurant which led to the trial of the so-called Mangrove 9; or the emergence of a new British-born rather than migrant generation of black Britons – youthful, uncompromising and militant – who responded to discrimination with outrage and action, as evidenced at the 1976 Notting Hill Carnival by the violence which erupted between carnival-goers and the Metropolitan Police; or the fledgling black women's political organizations. Reading most popular accounts of the 1970s, it is quickly forgotten that this was the decade when the divisive impact of race in the articulation and imagining of national community in the wake of Enoch Powell's 1968 comments on immigration became spectacularly visible in conflicts such as those witnessed at the 1976 Carnival, or between the National Front and the Anti-Facist League in Southall in 1979 where the New Zealand activist Blair Peach was killed. Marginalized at the time, the struggles of black Britons (and their supporters) are sidelined again in those accounts of the seventies which do not illuminate the significance of black British politics and of black cultural transformation without which any cultural or social history of the decade appears impoverished. As regards these matters, and to rent Beckett's titular formula, the lights remain out.

However, in truth there is so much to see. In many ways, the 1970s was something of a watershed in the fortunes of post-war black British culture, and especially as regards literary production. It is the purpose of this chapter to bring illumination to an otherwise shaded terrain, and in so doing I want to focus upon some of the literary-fictional activities of the seventies that are neglected unlike the more historically luminescent black British cultural endeavours of popular music and poetry. While it is something of a cliché to talk about the seventies more widely as a transitional moment between the revolutionary sixties and the individualism of the eighties – a cliché which the present collection of essays determinedly seeks to contest – it is fair to say that, as far as literary fiction is concerned, at first sight the horizon of black British fiction in the seventies can seem somewhat crepuscular. One is hard-pressed to find mention of seventies black British texts in just about any existing historical account of British writing since 1945, while scholarly accounts of black British writing also reveal the lacunae of the seventies, not least because literary endeavours from the decade can seem dwarfed by the gathering of creative energies that come immediately before and after. As I have claimed elsewhere (McLeod 'Lessons'), the mid-century decades of the fifties and sixties are especially rich ones for black British fiction, with the arrival in the UK of a new generation of writers often from the Caribbean – E. R. Braithwaite, George Lamming, V. S. Naipaul, Andrew Salkey, Sam Selvon – who formulated vivid reflections of migrant life in Britain in a clutch of fascinating and influential novels in the initial post-war years. The 1980s welcomed the advent of a new generation of writers – Hanif Kureishi, Timothy Mo, Caryl Phillips, Joan Riley, Salman Rushdie – born or raised in Britain and designated as distinctly postcolonial, whose writing about colonialism's unhappy pasts and present consequences helped establish a sharp sense of what Randall Stevenson labels 'the "pluri-culture"' (521) of English life in later years, and arguably more broadly throughout the British Isles too. Consequently, the seventies can seem devoid of significant fiction writing, and it must be acknowledged that the decade does not contain the same sense of richness identified with previous and subsequent decades. James Procter's richly authoritative anthology *Writing Black Britain* (2000) includes a long section of entries in its section 'late 1960s to mid-1980s' but features very few examples of 1970s fiction, and this allows us to see in snapshot how many black writers were turning to other genres – poetry, autobiography, political polemic and essay – as a way of contending with the increasingly vexed atmosphere of Britain at the time.

In addition, on the whole, those writers who became established in the mid-century were turning away from Britain in their work and in their lives by travelling extensively overseas or moving back to once-colonized locations. George Lamming, whose novel *The Emigrants* (1954) gave a coruscating account of metropolitan migrant life, had become primarily concerned with the Caribbean and published effectively his last novel, *Natives of My Person*, in 1972. V. S. Naipaul's writing of the 1970s reflected his growing intimacy with India and his Indian heritage in his travel book *India: A Wounded Civilisation* (1977), and he portrayed his jaundiced disillusionment with postcolonial politics in his three novels of the decade – *In A Free State* (1971), *Guerrillas* (1975) and *A Bend in the River* (1979) – which roam the globe and in which Britain is hardly glimpsed, although admittedly later he would come to reflect on post-war Britain in works such as *The Enigma of Arrival* (1987) and *Half a Life* (2001), but such fictions looked back to the days prior to the seventies. The momentum effected by post-war migrant writers immediately after the war appears to dissipate in the seventies. Institutions such as the BBC had enabled black writers to encounter each other and come together in informal networks, such as the affiliations engendered by the *Caribbean Voices* radio programmes which connected writers from disparate parts of the Caribbean, while the late-1960s Caribbean Artists Movement (CAM), which was brokered in Britain and owed much to the confluent energies of British-based figures such as John La Rose, Edward Kamau Brathwaite and Andrew Salkey, had effectively finished its activities by 1972. In one respect, the advent of the 1970s marks an ending of a particular moment in the history of black British writing with many of those identified with the post-war migrant generation of writers moving away from Britain, both on the page and in their travels. From the eighties new constellations of black writing in Britain would emerge supported by mechanisms such as the

Booker Prize – which encroached increasingly in public consciousness in the wake of Salman Rushdie's 1981 success (Huggan 105–123) – and Granta's ten-yearly 'Best of Young British Novelists' list of 20 exciting writers under the age of 40, which brought the work of figures such as Ben Okri and Caryl Phillips to wider attention (and it would be this generation that would put the category of 'black British writing' under unbearable pressure).

While it is possible to speak of black British *writers* of the 1970s, it is much harder to identify a distinctive black British *writing*, formulated (contentiously or confluently) across a body of writers who interacted with each other or wrote in the cognisance of the examples of others. Black British writers of the 1970s were far more isolated figures, siloed within an often unaccommodating political and cultural landscape, whose work often depicted the grimness, loneliness and pessimism of trying to reckon with and live within an increasingly racist and prejudicial environment long after the initial excitements of migrant arrival had paled. But if we align them retrospectively, historical hindsight enables us to see how they comprised quite a busy constituency of literary endeavour. The seventies may look arid for black British prose at first glance, but this was the decade of significant works that include Buchi Emecheta's early novels *In The Ditch* (1972) and *Second-Class Citizen* (1974), Wilson Harris's British-based fictions such as *Black Marsden* (1972) and *The Tree of the Sun* (1978), Sam Selvon's *Moses Ascending* (1975), Beryl Gilroy's *Black Teacher* (1976), Farrukh Dhondy's *East End at Your Feet* (1976) and his novel for young adults *The Siege of Babylon* (1978), E. R. Braithwaite's *Reluctant Neighbours* (1972) and Kamala Markandaya's *The Nowhere Man* (1972); although the publication of the debut novels by two writers identified more with the new generation of the eighties – Timothy Mo's *The Monkey King* (1978) and Salman Rushdie's *Grimus* (1975) – should remind us of the essential untidiness of attempting to separate decades, or generations of writers, into neat distinctive units, of course.

The work of these writers owes something to the changing cultural and political energies of the decade. As Anne Walmsley summarizes, '1972 proved in many ways to be the end of an era in the life of West Indians in Britain. […] This was the year in which the 1971 Immigration Act came into force, bringing all primary black immigration to an end. The Caribbean community gradually became less one of immigrants and exiles, more one of black British. […] [I]t is reckoned that, by the mid 1970s, two out of every five black people in Britain were born there' (300). These demographical shifts impacted tectonically on the terrain of black British cultural production as the decade unfolded. The art of fiction seemed at the time less attractive than other cultural forms especially for both established migrants and British-born youth, and, as we shall see, much writing of the decade moved discernibly away from experimentally creative modes and towards the documentary or chronicle, as in the work of Emecheta, Gilroy and Braithwaite, to the extent that fiction writing sometimes became documentary-making by other means or gave way entirely to the prose memoir (the dissolving of a clear line between novel and memoir/chronicle will be a preoccupation of this chapter). In the seventies popular music became perhaps the most significant creative outlet for youthful black British voices, especially towards the end of the decade with the rise of bands such as The Selecter, The Specials and UB40, in which young white and black Britons blended a range of musical styles (reggae, rock, ska) and sang in protest to the racism, discrimination and poverty at large on Britain's streets. As Pauline Black, the mixed-race lead singer of The Selecter recalls, 'we were all so earnest about society's ills. We wanted to write political songs about socially charged stuff. We were talking about the life on the street from a largely black perspective' (160). Not surprisingly, the most important writer to emerge from the decade – dub poet Linton Kwesi Johnson – brought together poetry and music in his verse which, more than any other literary output from the decade, captures the political militancy and aesthetic creativity of young black Britons at the time. Black British fiction remains at a remove from these youthful militant activities partly because much of it was produced *not* by the British-born but by an aging migrant generation that was at times either alarmed by their children's aggressiveness, satirical of their political militancy, or unwilling to release them from their metaphorization as part of a future post-racial community that might arrive eventually. As we shall see, much seventies black British fiction is distinctly concerned with the bleak, racist social landscape of the time and the political necessity of challenging prejudice, as was black British youth; yet it rarely possesses the ardent experimentalism of youth and seems much more wearied when contemplating the enormity of the task facing those who wish to destroy once and for all the pernicious discourses of race in British life. The challenge of taking on discrimination at the levels of state and street was discovered more in popular cultural endeavours, especially in the latter half of the decade, with rock ready to take on racism in acts of political and collective solidarity.

But while literary fiction sat to one side of the mainstream thrust of black political culture of the time – and, as in Sam Selvon's work, openly satirized it – it nonetheless constituted a political micro-culture of its own. To be sure, in writing from the time one might discern literary responses to social conditions that dispiritingly marked the disempowering prejudices of Britain and offered very little faith in the possibility of postcolonial transformation. That said, sometimes black British writing pointed in a more progressive direction as writers dealt with matters often missing from more robust and distinctly macho forms of social protest and black political culture at large. This is especially true of black British women's writing as will be noted towards the end of the chapter. Yet even here optimism is hard to find, and it is an unhappy truth of so much black British fiction and prose of the seventies that a sense of progressive, productive change for the better is difficult to discover or, when envisioned, to sustain. Little of the revolutionary energy and confidence within youthful popular cultural endeavours can be found in these texts, partly because the new energies of younger British-born fiction writers would not be established until the eighties.

As Mark Stein has counselled, '[g]rouping texts together as black texts, or women's writing, as post-colonial, or gay, is an act in history – an intervention – that conditions its significance and the meaning that texts will attain in a reading' (9). The emergence of a distinctly black British literature is indebted to the conditions of possibility which obtained in the 1970s, where the term 'black British' accrued particular significance and currency. While the terms 'black British literature' and its sub-set 'black British fiction' have been used to gather together a range of texts by black writers in Britain, migrant or British-born, published since the end of the Second World War to the present day, most scholarly discussions of these terms make a number of important points which sharpen their conceptual focus. The 1970s saw the productive articulation of 'black' as a politicized sign of racial pride and political dissidence often by the British-born descendents of New Commonwealth migrants, one that boldly stressed their right to belong to the imagined community of the British nation rather than their ancestral affiliations to locations overseas. This new inflection of race could be found in street-level popular political protest and vernacular cultural activities – anti-racist demonstrations, popular musical endeavours – and expressed something of (in A. Sivanandan's phrase) the 'different hunger' (49) of black British youth, sometimes working in concert with white supporters. Yet it also took hold in the academy, in the activities of journals like *Race and Class*, the title of which was coined in 1974 to capture the increasingly politicized sense of race which emerges in the seventies (the journal had been titled *Race* since its inception in 1959), and in the work of intellectuals such as Stuart Hall who was head of the influential Centre for Contemporary Cultural Studies in Birmingham between 1969 and 1979, and which produced in 1978 one of the most important critiques of state authoritarianism in 1970s Britain and its impact on immigrants and other demonized figures, the collection *Policing the Crisis: Mugging, the State, and Law and Order*. As Kwesi Owusu argues, this was the decade in which was formulated a 'systematic engagement with "race" and the black presence in British cultural studies' (2), one that sought to answer back to the increasing obsession with race in formal politics and the media concerning 'issues about "blacks and crime", "black youth policing", "rise of the fascist National Front", "Mrs Thatcher's fear of being swamped by foreigners", "Enoch Powell's legacy" and so on' (3). Indeed, the seventies was a decade in which a politicized articulation of race could be found on both sides of the political divide, in the speeches of Margaret Thatcher and the editorials of A. Sivanandan, and which betrays the increasingly polarized and embattled terrain of race-thinking which became increasingly central to British political life during these years, and which helped make seventies Britain seem almost as a warzone for black Britons. Andy Beckett soberly notes that between 1975 and 1977, 'the number of assaults, robberies and violent thefts suffered by Asian and Afro-Caribbean Britons increased by almost a third' (368); by 1982 Sivanandan had come to view the nation-state as fatally authoritarian in its relations with black people, with the police acting as 'a foreign force, an army of occupation' (48).

In addition, as a tool of political anti-racist dissent 'black British' was a stratagem of political solidarity intended to bring together black people of different ethnicities, faiths and ancestral locations who were oppressed in Britain as immigrants or members of embattled minority communities. Primarily, the term enveloped those from Africa, the Caribbean and South Asia, but it could also be extended to other migrant communities such as the overseas Chinese. My inclusion of Hong Kong-born novelist Timothy Mo in the list of black British writers I gave above might strike one today as slightly odd, but in the black British seventies, this issue would have been less immediately contentious: the overseas Chinese, like South Asian Britons, were black 'politically'. As it transpired, alliances between black Britons from across these regions were often uneasy: as James Procter remarks, '[i]f the label was politically successful in bringing about an alliance and exchange between Britain's different migrant communities, then this conversation was often uneven and one-sided' (*Dwelling* 6). Ultimately, tensions both within and between different constituencies of black Britons would prove overwhelming by the end of the 1980s. However, it is important to remember, following Alison Donnell's assessment, that the 'politicisation of black consciousness in the 1970s – when the media cocktail of race riots, mugging and carnival led to a powerful and damaging representation of black youth as criminalized and subcultural – was clearly a reaction and opposition to state racism and offered a vital, if limited, platform for self-representation' (xii).

Black British literary endeavours of the seventies were inflected by, and never far away from, the distinctly politicized social and cultural landscape of the time, in which race and resistance loomed large. The emergence of a self-declared 'black British' response to the racism and intimidation that had acquired political legitimation in the speeches of Powell and Thatcher marked a shift from a politics of resistance to one of rebellion, a process Sivanandan details (3–54), so that during the 1970s, the activities of state apparatuses such as the Metropolitan Police force in London were met by an equally incendiary response from Britain's youth. In terms of literary culture, it was black British poetry rather than fiction, perhaps, which constituted the vanguard of the shaping of an anti-racist literary consciousness. Linton Kwesi Johnson's milestone collection of dub poetry, *Voices of the Living and the Dead* appeared in 1974, with his *Dread, Beat an' Blood* appearing in 1975 (an album recording was released in 1978), while James Berry's influential anthology *Bluefoot Traveller: Poetry by Westindians in Britain* was published in 1976. Although sometimes seeming at a remove from an overtly rebellious standpoint, much black British fiction was not ignorant of the consciousness and frustrations of the time voiced more effectively and ardently elsewhere, as we shall see – although the anti-racist activities of the decade were satirized as well as supported, critiqued as well as condoned.

Settling and reckoning

Black British writers were under few illusions about the grim conditions of Britain in the 1970s especially for migrants and their British-born children. Twenty-five years after the end of the Second World War and the beginning of mass migration from the colonies to the motherland, the longstanding colonial myth of Britain as a welcoming homeland for colonial peoples had been well and truly dispatched. The cosmopolitanism of its big cities was hemmed in by poverty, racism and hostility. The Trinidad-born novelist Shiva Naipaul had this to say about Earls Court, London, in an article from 1973:

> Earls Court is nothing if not Cosmopolitan. Long-haired students from the Continent weighted under rucksacks studded with the flags of their countries of origin pore over street maps. Bearded Australians study the poster that invites

them to join the Zambesi club – Rhodesians, South Africans, New Zealanders are also welcome. West Indians – lithe black bucks dressed in the height of fashion – parade aimlessly. […] From the hamburger joint not many yards away throbs a delirium of pop music. Hippie-clad young men and women swagger in and out. Those of the tribe who congregate in Earls Court have a tough vacancy of expression: they represent the fag end of that particular dream of gentleness. (212–213)

This references a number of dreams that appear to be ending: hippie optimism, multicultural conviviality, a life of cultural substance rather than aimless urban vacuity. Earls Court is tribal rather than tolerant, culturally balkanized rather than convergent. The 1970s is a profoundly post-mythological decade: there appear virtually no illusions of tolerance or belonging available to migrants and their descendents who instead have to make their way in the kind of brittle social and cultural milieu evoked so vividly in Naipaul's Earls Court.

Much of the decade's black British writing conveys a scene of migrant life as one of settling and reckoning. Long after the youthful exuberance of initial migration has passed and its dreams of forging a better life in a welcoming country have expired, there remains a generation of migrants now approaching middle age who have tried to settle over many years in Britain and whose lives are still being shaped by the perpetual reckoning with long-standing prejudices, with little sense of postcolonial transformation or diasporic conviviality arriving anytime soon. The muted hue and often pessimistic tone of several black British texts from the time give literary shape to these experiences, while the disavowal of fictional creativity and innovative confidence evidences the sense felt by many that Britain as a progressively creative or transformative space for black Britons had been short-circuited. Some of the most important writing of the decade either dispenses with fictional modalities – as in Braithwaite's *Reluctant Neighbours* or Gilroy's *Black Teacher* – or chooses a documentary realism where the inventive possibilities of metaphor are kept to a minimum, if not entirely absented, as in Emecheta's *In the Ditch* and *Second-Class Citizen*. Each in their different ways reckons with that 'fag-end of gentleness', the expiration of which Naipaul sees at large in London; but still, there is a little evidence amidst the gloom of a dissident consciousness that offers something more than a 'tough vacancy of expression'.

We can get the measure of the sobering, dejected optics of the 1970s in Braithwaite's gravely titled documentary of British life, *Reluctant Neighbours*. A migrant from Guyana and former RAF serviceman, Braithwaite's previous work includes *To Sir, With Love* (1959) and *Paid Servant* (1962); the former dealt with his work as a teacher in a tough East End school, while the latter described his life as a Welfare Officer helping to place black children for adoption. Braithwaite's initial documentary approach to writing black Britain seems unusual when set against the creative exploits of his fellow migrants (Lamming and Selvon in particular), but it is significant that by the seventies it seems to reflect something of the dominant mode. Each of his earlier two books certainly portray a cruel, racist Britain in the fifties and sixties; yet their conclusions are ultimately hopeful and both texts tentatively celebrate overcoming an environment of prejudicial contempt. In *To Sir, With Love* Braithwaite's textual alter ego, Ricky, eventually conquers his often racist and aberrant pupils (and indeed, the romantic interest of a fellow teacher) and the book ends with recognition and reciprocity, as Braithwaite receives a gift from his students on which is written the phrase which becomes the book's title. In *Paid Servant*, for all of its gloomy evocation of London's most vulnerable, the ending sees a young black child delivered into the care of well-meaning white parents, a sign perhaps of the small acts of love upon which a multicultural future depends. But *Reluctant Neighbours* seems to have no such hope to offer.

In *Reluctant Neighbours* Braithwaite uses the occasion of a chance encounter between himself and a white American man on a train heading to New York City to indulge in his memories of living and working in post-war Britain. The American asks a series of intrusive questions about Braithwaite's life which provoke the latter's growing upset and anger, and these feelings inflect the outraged vision of Britain which emerges in the book. The 'reluctant neighbours' of the title refers both to the two men on a train, forced to travel uncomfortably together, and the black and white communities of Britain (and, later, France and America) on which Braithwaite reflects. As the journey proceeds and Braithwaite's reflections grow, there emerges a mounting sense of frustration with the racialized character of British life for which there seems to be little outlet, either emotional or political, which might trigger a process of change. He recalls a series of lecture tours in the wake of *To Sir, With Love*, when he struggled to make contact with black Britons who remained wary and mistrustful of him, due in part to Braithwaite's Cambridge-educated and relatively privileged status which marked him out from most post-war migrants, but also because they 'had themselves been so often deceived and exploited that there remained no trust. For anyone' (89). The book's portrayal of the landscape of post-war black Britain as so isolating and fractured, united coincidentally rather than cogently by 'our common experiences, our common pain' (89), reminds us that black British literary contacts and activities in the post-war years were in many ways not entirely reflective of the more cellular social realities of black British life, as well as underlines the vital significance of those initiatives which eventually grew, often in the face of hostility, as the century progressed – such as the political consciousness raising both within and beyond the trades union movement (which was initially ambivalent towards Britain's new black working-class) and the youthful advocacy of anti-racism in popular culture. Braithwaite's black Britain is glimpsed as disorganized, with little hope of progressive co-ordinated political change.

Interestingly, a key moment of revelation occurs on a visit to Ghana, where Braithwaite indulges in an Afrocentric confection of black nobility and, after visiting an open air market, speaks that 'blackness was beauty, blackness was nobility, blackness was grace, blackness was humour, blackness was pride, blackness was all those things for which I had been hungering for so long' (108). Inadvertently perhaps, Braithwaite touches upon a tactic of black survival that would spread in the decade: the endorsement of an ancestral nobility of blackness which seeks to endorse rather than denigrate blackness, evoking it as a sign of proud being. (The seventies dub poetry of Linton Kwesi Johnson determinedly articulated 'black' in productive terms as an anti-racist mantle of identity to be worn proudly at large.) But on the whole, Braithwaite's story is one of arrested emotional and identitarian development, with the wounding experiences of his initial years in Britain having congealed into a self-lacerating rage and anger that seems to have no means of release in 1972.

When recalling his early days as a teacher, Braithwaite remembers again receiving the gift from his pupils, signed 'To Sir, With Love' (152), which he took as the title of his successful debut book. He presents that phrase, and especially the choice of the word 'love' as offering a challenge: 'Its challenge to growth, its challenge to stature; its challenge to live' (152). In the ensuing years, attempts to live and grow have been ever thwarted, pushing Braithwaite away from the polycultural potential of the fledgling community which is imagined in *To Sir, With Love* to a much more heated separatist political position, where racial brotherhood has gazumped transracial convergence. At the climax of *Reluctant Neighbours*, Braithwaite conducts a discussion with his train-bound neighbour about the violence and rage which both mark and mar contemporary black people's lives, and demands the need for 'a new appreciation of ourselves, expressed among us, understood by us, inculcated in our children. An appreciation of our worth and our ability to direct and exploit that worth to our advantage' (146). This sentiment is of a part with those several occasions in the book when Braithwaite reflects upon his decision to engage more and more with black people across Europe, Africa and America. Whereas his earlier work ironically upheld colonial visions of British civitas and reached for polycultural understanding as the best response to Britain's cultural austerity and myopia, by the 1970s Braithwaite has rejected such utopian visions and has embraced a more militant and separatist position where race consciousness is in the ascendency. It is both a symptom of, and a reflection on, the corroded cosmopolitanism which Shiva Naipaul witnessed in Earls Court, and acts as an unwitting prelude to the separatist militancy of the so-called second generation. Braithwaite's text is one of several such 1970s books which reflect unhappily on the dire experiences of settling and reckoning in Britain that seem to lead only to divisiveness and separation than any kind of redemptive mutuality. The earlier postcolonial transformative projections found in the initial phase of post-war migration have been replaced by a bleak, pessimistic and separatist pragmatism.

Reluctant Neighbours is not a political polemic, and its advocacy of black politics of resistance emerges implicitly rather than is voiced upon a literary soapbox. Its dispiriting sensibility, weary of the ongoing mechanics of prejudice in seventies Britain, can also be found in one of the best and also oddest of the decade's black British novels, Sam Selvon's *Moses Ascending* (1975). Like Braithwaite's text which looked back to his earlier writing, Selvon's novel also recalls his previous literary career, in offering a sequel to his landmark novel of migrant Britain, *The Lonely Londoners* (1956), arguably the most significant of all the novels produced by the so-called Windrush generation. *Moses Ascending* features the two key figures from the previous novel, namely Moses Aloetta and Sir Galahad, but there the resemblances cease. Whereas *The Lonely Londoners* renders the hardships of migrant life in an often ebullient tone in keeping with the migrants' initial *joie de vivre* and imagines a cosmopolitan future glimpsed at a fete at St Pancras Hall, *Moses Ascending* is much more cynical and tired than its illustrious predecessor, despite its presentation of the vicissitudes of black British life ostensibly in comic terms. It both shows and satirizes the increasingly separatist and political militancy of black political groups at the time, while also calling into question the possibility of a black British community or brotherhood which reached across ethnic and cultural differences. As arguably the most artful black British novel of the decade, it deserves pausing over not least because of the problems it both articulates and suffers from.

Moses Ascending concerns the fortunes of long-time London resident Moses Aloetta, a Trinidadian migrant, who decides to buy a condemned house in Shepherd's Bush as a rental property in order to make some money. Installed as landlord on the top floor of the house, Moses hires an illiterate white British youth, Bob, as his assistant, and he also gives lodgings to his old friend Sir Galahad and his companion Brenda, both of whom have become avid activists in London's Black Power movement. The rest of his tenants comprise a cosmopolitan collective which recalls Naipaul's vision of Earls Court, but their rendering suggests something of the inter-racial prejudices which exist amongst London's residents and which ultimately challenge any pan-racial collective of black Britons from forming a subaltern political community. Bob informs Moses that the tenants include a woman from Barbados, a Cypriot, an African, an Australian and 'Two Pakis. Faizull and Farouk' (32), the news of which Moses finds 'disturbing' (32) as he presumes they may be illegal immigrants: '"Black power in the basement", I muse, "and Pakis in the residence – no wonder my house is under surveillance!"' (32). The casual racism in Bob's and Moses's denotation of their South Asian tenants betrays the fractured and cellular character and corroded cosmopolitanism of black British life in the seventies, and suggests a distinct gap between the collective aspirations of the political term 'black British' and the social constraints and intolerances within black British communities themselves.

As always with Selvon's London writing, it is not very easy to establish the extent to which he is complicit in or critical of the often chauvinistic attitudes he voices through the mouth of Moses, Sir Galahad and others, but it is clear that Moses is a figure whom readers are invited to hold up to the light for questioning. On the one hand, he offers poignant moments where the plight of black Britons is sharply drawn: in one vivid scene near the novel's beginning he attends to the legions of black cleaners and domestic workers who travel to work in London while the rest of the city sleeps, and without whom London could not function:

> [The black man] is the first passenger of the day. He is the harbinger who will put the kettle on to boil. He holds the keys of the city, and he will unlock the doors and tidy the papers on the desk, flush the loo, straighten the chairs, hoover the carpet. He will press switches and start motors. He will empty dustbins and ashtrays and stack boxes. He will peel spuds. He will sweep the halls and grease the engines. (6)

This vision of black domestic servitude is seen as part of the predicament of black life in Britain which Moses sums up a few pages later when he admits to 'a kind of sad feeling that all black people was doomed to suffer, that we would never make any headway in Brit'n. As if it always have a snag, no matter how hard we struggle or try to stay out of trouble' (35). This perceived lack of progress leads Moses not to action but to a kind of political quietism. Dismissive of the Black Power activities of Sir Galahad and Brenda, he yearns only for a quiet life – 'I just want to be left in peace' (12), he tells Sir Galahad – and the chance to indulge his youthful passions for wine, women and song exactly as he and others did in *The Lonely Londoners*. Although as the novel's entertaining narrator the action is framed and filtered by Moses's consciousness and standpoint, it is not unlikely that Selvon vents a little frustration at his narrator's placidity and uses it to point to a wider failure of political integrity amongst long-established migrants. Antipathetic to the world of demonstrations and political rallies, Moses objects to 'men [who] would come and ask you if you voting, or if you going to contribute, or if you going to join the rally in Trafalgar Square and march with the masses to number ten Downing Street. Suppose, just suppose, you don't want to do any of them fucking things' (14). Moses's fortunes in the novel are at best mixed: he finds himself working for the Black Power movement under duress and gets mixed up in the sinister illegal immigrant operation run by 'Faizull and Farouk' (who are in actuality the same person), and he ends the novel living in the basement with Bob installed in the room at the top. 'It occurs to me', Moses concludes, 'that some black power militants might chose to misconstrue my Memoirs for their own purposes, and put the following moral to defame me, to wit: that after the ballad and the episode, it is the white man who ends up Upstairs and the black man who ends up Downstairs' (139–140). But given the fact that Moses's memoir suggests little tangible 'headway' for black Britons by its close, it is difficult to find another moral amidst the comings and goings at Moses's Shepherd's Bush house.

The fortunes of Black Power also fail to have significant impact according to the narrative, however, and Selvon reserves much of his satirical energy for its depiction. Although a long-standing migrant himself, Sir Galahad is identified with the new Black Power militancy of the seventies, along with his young companion Brenda. 'The time is ripe now', declares Sir Galahad to his old friend: 'Long ago we had a chance to stand up and take the blows, but these days we have a chance to fight back. Black Power! All over the world the cry is going up' (12). Selvon belittles the political integrity of Black Power first by underscoring the movement's constant need for funds, as if it is first and foremost a money-making racket for the activists, and second by underscoring its chauvinism. As regards the former, in a key scene in the novel, a distinguished Black Panther from the United States gives a speech at a community hall in North Kensington and rouses the audience into a frenzy, at the climax of which he urges those gathered at the meeting to contribute to the party's funds. The scene descends into chaos when the police attempt to break up the meeting by unleashing Alsatians which attack the gathered militants. Sir Galahad, Brenda and the

Black Panther are arrested for inciting a racial riot, and – incensed that all black Britons are seen as default criminals in the eyes of law – Moses posts over £300 of bail money to get them released and asks that when the money is returned it is used to fund their defence. However, if this looks like the beginnings of Moses's political consciousness at last, it is short-lived: the Black Panther absconds with the party's funds and Moses is left broke and disillusioned again.

If the Black Panther's theft of funds mocks the political integrity of racial brotherhood spanning the diaspora, the chauvinism of the black Britons in the novel adds another element to the critique of Black Power. For all Sir Galahad's enthusiasm for collective political action which brings black Britons together – 'We shall overcome!' and 'We is we' (13) he cries – his prejudice to others in a predicament like his own is repeatedly emphasized. During a squabble with Moses he rejects his friend's assertion that 'the black man cannot unite' (43) by declaring that 'the black man these days is a different creature. He realizes that if he doesn't co-operate and cling together, all is lost' (42). And yet his racist rejection of South Asians as 'Pakis' who 'do not know their arse from their elbow' and who 'need a man like me' (77) indexes his complicity in British racism as well as the extent to which this epithet, always pejorative, was worryingly normalized in popular speech in the seventies (and significantly early episodes of the BBC TV comedy *Only Fools and Horses* that featured the beloved figure of Del Boy using this term have since been edited for DVD release). Sir Galahad chastizes Moses for getting involved in the illegal activities with 'bloody Pakis' and not keeping to 'Our People. If you had stuck to your own kind, you wouldn't have been in this shit' (78). Indeed, it is the 'cynical' Moses rather than the 'political' Sir Galahad who seems more interested in the lives of others oppressed in seventies Britain, as when he asks Faizull how 'does the Pakistani community react to Black Power? What trials and tribulations do they have to overcome?' (51). Selvon's critique of the racist chauvinism of both Sir Galahad and Moses is pronounced when we remember that, as a Trinidadian-born writer, Selvon was descended from Indian and not African ancestral families in the Caribbean (his grandfather was from Madras), and throughout his life he advocated the benefits of creolization against the separatist standpoints of the Caribbean's myriad cultures.

Less easy to establish is the extent to which *Moses Ascending* offers a critique of the sexist as well as the racist chauvinism of Black Power. In the novel the party is often represented by the dynamic young 18-year-old Brenda, but she struggles to escape the sexist designs of the male characters and indeed perhaps the novel itself. Moses initially describes her significantly as 'a Black Briton [...] with Afro hair, Afro blouse, and Afro gleam in the eye' (17), born in the country to Jamaican parents and with an accent distinctly English rather than Jamaican-inflected. Confident, assertive and bold, in one comical scene she repels an attempt by Bob to seduce her by striking him repeatedly while telling him to 'respect womanhood' (23) and that it is not the case that 'because I am black I am easy to get' (23). Yet a few minutes later, after Moses attempts his luck, Brenda is quickly compliant, enabling Moses to reflect that his vast sexual experience of women meant that he 'was not to be carfuffled by a new breed of Briton' (25). Keen to have Brenda 'on the spot' for similar 'strokes', he offers her the basement room. When Moses confronts Bob that Brenda has promptly turned the basement room into a meeting centre for the party – 'it appears you are turning a blind eye because of a bit of black pussy' (31), he charges – it is implied that maybe the party has been using Brenda's attractiveness in the eyes of Bob and Moses for its benefit. So if Brenda appears to a degree as an independent and politically savvy figure in the novel, she remains contained by the chauvinism of the main male characters and by Moses's narrative framing, and she struggles to free herself from being seen primarily in sexual terms. Ultimately, the new Black Power movement of the 1970s is critically illuminated by Selvon as having little chance of changing or transforming black British life, menaced from without by the increasingly racist activities of the police, and fractured from within by prejudice, chauvinism and the exploitation of black people by members of their own constituency. Despite the comical and satirical agency of Selvon's writing, Moses's gloomy sense that no headway is possible seems to win out.

While one wants to read the sexist framing of Brenda as evidence of the novel's attempt to critique sexist thinking, there is little room in *Moses Ascending* for a vision of women alternative to the men's to be aired. Indeed, Moses offers a paean to black women, which focuses solely on their arousing bodily qualities:

> Blessed be the coming of this new generation of black Britons, and blessed be I that I still well and alive to witness their coming of age from piccaninny to black beauty. It is a sight for sore eyes to see them flounce and bounce about the city, even if they capsize on their platforms and trip up in their maxis. Be it bevy or crocodile, Women's Lib or Women's Tit, they are on the march, sweeping through the streets. You see one, you see two, you see a whole batch of them. There are no women in the world who could shake their backsides like a black woman. [...] It maybe that they inherit that proud and defiant part of the anatomy from toting and balancing loads on their heads from the days of slavery. But howsoever it come into being, it is good to look at. (15)

This perspective on young black British womanhood converts ancestral connections and pride, as well as the new fashions of black British women, into the stuff of lecherous applause. And while one would want Moses's standpoint to be effectively critiqued by Selvon, an alternative vision of black womanhood to this one hardly emerges in the novel, so that it remains ultimately too firmly bound up in the sexism of this perspective. In a parallel fashion to Sir Galahad, Moses falls foul of an illiberal notion of 'our people' in launching this praise of marching women, where the emphasis falls on the body in motion rather than politics which these women wish to set on the move. For a different rendering of black British women in the 1970s, other voices are needed.

Finding their voice: Black women writing

In 1978 Amrit Wilson published *Finding a Voice: Asian Women in Britain*, which called attention to the particular predicament of Asian women in the wider landscape of racial and class divides. Mindful of the those who mounted the strike at Grunwick Photoprocessing in 1976–1977, she wrote of 'a sub-proletariat, a sub-class of the working class who are far worse off than the main body' that was historically constituted by white British women but which was now the terrain of 'Asian women [who] have taken over their positions' (31). Wilson's book spoke of the specific challenges and needs of Asian women in Britain and helped bring into focus the particularities of black women's experiences more broadly – matters which were not necessarily at the heart of the arguably more male-centred activities of black British politics at the time. As I have discussed elsewhere (McLeod *London* 93–94), the 1970s saw the advent of important black women's political movements that included the Brixton Black Women's Group created in 1973 and the Organisation of Women of Asian and African Descent (OWAAD) established in 1978. As Sonya Andermahr argues in her contribution to the present volume, the 1970s was an important decade for the furthering of feminism in Britain, and this was no less the case for black British feminism. If black British feminism challenged the perceived chauvinism of black British politics and society as well as the marginal position assigned to black women in feminist politics, then black British women's writing also participated in critiquing the patriarchal character of black life as well as glib notions of sisterhood which had little to say about race.

The most distinctive black woman's voice from the 1970s was Buchi Emecheta's. Emecheta arrived in Britain to join her husband; after only a few years later she decided to leave him, due to the abusive nature of their relationship, and while in her early twenties she raised her five children as a single mother on a council estate in North London. Her novels *In The Ditch* and *Second-Class Citizen* depict the fortunes of a young Nigerian migrant, Adah, a fictional surrogate of the young Emecheta, struggling to make ends meet as the mother of five children who has suffered at the hands of her abusive husband, fellow-migrant Francis. The documentary mode of each novel was a product of the conditions of their genesis as well as a literary stratagem to secure an 'informative' (*Head* 58) fictional mode that exposed hitherto little-known difficulties faced by many black British women. *In the Ditch* was initially a series of articles Emecheta wrote for the *New Statesman* in the early 1970s while taking a part-time Sociology degree at the University of London, and deals with her post-marital settling in the city, especially Adah's narrow life as a resident of Pussy Cat Mansions struggling to make ends meet as a single mother of five children. *Second-Class Citizen* acts as its prequel and concerns Adah's coming to Britain, Francis's abuse and Adah's decision to leave him – its writing was prompted, Emecheta alleges, after she read cynical reviews of *In the Ditch* which doubted the basic premises of Adah's impoverished situation and presumed 'that women did not live as I described' (*Head* 104). The grim vision of Britain it offers maintains the sobering rendering of the nation in *Reluctant Neighbours* and which inflects *Moses Ascending* with its moments of sobriety. But fresh attention is given to the particular challenges for black women and mothers in attempting to reckon with the hostile environment of a prejudicial country, while the arguably sexist optic of Selvon's novel is categorically disavowed.

In the Ditch's sobering tale of black female survival in the working-class enclaves of North London concludes with a fascinating representation of Queens Crescent market that we might read as an index of the tensions and corrosive cosmopolitanism of London, and which holds in check the novel's more optimistic story of Adah's unvanquished spirit and determination as a black woman not to succumb to the immiseration of her social conditions. One of the novel's most significant elements is its mooting of how working-class women across a number of ethnic groups might come together to form a fledgling polycultural network of support and resistance less wedded to the banner of blackness that challenges racial divisions and suggests female solidarity which is not led by the actions and agenda of middle-class white women. But the fragility and short life of this network is emphasized in the closing pages. The narrator comments upon the multicultural shoppers at the market and teases us with a quick-glance confection of cultural plurality:

> The noise, clatter and bustle was like that of birds in an aviary. People screamed and tumbled into each other, arguing and protesting over rising prices, filling

the air with their shouted communications. [...] Africans, Pakistanis and West Indians shopped side by side with the successful Jews, Americans and English from Highgate, Hampstead, Swiss Cottage and other equally expensive places. (131–132)

This multicultural confection is something of an empty promise. The language of this passage reinforces the impression of the crowd as one of coincidental cultural diversity, while the references to screaming, arguing and protest maintain a sinister impression of submerged violence. The class dynamics here emphasize distance as well as difference. Immediately after this moment, three women who have recently been living in Pussy Cat Mansions talk about how their rehousing has in some cases added to rather than alleviated their woes. While much of the novel moots a fledgling supportive community of women forged at the Mansions, by the novel's close it has quickly broken up as the women go their separate ways. The text's final passage underlines this sense of brokenness and apartness; the central character, Adah, invites her friend Whoopey to visit, but Whoopey retorts 'Yes, I'd like to do that, but you're always out, aren't yer' (135).

In a similar vein, as the novel closes Adah witnesses '[a] group of white and black regulars' leaving a pub which smells unhappily of alcohol and urine, one of whom offers a leery 'Hello, sister' to her (134). Adah replies laughingly, acutely aware of the danger of blanking a black man when in white company. As with the scene in the market, the vision of cultural exchange here is more endangering than encouraging, and points to the enduring divisions of gender which glib confections of racial solidarity obscure. While a significant element of *In the Ditch* wants to expose the possible new modes of cultural and racial affiliation being opened in Britain amongst women, Emecheta's understanding of the grim realities of the 1970s effectively counteracts and circumscribes such transformative utopianism. As her next novel *Second-Class Citizen* (1974) also proved, despite capturing much better the trials and tribulations of black British women's lives than in writing by men, Emecheta's progressive visions of a transformed Britain in which the protocols of class, race and gender no longer obtain are infinitely suspended or are unhappily ditched. Ultimately, in each novel, the focus remains upon Adah's seemingly unending struggle to survive within in an enduring racist and sexist milieu. While these novels can imagine and record moments of solidarity and resistance which challenge chauvinism, these are forever fragile and grimly, perpetually attenuated.

One can discern a similar envisioning of black British women's lives in Beryl Gilroy's account of her work as one of London's first black educators, *Black Teacher*. Like Braithwaite's work, Gilroy's book is a primarily documentary account of life in Britain since her arrival in the early 1950s and the struggles she encountered in gaining work as a teacher caused through the operation of the infamous colour bar and the institutionalized racism of British employees. As a much-forgotten landmark text from the 1970s, it is productive and provocative to bring it to a discussion of black British fiction, not least because it blends a documentary impulse with a novelistic attention to formulating experience which we also find in novels such as Emecheta's that declare themselves as fiction despite their documentary necessity – reminding us, again, of the often highly porous border between fiction and documentary in much 1970s black British writing. Gilroy too is concerned with settling and reckoning with Britain, long after the initial excitement and disorientation of migrant experience has been becalmed. The merits of her book have been applauded by critics such as Sandra Courtman (2006) as part of a celebratory attempt to retrieve forgotten black women writers and reinstate them into the wider story of postcolonial and diasporic British writing. While one would want to support this endeavour, it is also important to recognize how Gilroy's often steadfast challenge to prejudice and racism as described by the book often pulls forlornly against the tightening noose of racialized thinking in Britain in the 1970s. In *Black Teacher* any hopeful vistas of multicultural conviviality seem circumscribed by an insoluble racial realism that keeps any such optimism for change in check.

Black Teacher begins with Gilroy being confronted by the parent of a new pupil, Sue, whom she immediately recognizes as a one-time co-worker at 'a sort of Mail Order sweatshop' (9) in Central London, where Gilroy was employed on arriving in Britain. The parent does not recognize Gilroy when she speaks to her; but this chance encounter prompts Gilroy to narrate her early days in London, which preoccupy a large section of the book. Much of this narrative concerns the racism which she experienced, often through the nosey questions of her white female co-workers – one colleague is very interested to learn about black women's menstruation and how it compares with white women's. The friendships she makes at the sweatshop are at best temporary and quickly soiled by bigotry: when Sue moves to Swiss Cottage after winning the Pools, she tells Gilroy ' "we been mates, but I don't want you to come visitin' me, see? Wouldn't do", she explained, "not with the sort of people where I'm goin'. I don't want to them to see me 'ob-nobbin' with nigs and such. Get it?" ' (28). The scene vividly articulates the ways in which race corrupts the possibilities of female solidarity and sisterhood, as well as underlines the complicity of white women in racial oppression.

During her work as a teacher, Gilroy spends much time teaching London's polycultural offspring and she makes a great deal of headway in suggesting to them different ways of thinking about people that are not indebted to their parents' prejudice. The cross-cultural relationships built between the children is mooted as encoding a possible alternative to the separatist and prejudicial world of parents like Sue, and *Black Teacher* is at its most optimistic when dwelling on the successes of this. At one memorable moment, Gilroy recounts the visit of one of her classes to her house for an impromptu party. Beryl's son, Paul, is very excited by the visit:

> 'Come on!' said Paul. 'We'll all have a super game!'
> And that was what happened, with Tizer and crisps and soggy swiss rolls to add to the party. As I looked out of the kitchen window at the children playing in the back garden, it was as if, for a moment, I saw beyond them and caught just the faintest, faraway glimpse of a multi-racial society. (157)

However, such a glimpse is not necessarily a gain. The return of Sue from the beginning of the book makes it temporally recursive: it begins and ends at the same moment on the cusp of the 1970s, and structurally circumscribes any gains of the recent past within the persisting prejudices of the present towards race and gender. For Gilroy, the present moment of the early 1970s is one that seems both too late and too soon for the 'multi-racial' alternative she glimpses in her garden. By the book's close, she is working just as hard as she was at the beginning to break down the children's prejudices they have inherited from their parents, but a new separatism seems to be emerging amongst her latest pupils. Gilroy notices with sympathy that the new Asian children seem to find it harder 'to mix with the rest of the school. They would hang together, prattle away in their several languages, and defy any intrusions by what seemed to the English despicable methods' (187). New arrivals bring new challenges and more barriers to overcome; at least Gilroy's pragmatism fuels her commitment to pursue such tasks. Meanwhile, the adults appear to be making only the most infinitesimal steps away from bigotry. The last adults we see visiting Gilroy in her office are unhappy with a letter which she has written to them about their child's behaviour. While the child's mother seems more reasonable, the grandmother has this to say to Gilroy: 'You know where you ought to be? You ought to be on telly with them Brooke Bond tea chimps. That's where you bloody ought to be – not here, telling us' (196). The final moment of the book depicts one of Gilroy's pupils singing happily in the school and saying how nice he thinks is Gilroy as his head-teacher; but this sounds only a faint and entirely transitory note of hope amidst an otherwise bleak articulation of the nation's carcereal contemporaneity for black Britons. As *Black Teacher* sees it, race, class and gender will endure and congeal in the immediate future. The pessimism to be discovered in the frustrations of Braithwaite, the sardonic comedy of Selvon and the documentary pragmatism of Emecheta merge in Gilroy's poignant documentary. From the vantage of black British fiction and prose, there seems to be little way out of the deadlock which Gilroy laments.

Conclusion: Into the gathering storm

In terms of its literary output, the black British 1970s might be thought of as characterized by the emergence of a post-mythological realism which has two distinct elements: first, the attempt to bear witness to the fortitude of those diasporic Britons who have settled in and reckoned with the old colonial mother country; and second, the often jaded cancellation of any kind of convivial, 'multi-racial' or polycultural future for Britain due to the acceleration, not dispersal, of racist thinking. By the end of the decade, according to brief selection of texts I have engaged with in this chapter, few options for change seemed to exist: cosmopolitanism was either corroded or cancelled as a meaningful creative social possibility; sustained solidarity between women, or across men and women, seemed unavailable or susceptible to sexist dynamics; while the rebellious manner of black British politics gloomy indexed the enduring, and indeed, growing, centrality of race in political vocabularies and street-level experiences at large. The political preoccupation of race would grow with the election of Margaret Thatcher's first Conservative government in 1979, which quickly identified black Britons as an enemy within, supposedly challenging the social and moral fabric of an essentially white nation which, of course, had never shared the racial or cultural purity and exclusivity which was deemed under attack from sinister immigrant communities. Black British fiction shared little of the heady revolutionary energies discovered elsewhere in cultural production and cultural politics: its predominant tone was sombre and dispirited. In bringing such politics and culture out of the shade to locate them as a constitutive part of the social and cultural landscape of the 1970s, the particular realm of black British prose writing maintains a darkly sobering envisioning of a profoundly difficult decade for black Britons, even at those moments when it dares to moot more hopeful visions of how Britons might live otherwise.

Works cited

Beckett, Andy. *When the Lights Went Out: What Really Happened to Britain in the Seventies*. London: Faber and Faber, 2009.
Berry, James. *Bluefoot Traveller: Poetry by Westinidians in Britain*. London: Limestone, 1976.
Black, Pauline. *Black by Design: A 2-Tone Memoir*. London: Serpent's Tail, 2011.
Braithwaite, E. R. *To Sir, With Love*. London: Bodley Head, 1959.
———. *Paid Servant*. London: Bodley Head, 1962.
———. *Reluctant Neighbours*. London: New English Library, 1978 [1972].
Courtman, Sandra. 'Not Good Enough or Not Man Enough? Beryl Gilroy as the Anomaly in the Evolving "Black British Canon"', in *A Black British Canon?* Ed. by Gail Low and Marion Wynne-Davies. Basingstoke: Palgrave Macmillan, 2006. 50–73.
Dhondy, Farrukh. *East End at Your Feet*. Basingstoke: Macmillan, 1976.
———. *The Siege of Babylon*. Basingstoke: Macmillan, 1978.
Donnell, Alison. 'Introduction', in *Companion to Contemporary Black British Culture*. Ed. by Alison Donnell. London: Roultedge, 2002. xii-xvi.
Emecheta, Buchi. *In the Ditch*. London: Heinemann, 1994 [1972/1979].
———. *Second-Class Citizen*. London: Heinemann, 1994 [1974].
———. *Head above Water: An Autobiography*. London: Heinemann, 1994 [1986].
Gilroy, Beryl. *Black Teacher*. London: Cassell, 1976.
Hall, Stuart, et al. *Policing the Crisis: Mugging, the State, and Law and Order*. London: Macmillan, 1978.
Harris, Wilson. *Black Marsden*. London: Faber and Faber, 1972.
———. *The Tree of the Sun*. London: Faber and Faber, 1978.
Huggan, Graham. *The Postcolonial Exotic: Marketing the Margins*. London and New York: Routledge, 2001.
Johnson, Linton Kwesi. *Voices of the Living and the Dead*. London: Race Today, 1974.
———. *Dread, Beat an' Blood*. London: Bogle-L'Ouverture, 1975.
Lamming, George. *The Emigrants*. London: Michael Joseph, 1954.
———. *Natives of My Person*. London: Longman, 1972.
Markandaya, Kamala. *The Nowhere Man*. London: Allen Lane, 1972.
McLeod, John. *Postcolonial London: Rewriting the Metropolis*. London and New York: Routledge, 2004.
———. 'Lessons from London: E. R. Braithwaite and Black Writing in 1950s Britain'. *Yearbook of English Studies*. 42, 2012: 64–78.
Mo, Timothy. *The Monkey King*. London: Deutsch, 1978.
Naipaul, V. S. *In a Free State*. London: Deutsch, 1971.
———. *Guerrillas*. London: Deutsch, 1975.
———. *India: A Wounded Civilisation*. London: Deutsch, 1977.
———. *A Bend in the River*. London: Deutsch, 1979.

———. *Half a Life*. London: Knopf, 2001.

———. *The Enigma of Arrival*. Harmondsworth: Viking, 1987.

Naipaul, Shiva. 'Living in Earls Court', in *Beyond the Dragon's Mouth: Stories and Pieces*. London: Abacus, 1988 [1984]. 207–15.

Owusu, Kwesi. 'Introduction: Charting the Genealogy of Black Cultural Studies', in *Black British Culture and Society: A Text Reader*. Ed. by Kwesi Owusu. London: Routledge, 2000. 1–18.

Procter, James, ed. *Writing Black Britain 1948–1998: An Interdisciplinary Anthology*. Manchester: Manchester University Press, 2000.

———. *Dwelling Places: Postwar Black British Writing*. Manchester: Manchester University Press, 2003.

Rushdie, Salman. *Grimus*. London: Gollancz, 1975.

Selvon, Sam. *The Lonely Londoners*. London: Wingate, 1956.

———. *Moses Ascending*. London: Heinemann, 1984 [1975].

Sivanandan, A. *A Different Hunger: Writings on Black Resistance*. London: Pluto, 1982.

Sounes, Howard. *Seventies: The Sights, Sounds and Ideas of a Brilliant Decade*. London: Simon and Schuster, 2006.

Stein, Mark. *Black British Literature: Novels of Transformation*. Columbus: University of Ohio Press, 2004.

Stevenson, Randall. *The Last of England?* Oxford: Oxford University Press, 2004.

Walmsley, Ann. *The Caribbean Artists Movement, 1966–1972: A Literary and Cultural History*. London and Port of Spain: New Beacon Books, 1972.

Wilson, Amrit. *Finding a Voice: Asian Women in Britain*. London: Virago, 1978.

5

'This Time It's Personal': Reliving and Rewriting History in 1970s Fiction

Sam Goodman

Although reliable sources indicate that according to the Gregorian calendar the 1970s began on a Thursday and lasted precisely ten years, no decade really begins nor ends with a countdown from ten and a hangover the following day. The origins of each new decade are found in those which precede each successive period. Similarly, the events which transpire decade to decade do not spring forth spontaneously; their roots too often run far deeper, their beginnings being found many years prior, sometimes in the unlikeliest of places. This, though, is not to suggest that examining a decade in isolation is simply an artificial or arbitrary process; far from it. The division of time is something that people often take for granted and even consider, somewhat paradoxically, natural. Few question the neatness with which yesterday becomes today and today, tomorrow; almost with relief, the past is chronologically ordered, structuring our misshapen, unruly lives. But history never stays where it is meant to. It becomes spoken of, written about, remembered. To paraphrase Pierre Nora, something that seemingly no longer exists remains constantly on our lips (1).

One example that illustrates this capacity of past events to continue impacting on the present was British entry into the European Economic Community (EEC) in 1973; a central plank of Ted Heath's Conservative government policy. This decision was an indication that the historical alliances of the post-war world, specifically that of Britain and America, were being redrawn. Tom Nairn (1977) posited a 'break up' of Britain; it could be argued that the first stage of this break up was the (temporary) end of the 'special relationship'. In 1946, Labour MP Benn Levy (with all the uncompromising austerity of that age), according to David Kynaston's account, stated that there were two roads open to the British – the Russian or the American – and that the country had to choose which one to travel (223). However, Levy was, along with many other politicians at the time, struggling with the reality that the nation had made its choice as early as 1941 with the Lend-Lease Act which supplied $31.4 billion of war materials to Britain, the final payment of $83.3 million (£42.5 million) occurring on 29 December 2006.[1] Once that agreement had been put in place, Britain was entwined with American policy, and the need to support American authority, sustained in most matters until the point when Labour Prime Minister Harold Wilson declined to send British troops to fight in Vietnam. Even then, in the mid-1960s, it was only the fact that manufacturing industries were declining and economic tensions were growing, which provided Wilson an adequate sicknote. British entry to the EEC is just one example of how modernity retains a historical quality; how the present always contains an element of the past. How a country looks forward cannot be explained without also looking back. The 1970s became the point at which Britain abandoned the American road, turned back and looked for itself.

If the process of examining and re-examining history is fraught with complications, then so too is establishing precisely what constitutes history. When asked this question in first year History modules, many undergraduates rely on the *Oxford English Dictionary* definition that it is 'that branch of knowledge which deals with past events ... the formal record of the past, esp. of human affairs or actions'. Whilst this is perhaps a very general set of parameters, at least it is an egalitarian view, suggesting a history that encompasses all things regardless of their magnitude and remains accessible to all regardless of their origin. I hesitate to use a word as loaded as 'democratization', but the idea that there is an 'openness' to history is crucial and contextually relevant to study of the 1970s. As other chapters in this volume suggest, the 1970s was a decade in which the boundaries affecting ethnicity, gender and other similar conventions began to be openly and widely challenged or redefined. In the same vein, the openness of history was also a relatively recent phenomenon. New academic approaches to history had responded to the declining state of Britain, re-examining the traditional narrative of British history and seeking answers to why the country that had until just recently governed a quarter of the globe had come to find itself in such a state of political decline, social division and economic paralysis. As a consequence of this re-examination, even as a new decade the 1970s was profoundly historical.

Having never wholly recovered from the war, the nation had never forgotten it either. Indeed, the Second World War became enshrined in the collective social memory of Britain, overshadowing so much and influencing so many.[2]

The influence of new developments in historiography, specifically Marxist and poststructuralist schools of thought, on literature in the 1970s meant that the Second World War retained its cultural relevance as it was rewritten and examined in different ways. In the same fashion that historiography began to reassess the past, fiction and novelists did also. The work of novelists such as John Berger, Thomas Keneally and Paul Scott all displayed a preoccupation with history and retelling familiar stories of the past from unfamiliar perspectives.[3] It is of further interest to note that in the first decade of the Booker Prize, six winning entries were historical novels. One of these, J. G. Farrell's *The Siege of Krishnapur* (1973) was part of a loosely structured series including *Troubles* (1970), and *The Singapore Grip* (1978) known as his 'Empire' trilogy. In the Empire trilogy, Farrell chose three key moments in the construction of modern Britain as a means of ascertaining how the British nation state arrived at the degraded circumstances of the 1970s.[4] These fictional re-engagements with Imperial mythology are sometimes shocking (in the case of the Mutiny) and sometimes embarrassing (in the case of Singapore) but are written with a sense of instructive contemporary relevance. For Farrell and many others, an overwhelming feeling of ending occupies a central position in 1970s fiction and in the cultural fabric of the nation.

In this chapter, I will examine the circumstances of Britain in the 1970s, arguing that whilst the understandable preoccupation of post-war Britain was the dissolution of Empire and the search for place, this obscured the underlying, and more vital, issue of struggle and difference in British identity. Whereas a great deal of existing literature and criticism focuses on the issue of place in post-war Britain, the division inherent to identity is not only a crucial concern of the period, but an acutely historical one. New approaches to history emphasized a more personal involvement with the past, one that manifested itself in deeply historicized fiction. Focusing on a range of contemporary authors, I will illustrate how the literature of the 1970s indicates an almost bi-polar split in the contemporary historical consciousness of the nation; one that is relative to the fragmenting of male British identity. The representation of history in 1970s fiction becomes as divided as Britain; the past is alternately re-inscribed or dismissed in the search for a secure sense of self.

My analysis will be concerned with the consequences of movements in history and historicized fiction connected to the theme of British identity in the 1970s. Initially, I will briefly examine the social, political and economic circumstances of the 1970s in greater detail in an attempt to establish why the applications of new methods of historical enquiry were able to gain such ground in literature also. Secondly, I will engage with instances of historicized fiction, including David Lodge's *Out of the Shelter* (1970), Martin Amis's *The Rachel Papers* (1973), Malcolm Bradbury's *The History Man* (1975) and others. Using these novels, I will explore the way in which identity is created through an engagement with history and historiography within an overarching narrative of collective disintegration. The past becomes either wholly appropriated as it is rewritten and re-inscribed or ostensibly rejected, despite still retaining a sense of relevance. History, and the representation of history, is either embraced or dismissed but the past is always present.

Crisis? What crisis?[5]

Popular historical representation typically tends to neglect the 1970s in favour of the 1960s; a time when traditional Britain and what it had meant to be British experienced a process of slackening and relaxation. Until fairly recently, retrospectives on the 1970s have typically blurred the decade between the so-called 'fairground' of the 1960s and the avaricious consumerism of the 1980s.[6] Such perspectives overlook the crucial place that the 1970s occupy in the history of post-war Britain. It was in the 1970s that so many of the decisions made immediately post-war came to often debilitating fruition and when the relaxation of social sensibilities, beginning in the 1950s, grew into more widespread feelings of disenfranchisement, prompting the demand for the redefinition of identity.

What little contemporary cultural representation there is of the 1970s tends to differ quite greatly. The most notable trend in recent years is the recurrent and popular tendency towards a revisionist process of historical gentrification of the 1970s; a kind of 'Life on Mars' effect, in which the decade is represented as safer, simpler times with a better soundtrack than that of our own.[7] The gloss of nostalgia and the elision of popular memory attempts to convey the message that somehow the 1970s are no longer as bad as they used to be. A brief scan of the decade's major political events, however, reveals that the 1970s are still as grim as they have always been. As discussed in the introduction to this book, the 1970s were a decade of iconic cultural incidences such as the Miners' Strikes; the Three Day Week; the Winter of Discontent; the Birmingham Six; the IRA struggle; the National Front; the Cod War; rubbish in the streets, the break-up of the Beatles, the end of *Monty Python's Flying Circus* and the beginning of *Fawlty Towers*.[8] Writing at the end of the decade, Nairn argued that Britain was a society experiencing 'rapidly accelerating backwardness, social decay...and cultural despair' (51). The 1970s were seemingly characterized by a feeling of impending conflict and the threat of potential annihilation, largely as a result of Cold War tensions reinforced by the popular culture of the era such as Terry Nation's *Survivors* (1975–1977). The atomic tensions of the Cold War had also served to nurture the backward-looking memorial culture of Britain which had developed in the wake of the Second World War.[9] As a consequence of total mobilization, the war acted as a social denominator in the decades that followed; evoking the war became a method of popular appeal which found expression in multiple formats ranging from political manifestoes through to the surrealist comedies of the Pythons.[10] The overall effect was a desire for commemoration, veneration and preservation of a range of values, attitudes and events from the British past, and, of course, a backlash against them.

To place responsibility for this retrospective stance solely at the door of social tension and national political vicissitude is to ignore crucial developments in wider fields of contemporary critical scholarship. Put plainly, there were a number of forces at work on the state of British fiction of the 1970s; not least of these was a major rethinking of the contemporary relationship to the past. The redevelopment of historical study in the 1960s is typically connected to the so-called Cultural Turn, a term used to describe the widespread shift towards cultural history that originated in academic circles in France and the United States in the post-war period.[11] As a consequence, the examination of history began to be conducted from new and oblique theoretical viewpoints. Foremost among new, and in the early 1970s 'popular', interpretations of history and historiography were Marxist and poststructuralist philosophies such as those of Herbert Marcuse and Michel Foucault. Rethinking the discipline of history through unexplored theoretical means allowed for re-engagement with and re-evaluation of accepted positions on historical events and their effect on the present. The use of these concepts as theoretical lenses enabled the examination of the past from fresh and radical perspectives, unencumbered by the typical deference of conventional historiographical study.

The advent and popularization of 'history from below' – the approach whereby attention was focused on those sections of society, such as women and the working class, seemingly marginalized by the grand narrative or 'great man' approach of conventional historiography – is an integral part of the way in which the average person's relationship to history was reshaped in this period. 'History from below' was ostensibly Marxist in construction, although not always based on economic exclusion. If perhaps the beginnings of 'history from below' are in the publication of E. P. Thompson's *The Making of the English*

Working Class (first published in 1963 but, significantly, revised in 1968 and subsequently published in paperback), then in the decade that followed it could be argued that Thompson's ideas on class became the element of Marxism which reinvigorated the common relationship to the Second World War. Thompson wrote of an affinity between men who 'as a result of common experiences (inherited or shared), feel and articulate the identity of their interests as between themselves' (9); the relationship between shared history and shared identity began to be drawn into sharper focus.

There were other contributing contemporaneous factors which lent the wartime experience of the individual new life. By the late 1960s, a number of the 'great men' of the war were dead or, as the case of the 'Hero of Alamein' Field Marshal Bernard Law Montgomery of former SAS commander David Stirling, had not weathered well in public life due to their questionable political affiliations.[12] The conflict that had perhaps defined the modern era, the First World War, was passing into history and out of collective living memory. Similarly, the conflict that had defined the adult population of Britain, the Second World War, was gaining memorial currency as its participants also began to age and die. The Imperial War Museum's 'Forgotten Voices' project of 1972 supervised by then director Noble Frankland, coupled with Jeremy Isaacs's groundbreaking documentary series *World at War* in 1973 (again with Frankland as series advisor), contributed to the popular spread of memorial culture, satisfying a deeply felt need to preserve individual and shared experiences.

Indeed, media representation of the war and public interest in it had appeared to be a wholly reciprocal relationship in the 25 years since the war ended, with a range of varied sources satisfying a collective national preoccupation. These sources ran the gamut; representation of the Second World War ranged from the then authoritative five-volume history published by Winston Churchill between 1948 and 1954, to the pulp press of the Commando comics, responsible for underwriting the popular xenophobia of a generation through their tales of triumphant British grit over bucktoothed, bespectacled Japanese and square-headed Germans.[13] Though very different, the Commando comics and Churchill's panegyric indulged similar sentiments – that of the essential righteousness of British conduct and victory over inherently 'evil' regimes. Though not given to the same crude absolutes, academic publications also performed a prominent role in substantiating public conception of the country's wartime role. In his later work, *The Myth of the Blitz* (1991), Angus Calder would acknowledge his own part in the myth-making process of post-war Britain; his earlier and, for many, definitive work *The People's War* (1969) championed the tremendous collective effort of Britain and celebrated the nation's wartime unity as an overwhelming force for good in the face of adversity.

In a nation beset with fears of 'disintegration' and collapse, a historical and moral centre such as the war fulfilled a vital function. It provided evidence that far greater threats to national stability had been experienced and survived. However, though the war was viewed by many as a point of national historical and memorial communion, the increased emphasis upon it also exacerbated the existing gap and disenchantment of those who perceived that they had no connection to it. The polarization of opinion on the war is perhaps crystallized in the contemporary expression 'Never trust anyone over thirty', a phrase that appears in both *Out of the Shelter* and *The History Man*. For as many people who found an affinity with the memorial culture of the war, just as many were excluded from it. The shared common experience Thompson describes appeared to exert a greater pull on the individual than an inherited one.

The perceived gap between the generation involved in the war and those who were its inheritors was only widened by the nascent popularity of post-structuralist discourses, which were beginning to receive greater recognition at the time. The advent of new discourses within social history and historiography placed the moral centre back into question; the meaning and purpose of the war was being read as originally inaccurate, the state of the nation affirming its debilitating and not empowering effect.[14] In this vein of reassessment, the moral sureties of the war were also rendered questionable, undermined by the focus on the conduct under arms of operations such as Bomber Command and their responsibility for the unnecessary firestorms in Dresden and Hamburg resulting in the deaths of tens of thousands of German civilians.[15] Bearing only an inherited relevance to the lives of millions, the Second World War, and the supposedly glorious chapter of British history it belonged to, was only accessible through means of discourse and an analysis of available historiography. The disenfranchisement from shared memorial experience that resulted from challenging the central position the War had hitherto played in post-war British society became another factor in an understanding of modern British history and contemporary malaise.

The effects of these conflicting positions on the defining event of mid-twentieth-century history were refracted through revisions of accepted record. Marxist historiography asserted that the war, and the culture of porous heritage it proffered, should be celebrated as an ordinary people's triumph; after all, they were the ones who did the fighting and the dying. Raphael Samuel's identification of their reward is the enshrining of contemporary myth at the heart of post-war British identity (208). However, the oppositional view was that over-emphasis of this myth was the very bar holding back the progress of Britain. The war was instead to be rejected utterly in the pursuit of future history and progression. A reappraisal of history in this fashion led inexorably to a reappraisal of what is understood by the individual in terms of their personal and national identity. The oppositional nature of traditional and radical revisions of history were responsible for the polarization of British identity encapsulated in Lodge's and Bradbury's use of the popular aphorism concerning not trusting anyone over 30; an opposition both authors would, along with others, explore in popular fiction. Though the objectives of each philosophy may differ, the means and need for revisiting the past share a great deal of similarity; only through reliving and rewriting history could an accurate sense of contemporary identity be fully determined.

Re-inscribing Janus

Building on the identification of these new trends, in this section I will focus predominantly on David Lodge's *Out of the Shelter*, a novel so totally pre-occupied with history, personal and (inter)national that its structure, publication and construction read as though it is an artefact of historiography. In his introduction, Lodge asserts that although not intended to be 'confessional' in the revelatory sense, the novel is deeply autobiographical and makes identity in relation to history its central preoccupation (ix). Lodge's novel is less about invention as it is representation. In looking back, Lodge seeks to reassess his part in a world of 'simple patriotic ethic and mythology […] not easily or lightly discarded' (x). He positions his novel as an alignment of personal history and a personal construct of history. By this I mean that Lodge seeks a correspondence between his own past and how he perceives his experience to play a part in modern history. In doing so, he privileges the record of the individual connection to historical events, stating that the experiences he fashioned into the novel 'had a representative significance that transcended [their] importance for me personally' (x). Lodge attempts to create a consensus of identity at the outset of the 1970s through emphasizing common connection to a greater ideal. The reappraisal of his childhood past from an adult perspective is an affirmation of dual relevance; first of the relevance of history and second of his own part in it.

Out of the Shelter describes the experiences of a boy growing up in wartime Britain, passing exams, enjoying the material excesses of American occupation, accessing higher education and then entering the rosy world of Britain's archetype of the middle-class, nuclear family. In many ways, Lodge's narrative is mundane and today's readers might be forgiven for thinking so far, so typical; so far, so what? Though the novel may appear banal to a modern eye, its underlying instances of social mobility allow it to transcend mere personal relevance; it is a story familiar, albeit with natural variations, to a generation. The connection to the past that Lodge describes is the same one held and felt by the adult demographic to whom he is writing; the supposed untrustworthy generation of Britons over 30. As a childhood world of deference and war mythology begins to dissolve, there is a perceived need on the part of the author to reinforce it. The events of Lodge's novel are unexceptional, but then so were the experiences of millions in the impoverished Britain of the post-war period. In affirming the ordinariness of their lives, Lodge also validates the extraordinary circumstance of war.

The central figure of Timothy Young, a literary counterpart to Lodge himself, reassures a readership unsure of itself by providing a lower-middle-class everyman figure. Lodge's novel becomes an act of reclamation in that it privileges the currency of personal recollection over that of the grand narratological one. The universality of the Young/Lodge character emphasizes the openness inherent to 'history from below', instructing a readership that their experiences are just as valid as the accepted historical record. The question of how and who best to represent historical experience is brought up directly throughout the novel, such as when its narrative argues, 'History is the verdict of the lucky on the unlucky, of those who weren't there on those who were. Historians are so goddam smug' (185). In this statement Lodge not only seeks to privilege personal connection to historical events but also, by placing these words in the mouth of an American conscientious objector, to assuage the guilt of those who had been unable to participate directly. In doing so, Lodge marshals the values of the war – unity, comradeship, purpose, sacrifice – and makes the representation of History instructive to contemporary identity. It is in this usage that the power of the past lies for Lodge; identity in modernity, namely the 1970s, is constructed through the individual's perception and identification with the nation's immediate past and the way in which it relates to their own. The mantra for the generation that Lodge addresses is repeated throughout the novel: 'we shall drag a world with us; a world in flames' (252). Memory and history are not relinquished or lost; the individual carries them forth into modernity.

The continual re-inscription of memory and history creates a feeling of unending in Lodge's novel. Young/Lodge considers the 'imperfection' of the victory, resenting it as 'a piece of mismanagement on the part of God' (29). The war did not end as planned, and the peace that followed it did not proceed as intended into bright, sunlit uplands. Rather, the post-war world is shown to have been deeply imbued with nostalgia for the war, endlessly replayed. In terms of historiography, *Out of the Shelter* and Lodge suffer from what is termed 'composure' by psychologists and social scientists such as Perks and Thompson (300). This is the process by which individuals can be seen to 'compose' or selectively re-edit their self-narrative to fit with changed conditions. Lodge sites the novel in a number of temporal co-ordinates. The majority of the narrative is set between 1939 and 1951; the epilogue takes place around 1965 and the book itself was published in 1970. Also, dependent on which edition one acquires, Lodge amended the original text and added an introduction in 1984. The effect of this temporal jumble is that the past is 'composed' in order to better fit with the current picture, suiting subsequent sensibilities. The fiction-as-fact-as-fiction status of the work means that Lodge, somewhat unwittingly, affirms the maxim he disdains: never trust anyone over 30. His repeated revisiting of his novel continually casts doubt over the authenticity of the recollections it is based on. Lodge revisits the text and the past in search of the most effective version of remembered events. The revisiting and rewriting of his personal past belies the subjective objectivity that Lodge sets up as opposite to the 'smugness' of history. Lodge's 'trust me – I was there' reliability suffers in that the reader is never quite certain where 'there' is.

Lodge's contribution to the canon through this novel is perhaps negligible, but *Out of the Shelter* contributes a great deal more to the myth of British identity as defined by the Second World War. In his article 'The Moment of British Nationalism 1939–70', Christopher Harvie argues that post-war evocations of British identity continually reference pastoral and parochial images of the nation mythologized through films, poetry and other media produced before and during the Second World War; Harvie illustrates how a range of sources, from T. S. Eliot's *Four Quartets* (1943) to Olivier's *Henry V* (1944), influenced post-war culture, to the point where he argues that Britain as 'living obsessively off the war' (333). Perhaps nowhere is this as true as within Lodge's novel. The book appears a final act of deference and gratitude to the dream of a New Jerusalem and one in which British identity fixates itself on an ideal of austere national solidarity, pre-Suez, Aden or Kenya. Its epilogue hints at the prospect of realizing this dream anew, in that with the application of the values Young/Lodge describes, Britain could once again find security, identity and purpose in the pages of its history. In order for the nation to look forward, it had to simultaneously look back.

Bi-polar Britain

I know that this is paradise everyone old has dreamed of all their lives.
Philip Larkin, 'High Windows', 1974

In reading *Out of the Shelter* it is perhaps possible to imagine the beginning of the 1970s as the threshold to a better time; the prosperous vision of comfortable middle-class living in its epilogue, the new and socially beneficial occupation of its protagonist (who has a PhD specializing in the eradication of planning blight and works in Environmental Studies) and the conspicuous leisure in which he and his family indulge indicates a British identity at ease with itself. The past had been reconciled and social mobility, if not the fully realized project that had been envisaged as succeeding the age of austerity, had nevertheless secured a little something for everyone. But for all of Lodge's reinscription of the glory of the modern past, the gulf between those who venerated it and those who didn't kept on growing. For every Lodge, there were a growing number of Britons who saw the past as no more than the stuffy, stagnant rigidity of Imperial mythology. It is perhaps a detail worth noting that a couple of years after its publication, *Out of the Shelter* went out of print for over a decade.

Malcolm Bradbury's *The History Man* examines a character of contemporaneous origin to that of Young/Lodge, but one that interprets his relationship to history in a very different fashion. Howard Kirk comes from a similarly lower-middle-class background and, through his own hard work and the opportunities of socially mobile post-war Britain, accesses higher education. He becomes a lecturer in Sociology, first at the University of Leeds (incidentally, and, one imagines, deliberately referenced, where E. P. Thompson wrote *The Making of the British Working Class*) and then at the fictional University of Watermouth based on the University of East Anglia where Bradbury worked. Kirk and Young share a great deal in common in terms of the opportunities afforded to them by history but most similarities end there. Kirk, unlike Young, views the accepted notion of past history, as something to be rejected in favour of a sense of history to come. Bradbury's narrative introduces Howard and his wife Barbara as 'true citizens of the present', committed to change and to the escape from a past they see as oppressive (2). Yet, paradoxically, they also lay claim to their 'historical rights'; namely the very social developments which permit them to be ahistorical. Howard Kirk sees the 1970s as a threshold too, but to a future in which history will be determined in the present, as it is experienced as opposed to when it has passed. History, for Howard, would no longer shape identity; identity in the present would instead allow for history to be determined through the application of new discourses.

For a couple who profess to be disinterested in history, in a traditional sense, the Kirks seem curiously unable to stop discussing it. Howard's sense of identity is determined by re-engaging with his personal past through new means of analysis. Howard seeks to interrogate the past using his own private method, namely the judicial application of 'a little, Marx, a little Freud and a little Social History' (22). Despite Howard's assertions, however, it is not any of these three disciplines that take precedence in his outlook. Though ostensibly rejected in favour of the dynamism of the present, history in *The History Man* is rewritten and re-ordered. Rather than the situation that Young/Lodge fears, that emphasis on history is diminishing, instead its authority is no longer simply held to be definitive. Whereas Lodge constructs Young's identity through a privileging of his voice within history, Bradbury allows Howard to question the meaning of his identity, and the historical forces behind its creation, through language.

Bradbury's novel is primarily satirical and focuses on the peculiar absurdities of campus life. However, beneath the self-assured, leather-jacketed swagger of Howard Kirk and his Zapata moustache, Bradbury invites the criticism of wider British middle-class identity and a need for reassessment of how it came to be that way. Howard perceives the watershed moment in his own life as motivated by two significant events; firstly his cuckolding by an Egyptian student and secondly, the 'liberating' death of his father. If these events are to be read allegorically, and indeed, through application of Howard's own method, then they could be argued to specifically represent the decline of British authority over the Middle East (or the empowering of the Third World as Howard describes it) and the more general collapse of the old world of Empire as represented by his father's generation. Bradbury's novel allegorizes the humiliation of post-war Britain after the Egyptian annexation of the Suez Canal in 1956, and the decline of Empire in the era of decolonization that followed.[16] Howard's analysis lends itself to the determination of tremendous individual freedom of being, or as he puts it, 'One inevitably recognizes the removal of the psychic focus of paternalist constraint' (27). Without the strictures of the past, here represented by Britain's imperial role and the traditional structure of deference, Howard perceives the disassociation of personal history and personal constructions of history. For him, it is the prospect of anti-Hegelian fulfilment; no longer was mankind sentenced to history.

Howard's revisionism when narrating his past can be read as a similar process to the rewriting present in *Out of the Shelter*; Howard uses method and experience to assemble a more effective version of the past in the present. Bradbury, however, indicates the inherent danger of ideology in this practice. By eliminating the relevance of history in favour of the pre-eminence of the language used to relate it, Bradbury suggests that there is a danger of removing personal responsibility and dissolving all meaning associated with the consequences of one's actions. One character, when asked what she has learnt so far, replies: 'I think you're very interesting characters, but I haven't discovered the plot' (106). Howard spends the majority of the book deluding himself with his own solemn responsibility to forge history and with the supposed gravity of his ideals. The bathos of his breakfast-time watershed moment, 'He poked a sausage; he recognised historical inevitability', is lost on Howard. Bradbury asserts that the 'inevitability' that Howard perceives in modern history is not the liberating force he imagines, but something as repressive and flawed as that which it seeks to replace. Far from representing the end of grand narratives and repressive structures, Howard's hypocritical view of identity imposes a new narrative in which dissent and disunity are inevitable and unavoidable. When one of Howard's students, George Carmody, opposes his consensus of opposition, Howard has him removed from the course and later the university, stating that George, and the 'outdated' style of dress, thought and historical enquiry he represents, has 'reached the end of the line' (205).

In many ways, Howard Kirk's philosophy in Bradbury's *The History Man* is a counterpart to the thematic concerns raised in *Out of the Shelter*. Whereas the characters of Lodge's novel are preoccupied with looking back, Bradbury's are only concerned with looking forward; although the consequence of such temporal thinking is equally delusional in both works. The Kirks believe that they occupy a position of historical transcendence, that their past selves remain relegated to the confines of history. But they too are guilty of the self-mythologizing practices they deplore in others. Perhaps, though their means are different, the Kirks are not as dissimilar to Timothy Young as they might well wish to be. Despite the typically perceived oppositional nature of Marxism and poststructuralism, both perspectives reveal a malleable approach to the past and a utility in historical representation resistant to any definitive record. Through Howard Kirk's emphasis on discourse, British identity is reduced to what the narrative describes as 'a particular type of relationship to the temporal and historical process, culturally conditioned and afforded […] a particular performance within the available role sets' (33).

First as tragedy, then as farce?

As the litany of British imperial history was re-examined and re-evaluated by authors such as Lodge, Bradbury and others, the protagonists that populated the 1970s novel underwent a dramatic shift in characterization. The sixties and seventies have been long regarded as decades in which seminal feminist texts pursued a revision of female social identity, both in the present and in the past. However, the end of Empire and the consequent erosion of its traditionally inculcated codes of masculinity forced an equally dramatic reorientation of male identity also. Indeed, the common developing theme in the novels I have examined in this chapter thus far is arguably that of the unsettling effect that the disintegration of Empire and the rejection of history have on central male figures. Although the manner by which authorial engagement with the dissolution of male identity and masculine roles differs greatly, nevertheless their methods encompass many of the analytical and critical approaches brought to bear on the Empire itself, reinforcing Bradbury's equation of paternalism with empire and suggesting a further correlation between their parallel downward trajectories.

In many instances of contemporary fiction, the figure of the male protagonist is the means by which novelists sought to engage with wider concerns, preferring a more oblique route than attempting to tackle many such issues directly. Such indirection is deployed with great subtlety by Bradbury, who uses such nuances to great satirical effect in *The History Man*, and thereby illustrates the danger inherent in deliberately dismissing all established cultural values particularly of the Empire and of the past. However, although one is not led to applaud the kind of liberation Howard Kirk pursues, the end of Empire and shifting of social sensibilities it produces is still not a counterbalance of revered tradition, and not presented necessarily as something to be actively mourned. Instead, that ending of imperial values might still be seen as a potential step towards an empowerment of sorts, creating a space for a British cultural awakening in the 1970s, albeit one abused by Kirk.

If political difference is often the catalyst that produces a radical shift in art and literature, then perhaps the most readily identifiable difference between the

1960s and the 1970s is the rapid removal of African and other overseas colonies; after 1956, British colonies diminished at the rate of approximately one per year for a decade, thereby removing the last remaining pretence of Empire.[17] Despite efforts by successive governments and contemporary historians, the British Empire had effectively ceased to exist by the 1970s.[18] However, unlike Britain's former European compatriots, France, and opponents, Germany, the manner in which the Empire evaporated was marked by enervation rather than any great catastrophe. With Germany's territorial pretensions ending at the Potsdam conference of 1945 and France's in the bitter struggles for Indochina and Algeria during the 1950s, the late and relatively bloodless denuding of the imperial map, again along with entry to the EEC, created an atmosphere in which Britain seemed belated, anachronistic, one of the last European colonial powers to adapt. In the fiction of the period, significantly in a historic and symbol, male characters, in particular English ones, often appear confused and adolescent, coming to maturity only gradually and somewhat later than those around them. This theme of tardiness used in characterizing male figures is embodied in Howard Kirk, with Bradbury illustrating how his personal reinvention as swaggering political philosopher is Kirk's attempt at catching up with the spirit of 1968 and effectively an admission he had missed those revolutionary times whose dynamism he co-opts negatively, a parody of radicalism.

In many instances, however, other novelists of the 1970s would find themselves unwilling or unable to go as far as Bradbury in disassociating their male characters so greatly from tradition and convention. Martin Amis's *The Rachel Papers* tells the story of Charles Highway and his pursuit of the titular Rachel. Told, or more tellingly retold, in first person, the novel follows Highway's attempts to reassess both his own persona and his understanding of various conventions. Amis sets the novel in the liminal period between Highway's graduation from school and departure for university, awarding a transitional quality to his protagonist as he adapts to a world beyond the one he has outgrown since childhood; much like Lodge and Bradbury, Amis's novel acts as a bildungsroman of sorts. Amis's protagonist shares a similar identity crisis to that of Bradbury's, illustrating the discrepancy between appearance and reality. Highway states at the novel's opening that he suffers from 'such a rangy, well-travelled, big-cocked name, and to look at, I am none of these' (7). The implication is that despite not appearing as the impressive physical specimen that his name signifies, Highway will act as such regardless. He goes on to mythologize the circumstances of his birth, using a distorted version of his personal history to counteract the shortcomings of reality. In doing so, Highway acts as a metaphor for a nation broaching its own difficult coming of age in the 1970s, since suffering from the expectation created by a well-travelled, big-cocked name, Great Britain would similarly indulge in compensatory self-mythologizing.

Where Amis's novel differs from Bradbury's is in the inability of his central character to redefine himself in the fashion that Howard Kirk manages. Highway seeks to disavow the world of academia and the specific establishment, Oxford, that he attempts to enter, assailing it as full of 'tarts' and 'dotards' (9), but is unable to entirely do so. In spite of his disdain, Highway finds himself still deriving value from the status that a place at Oxford would confer upon him. Despite attempting to reject certain conventions as a means of seeming modern or fashionably self-destructive (he confesses to wishing to die in a Keatsian fashion before the age of 26), Highway's weapons are the conventions themselves, as evinced by his continual diarizing. He admits that his only real skills lie in 'English Literature and language, which, or so it seemed to me, I was really fucking good at' (64). However, when he goes for his interview at Oxford, Highway finds that it is he who is the old-fashioned one. Lectured into silence by the young and punningly named Dr Knowd, all 'beetle-crusher, pig-stomper boots; beret. Jack-Christ face and hair', Highway is confronted on his traditional choice of literature and his heavily plagiarized views on it (210). Highway's transition to adulthood, university and the wider world is as unsettling as Howard Kirk's, resulting in a need for the reappraisal of his personal history.

Amis, who later acknowledged in an interview with *Esquire* magazine that he was writing from a largely autobiographical perspective in his debut novel, suffers a similar fate to his protagonist.[19] In much the same fashion as Charles Highway, Amis's writing style, his means of expression and many of the episodes in *The Rachel Papers* are often reminiscent of earlier writers; in this particular case, most notably Kingsley Amis, his father. More so in this novel than any of his later work, Amis junior often appears to mimic the exaggerated farce and the linguistic tics of Amis senior. Amis's mimicry results in a temporal and literary irony in that just as Jim Dixon attempts to fight against conformity and convention in *Lucky Jim* (1954), Highway and Amis do the same in *The Rachel Papers*. Both Amis and Highway attempt to break out of the paternalistic constraints they perceive themselves bound by but never quite manage to do so fully. Despite Amis's clear desire to break with tradition through his characterization of Highway, a complete rejection of history is not possible and, even in his dismissal of the past, Amis creates a relationship with it.

After the initial success of his first historical novel, *Troubles*, J. G. Farrell's follow-up, *The Siege of Krishnapur*, delved further into British Imperial history with its depiction of the Indian Mutiny of 1857. Perhaps wary of the difficulties in adequately satirizing the present state of Britain, Farrell employs a technique of historical distancing to enact such a critique. *The Siege of Krishnapur* has been criticized for its lack of representation of Indian characters or colonial perspective; however, this is not simply a case of narrative oversight on Farrell's part, but is rather, as John McLeod argues, a deliberate stylistic decision (72). With characteristic irreverence, Farrell brings focus to bear on the men of the Empire at its historical high-water mark as a means of critically engaging with the political present. Farrell's intention, borrowing a phrase from Jean Paul Sartre, was to show ordinary 'people undergoing history' (qtd in McLeod 37). In *The Siege of Krishnapur*, Farrell takes an episode of supposedly glorious British victory in the form of the Indian Mutiny, a much mythologized episode of late-Victorian history, and subverts it, intimating that the more distant past required a degree of re-appraisal similarly to that undertaken in *Troubles*. Just as he did in *Troubles* with the origins of the IRA, Farrell uses the instance of a British garrison under assault in India as a way of assessing the contemporary state of British institutions, and as symbols of failure and crisis, the shortages, privations and collapse of social order within the town of Krishnapur echo those of Farrell's contemporary Britain in the early 1970s.

Farrell directly questions the traditional historical narrative of Empire and its popular representation as part of his critical re-engagement with the past. During the relief of Krishnapur, the General commanding the reinforcements notes that '[e]ven when allowances were made, the "heroes of Krishnapur" [...] were a pretty rum lot. And he would have to pose for hours [...] whilst some artist-wallah depicted "The Relief of Krishnapur"! With any luck this wretched selection of heroes would be given the soft-pedal' (310-11). Farrell's novel emphasizes how fiction, in this case artistic celebrations of British heroism during the Indian Mutiny, has been used to distort the facts of history and conceal the shortcomings of the Empire in the national consciousness; Farrell's intention is to show how historical fiction can seek to redress the balance and actively apply new scrutiny to Britain's Imperial legacy.

Farrell further examines the attitudes and, in particular, the weaknesses of Imperial subjects throughout his trilogy. In *The Siege of Krishnapur*, he gives a great degree of attention to the Magistrate, notoriously dismissive of anyone else's opinion but his own, and to the romantic, idealistic young poet George Fleury as a means of illustrating the danger inherent in both arrogance and ignorance. Farrell uses similar polarizations of Imperial characters throughout the trilogy to further satirize the 1970s attitudes towards British status in international and domestic affairs. His characters, from the leonine Edward Spencer and dissolute Ripon in *Troubles* to the colonial robber-baron Walter Blackett and the politically active yet naive Matthew Webb in *The Singapore Grip*, appear unprepared to cope with the exceptional circumstances occurring around them. Farrell repeatedly presents the reader with the best and worst of British character in equal measure, and their short-sightedness in either politics or awareness of the implications of their actions are used as indications of his dismissal of on the parallel complacencies he identifies in contemporary Britain. Despite the occasional savagery of Farrell's satire, *The Singapore Grip* is perhaps the most unflinching in charting the venal conduct of Britons in Asia; his re-examination of imperial history and the men that made it is always in pursuit of a better understanding of the contemporary British malaise. His men of Empire may be far from perfect but they remain essentially patriotic. Farrell's historical forays challenge the assumption that greatness always precedes Britain and that the past and its characters are similarly made up of the great and the good.

Aside from Farrell's use of the historical novel to explore traditional evocations of the past, other contemporary authors used radically different genres to similar effect. John le Carré, in what is possibly his most personal novel based on his time in British secret service, chooses to question the validity of current British political values through an examination of the nation's recent clandestine past in *Tinker, Tailor, Soldier, Spy* (1974). Le Carré fictionalizes the actions of Kim Philby in the central narrative of the novel, whose betrayal of the nation became evident when he blew his own cover, as well as that of le Carré's, during his time with MI6 in the early 1960s.[20] Le Carré's mole, Bill Haydon, is a literary caricature of Philby, being Oxbridge educated, effortlessly intelligent and well-connected throughout the British political establishment. Le Carré uses the novel to engage with the pre-war past of British appeasement and the swing to the Left of many of Philby's generation. In doing so, he reveals the men of the Empire as inherently rotten, lacking in either principle or scruples.

Le Carré's espionage novels mark the end of the genre's traditional place as a patriotic mode of production. Instead of the popular fantasies of Ian Fleming, le Carré reorients the spy novel as a means of interrogating the downgraded position of British authority and to lament the contemporary state of British fortunes. Le Carré problematizes the typical approach to patriotism in the spy novel by making his protagonist, George Smiley, occasionally as dislikeable as Bill Haydon. Smiley eventually captures Haydon but only does so by employing the same duplicitous means as his adversary. The figure of the 'gentleman spy' is rendered outmoded in le Carré's fictional espionage network, and in this retrospective on the nation's secret past he writes of only ignominy and shame where there was once a perception of glory.

Beyond his criticism of past generations, le Carré finds little hope for the nation's future either: his novel includes a lament to a disappointed generation, described by le Carré as 'Poor loves. Trained to Empire, trained to rule the waves. All gone' (70). By setting a large portion of the novel in a public school, the archetypal breeding ground of Empire-builders since the late-nineteenth century, le Carré compounds the historical irony of these future servants of Empire left without a literal, geographic Empire to serve. The final line of the novel appears to represent le Carré's assessment of the now redundant militarism of the nation's past; 'The gun, Bill Roach had finally convinced himself, was after all a dream' (210). With the nation's capacity for aggressive international action severely curtailed, the gun has been placed out of bounds.

Despite the variety and difference in style, genre and approach between each author, the unifying aspect of the fiction of Amis, Bradbury, Lodge, Farrell and le Carré lies in their reaction to historical figures and events. In all of their historical rewritings, reassessments or re-enactments, each author offers an alternative to the 'Great Man' approach to history by presenting the reader with a range of anti-heroes. Writing in a time of national denigration, the novelists of the 1970s seek to further blur historical and moral sureties through the use of such antiheroic protagonists. In some instances, male figures in the 1970s novel are rendered decidedly ordinary, successful by accident or good fortune; in others, they are simply appalling. In their efforts to explore the range of personalities in both the national past and present, these authors appraise and criticize not just the supporters of the Empire but also those that fought against it. The death of absolutes is enacted in 1970s fiction; no-one escapes a certain degree of historical or moral culpability.

Things fall apart ... the centre cannot hold

In the same way that decades do not start precisely when historical record states they do, neither do they conclude as neatly. Many of the approaches to the fusion of literature and history that began to be explored in the 1970s novel had far-reaching consequences in the decade that would follow. Whilst not necessarily claiming the existence of a 'long' 1970s stretching from 1968 through to the Falklands Conflict of 1982 or to Margaret Thatcher's subsequent re-election in

1983, there is a clear sense of political, social and cultural continuity throughout this period in that the origins of concerns and styles which reach maturity in 1980s fiction can be found in their infancy in the 1970s. Similarly, there is a tangible process of development occurring within the 1970s itself, whereby fiction produced in the latter part of the decade illustrates how many of the themes associated with historicity and the re-examination of the past had been pursued to ever more extreme, and occasionally contradictory, conclusions.

In comparison to the critical approaches to the British past in the novels of Bradbury and Farrell, Lodge's deference to the myths of Empire and the Second World War sits uneasily within the literary climate of the late 1970s. Instead of the 'simple patriotic ethic and mythology' Lodge sought to uphold in *Out of the Shelter*, successive novelists such as Paul Scott and Timothy Mo would create a far more complex and deeply subjective approach to the representation of history, both distant and recent, in their work; Scott and Mo, in particular, would seek to explore the post-war days of India and Hong Kong respectively. As the decade progressed, the onus of responsibility on the contemporary novelist towards engagement and activism grew ever more visible. For instance, both Farrell's and John Berger's use of their Booker Prizes as platforms for commenting on political causes, colonial oppression and the Black Panther movement respectively, suggested that the irreverence of the 1970s was fast becoming symptomatic of a larger, more general antipathy towards the perceived political apathy of the previous generation of writers.

In as much as authors such as Farrell and Berger would increasingly amplify their polemic, again especially so in a novel such as Farrell's *The Singapore Grip*, the general and widespread irreverence of 1970s literature would also just as often result in indifference to overtly political causes. However, irreverence, pursued through pastiche and parody, remains a politically subversive form despite assertions to the contrary. A very popular and superficially apolitical example of such 1970s flippancy was George MacDonald Fraser's *Flashman* series. Though the first of these ostensibly factual historical novels was published in 1969, it was in the following decade over the course of five volumes that the series' popularity was cemented in the public domain. Fraser used a form of ironic historical distancing not unlike that of Farrell's to engage with culturally produced and redundant Victorian social mores. The result was a seemingly innocuous yet highly cynical form of historical parody which conceals its teeth beneath sardonic humour. Fraser positions himself as the editor of the late Flashman's recently discovered memoirs, which allows him to suggest authenticity whilst also enabling him to exercise literary licence in his portrayal of history; writing up any errors as the mistakes or exaggeration of the memoirs' 'true' author, Flashman.[21] Fraser as author, however, makes his position on history clear in the opening pages of *Royal Flash* (1970): 'great events are decided by trifles [...] Scholars wouldn't have it so [...] but in my experience, the course of history is as often settled by someone's having a bellyache, or not sleeping well, or a sailor getting drunk, or some aristocratic harlot waggling her backside' (2). Fraser's novels create a literary space in which the values and morals of empire are subverted and parodied through the use of false documents. In this sense, history from below allows Fraser to expose the hypocrisy of conventional history; Flashman, supposedly a 'great man' of the Victorian Empire, reveals himself as a 'scoundrel, a liar, a cheat, a thief, a coward – and oh yes, a toady' (13). The success of Fraser's novels is achieved through inducing the reader to identify with everything that is counter to the deferential expectations of their setting; in rooting for such a deplorable anti-hero, Fraser offers his readership the opportunity to become complicit in Flashman's adventures and enjoy the subversion as their own.

Despite the wide variety of style and setting that their authors employ, the majority of the historical fictions I have examined in this chapter conform generally to realist modes of production. Though there are hints of intertextuality in the work of Fraser, the central conceit of Flashman as a character from *Tom Brown's Schooldays* (1857) for instance, or self-reflexivity in Bradbury's knowing construction of Howard Kirk as a conglomerate of fashionable discourses, most historical fiction of the 1970s would adhere to naturalistic mimetic accuracy. The commitment of 1970s novelists to realist modes of literature does not signify an unwillingness to experiment but represents a deliberate choice of form to suit authorial intent. For example, McLeod has argued that Farrell's mimicry of the imperial adventure novel in *The Siege of Krishnapur* has led to critics including Bernard Bergonzi to categorize him alongside those post-war novelists such as John Masters who kept 'faith with the discredited certainties of the traditional historical novel' ('Post-Imperial' 180).[22] In pursuit of satire or parody, authors would of course have to emulate their intended targets. Moreover, by couching an unsettling message within a familiar form, the act of parody becomes a novelistic Trojan horse, subverting mainstream literature from within.

Alongside the parody of mainstream literary realism, a range of authors were similarly engaging with other genres as a means of rewriting established narratives. Angela Carter began the 1970s by writing magical realist novels such as *The Infernal Desire Machines of Doctor Hoffman* (1972), heavily influenced by continental philosophy and literary theory. However, by the close of the decade,

Carter had crystallized the element of feminism, developed further through *The Passion of New Eve* (1977), within the political bent of her earlier work, adding a dose of shock-value for good measure. Carter's volume of short fiction, *The Bloody Chamber* (1979), continued her preference for the macabre by rewriting a succession of fairytales in a horror-Gothic style, placing particular emphasis on the more shocking and explicitly sexualized elements of the original narratives. Aidan Day argues that Carter's writing was away of 'reclaiming a past from which standard history had largely banished women' (167). Indeed, in this regard Carter's intention in *The Bloody Chamber* is perhaps best encapsulated in a line from 'The Lady of the House of Love' taken from this collection: 'Nervously, to conceal her inner voices, she keeps up a front of inconsequential chatter ... while her ancestors leer and grimace from the walls' (103). Whilst she would go on to develop her position in more evidently postmodern historical novels such as *Nights At the Circus* (1984) and *Wise Children* (1991), Carter's writing in *The Bloody Chamber* suggests a subject in conflict, overtly conscious of the weight of history bearing down on them; her solution, via shock and gore, is to leer and grimace straight back.

Though there appears little to link the highly critically regarded Angela Carter with the more populist Jack Higgins and Frederick Forsyth, all three authors attempt to rework contemporary and traditional myth in their own way. Carter's role as a fabulist, although in a fundamentally different genre, shares similarities with that of Forsyth's and Higgins' tall tales of the war and after. Higgins's *The Eagle Has Landed* (1975) narrates a wartime Abwehr plot to capture Winston Churchill in the same manner that Mussolini was rescued from Greece in 1943. After a pitched battle between German infiltrators and British troops, Churchill is rescued in the nick of time and the Nazi plot foiled. Written in a mock-factual tone, Higgins invents historical evidence and oral testimony from supposedly surviving participants to frame the story within the borders of plausibility; Higgins, much like Fraser, recognizes the utility and importance of history from below. Forsyth's *The Odessa File* (1972) concerned the network of former Nazis that assisted various war criminals in obtaining new identities and helped them either flee Germany or assimilate into post-war German society. The plot centres on the crime reporter Peter Miller's pursuit of the SS Commandant of the Riga concentration camp, Eduard Roschmann. The novel's dénouement fuses the personal and the political in myth as it is revealed that Miller's father, a Wehrmacht officer, was killed by Roschmann in the retreat from Riga and that the pursuit of justice for the victims of the holocaust was no more than cover for Miller's real purpose.

By appearing to invoke values of duty, honour and self sacrifice, Higgins's and Forsyth's novels superficially recall Lodge's simplistic moral viewpoint outlined in *Out of the Shelter*. The novels indeed share similarities but where Lodge was attempting to record an objective truth as he saw it, Higgins and Forsyth indulge lurid morality tales in which the good are lionized and the wicked are, by and large, punished. In their creation of new myth, Higgins and Forsyth adopt the fabulist persona that Carter also employs in *The Bloody Chamber*. The crucial difference between them, however, is that Higgins and Forsyth concoct myth to preserve the mystique of their subjects whereas Carter does so to destroy it. Carter's commitment to the debunking of myths and exposure of the fairy tales of patriarchy and Empire would eventually reach its satirical peak with *Wise Children* in which outdated circus freaks like Gorgeous George, tattooed with the map of the Empire and almost unrecognizable in a contemporary setting, are juxtaposed with the Chance sisters. Claiming that all women look like female impersonators after a certain age, Carter's characters are the daughters of another elderly lady, Britannia, similarly still attempting to impersonate her younger self.

However, and in spite of the continuation of overtly realist forms of literature, the breaking down of traditional absolutes and the continual rewriting or re-orienting of history leads to many instances where conventional narratological rules are suspended and strict stylistic convention ignored. For example, though Salman Rushdie's greatest successes would occur in the following decade his published work in the seventies, *Grimus* (1975), not only illustrated the beginnings of the magical realism that he would typically come to be associated with but also incorporated elements of mythological fantasy and science fiction. Amis too pursued a similar progressive approach to stylistic matters after *The Rachel Papers* and *Dead Babies* (1975), with novels such as *Other People* (1981) that deliberately unbalance the expectations of consistent form and genre.

Beyond the indifference of contemporary authors to matters of conventional style, however, the deliberate re-examination of form changed the authorial relationship to the use of history within fiction. Although strictly speaking it belongs to the following decade, Rushdie's *Midnight's Children* (published in 1981, but begun in 1976 and delayed, somewhat ironically given its preoccupation with time) illustrates how ideas of 'undergoing history' had been developed further. In a logical extension of Farrell's dictum, Rushdie portrays history as an active force within his novel which affects each individual in a way uniquely experienced by them. History for Rushdie has ideas of its own, seemingly in possession of intent and power beyond that of the history encountered in the work of other novelists. The theme of active history is one that Rushdie would again revisit in the follow-up to *Midnight's Children, Shame* (1983). By splintering the experience of undergoing history from a totalizing narrative to a multiplicity, Rushdie further strengthens the relationship between individual experiences and events of national importance (Bowers 78). Consequently, all histories are rendered equally valid in Rushdie's work; the egalitarian interlinking of personal and political concerns in 1970s fiction would be preserved in the decade to follow.

Conclusion

In many ways, the 1970s was the last period in British history in which a general sense of consensus was possible. Many critics and commentators such as John Nagle and Richard Lewis have noted that with the developments in immigration, multiculturalism and the disassociation of many traditional communities, the fragmentation of the 'general viewpoint' has progressed to the point of collapse.[23] Historical representation in 1970s fiction suffers from much the same problem; the advent of new theoretical discourses resulted in the splitting of the British relationship to the past and the means of representing it. However, despite the varied nature of the relationship between historicity and literature, the pull of the past remained undiminished. Edified or deconstructed, mythologized or marginalized, the panoply of British history endured.

Despite the best efforts of 1970s novelists to highlight British history for the production it was and still is, the spectre of the past would remain, not static but dormant, until it was subjected to another new interpretation. Not so far into the future, in the early 1980s, Margaret Thatcher would reawaken and rejuvenate the memorial culture of British history for use in the Falklands campaign; the significance of such a move was not lost on David Lodge, who, in a new introduction to the reprinted version of *Out of the Shelter* noted how 'the old emotions welled up again in the Falklands War!' (x). Thatcher's actions would provide Linda Hutcheon grounds to observe that through selective, politically motivated emphasis on certain elements of the past 'The representation of history becomes the history of representation' (58). The past, and the way it is constructed, is again composed to fit best with the present picture; during and after the 1970s, the past, to paraphrase Umberto Eco, is never revisited innocently.

Notes

1. The Lend-Lease Act of Congress in 1941 concerned the supply of essential weapons and supplies to Britain during the period of United States neutrality. As the war developed, this legislation was modified to include the ceding of British territory to the US for the construction of airbases during the war and a range of other provisions; the legacy of Lend-Lease would influence and restrict British sovereignty for decades afterwards. For a comprehensive, if occasionally vitriolic account, see Correlli Barnett, *The Lost Victory: British Dreams, British Realities 1945–1950* (London: Macmillan, 1995).
2. See Raphael Samuel, *Theatres of Memory: Past & Present in Contemporary Culture Vol. I* (London: Verso, 1996) or Angus Calder, *The Myth of the Blitz* (London: Jonathan Cape, 1991) for interpretations of Britain's preoccupation with the Second World War.
3. See Scott's *The Towers of Silence* (1971) and *A Division of the Spoils* (1975), Keneally's *Gossip From the Forest* (1975) and Berger's *G.* (1972).
4. The trilogy was, in fact, designed to be at the very least a quartet; at the time of his death, Farrell was working on another novel set in British India in 1871 which featured characters from *The Siege of Krishnapur*. The work was posthumously published under the title *The Hill Station* in 1981.
5. *The Sun* headline of 11 January 1978 famously attributed Labour Prime Minister Jim Callaghan with this blasé response to the nation's 'mounting chaos'.
6. Dominic Sandbrook's two-volume series on the 1970s, *State of Emergency: The Way We Were, Britain 1970–1974* (London: Allen Lane, 2010) and *Seasons in the Sun: The Battle For Britain 1974–1979* (London: Allen Lane, 2012) have more recently given the 1970s further scrutiny.
7. The BBC's *Life on Mars* (2006–2007) popularized contemporary views that the 1970s were somehow a more innocent, straightforward time, devoid of the complications of health and safety and red tape, albeit one with questionable attitudes towards gender, race and sexuality.
8. *Monty Python's Flying Circus* (1969–1975) and *Fawlty Towers* (1975–1979) are, along with Morecombe and Wise and *Dad's Army*, the best known British comedies of the 1970s; *Fawlty Towers* in particular was voted the best British sitcom of all time by the British Film Institute in 2000. See Marcia Landy, *Monty Python's Flying Circus* (Detroit: Wayne State University Press, 2005).
9. Samuel, *Theatres of Memory*, 208. Samuel analyses the post-war boom in both heritage and nostalgia, suggesting that the war had prompted the widespread cultural shift towards preservation of all sorts.
10. Sandbrook's *Seasons in the Sun* explores the multitude of television programmes which directly represented or were influenced by the Second World War. He quotes

from Gerard Glaister, producer of the BBC's *Colditz* (1972-1974) and former RAF pilot, who recognized his own part in turning the Second World War 'from history into myth' (317).

11. Chiefly associated with the Cultural Turn are various members of the Frankfurt School, including Theodor Adorno and Herbert Marcuse, and other prominent academics such as Clifford Geertz working in the United States during the 1950s and 1960s. See Frederic Jameson, *The Cultural Turn: Selected Writings on the Postmodern, 1983-1998* (London: Verso, 2009) and Victoria E. Bonnell, *Beyond the Cultural Turn: New Directions in the Study of Society and Culture* (Berkeley: University of California Press, 1999).

12. During the 1960s, Montgomery had publicly expressed support for South African Apartheid and had been openly critical of Britain's chief ally, the United States. Similarly, in the mid-1970s, Stirling lent his support to the radical civil defence organisation GB75; though the group was never any serious political entity, it nonetheless damaged his credibility. See Philip Whitehead, *Writing on the Wall: Britain in the Seventies* (London: Michael Joseph, 1988), 211 or Sandbrook, *Seasons in the Sun*, 139-140.

13. The Commando Comics series is still in print today. Collected volumes have been published in recent years capitalising on a resurgent interest in the Second World War, prompted by the larger commemorative celebrations of the Normandy Invasion and the Battle of Britain in 2004 and 2010, respectively.

14. Though they precede the chronology of this volume, the scholarly impact and controversy of A. J. P. Taylor's *The Origins of the Second World War* (1961) and E. H. Carr's *What is History?* (1961) was particularly seismic and both works remained influential for many years afterwards. Keith Jenkins's *On 'What Is History'; From Carr and Elton to Rorty and White* (London: Routledge, 1995) provides a useful overview of historiographic debates from the 1960s to 1970s.

15. Surveys of the historiographical debate over the bombing of Dresden can be found in A. C. Grayling's *Among the Dead Cities: Is the Targeting of Civilians in War ever Justified?* (London: Bloomsbury, 2006) and Frederick Taylor's *Dresden: Tuesday 13 February 1945* (London: Bloomsbury, 2005).

16. See Keith Kyle, *Suez: Britain's End of Empire in the Middle East* (London: I.B Taurus, 2011); W. M. Roger Louis, *Ends of British Imperialism: The Scramble for Empire, Suez and Decolonization* (London: I.B. Tauris, 2006); Scott Lucas, *Britain & Suez: The Lion's Last Roar* (Manchester: University Press, 1996).

17. For instance, in 1957 the Gold Coast and Togoland became Ghana, in 1958 Singapore achieved home rule and Cyprus gained independence in 1959. Next to go was British Somaliland in 1960 followed, much to Ian Fleming's dismay, by Jamaica in 1962 with Kenya and Zanzibar in 1963. See Lawrence James, *The Rise & Fall of the British Empire* (London: Abacus, 2001), 559-588.

18. In many instances, historians such as Piers Brendon and Niall Ferguson have argued (somewhat unconvincingly) that the handing back of Hong Kong in 1997 as the official end of the British Empire; however, Hong Kong, British territory only under lease, was not part of the Empire in the same way as other colonies and did not seek decolonization.
19. See Charles Michener. 'Britain's Brat of Letters: Who Is Martin Amis, and Why Is Everybody Saying such Terrible Things about Him?', *Esquire*, January 1987: 107.
20. Harold Adrian Russell Philby, known as Kim, was part of the so-called Cambridge Ring of spies which also included Guy Burgess and Anthony Blunt. Philby told his version of events in *My Secret War* (London: Granada, 1969) complete with an introduction written by his former wartime agent Graham Greene.
21. In the explanatory note that precedes the fifth volume of the Flashman papers, *Flashman in the Great Game* (1975), Fraser thanks those readers who had written to correct 'curious discrepancies' in Flashman's recollections and excuses 'such lapses' as 'understandable, if not excusable, in a hard-living octogenarian'. Whether readers around the globe really believed Fraser's novels were authentic memoirs as he claims is open to question.
22. For a comprehensive survey of how Farrell in particular has been miscategorized see John McLeod, 'J. G. Farrell and Post-Imperial Fiction' in Ralph Crane *J. G. Farrell: The Critical Grip* (Dublin: Four Courts Press, 1999), 178–195.
23. See Richard Lewis, *Multiculturalism Observed: Exploring Identity* (Brussels: University of Brussels, 2006) and John Nagle, *Multiculturalism's Double-Bind: Creating Inclusivity, Cosmopolitanism and Difference* (Farnham: Ashgate, 2009).

Works cited

Amis, Kingsley. *Lucky Jim*. London: Penguin, 1964 [1954].
Amis, Martin. *Other People: A Mystery Story*. Harmondsworth: Penguin, 1982 [1978].
———. *Dead Babies*. Harmondsworth: Penguin, 1984 [1975].
———. *The Rachel Papers*. Harmondsworth: Penguin, 1984 [1973].
Bowers, Maggie Ann. *Magic(al) Realism*. London: Routledge, 2005.
Bradbury, Malcolm. *The History Man*. London: Secker & Warburg, 1975.
Calder, Angus. *The Myth of the Blitz*. London: Jonathan Cape, 1991.
———. *The People's War: 1939–1945*. London: Pimlico, 1992.
Carter, Angela. *The Infernal Desire Machines of Doctor Hoffman*. London: Penguin, 1982 [1972].
———. *The Passion of New Eve*. London: Virago, 1982 [1977].
———. *The Bloody Chamber and Other Stories*. London: Penguin, 1986 [1979].
———. *Wise Children*. London: Penguin, 1993 [1991].

Day, Aidan. *Angela Carter: The Rational Glass.* Manchester: Manchester UP, 1998.

Farrell, J. G. *Troubles.* London: Phoenix, 1993 [1970].

———. *The Siege of Krishnapur.* London: Phoenix Press, 2007 [1973].

———. *The Singapore Grip.* London: Phoenix Press, 2007 [1978]

Forsyth, Frederick. *The Odessa File.* London: Random House, 1998 [1972]

Higgins, Jack. *The Eagle Has Landed.* London: Penguin, 1998 [1975].

Hutcheon, Linda. *The Politics of Postmodernism.* London: Routledge, 1988.

Kynaston, David. *Austerity Britain: 1945-51.* London: Bloomsbury, 2007.

Larkin, Philip. *High Windows.* London: Faber & Faber, 1991 [1974].

Le Carré, John. *Tinker, Tailor, Soldier, Spy.* London: Octopus Group, 1988 [1974].

Lodge, David. *Out of the Shelter.* London: Secker & Warburg, 1985 [1970].

MacDonald Fraser, George. *Flashman in the Great Game.* London: Collins, 1985 [1975].

McLeod, John. 'J. G. Farrell and Post-Imperial Fiction', in *J. G. Farrell: The Critical Grip.* Ed. by Ralph Crane. Dublin: Four Courts Press. 178-195.

———. *J. G. Farrell.* Tavistock: Northcote House Publishers, 2007.

Moore-Gilbert, Bart. *Cultural Closure: The Arts in the 70s.* London: Routledge, 1994.

Nairn, Tom. *The Break-Up of Britain: Crisis and Neonationalism.* London: NLB, 1977.

Nora, Pierre. *Realms of Memory.* New York: Columbia Press, 1996.

Oxford English Dictionary. 12th June 2010. http://dictionary.oed.com/cgi/entry/50106603

Perks, Robert and Alistair Thompson, eds. *The Oral History Reader.* London: Routledge, 1998.

Rushdie, Salman. *Midnight's Children.* London: Pan, 1983 [1981].

———. *Shame.* London: Jonathan Cape, 1983.

———. *Grimus.* London: Random House, 2003 [1975].

Samuel, Raphael. *Theatres of Memory.* London: Verso, 1996.

Sandbrook, Dominic. *State of Emergency: The Way We Were, Britain 1970-1974.* London: Allen Lane, 2010.

Thompson, E. P. *The Making of the English Working Class.* Aylesbury: Pelican Books, 1968.

Ward, Paul. *Britishness since 1870.* London: Routledge, 2004.

6

Turbulent Times: Conflicts, Ideology and the Experimental British Novel, 1969–1979

Philip Tew

As a wide-ranging genre, the novel evokes, charts and even contributes to a plethora of intersecting social narratives, which relate and respond variously to an overarching and complex flux of human experience that surpasses any particular account, yet which are inevitably distilled down into particular historical perspectives, allowing an individual understanding, but in doing so one risks simplifying the potential scope for knowledge. In an aesthetic sense as a result of such repeated narrowing when society is habituated to current literary stylizations, a familiarity masking both the presence and significance of formal devices, experimental novelists seek to interrogate and undermine existing generic boundaries. Such a shift may explain the sense of crisis at the beginning of the 1970s alluded to by Gabriel Josipovici in *The World and the Book: A Study of Modern Fiction* (1971), 'It is sometimes said by literary people that the novel is dead. What they mean by this is that the form has run itself into the ground or is somehow no longer relevant to the present age. This of course is nonsense' (286). An active avant-garde writer, Josipovici believed experimentalism sustained the form, and understood its proponents were committed to the genre's survival and adaptation. Many such authors considered below were part of overlapping coteries, sharing ideas, at times projects. Between 1960 and 1963 for instance Zulfikar Ghose collaborated severally with B. S. Johnson. Their circle included Alan Burns, John Berger, Rayner Heppenstall, Stefan Themerson, Ann Quin and Wilson Harris among others. Johnson, whose own life would end tragically in 1973, edited *London Consequences* (1972) with Margaret Drabble, and in *Aren't You Rather Young To Be Writing Your Memoirs?* (1973) argues for the evolution of the novel beyond 'exhausted forms' (16). He named authors 'who are writing as though it mattered, as though they meant it, as though they meant it to matter' (29). Additional to the circle cited above (but excluding Drabble), he included Anthony Burgess and Christine Brooke-Rose. All feature, alongside others, in this reconsideration of 1970s experimentalism, assessed largely in terms of underlying conflicts and ideologies. Such writers and their peers could draw upon both formal and ideological innovations stretching from the novel's origins in the eighteenth century to the so-called postmodern self-reflexive novel. This broad genealogy begs the question of where exactly might the boundaries of such 'experimentation' be defined in terms of textual dynamics or acts of authorship, ever an elusive matter. Josipovici comments that the novel form 'is entirely free to do what it pleases, to move in any direction it wants' (286). If this is true of more traditional, mimetically inclined texts, then the elements that constitute avant-garde practice cannot be easily settled nor precisely defined; rather there exists a constant series of aesthetic challenges and adaptations some of which we award experimental status.

As Émile Zola expounds in *The Experimental Novel and Other Essays* (1893), the naturalistic novel with its panoptic vision was originally considered experimental, although Zola concedes such fiction can never finally create an entirely faithful mimesis that many assume to be its ambition.

> The idea of experiment carries with it the idea of modification. We start, indeed, from the true facts, which are our indestructible basis, but to show the mechanism of these facts it is necessary for us to produce and direct the phenomena; this is our share of invention, here is the genius in the book. Thus without having recourse to the questions of form and style, which I will examine later, I maintain even at this point that we must modify nature, without departing from nature, when we employ the experimental method in our novels. (11)

Hence later avant-garde novels simply exaggerate certain failings underlying the genre's apparent ambitions towards verisimilitude. Subsequent modernist experimentalists rejected Zola's sense of an innate and underlying factuality, overturning concepts based upon the solidity of nature and fixity of time, highlighting both the text's artefactual nature and the limitations of human perspectives. Josipovici offers a workable categorization: 'The modern novel draws attention to the rules which govern its own creation in order to force the reader into recognising that it is not the world' (298). However, as Brian Stonehill indicates in *The Self-Conscious Novel: Artifice in Fiction from Joyce to Pynchon* (1988), if complex modes of reflexivity are central to the avant-garde novel, they simply exaggerate elements that occur in *all* fiction, and 'As a concept and a genre, the self-conscious novel makes salient fiction's dual nature – its ludic and its mimetic mission' (47). And even though it is suggested by many, including Patrick Parrinder in *Nation & Novel* (2006), that fictional narrative can only represent what he describes as 'imagined communities' (14), yet fiction clearly and often volubly draws from concrete cultures of eventfulness, evident in the 1970s, as demonstrated below, where the interpenetration of real and written worlds was very much part of the cultural zeitgeist. By this time – reflecting an increasingly accelerated sense of progressive developments, a rapidity of generational responses and an acceleration of changing fashions – decades were increasingly used as markers to identify certain clusters of emerging opinions and actions. Despite risking arbitrariness, fictionally such a strategy potentially accentuates both correlations of key historical factors and offers focused possibilities in charting such cultural contexts and additionally key thematic and formal responses to them. Bearing in mind Parrinder's claim that 'Novels exert a powerful influence on our perceptions of society and of our individual selves precisely because they lack any official sanction' (9), I seek to demonstrate below how in a decade as uncertain as the 1970s, the experimental novel sustained thought-provoking challenges, despite a critical establishment that had declared the form's demise. It incorporated intensifications of what Michel Butor describes in 'The Novel as Research' as a literary-social 'exploration', one which

> reveals what is contingent in the form we are used to, unmasks it, releases us from it, allows us to rediscover beyond this fixed narrative everything it camouflages or passes over in silence: that fundamental narrative in which our whole life is steeped. (50)

Clearly, the experimental novel is never singular, its innovations and possibilities engaged variously to abjure traditional modes of writing: formally through innovations and self-conscious devices; thematically through ideological intensity or disruptions of the status quo; or by combining a number of these responses. The latter propensity or synthesis as I will demonstrate below becomes more marked in 1970s avant-gardist writers. However, the academic critic and experimental writer, Christine Brooke-Rose makes a significant observation in 'Illiterations': 'Clearly there can be trivial as well as truly innovative experiment just as there can be trivial as well as important writing in wholly familiar forms' (62).

Like all periods, the 1970s emerged from and responded to the remnants of an anterior consciousness. However, tentatively, the post-war years had seemed variously to promise economic growth, greater leisure and increasing social equality. Both radical Sartrean philosophy and the *nouveau roman* defined the period's cultural, intellectual and literary identity, foregrounding existential angst and alienation as key contemporary experiences, expressed in a troubled aesthetic. The ideological quest for existential authenticity generated a perspective divergent from both high modernist and realist perceptions. As James Gindin says in *Postwar British Fiction: New Accents and Attitudes* (1962), 'the existentialists insist on dealing with concrete facts of experience, multiple and unsystematic though they may be, rather than theorizing about the general nature of essences' (231). Many writers were compelled by the obsessive objectivity of the *nouveau roman*, about which Bernard Bergonzi is sceptical, most particularly regarding 'Robbe-Grillet's commitment to constant evolution' (30). One English conduit for such ideas had been Heppenstall, who was intimately involved in existentialism's emergence, influencing its alienated despair. The post-war world resisted traditional moral perspectives, exploring the aesthetics of ideological engagement. Rather than adopt modernism's formula of making things new, this later phase pursued theoretical concepts of freedom; apparent pathways where through various critical perspectives the oppressed might be liberated, chiefly by a Marxist critique or that of a supposedly radicalizing identity politics. In essence, too, the crisis of existential doubt that characterized the 1950s and 1960s gave way to an increasing historicity and reflexivity of the 1970s and 1980s because of an underlying confidence that individuals might liberate both themselves and the social order, even without religiosity and faith.

Hence against these concerns of the preceding decades, the 1970s novel popularized historicity and introduced reflexivity, although the latter only became fully developed in the following decade. If the 1970s was marked by literary *and* cultural transitions, for A. S. Byatt in 'People in Paper Houses', a profound aesthetic shift, which paradoxically brought 'certain firmly "realist" works and certain declared experimental works curiously close together' (27), was exemplified by John Fowles's *The French Lieutenant's Woman* (1969). Byatt assumes 'Fowles's understanding of Victorian life and literature is crude and derived from the Bloomsbury rejection of it, which makes his technical nostalgia fascinating as a phenomenon' (28). Yet Fowles demonstrates copious research in his prefatory material to various chapters; he seeks to parody the mid-twentieth-century view of the past and its privileging of its contemporary mores. He adapts archetypes and furthermore he condemns the Victorian 'battle for universal masculine purity' (238) which led to the social rejection of so many women. Certainly, this seems to qualify as parody according to Brooke-Rose's summary of Bakhtin's view of the concept in *Stories, theories and things* (1991): 'And for him *parody* appropriates, as object, an already artificial discourse, but introduces into it an orientation diametrically opposed to its own' (192). Byatt finds the novel stylized and inseparable from the dynamics of Victorian narratives, but surely Fowles consistently undermines and opposes much about the Victorianism he absorbs into his parodic model, not just in terms of content, but also with regard to the neo-Victorian rhetoric and style which he adopts only to subdue and subvert it.

The French Lieutenant's Woman is explicit in its formal challenges to tradition, incorporating devices such as multiple endings (only one of which sustains conventional romance and traditional motherhood as satisfactory for one of its protagonists, Sarah Woodruff) with a historical neo-Victorian narrative running parallel to ideological reflections on contemporary feminism and sexuality, the era of burning bras and free love. The multiple endings emphasize both the contingency of one's fate, but also the performative nature of identity. The narrative consciously contrasts the apparently *laissez-faire* sexuality of the 1960s with the intensity and restrictions of the Victorian era, where sex was profoundly significant in very different ways. Despite Byatt's objections, Fowles's ahistorical qualities are intended, the text's anachronisms deliberate. Fowles's historical narrative may initially appear realist, but is progressively concerned with self-narratives that constitute both social identity and challenges to the established order. The plight of Sarah Woodruff, one of the two protagonists, appears to mirror the experiences of Thomas Hardy's Tess, although Sarah's social exclusion is a state that she is revealed to have sought for its notoriety and capacity to challenge. In an apparent condition of depressed vulnerability and passivity, actually she attracts, courts and seduces Charles, the other main character, performatively bringing about a brief romance and her conception of a child. She rejects Charles's offers of help precisely because it is she that is in control of the situation. The text may be deeply, darkly and insistently ludic and provocative, contemporaneous readership and misapprehension informing its historicity, and in so doing heralding a more contested, self-knowing and ironically doubtful avant-gardism. Nevertheless in countering traditional forms, writing can still be focused on seeking different modes that offer versions of verisimilitude, for as Brooke-Rose says in 'Illiterations' 'It is often forgotten for instance that the *nouveau roman*, when it burst out in the fifties, first acquired the label, *nouveau réalisme*, and was linked to phenomenology, just as earlier literary "revolutions" since Wordsworth had been made in the name of greater realism' (63).

Rather than offer crude Victorianism, Fowles layers its fictional breadth with both reflexive and self-parodic characteristics, which aspects Byatt concedes do not necessarily negate the solidity of eventfulness (31). At the end of the twelfth chapter the narrator supposedly avoids but states the extremes of emotion and hysteria that Sarah Woodruff suffers after the moral opprobrium of her employer, Mrs Poulteney, for being on the Ware Commons in Lyme Regis, a place inappropriate for a single woman according to respectable mores. Fowles explodes the conceit, the narrator asking:

> Who is Sarah?
> Out of what shadows does she come? (84)

The same voice declares at the beginning of the 13th chapter, in a strategy that compounds the sense of self-awareness and narrative contrivance:

> I do not know. This story I am telling is all imagination. These characters I create never existed outside my own mind. If I have pretended until now to know my characters' minds and innermost thoughts, it is because I am writing in (just as I have assumed some of the vocabulary and 'voice' of) a convention universally accepted at the time of my story: that the novelist stands next to God. He may not know all, yet he tries to pretend that he does. But I live in the age of Alain Robbe-Grillet and Roland Barthes; if this is a novel, it cannot be a novel in the modern sense of the word. (85)

Fowles – writing a century after the period he describes (238) – indicates his fiction is a hybrid form, framed by irresolution, mixing populist elements with a high seriousness matching that of the Victorians. Contingency is significant both structurally and thematically. Although seemingly bucolic in its setting and historicity, Fowles problematizes both any idealized notion of the Victorian past and the contemporary condescension which labels this period as simply repressed sexually. His narrative also vociferously challenges the Victorians' view of themselves as fundamentally bourgeois, a perspective that colours every age including by implication the present; a point made by stating that the Victorians 'were quite as highly sexed as our own century – and in spite of the fact that *we* have sex thrown at us night and day (as the Victorians had religion), far more preoccupied with it than we really are' (232). Later, Fowles deploys evidence of the unabashed sexuality of the working classes and farm labourers where overcrowding inculcated incest (234–235), ending his novel enigmatically with its doubled final endings, matching the third of Charles's earlier daydreams. Charles has faced an existential crisis in the church in Exeter, questioning the tenets of his world and its constraints, glimpsing 'a new reality, a new causality, a new creation' (316). Fowles comments on this struggle: 'A modern existentialist would no doubt substitute "humanity" or "Authenticity" for "piety"; but he would recognize Arnold's intent' (398).

Both Fowles's doubts about 1960s culture and his fictional hybridity became ever more widespread in the following decade. As Alwyn W. Turner comments in *Crisis? What Crisis? Britain in the 1970s* (2008), 1960s euphoria had faded:

> The country was confronted by a series of crises that set the tone for the remainder of the century and beyond: crises about natural resources, about race and immigration, about terrorism and environmental abuse, about Britain's position in Europe and that of nationalisms in Britain, crises in fact about everything from street violence to class war and even to paedophile porn. (ix)

The 1970s continue to be resonant aesthetically and culturally, initiating certain themes and transitions which swept aside the previous consensus, thereby creating a new social order. Responding to the period's consequent sense of accelerating crisis, experimental writers were drawn to the recurrent features, many of which were at least putatively present in Fowles: a mixture of dark comedy with an intensity and perversity of themes; interrelated and overlapping vignettes or episodes that abjure traditional narrative progression and teleology; themes made emphatic through insistent symbols and motifs; a notion of cultural and economic bankruptcy; a sense of social disintegration challenging decaying traditions; a notion of personal entrapment by larger forces; and a crisis of bourgeois identity. As opposed to the intensities of modernism's inner, aesthetic struggles, 1970s writers grapple more with an objective world of events, its moral and ideological struggles staged through traumatic confrontations. In terms of violent death, for instance, 1972 alone saw the IRA kill 100 British soldiers in Northern Ireland, wound 500 more, and cause 1,300 explosions with 90 of their own members killed too. The Republicans controlled large parts of Belfast and Derry, effectively removing them from government control. The decade was characterized by further political trauma and social strife as manifested by such examples as the case of the Pentonville Five, in which trades unionists imprisoned for picketing were freed only after the threat of a general strike (80), Enoch Powell's 'Rivers of Blood' speech (29–31), the troubles in Northern Ireland which included the infamous 'Bloody Sunday' (70) and the IRA mainland bombing campaign. Add to that corruption in the Metropolitan Police (61–2), the Angry Brigade bombings, the Miner's Strike of 1973–1974 that forced an election, a frequently articulated fear of an impending authoritarian government and more generally economic turbulence and instability throughout the period; in many ways Britain seemed like a country tearing itself apart.

Drabble and Johnson's *London Consequences* (1972) was an unusual novel project involving anonymously various avant-garde and associated writers, consisting of a palimpsest or pastiche of 20 different chapters written in succession, the previous ones handed on, by 20 writers each progressively supplementing a narrative set in London at Easter 1971. Melvyn Bragg's fourth chapter summarizes many of the tensions and traumas of the time. 'Society – yes; 250 years and more of civil peace – yes; Northern Ireland and Vietnam and build-ups and returning troops – yes; bombs in Parliament and at private houses; Duty of the Press; political journalism in the streets as well as in the committee rooms […]' (36). Fictionally, the decade's mood is expressed in discordant and intersubjective social interactions that go beyond personal alienation, concerned with profound individual and collective threats. Society seemed to face an abyss, which individuals encountered variously. The characters in 1970s experimental fiction are typically deeply unheroic, inhabiting social and economic conditions that become disturbing and strange, the plight of the individual often intensely violent, either literally or psychically. In *Christie Malry's Own Double-Entry* (1973) Johnson's protagonist is an urban terrorist working as a single cell, responsible ultimately for killing hundreds of thousands. Johnson polemically reminds the reader, despite the self-parodic brevity and cursory nature of his text, that life is never in truth full of open choices: 'Christie, like almost all of us, had to think of earning a living first; the economics dictate to an extent sometimes not fully realised the real (as distinct from the imaginary) possibilities open to one to move in other directions' (12). Work as described by Johnson is an embittering experience for the ordinary worker. Changing social conditions, shifts in general moral codes and the commodification of values recur as the social substrata to such conditions.

Violent undercurrents subtend the narrator of the initial anonymous chapter of *London Consequences* (written jointly by Drabble and Johnson), whose contributions also curiously served as a Greater London Arts Association competition. Readers were invited to work out which writer composed which chapter (none were identified on publication), an entry form printed after 'Biographical Notes' of contributing writers. The first chapter opens with double columns representing the inner thoughts or dreams of a married couple, Judith and Anthony Sheridan. Subsequently Judith worries about her political journalist husband:

> Easter was a violent time. The thought licked over her mind. Annoying as Anthony could be, she wouldn't like him crushed to death by a police horse, picked off by a sniper, hunted by the mob. Easter was a time for civic unrest. (16)

This sense of violence and unrest persists. The various contributors include thematically various points of contemporaneous public debate: terrorism, demonstrations, immigration, race relations and threatened lay-offs (redundancies). A reflexive and ludic quality permeates many of the chapters, as with the final twentieth (also by Johnson and Drabble) where the couple return home in neo-Woolfian fashion after a day's expedition in town, back to where the narrative had commenced that morning:

> 'I've never had a worse day in my life', he said.
> 'Neither have I', she said.
> 'All those novellers at us, one after another'.
> 'I'm absolutely knackered'.
> No physical reconciliation tonight, then, she thought, half relieved and half saddened.
> Then the questions began.
> [...]
> 'Do you think the violence in this novel reflects the violence in the life of the average novelist?' (149)

In terms of violence perhaps the most extreme example is Alan Burns's 11th chapter where Judith traverses ghettoes, and engages in multiple criminal acts including shoplifting, breaking shop windows and attempting to burn two fire engines while trailed by detectives. The logic of these acts is obscure and somewhat provocatively Burns uses Judith to catalogue acts of transgression and rebellion. Like some underground urban terrorist 'She carried a home-made banner reading: "Do you need bloodshed to make you understand"' (85). In the 13th chapter, Heppenstall responds (despite the mathematical miscalculation that commences his contribution) by self-consciously incorporating into the opening both his relationship as a writer among the other contributors and that which he perceives as existing between them and the protagonists, before implicitly rebuking those such as Burns for stretching credibility beyond its usual coordinates. His mild and good-humoured rebuke is implicit, but also serves to foreground the artefactual and eventful qualities of this book.

> Don't Mrs Sheridan, please. It isn't your fault, and you aren't mad. You have simply been mauled by novelists, five so far. I cannot guarantee what your evening will be, but I assure you that for two hours nothing untoward will happen or even seem to happen to you, nor will you behave or be thought to behave oddly. You will live in the present, your present. Your personality will have time to recover and heal. (97)

Despite this authorial effort at collaborative creativity, clearly by the 1970s more broadly any lingering sense of Britain as a collective progressive social enterprise was being challenged. The erosion of such certainties began as the decade approached, epitomized well by the Labour party's inner debates and infighting about limiting union power; its official line published as Barbara Castle's Government white paper *In Place of Strife* (1969). Perhaps the 1970s became less optimistic because, as Iris Murdoch points out in *Existentialists and Mystics: Writings on Philosophy and Literature* (1997), 'The existentialist may become so obsessed with the powerful self-assertive figure of his hero (or anti-hero) that he presents a mediocre person as being important and valuable simply because he is contemptuous of society and gets his own way' (226). This is suggestive as in the 1970s a certain lack of discrimination and a certain underwhelming mediocrity and sense of failure prevailed despite the apparent search for authentic being. This bathetic tendency, in conjunction with the continual social strife, explains why the decade's legacy was subsequently regarded in mostly negative terms; responses akin to that Andrew Spicer who describes in 'British Culture and Society in the 1970s' the decade as being retrospectively for many 'tasteless, uninteresting, economically and artistically moribund –marooned between the vibrant 1960s and the entrepreneurial 1980s' (134).

In many ways one might argue that after the cultural exuberance of the 1960s, the 1970s celebrated the banality of life, foregrounding its conflicts and vicissitudes, and the failings of dreams of escape or transcendence. Certain of these cultural obsessions are incorporated in Rayner Heppenstall's largely semi-autobiographical and quasi-documentary novel, *Two Moons* (1977), which reflects on Britain in the world of the early 1970s, incorporating its social and industrial conflicts, ending with reference to the Munich massacre in which Israeli athletes were 'butchered' (194) at the 1972 Olympics. Set against multiple events drawn from reports, some minor, others like assassination attempts more momentous, are records of the implacable movement of celestial time charted against the moon's progress. The text is 'dominated by impenetrable astrological rhetoric' (77) according to G. J. Buckell in *Rayner Heppenstall* (2007). The effects of this and the myriad points of factual reference are cumulative, in excess of any particular experience, suggesting an underlying collective and interrelated commonality, a part of the unachievable totality of historical being itself. This applies across time, linking the phases of life as if by both chance and design. This can be viewed literally at times, since in the novel each side of the page offers different, yet continuous and interrelated narratives where the verso account precedes the recto, demanding 'parallel reading [which if] burdensome the author suggests that he (the reader) should read all the left-hand pages in the book and then all the right-hand pages' (11). In the record of the Atha family, life's minutiae, variously global, local and personal, offer fragmented pictures of existence, not inchoate but redolent of the struggle for meaning amongst a cacophony of events. In the novel any grandiose sense of historicity is overwhelmed by life's detailed malice and contingency, which is reflected in the book's unusual presentational structures, for instance the verso tale at one point highlights a series of murders and acts of violence, including:

> Murder was unsuccessfully attempted that evening in Olney Place, Stepney. There, a middle-aged intruder from over the river was discovered with six gunshot wounds. Of the two young men arrested and charged, one was described as an insurance broker. (158)

As with much thought of the time, the personal incorporates the avowedly political and the latter is personal. Opposite from this passage is the narrator, Harold Atha, drawing from his *Observer*: 'Pakistan had accused India of shelling her territory. Denmark had voted to join the Common Market. There had been more fatal shootings in Belfast and Mr William Craig was threatening a Protestant U.D.I. if we did not do something' (159). Interestingly, Heppenstall repudiates fuller detail, any hierarchy of meaning or even editorial intervention and guidance, since what Buckell describes dismissively as 'endless arbitrary details' (77–78) surely must represent a strategy to convey the plenitude of data of any passing historical moment, of potentially any consciousness, full of the plethora of elements that signify various lives intersecting and seeking meaning, from channel swimming through industrial unrest to terrorism on the one hand and immigration, politics, personal tragedy and home life on the other. Like much of the experimental imagination of the period, social conflict, violence, injury and death are all foregrounded, a macabre matrix tying together the narrative sensibility.

Underlying gender conflict lies at the heart of Iris Murdoch's *The Black Prince* (1973), which attempts a self-reflexive narrative, although in some senses following a relatively traditional strategy, in that an 'Editor's Foreword' by P. Loxias is followed by 'Bradley Pearson's Foreword' which is purportedly that of the ensuing book. On a (second) title page the reader (addressed variously and directly throughout the novel) encounters:

> NOW FOLLOWS BRADLEY PEARSON'S STORY, WHICH IS ENTITLED:
> THE BLACK PRINCE: A CELEBRATION OF LOVE. (1)

These features are not emphatically innovative, since informally addressing readers was common in the novel from the eighteenth century, and similar prefatory material appears, for instance, before the main narrative in Nathaniel Hawthorne's *A Scarlet Letter* (1850), including his discursive 'Custom-House sketch'. Murdoch's novel may be replete with a variety of reflections on the meaning and experience of love, but the book also considers first the process of writing and the meaning of art, and second it conveys some sense of the arrogance underlying the residual patriarchal masculinity still common in a decade where such attitudes continued to be radically challenged by feminists. Murdoch's shifting of genre boundaries lies in blending dark comedy with a mystery story. Murdoch remains sceptical of claims of self-knowledge. Bradley says that 'no philosopher and hardly any novelist has ever managed to explain what that weird stuff, human consciousness, is really made of' (157). Certainly Murdoch has Bradley fail spectacularly in this context. Women confuse him. Bradley has an affair with Rachel, wife of fellow writer, Arnold Baffin, and later his extra exam tuition with the couple's daughter, Julian, leads to passion with the latter. The second affair has obvious complications, since Julian is much younger than him, a matter of great consternation to her parents. Concurrently, Arnold has an affair with Bradley's former wife, Christian. Bradley recognizes the wrong tensions and complications. His obsessive and unrealistic love for Julian allows him to be framed by Rachel for murder. The narrative is told from prison, followed by Bradley's postscript and 'Four Postscripts by dramatis Personae' (343). Throughout Murdoch conveys a sense of Bradley's ironic literary mediocrity, his hubristic arrogance and his inability to transcend his previous life as an Inspector of Taxes even in retirement. Murdoch represents a covert challenge to patriarchal self-obsession, where objectifying male desire leads to a limited vision of the world, and Bradley's hubristic downfall is that of men generally.

During the 1970s, aesthetically it was open season on middle-class masculinity, whose certainties are parodied in Christopher Priest's *Fugue for A Darkening Island* (1972). As a first-person narrator, Alan Whitman's decreasingly assured voice describes in fragmentary episodic style a dystopic vision of societal breakdown in Britain with an extrapolation of its fears of mass migration. The narrative deconstructs both his male bourgeois perspective and associated identity. As protagonist he describes in impressionistic and highly personal fashion numerous elements in the decline of civil society, where order collapses and civil war rages. The nation descends into chaos after Britain has been subject to large-scale immigration after Africa has been attacked by nuclear weapons. After their arrival the two million plus survivors or 'Afrims' arm themselves and a complex civil war ensues between British National forces and Secessionists.

If the migrants have destabilized the political and economic situation, to explain Britain's particular problems in a worldwide crisis, Whitman identifies a particular form of extremism as catalytic. Prime Minister John Tregarth has propounded effectively a Powellite rejection of migrants and concurrently avows a radical Powellite economic and monetary reform (the latter mirroring Edward Heath's Selsdon policy document) that increases poverty:

> The Africans, the Afrims, were welcome nowhere. But where they landed, they stayed. Everywhere they caused social upheaval; but in Britain, where a neo-racist government had come to power on an economic-reform ticket, they did much more. (69)

Whitman is a lecturer but unemployed after cuts and rejected by the British Nationalist Army because of his 'former membership in the pro-Afrim society at the college' (71); he loses his professional status and takes on a succession of menial jobs, where he is distrusted by his fellow workers. The dynamics of Priest's economic world mirror the albeit reluctant interventionism of the Heath Government (such as in the Upper Clyde Shipbuilders dispute). 'Following government restrictions it was not possible to make staff redundant, except at the cost of high financial penalty, and our labour-force was not reduced in any way' (83). Plagued by serial infidelities on Whitman's part, his marriage splinters rapidly, and his relief seems palpable. The narrative's various episodes are non-sequential, overlaying each other, revolving around the loss by Whitman, his wife and daughter of their middle-class suburban home in Southgate, their flight across country, the hopelessness of a 'U.N. camp' (25), the subsequent loss of his family, and finally his discovery of their bodies. If the individual episodes are largely realist, their accumulation and adjacencies create a meta-framework, where the phases of decline and chaos can be seen in parallel. Loss of values, tolerance and respect lead directly to images of violence and trauma. Towards the end, Priest moves through chapters episodically from Whitman's infidelity before the crisis, to his joining a group led by Lateef still with his wife and daughter, to his abandonment of Lateef in search of them in Afrim brothels, to walking home from a pub during the initial crisis past an Afrim settlement: 'I felt distinctly that events were picking up a self-destructive momentum, and that no longer was a humane resolution possible' (109). At the end, Whitman stops in a middle-class enclave, but cannot abandon his quest. Finally the dark vision of this fractured world cannot sustain the illusion of bourgeois life, reflecting the dark undercurrents and fears of the 1970s aesthetic psyche, belief that chaos was threatening social values, its intangible anchoring points being ineluctably eroded. Priest's experimentalism lies in moving from the domestic to the chaotic, and the breadth of his futuristic portrayal of contemporary extremes in this predictive vision of widespread cultural collapse.

Similar dark tensions and challenges to masculinity underpin Doris Lessing's dystopia, *The Memoirs of Survivor* (1974), although less explicitly, insistently and realistically evoked. Lessing emphasizes a general, underlying and understated fear of social breakdown and conflict, but in flattening these crises she indicates exactly how people unconsciously adapt to them by suppressing their appalling nature. At the beginning she writes 'we – everyone – will look over a period in life, over a sequence of events, and find much more there than they did at the time' (7). The possibilities that underpin the middle-aged world of householders haunt them, since like the unnamed female protagonist, they face the collapse of the social fabric and civil order, where 'all public services had stopped to the south and to the east, and that this state of affairs was spreading our way' (12). Towards the end, she reflects obliquely on 'our descent into anarchy' (147). Her status feels like that of an observer, although clearly this extrapolates political, ecological and social tensions of the early 1970s. Reluctantly, and without full explication, the anti-heroic narrator is forced to adopt a displaced child, Emily, who has Hugo, 'this botch of a creature' (72), a beast seemingly part cat and part dog. As the girl matures at 15, she is attracted to Gerald, a youthful member of one of the many gangs. The streets are increasingly threatening, with the young, including children, living feral existences, some migrating from the town, others aggressive and violent. In the face of lawlessness, the narrator becomes instinctively obsessed with the wall of her ground-floor flat, first seeing beyond to another room. Drawn irresisitably, she looks 'And again the wall dissolved and I was through' (15). She discovers an indeterminate, shifting alternate and parallel realm, an occasionally prelapsarian land of plenitude (135–6), but mostly a troubling and seemingly phantom dream environment. Here she has glimpses of scenes from Emily's childhood, of her parents, of the mostly decaying house, a place 'with no boundaries or end that I could find, much larger than I had ever understood' (87). Its status is unclear, but the links to unconscious symbols of the time are evident, perhaps even the image of 'stinking piles of rubbish' in many rooms reflecting not only the state of the nation, but the conditions endured during the council workers strike in 1970 when rubbish literally rotted in the streets, as recorded by Mexican avant-garde artist and filmmaker Felipe Ehrenberg in his documentary *La Poubelle: It's a Kind of Disease* (Gilbert, 44). In Lessing's novel Gerald attempts vainly to maintain order for a band of children, but the anarchic, chaotic forces prove centripetal; the authorities very largely abandoning people apart from the occasional draconian, undifferentiating incursion into the chaos, where civilization has collapsed. As the protagonist reflects of both worlds, 'one took what came, did not criticise the order of things [...]' (157). Gerald's neo-patriarchal ambitions and desires fail, seeming anachronistic in their refusal of change and symbolizing the period's crisis in masculinity. The dual worlds blur at the end, the narrative undermining any remaining solidity and certainty both by the extremes of the historical moment, but also through the literary strategy of the fantastic and the dreamlike acquiring equal solidity.

Both Lessing's central theme and her literary disruption of the boundaries between fantasy and reality recur in various other authors of the period. However, by the mid-1970s, the cultural zeitgeist was more shaped by the paradoxes and dilemmas of a culture of self-obsession, and various crises of identity. In psychic and technological terms, a similar obscuring of distinctions between apparent solid reality and dream-like or paranoid projections occur in Gabriel Josipovici's *The Present* (1975), Christopher Priest's *A Dream of Wessex* (1977) and J. G. Ballard's *The Unlimited Dream Company* (1979), both of the latter texts sharing Lessing's dystopic framing of events. These employ disruptions of perspective involving both rejecting readers' formal expectations as well as assuming thematic and geographical dislocations within the narratives. Josipovici's narrative is more domestic; although that setting's apparent banality becomes comically surreal. The plot revolves around a shared flat in Hampstead, where Reg and Minna are married, and their lodger Alex is a teacher, whose perspective unsettles the wife. At the beginning, he refers to an accident, doubted by the other two. The playful interplay of the dialogue becomes oppressive, the ménage constricting, at least for Minna, while the men sustain a curious verbal intimacy created from a series of non sequiturs and almost slapstick exchanges:

> 'What we must do', Alex says, is something exciting. We must go out and wring the neck of the world. Stamp out mark upon it. Impose our desires'.
> He takes a turn around the room. 'Well?' he says, seeing them watching him.
> 'Mustn't we?'
> 'Yes', Reg says.
> 'Yes', Alex says. 'Yes, yes, yes, and yes'.
> Reg shrugs his shoulders.
> 'All he can say is yes', Alex says to Minna.
> 'What do you want him to say?' (53)

The inconsequentiality and the closeness become claustrophobic. Minna becomes radically disoriented, especially after it seems Alex has committed suicide, jumping from a window while the others are out. These scenes are intercalated with others, the normal novelistic progression disrupted, some vignettes based on visions of children, Isabel and Hattie, where Alex is her husband, others where the latter's suicide is the subject of examination by a police inspector, others in a hospital or asylum, others where Alex is still present. In Josipovici's narrative, violence and conflict remain largely that of the inner consciousness, especially Minna's, whose interiority may dominate, yet seems incapable of assimilating or stabilizing externalities. Certain vignettes revolve around a vision of her screaming in the asylum. The discrete environments coalesce, the asylum doctor singing in a choir as Alex has claimed to do (101), a bookshelf being brought into her room as had happened in the narrative of the shared flat (102). That flat becomes nightmarish, her coordinates uncertain, the existential unreal; yet the narrative returns her there, as if negating any resolution of truth and reality in narrative. Clearly, the possibilities are multiple even in this brief, laconic tale. One might reconstruct the hierarchy and development of events, so that Alex's suicide triggers her breakdown with her regressing afterward, or see the flat as a projection of her fears from another life with Alex and the children, or see these as intersecting possibilities. Josipovici resists any commonality of meaning, prioritizing the strangeness of the familiar, the lurking fears, the possibility of apparent normality collapsing in upon itself.

Like Ballard, Priest projects the traumatized self onto the world in a search for inner truth expressed in outward symbols of unease and violence. *A Dream of Wessex* highlights particular ideological contexts, featuring a government experiment in which a collective psychic projection creates an alternate twenty-second-century world where Wessex and the South west have been separated seismically from the UK mainland, both ruled by a Soviet administrative system that has superseded capitalism. Islam has colonized the United States. As the narrative commences in the apparent real world beyond the projector 'The Tartan Army had planted a bomb at Heathrow [...]' (9), a world protagonist Julia Stretton happily escapes. On many levels, bourgeois dissatisfaction with the conflicts of culture and the bureaucracy of contemporary life underpin even the alternate projected reality, where curiously any changes in the projection seem to be forgotten, which with the projection itself mirror the Orwellian fears of many in the 1970s of manipulation of the media and history. Finally, however, after a confrontation with a former boyfriend who permeates and distorts that reality, by the end Julia and her lover, Harkman, seem uncertain as to whether that past was a projection of their future states. She concludes '"Neither of us is real, but it doesn't matter! We are real to each other. I saw what was happening in the present, and I couldn't stand it. I had to come back"' (205). Perhaps unconsciously, Priest recognizes that the zeitgeist of the period was imbued by an idea of the insufferable quality of the present, at least for those used to setting cultural and social norms. In Ballard's *The Unlimited Dream Company*, the other reality seems to be some kind of afterlife. After crashing a stolen Cessna into the Thames at Shepperton, the pilot, Blake, ought to be dead, but is resurrected. He 'obsesses with man-powered flight' (13) and 'a Pied Piper complex' (13), believing in his power to transcend and lead others to a paradise. Plagued by visions of his corpse submerged in the cockpit and 'messianic delusions' (82), he feels trapped by 'this nondescript suburb' (68), yet feeds upon its inhabitants' energy seemingly to enact their dreams. The culture seems entropic; Blake's sense of entrapment represents perhaps the implicit state of Britain subtending Ballard's text, emphatically contrasted by a metaphysical sense of soaring above, a preternatural state that defines Blake's ambitions. The individual is enmeshed in a failing culture and set of relationships. Similar feelings of entrapment and imprisonment inform *Concrete Island* (1974), one of a flurry of innovative novels that mark Ballard as a prominent experimental writer of the 1970s. It is set on an isolated triangular 'island' beneath and between intersecting motorways, where Robert Maitland is marooned after a car crash. The text foregrounds allegorical, intertextual and symbolic dimensions; Robinson Crusoe's abandonment and desire for self-sufficiency subtending Maitland's fate. After injuring his leg in his initial attempt to escape, surviving on the contents of his Jaguar's boot, but liberated from his infidelity, Maitland painfully acclimatizes:

> He spoke aloud, a priest officiating at the eucharist of his own body.
> 'I am the island'. (71)

Later, post-delirium, he encounters the other inhabitants of the wasteland, Jane Sheppard and Proctor, Maitland's brain damaged 'Man Friday'. Ballard uses the three to rework Shakespeare's *The Tempest*, with the Calibanesque tramp, Proctor, initially free only to be subdued by Maitland's assumption, despite his physical weakness and injury, of the role of magus or hierophant. Ballard's most innovative aspect is to subvert the very realism of the novel's surface descriptive tone, creating an archetypal ideological struggle between the two men, with their economy of parodic exchange culminating in Proctor's oppression and his death in a final attempt to escape. Maitland is curiously determined:

> He would stay there until he could escape by his own efforts. [...] In some ways the task he had set himself was meaningless. Already he felt no real need to leave the island, and this alone confirmed that he had established dominion over it. (175–176)

Effectively the architect has reasserted his sovereignty; a middle-class hegemony that refutes his previous sense of emasculation and so symbolizes the wider struggles and social attitudes of the 1970s.

As many other experimental texts demonstrate, during this decade there were numerous aesthetic and eventful upheavals, including radical challenges to tradition and order, such as the increasing cultural dominance of technology including cars and planes, the centrality of urban culture with its incessant upward developments, celebrity culture, an overwhelming sense of cultural trauma and malaise, and an obsessive sexual self-identification explored in J. G. Ballard's other earlier fiction of the period: *The Atrocity Exhibition* (1970/rev. 1991), *Crash* (1973), and *High Rise* (1975). *The Atrocity Exhibition*'s fragmentary nature and style evokes the writing of William Burroughs, an American experimentalist much admired by Ballard and who later became greatly influential in Britain after 1980. Ballard's novel sifts the cultural iconography of the 1950s and 1960s that shaped the culture that followed. The very name of Ballard's protagonist is unstable – moving from a first section labelled 'Apocalypse' (1) – as are the impressions of the various elements of the text, with explanatory marginalia added for the 1990 republication intervening in or supplementing these original avant-garde fragments retrieved from Ballard's non science fiction small journal publication of the 1960s and expanded to offer a view of the world from which the texts emerged. In the second chapter 'The University of Death', Dr Nathan and Karen Novotny appear, persisting as nomenclatures throughout, but the male protagonist mutates through various names, guises or faces: 'Travis' (1), 'Talbot' (13), 'Tallis' (39), 'Talbert' (55) and 'Travers' (73). As Ballard clarifies in an annotation,

> The core identity is Traven, a name taken consciously from B. Traven, a writer I've always admired for his extreme reclusiveness – so completely at odds with the logic of our own age, when even the concept of privacy is constructed from publicly circulating materials. It is now impossible to be ourselves except on the world's terms. (13)

The narrative returns recurrently to one central event which obsesses the protagonist, the assassination of J. F. Kennedy and its aftermath. In the Canaries, 'The inhospitality of this mineral world, with its inorganic growths, is relieved only by the balloons flying in the clear sky. They are painted with names: Jackie, Lee Harvey, Malcolm. In the mirror of this swamp there are no reflections. Here, time makes no concessions' (29). Culture can finally only respond with the iconography of the theme park. Repetition, reiteration, slight modification and variation return the reader to images of violence, penetration and sexual excess. The many lists in *The Atrocity Exhibition* were produced by free-association. Ballard comments, 'What I find surprising after so many years is how they anticipate the future themes of my fiction' (57). Throughout the novel, Ballard is drawn to contradictions and extremes, even in the reconstruction of fragments of the cultural and literary scene in which he wrote, evidenced by his recollection of Ann Quin winning a short story prize for *Ambit*, an experimental journal he edited:

> She herself was a tragic figure, a beautiful but withdrawn woman who might have strayed from the pages of *The Atrocity Exhibition*. As her schizophrenia deepened she embarked on a series of impulsive journeys all over Europe, analogues perhaps of some mysterious movement within her mind. Eventually she walked into the sea off the south coast of England and drowned herself. (100)

Crash (1973), Ballard's other extreme novel, glorifies in transgression as offering a true sense of the depths of human desires. The narrator, James Ballard, is induced by Dr Robert Vaughan into the possibilities of sexual desire to be found by staging car crashes, and a perverse love triangle is formed with Catherine, Ballard's wife, who is scarred and exploited. Wounds become associated with a culture of spectacle, distortion and damage. The two men glory in the automobile as one of the central if ambivalent symbols of twentieth-century progress and masculinity, unifying its destructiveness with its capacity for erotic projection. 'For Vaughan the motor-car was the sexual act's greatest and only true locus' (131). Much of Ballard's innovation lies exactly in the extremes of his vision of the underlying realities of contemporary Western culture. The excess is revealing, for as Josipovici (1971) says, 'Reality has to be worked for, habit and the wiles of the imagination have to be overcome before it can even be glimpsed' (301).

Even the extremes of documentary realism were co-opted by novelists to create an avant-garde statement. Alan Burns's *The Angry Brigade: A Documentary Novel* (1973) is a subtle blending of fact and imagination; the author's aesthetic re-renderings of real life drawn from national events. Hence the novel reflects the eventful upheavals of the period including an ideological shift in the early part of the decade to notions of direct action and revolution, an aspect explicit in the aesthetics of the narrative, both formally and thematically. Both the structure and content highlight such engagement. The novel was inspired by the so-called Stoke Newington Eight trial which B. S. Johnson attended, and to which Heppenstall alludes in *Two Moons* (173), and during which proceedings the bombing of the Post Office Tower occurred (Crews, 222). Burn's text is ostensibly compiled from transcriptions of interviews with those revolutionaries both untried and unconvicted, who are committed to violence as a means of political change. This is evident in Barry's account in the final fifth section, 'Revolutionize':

> I could understand Ivor because killing, especially killing civilians, is immediately dramatic, powerfully dramatic. I don't care what people say, it gets things done. As does any violence, the less the violence, the less gets done, until we come down to the nth degree, voting, which gets absolutely nothing done. Right? (163)

This passage reflects the tenor of actual communiqués issued that insisted, 'The AB is the man or woman sitting next to you. They have guns in their pockets and anger in their minds'.

Both Burns's novel's apparently factual yet mannered structure and its attitudes explode (at times literally) the almost contradictory post-war zeitgeist made of a combination of consensus politics and individual angst that had previously permeated literary circles, often expressed in terms of loss of Empire and a sense of disentitlement accelerated by regretful inscriptions of cultural decline. In contrast, for the majority, the mood had been more determined by the optimisms and expansions of the baby boom, economic advances and technological change, all part of the post-war political and cultural consensus initiated by the post-1945 Labour administration. Its landmarks included establishing the Health Service and the Welfare State, and a social agenda ideologically inspired by notions of collectivism. Any consensus these elements symbolized was also displaced by a sense of outrage and violent opposition to norms, acutely articulated by the character Barry in *The Angry Brigade*: 'We did the old Bailey because it was where Dave and Jean were tried, because it represented everything bad in the country, the stupid shit-arsed laws and the pigs who were stamping us down, so we blew the bastards up' (168–9). More generally, in response to such attitudes, any lingering post-war consensus was stymied and eroded subtly by right-wing opposition, economic difficulties and a general waning of optimism, so that by the 1970s in contrast to the engagement and politicization of leftist, revolutionary values as described by Barry, actually a sense of transcendent right-wing individualism resurfaced. Burns's aesthetic radicality lies in the overlapping accounts that imply a revolutionary consciousness emerging from social experiences and conditions on an individual level, often contradictory and fragmentary, but cumulative. Burns not only mirrors the raising of consciousness, predicated on given social facts, but, as Zulfikar Ghose explains in 'Right You Go, Left With Burns', he seeks both ideologically and formally to challenge traditional readerly and literary values, insisting on both a contradictory and radical aesthetic, a perspective where 'it is as if one directly witnessed the raw experience without the author intervening to color one's view of the events with his own prejudice' (201).

In 1973, active literary experimentation seemed diminished for many by the two suicides, months apart, of two relatively youthful proponents of the avant-garde, Ann Quin and B.S. Johnson. Anthony Burgess wrote of the latter, 'Novelists like B. S. Johnson were keeping the novel alive. And now Johnson is dead' (21). In *Two Moons*, as part of the incorporation of a plethora of factual coordinates into fiction, Heppenstall refers directly to Quin and Johnson. 'They had been much of an age and both experimental writers. She was a big, healthy-looking girl, clean and beautiful, but her imagination was morbid' (165). Like Burns, Johnson reflected on the Angry Brigade in *Christie Malry's Own Double-Entry* (1973), whose protagonist's name may have even been suggested by that of Stuart Christie, tried but not convicted at the Old Bailey for Angry Brigade bombings (Crews, 222). Using other references far more oblique than those of Burns, Johnson creates a brief, laconic and sparse novel that incorporates his own struggles into the narrative of a young man in clerical employment turning to extreme responses. Heppenstall is mentioned obliquely *en passant* in Johnson's novel in connection with the religious myth taught to the infant protagonist, something Johnson dismisses. 'Certainly Rayner's re-telling was better' (80). As ever, Johnson's savage social satire is combined with acerbic self-parody of the writer's function.

Johnson's text is overtly self-reflexive and innovative, and as Anthony Burgess says of Johnson in 'Foreword', 'he had the courage and the devotion to the fictional art which makes a writer turn away from the obvious and facile. Hence his restless searching after new things' (19). Much of the textual layout and emphasis of Johnson's novel and its protagonist's terror campaign are all based upon the bookkeeping double-entry system, appropriately enough, as it serves as one of the cornerstones of capitalism. The origin of this system in the early modern period is pointedly and explicitly indicated by Johnson, who cites in this context a significant mathematical treatise '*Suma de Arithmetica, Geometria Proportioni et Proportionalità*' (17) by the author, Fra Luca Bartolomeo Pacioli, in which he introduces what Johnson's novel refers to ironically as 'the sublime symmetry of Double-Entry' (23) quoting at length from a translation of the original (18–19). Christie adopts his own system of Debit and Credit relating to perceived examples of 'AGGRAVATION' and 'RECOMPENSE' in five reckonings set out in the text (47, 85, 119, 151, 187) to assess the value and treatment of his life by society, inflicting damage as recompense for slights and maltreatment. As Carol Watts reflects in '"The Mind Has Fuses": Detonating B. S. Johnson':

> What are at first trivial acts of retaliation, in which Christie operates a *quid pro quo* with the banalities of the world employing him, soon escalate into acts of terrorism, in which the deaths of thousands by cyanide poisoning mimics the indifference of society which regards human lives as easily replaceable. (90)

As Watts makes evident, the novel also responds to the growing militancy during this period in the conflict between government and employers on the one side and trades unions and workers on the other. Johnson decried the oppressive measures of the Heath government, particularly the Industrial Relations Act, later repealed by a Labour government. However the turbulence did not subside. The effects of the economic and cultural erosions of the early 1970s were accelerated by the economic tremors that ensued after the economic earthquake, the 1973 oil crisis, with a three-day working week imposed by Heath's administration. Johnson undercuts his fictional task variously, literally at times. Art and its artifice is the subject matter, but so too is its reception; its relevance in people's lives:

> An attempt should be made to characterize Christie's appearance. I do so with diffidence in the knowledge that such physical descriptions are rarely of value in the novel. [...] What writer can compete with the reader's imagination.
> Christie is therefore an average shape, height, weight, build and colour. Make him what you will: probably in the image of yourself. (51)

Johnson dismisses motives, guiding us to actions by which we might judge his protagonist, whose girlfriend, the Shrike, is indifferent to his accounting system when he ruminates generally on the concept, only to decide he must be singular in his actions, the scheme of which the text sets out in 12 points. Later Johnson includes in Chapter XVI, 'Keep Britain Tidy, or, Dispose of This Bottle Thoughtfully' (131), the detailed instructions of making Molotov cocktails or petrol bombs (133–134).

Christie's actions accelerate in terms of their increasing social impact. In the Fourth Reckoning one finds 'July 7/Socialism not given a chance/311,398' (151), a monetary figure located in the column for aggravations which is far higher than Johnson's assessment in the same table of the value of Christie's next act of mass killing. When using cyanide in a reservoir, he poisons '20,479 innocent west Londoners' (151), assessed at only 26,622.70 pounds, indicative of capitalism's propensity to undervalue individual lives. Soon after a dialogue occurs between author and protagonist, where Johnson concludes he has made his points as far as possible.

> 'Christie', I warned him, 'it does not seem to me possible to take this novel much further. I'm sorry'.
> 'Don't be sorry', said Christie, in a kindly manner, 'don't be sorry. We don't equate length with importance, do we? [...] The writing of a long novel is in itself an anachronistic act: it was relevant only to a society and a set of social conditions which no longer exist'.
> 'I'm glad you understand so readily', I said, relieved.
> 'The novel should now try simply to be Funny, Brutalist, and Short', Christie epigrammatized.
> 'I could hardly have expressed it better myself', I said, pleased, 'I've put down all I have to say, or rather I will have done in another twenty-two pages, so surely...'. (165)

This is multiply ironic, since Johnson is in effect being omniscient despite himself, since he is planning Christie's demise from cancer. And of course Christie, as Johnson implies, represents an act of ventriloquism. As demonstrated in the quotation above, the novel offers a recurrent commentary which serves to describe exactly the structure and tone of the text. Yet, something resistant about its characterization and dialogue is sustained, however artificial such a separation might be. Exactly that number of pages after 'Xtie died' (183), Johnson finishes with the final reckoning where the character is owed as indicated in the columns 'Aug 13/Balance written off as Bad Debt/352,392' (187). Christie has commented earlier as if unexpectedly '"Your work has been a continuous dialogue with form,"' (166) a concept the Johnson persona palpably resists. In life, Johnson objected to the term *experimental* precisely because many used it pejoratively, not because of its avant-garde possibilities, which are evident in all of his fictions. He disliked such dismissals, although he accuses himself with Christie's final words: '"In any case," he said, almost to himself, not looking at me, "you shouldn't be bloody writing novels about it, you should be out there bloody doing something about it"' (180). Given Christie's experiences of work, it is almost as if the younger Johnson is berating his older self. As Jonathan Coe insists in *Like a Fiery Elephant* (2004), his biography of the author, 'if Johnson's work stands up better today than most of the writing of his "experimental" peers, this has everything to do with the fact that he refused – or was unable – to sacrifice intensity of feeling on the altar of formal ingenuity' (29). As Brooke-Rose explains in *Stories, theories and things*, Johnson is 'being mimetic when larger and larger gaps represent breakdown and increasing vacuity' (210). Certainly, this may be reflexive, involving a mimesis of the imaginative process as Brooke-Rose suggests, but in Johnson's posthumously published *See the Old Lady Decently* (1975) there is something additional. The text is inflected by a wide sense of the world both geographically and historically; by its negation and fragmentariness. Absence becomes presence, at least in terms of evoking oppressive structures. For Coe, as he explains in '"Great spunky unflincher": Laurence Sterne, B S Johnson and me', Johnson's novel demonstrates:

> what he had absorbed from Sterne – a desperate, ironic awareness that any attempt to convey the real texture, the complexity, the simultaneity of human experience through the medium of fiction was doomed to hilarious failure – had taken hold of his writing, and informs the book at every level – from sentence to sentence, and in its overriding, fragmented, anti-linear structure. (n.p.)

And yet Johnson achieves more. He politicizes the aesthetic form, since certain fundamental values both pervade and mediate the more formal devices curiously in the very lacunae or gaps that occur throughout the text. In its erasure of specificity, the colonial discourse is shown to be hegemonic, representing a uniform mode of thought that does not rely upon specifics such as naming or contextualization. Thereby Johnson broadens the ongoing relevance of the elements of his texts. Johnson here conveys a sense of an observation by Josipovici (1971) that: 'An author is not the source of meaning, but rather an organiser of pre-existent material' (309), which in Johnson's case conveys a complex critique of the imperial and social order. As Tew explores (2007), the final posthumous novel analyses Britain's postcolonial past, mirroring the marginality of the nation's lower-class subjects. As Coe indicates in his biography, Johnson reveals his personal vulnerabilities far more radically than most writers, when directly quoting John Berger's account that Johnson

> lacked the protective carapace that other people have, but one has to add that his achievement wouldn't have been possible if he'd had that carapace. So that the lack of a carapace was intimately related – was the same thing, almost – as his talent and his vision and his originality. (415)

One is given the impression implicitly by Johnson's polemic that the past shares the same dynamic elements as the present by implication, since as Johnson indicates such various oppressions persist.

Berger produced perhaps one of the most remarkable fictions of the decade, *G. A Novel* (1972), which is characterized by the use of a bricolage effect and its strong ideological perspective, the latter even more focused than that of

Johnson, alongside a strong sense of reinventing the historical as experiential. It commences both traditionally, with parentage, and yet reflexively: 'The father of the principal protagonist of this book was called Umberto' (3). Berger's narrative loosely and innovatively charts the life and times of this culturally Anglo-Italian child, born in Italy long after the revolutionary year of 1848, whose life is overshadowed by the legacy of Italian nationalism and anarchism. The existence of his father, Umberto, a merchant from Livorno, is concealed from him by his mother, Laura, a feminist socialist, who reveals the truth after an absence of 11 years. The boy's journey to meet Umberto, the father, is described in relationship to the mother: 'The imaginary mothers he sees through the window are candidates for filling the absence which Laura represents' (59). The perspective and narrative viewpoint shift in numerous episodes and vignettes, in which issues of art, language and representation recur. The narrative comments of Leonie, one of the protagonist's many lovers:

> To express her experience it would be necessary for us to reconstruct around ourselves her unique language. And this is impossible. Armed with the entire language of literature we are still denied access to her experience. There is only one possible way of, briefly, entering that experience: to make love to her. (135)

Berger, who espoused Marxist humanism, in a sense prefigures the ironic self-awareness and ludic qualities that would come to the fore in the next decade. In *G. A Novel*, he blends historical fact into his fiction, including the improbable but true story of the first flight across the Sempione in the Alps. Berger extensively describes the events in September 1910 leading up to the death of Jorge Chávez Dartnell (known as Geo Chávez) from injuries he received during the crash-landing in Domodossola at the end of the flight. The husband of G.'s lover, Monsieur Hennequin, passes the hospital intent on shooting his rival:

> He walked into the old centre of the town where there is an irregularly shaped piazza and the pavement in front of the shops is arcaded. The blackboard on which was written last night's medical bulletin concerning Chavez had been placed under the arcades in case it rained at night. The writing was smudged at one corner. The instability and irregularity of the patient's cardiac functions give rise to continuing anxiety... (187)

This recovers the minutiae, including obsessions of the moment, the mores of the times (such as duelling), and life's contingency and immediacy. Another event is a subsequently portentous assassination and the events surrounding it: 'On 2 June 1914 Francis Ferdinand, heir to the Hapsburg throne, was shot dead with his wife, as they drove through Sarajevo in an open limousine by Gavrilo Princip, a Young Bosnian of nineteen' (226). One of G.'s lovers, Nuša, is the sister of a conspirator and her request for an Italian passport leads somewhat circuitously to his G.'s death in Trieste. Berger maintains self-conscious reflexivity, and in doing so creates a paradoxical account of the process of writing:

> If G. had struggled with the four men when they came up to him their fight might take several pages to describe. He did not struggle.
>
> If, on the other hand, he submitted to them without any resistance at all, several pages might be needed to describe his acceptance of death. He did not submit without resistance.
>
> What happened can be quickly told and the rest can be conveyed at last by my silence. (315)

The tensions and artificiality of fiction are the focus here, and yet other contradictory elements are sustained. Clearly, in both extended episodes, Berger's technique is to first humanize the historical, locating it in the immediacy of perception, second expand and elaborate upon personal details through relationships with his fictional protagonist, third thereby counter any sense of the monumental or coherent, and finally in the interstices of these narratives explicitly interrogate both historicity and the function of narrative itself. Underlying the narrative is G.'s growing political consciousness, ironically so in that he is finally martyred by hegemonic forces.

In *Stories, theories and things*, a volume of academic criticism, Christine Brooke-Rose concludes 'Fragmented ectoplasms, pale copies of case-histories or of ancient archetypes, our characters are either documented records artificially animated or ghosts of past fictions and strip-cartoons' (176–177). In her novel, *Thru* (1975), Brooke-Rose certainly minimalized characterization. Her narrative deploys disjointed lists, columns, diagrams and handwritten notes in facsimile as if marginalia to essays and other strategies to deconstruct the text, rendering as its backdrop the impressions and minutiae of university life in a linguistics department. As Sarah Birch explains in *Christine Brooke-Rose and Contemporary Fiction* (1994), the novel is intentionally esoteric and yet attempts to parody certain intellectual pretensions. '*Thru* enacts this strategy of "wild jay-walking" between theories by side-stepping their systematicity and making them into stories' (90). As Birch explains, the novel was finished in 1973 and responds to theoretical texts published from 1966 to 1972, including those of Barthes, Derrida, Irigaray, Kristeva and Lacan. Its critique is decidedly feminist, countering patriarchal discourses and structuralism's 'sexist bias' (91). Characterization is schematic in a sense, for as Birch specifies 'As in Propp's folk-tales, characters in *Thru* are variables while their functions are constants' (92). Certain sections appear to offer no more than notes, or authorial intentions sketched out roughly and provisionally. Academic concerns predominate, reflexively so at times:

> So that today we shall try to work out a typology of digressive utterance by a narrator like Tristram Shandy who inscribes himself into his text as subject struggling with various levels of his own discourse. But is he not also an intransitivised subject walking through the inaction with indirect objects or none? Every structure presupposes a void, into which it is possible to fall, rehandling the signifiers over and over into acceptability, itself subject to memory and constant mutation as the subject-actat undergoes its transformations, each level of utterance generating another. (617)

Throughout, the text is knowing, allusive and parodic, such as the literary allusions introduced by Armel in response to Ruth's argument with him; her accusations of objectifying her, assuming her availability (624–625). The logic of the text is tortuous and obscure, its meaning diffuse and decentred. Armel discusses authorship with Larissa, on seemingly first meeting her, the conceit being he is interrupting her in the act of writing, creating a text such as the one in which they are contained.

If Ballard's *The Atrocity Exhibition*, is grounded in the various absurdities and extremities of American culture, this continued to provide fertile ground for the imagination of a number of other 1970s experimentalists: Burns's *Dreamerika: A Surrealist Fantasy* (1972), Quin's *Tripticks* (1972) and Paul Abelman's final experimental novel, *Tornado Pratt* (1977), all of which at least obliquely convey some sense of the cultural and ideological dominance in Britain of America after the Second World War. Burns's *Dreamerika* is a Rabelasian, highly scurrilous and thoroughly epigrammatic account – which is far too fragmented, impressionistic and complex to fully summarize – of America's Kennedy clan, featuring JFK's assassination, its aftermath including Jacqueline's marriage to Onassis, and various other loosely associated aspects of American capitalism of the period. Violence, corruption and sexual perversions and longings are its major themes. The narrative is a palimpsest, consisting of a series of brief episodes and polemics which undercut the myth of sanctity surrounding the rich and powerful, questioning their importance and the nature of power through a series of explicit sexual episodes and accusations of corruption. The text is characterized by a plethora of headings akin to those from populist tabloid newspapers, and several black and white illustrations. Visually, and in terms of readerly expectations, the novel form is partially subverted, opened into populism and critique. The assassination offers an example of how rapidly the perspective and viewpoint varies, shifting constantly:

> **THE ONLY ONE?**
> Who saw the brute who fired from the window, the guy who shot our President? An unnamed man insisted: he knew Oswald well, he called him buddy, he was a pal of Lee. Lee had been the sniper in the window, but he did not shoot the President as he claimed, the bullets in the body were not his.
> **death man named**
> who died after falling
> They drove a car at the man, ran him into the earth. His lips were sealed forever, it happens all the time. (43–44)

The novel opens with the fate of Joseph and Jack in the war, the father, Joe, and his fortunes until 1945 when 'He offered to buy America for seventeen billion dollars and received assurances that the government would move out as their leases expired' (11). Bobby is depicted as a homosexual paedophile:

> The small black hands carressed him: 'I believe in Black Power, and if need be, violence; but now is not the time.
> **'IT WAS**
> **WORTH IT'**
> He was aged about twelve and looked pretty wild. 'You need money? Right, here's ten dollars'. (66)

Later, Teddy is described at Chappaquiddick, where Mary Jo Kopechne died of suffocation in a submerged automobile that had been driven and abandoned by him. His actions after the crash are itemized and ironized, as are the Senate hearings, the situation reduced to absurdities. Near the novel's end, Charles Manson makes a brief appearance, with an oblique allusion to the events leading to the murders at the Sharon Tate residence and Linda Kasabian's later evidence against the so-called Manson family, signifying perhaps the degradation of the hopes of the counter culture:

> **A SPECIAL MADNESS**
> Looking for social revolution, Manson found personal liberation. He discovered freedom and practised it one morning with Kasabian. (129)

Subsequently the narrative is reduced to incoherent headlines, sensationalist and finally apocalyptic; contrasting the hubris of the contemporary world with the description of the remnants of a past fallen civilization where 'Only ruins remain. Emptiness, Snakes. Silence under light' (135).

A cornucopia of contradiction permeates the American landscape in Quin's last completed and published novel, *Tripticks*, which explores that country's commodified and conflicted culture. Quin's technical challenges to tradition are multiple, various aspects drawn from elements of popular culture encountered during Quin's travels around the United States, many vividly conveyed in illustrations by Carol Annand. Quin's creativity was fractured and obsessional. As Brian Evenson and Joanna Howard explain in 'Ann Quin':

> Trying to juggle her writing with the need to work for a living, she experienced her first nervous breakdown. [...] Quin would struggle with mental illness throughout her life and was hospitalized several times. In 1972 while traveling in Switzerland, Quin suffered a breakdown so severe that she was unable to speak for quite some time and ended up hospitalized in London for a month. (51)

Her mental state permeates all of her writing. In the last unfinished novel, *The Unmapped Country* (1975), a woman interacts with her psychiatrist; one section being a transcription of dialogue from Sandra, the protagonist's journal. 'I see the whole situation as an outsider looking on. I have not felt myself as the individual in the situation' (259). Throughout her novels, she objectifies such intensities of emotion, her exuberant and vulnerable sexuality mapped onto numerous uncertainties about the validity of personal perception and the instabilities of the identity. The first-person narrator of *Tripticks* exemplifies these changing coordinates. 'I have many names. Many faces. At the moment my no. 1 X-wife and her schoolboy gigolo are following a particularity of flesh in a grey suit and button-down Brooks Brothers shirt' (7). Quin's title draws upon a 'triptych', a three-panelled painting, referring obliquely perhaps to the three ex-wives who together might offer significant perspectives on this elusive male. As Evenson and Howard comment:

> Nondifferentiation of the narrative [...] in *Tripticks* [is] amplified to the level of collage and pastiche: [...] in *Tripticks* any given paragraph can contain all sorts of narration, some of it appropriated from magazines or television and nestling uncomfortably against the narrator's own words. (52)

As they add, the text is like a huge 'collage' (66) and the plot 'very tenuous' (69). Lorraine Morley in 'The Love Affair(s) of Ann Quin' sees the novel as a 'textual bricolage' in a 'bleak landscape' (136) devoid of familiar cultural coordinates, that resists communication, speaking 'a language of desolation and despair; a language no longer sure of its own parameters and possibilities' (137). The narrator is dogged by the mysterious Nightripper, seemingly a potentially malevolent force, but the narrator by Evenson and Howard's account 'seems to be undergoing a breakdown, his selfhood dissolving in the flow of images' (7). As he recalls at one point apparently happy, 'then blap whamp whamp whomp sok thud whak zapp whokk thud bam zowie I got pushed on all sides' (66). Later Quin's narrator locates the centre of this trauma, reminding himself of his ex-wife, 'Did half of me want her back? No. No. Remember marriage, any relationship with a woman is a gruelling, dehumanizing trial' (184). His sexism is endemic and diagnosed variously by therapists as '"compulsive liar"' (175) and '"manic-depressive hysteric"' (175); he distrusts language and is plagued by doubts. His voyage reveals the contradictions and bizarre qualities of both counterculture and conventionally capitalist America, 'this Theatre of the Absurd […]' (156).

Apparently lighter in tone and far more thematically whimsical than either Burns's or Quin's American narratives, Paul Abelman's *Tornado Pratt* features an eponymous protagonist-narrator born in a time of meteorological excess in Kansas, as if nature itself mirrored the turbulence of his subsequent life, that of his narrative, and of experimental writing more generally perhaps. It proved to be the author's final published avant-garde narrative, after which, in disgust at the public's general indifference to experimental fiction, he turned to profiting from 'novelizations' of famous British television series and characters. In *Tornado Pratt*, Abelman evokes the life-history of a larger-than-life character, who after a troubled childhood and sexual initiation becomes at 23 'the youngest self-made millionaire in the United States' (15) before pursuing a programme of self-education. Abelman parodies the American Dream. Tornado pursues profit, passion and knowledge until his consciousness is raised about the imminence of a new world war responding to Fascism and Hitler. As with all of the episodes, the events are rapid, sweeping and intensely personal, but underpinned by an ironic reflexivity, expressed in a serio-comic tone yet exuding throughout great underlying portentousness historically. With an almost pantomimic gusto, Tornado joins the army and fights against such malevolent forces, as if single-handed, a harbinger of an age self-obsessed. 'I never doubted I could seat a dagger in a tyrant's back, but I felt small in the swarm of egocentric midges which is mankind, each the pride of his little globe of affairs and each essentially ludicrous and alone' (160). His subsequent missions are nevertheless narrated in terms of an economy of heroism, expressed with Flashmanesque irony. Post-war, he suffers his own personal existential crisis after experiencing the male menopause:

> I was reading Hume and it struck me that when Hume analysed the structure of reality, he couldn't be right because all he produced was a series of words. How could a series of words, any imaginable series of words, be congruent with the

universe? How could even the most resonant verbal evocations of reality be on the same plane as the reality itself which included the processes which generated the mind writing the philosophy? (175)

Thus Abelman encapsulates the novelist's aesthetic and theoretical dilemmas, incorporating the limits of the text and the creative imagination, where all experience and knowledge is interrelated. By the end the narrator recognizes the Shandean futility of his task, even the most 'trivial question' requiring one 'to tell everything and leave out nothing that is or was or even might be in space and time. And if you don't say it all why you have to lie. To isolate is to lie and yet without it nothing can be said' (223). Despite the fulsome, frenetic detail of the life described, the reader is confronted with this conceptual impasse, although finally Tornado returns to the act of compulsive narration, to his mother and his birth.

Another narrative that returns to the maternal, Johnson's *See the Old Lady Decently* (1975) was published posthumously. Many consider it as representing a swansong for this phase of structurally innovative and ideologically committed experimentalism; its political awareness to be displaced by the more ironic and postmodern self-awareness of 1980s fiction. Johnson blends various narrative fragments in strands set out schematically including: a main narrative reconstituting his mother Emily's early life, in which each section is headed by the year of the twentieth century concerned and parenthetically her age; sections headed 'GB' representing Britain's mores; others headed 'BB' are concerned with the Empire and its power structures; and various other sections headed by various descriptors, including 'V' for Virrels, the chef at his mother's first employment. As Michael Bakewell says in his 'Introduction', 'The GB and BB bits are intended to involve the reader – he has to supply information himself – what he knows of the Empire'. (10) Despite these categorizations, certain themes and contents recur, for instance Emily at 25 in 1933 is effectively displaced by or contextualized by the geopolitical:

33 (25)
Two strong men came to power this January; all would be well. Roosevelt won an election, Hitler was made Chancellor. (129)

Johnson complains regarding his task in reconstructing his mother's life, 'How little I have to go on!' (66). In contrast, in the BB sections the unsayable is represented in blanks. Thus, the lacunary, the absent and the implicit represent a powerful undercurrent; the unsaid paradoxically representing the particulars of the colonial as something suppressed, the very excision of such detail serves to confirm how in a whole variety of situations the hegemonic discourse of superiority can prevail. A voice (for these may be many, one is uncertain) reflects that 'some of us still possess maps where the blanks are filled in with vague descriptions, but now can sit and look comfortably at a photograph and know that our fellow-countrymen out there have settled down to a pleasant life under a fair sky' (115–116). As Johnson realizes, Empire was about taking possession; native otherness is objectified, becoming variously alien and atavistic, dismissed through an Anglocentric gaze such as in 'BB4' where its incompletions are suggestive:

> Perhaps the most situated town in all the, how is it that it is clearly not further?   It is due to the   mixture of.   They are lethargic and unprogressive.   The descendants of slaves   brought by the are without energy and leave as much work as possible to be done by the women.   (62)

Indeed, such an apparently official account is rendered without location or particularities, for it is a generic perspective, both dismissive of otherness and negating the native's capacity to give voice. Not only is the very land appropriated, but any account of it need only be impressionistic and fragmentary, given the abject dispossession of the original inhabitants by the colonial enterprise, whose grim, yet logical terminus would be genocide, a matter alluded to directly. 'BB9' ends 'There are no aborigines now left in the island' (116). Johnson reaches beyond the narrative frame, as with reflections on his writing life, with his daughter bringing coffee, the sharpening of pencils among other distractions (56–7) only to worry about that which has been excised. So despite the strengths of his narrative strategies, with their implicit and explicit critiques of power, and the text's complex bricolage, as with Berger and Abelman, for Johnson a potential overriding impasse in the act of accounting for things haunts the narrative. He returns continually to this narrative:

> If it is really impossible to know anything, then it is impossible to know even this.
>   Or even that.
>   Or even the other. (72)

Johnson's problem might be seen as part of a wider crisis facing the experimental mode in the 1970s, as despite Johnson's humour, a grinding seriousness possesses him, so that he can only conclude of the historical, of the incommensurability of the amount of subjects involved, 'How could anyone impose order on that multitudinous discontinuity? History must surely be lying, of one kind or another, no more true than what used to be called fiction?' (96). Albeit Johnson continues his experimental narrative, as did others after his death, such a critique undermined the experimental process. Such ideological and theoretical seriousness would later be less foregrounded, such existential commitments diminished after the 1970s in favour of ludic and playful aspects, specifically a generic vision through qualities that would be described as postmodern, a turn which clearly drew upon its precursors but also sought to reconfigure the emphases of experimental fiction. Historical authority and authorial knowingness were to be deconstructed, made subject to comic subversion, a seemingly radical reflexivity challenge the text itself. Such a shift would involve a far more fundamental avowal of heterogeneity and provisionality overshadowing what preceded such postmodern explorations. Hence for a long time, critics have diminished the influence of the avant-garde of the 1970s, seeing its proponents as simply mired in aesthetic and cultural crisis, although perhaps any such presumptions can hopefully be further interrogated in the light of my analysis above.

Works cited

Anon. 'Angry Brigade Communiqués' http://www.spunk.org/library/groups/agb/sp 000539.txt

Abelman, Paul. *Tornado Pratt*. London: Victor Gollancz, 1977.

Bakewell, Michael. 'Untitled Introduction', in *See the Old Lady Decently*. Ed. by B. S. Johnson. London: Hutchison, 1975. 7–14.

Ballard, J. G. *High Rise*. New York: Holt, Reinhart and Winston, 1975.

———. *The Atrocity Exhibition*, rev. ed. San Francisco, CA: RE/Search Publications, 1990.

———. *Crash*. London: Flamingo, 1993 [1973].

———. *The Unlimited Dream Company*. London: Flamingo, 2000 [1979].

———. *Concrete Island*. London: Harper Perennial, 2008 [1974].

Berger, John. *G. A Novel*. London: Bloomsbury, 1996 [1972].

Bergonzi, Bernard. *The Situation of the Novel*. London: Macmillan, 1970.

Birch, Sarah. *Christine Brooke-Rose and Contemporary Fiction*. Oxford: Clarendon Press, 1994.

Brooke-Rose, Christine. *Thru*. London: Hamish Hamilton, 1975.

———. 'Illiterations', in *Breaking the Sequence: Women's Experimental Fiction*. Ed. by Ellen G. Friedman and Miriam Fuchs. Princeton, NJ: Princeton U, 1989. 55–71.

———. *Stories, theories and things*. Cambridge: Cambridge UP, 1991.

Buckell, G. J. *Rayner Heppenstall: A Critical Study*. Champaign and London: Dalkey Archive Press, 2007.

Burgess, Anthony. 'Foreword' in *Beyond the Words: Eleven Writers in Search of a New Fiction*. Ed. by Giles Gordon. London: Hutchison, 1975. 18–21.
Burns, Alan. *Dreamerika: A Surrealist Fantasy*. London: Calder & Boyars, 1972.
———. *The Angry Brigade: A Documentary Novel*. London: Quartet Books, 1973.
Butor, Michel. 'The Novel as Research', in *The Novel Today: Contemporary Writers on Modern Fiction*. Ed. by Malcolm Bradbury, London: Fontana, 1977. 48–53.
Byatt, A. S. 'People in Paper Houses: Attitudes to "Realism" and "Experiment" in English Post-War Fiction', in *The Contemporary English Novel*. Ed. by Malcolm Bradbury and David Palmer. London: Edward Arnold, 1979. 19–41.
Castle, Barbara. *In Place of Strife: A Policy for Industrial Relations*. London: Her Majesty's Stationery Office, 1969.
Coe, Jonathan. *Like a Fiery Elephant*. London: Picador, 2004.
Crews, Brian. 'Writing Radical Protest: The Angry Brigade and Two English novels.' *Journal of European Studies*. 40 (3) September 2010: 219–29.
Drabble, Margaret and B. S. Johnson, eds. *Consequences*. London: Greater London Arts Association, 1972.
Ehrenberg, Felipe. *La Poubelle: It's a Kind of Disease*. http://channel.tate.org.uk/channel#media:/media/6376932001&context:/channel/related?video=46376938001
Evenson, Brian and Joanna Howard. 'Ann Quin.' *Review of Contemporary Fiction*. 23 (2) Summer 2003: 50–74.
Fowles, John. *The French Lieutenant's Woman*. London: Pan, 1987 [1969].
Ghose, Zulfikar. 'Right You Go, Left With Burns.' *Review of Contemporary Fiction*. 17 (2) Summer 1997: 200–5.
Gilbert, Zanna. 'The Eclectic World of Felipe Ehrenberg'. *Estro: Essex Student Research Online*. 2 (2) http://www.essex.ac.uk/journals/estro/docs/issue3/The_Eclectic_World_of_Felipe_Ehrenberg.pdf
Gindin, James. *Postwar British Fiction: New Accents and Attitudes*. Berkeley and Los Angeles: U. of California P., 1962.
Hawthorne, Nathaniel. 'The Custom-House: Introductory to "The Scarlet Letter."' *A Scarlet Letter*. http://www.bartleby.com/83/101.html [1850]
Heppenstall, Rayner. *Two Moons*. London: Allison & Busby, 1977.
Johnson, B. S. *Aren't You Rather Young to Be Writing Your Memoirs?* London: Hutchison, 1973.
———. *See the Old Lady Decently*. London: Hutchison, 1975.
———. *Christie Malry's Own Double-Entry*. Foreword by John Lanchester. London: Picador, 2001 [1973].
———. '"Great Spunky Unflincher": Laurence Sterne, B. S. Johnson and Me.' Laurence Sterne Annual Memorial Lecture. Friday 11th June 2004 King's Manor, York. http://www.laurencesternetrust.org.uk/downloads/24-2004CoeLecture.pdf
Josipovici, Gabriel. *The World and the Book: A Study of Modern Fiction*. London: Macmillan, 1971.
———. *The Present: A Novel*. London: Victor Gollancz, 1975.

———. *The Lessons of Modernism and Other Essays*. London: Macmillan, 1987.
Lessing, Doris. *The Memoirs of a Survivor*. London: Flamingo 1995 [1974].
Lodge, David. *Working with Structuralism: Essays and Reviews on Nineteenth- and Twentieth-century Literature*. Boston and London: Routledge & Kegan Paul, 1981.
Morley, Lorraine. 'The Love Affair(s) of Ann Quin.' *HJEAS: Hungarian Journal of English & American Studies*. 2, 1999: 127–141.
Murdoch, Iris. *The Black Prince*. New York: Viking Press, 1973.
———. *Existentialists and Mystics: Writings on Philosophy and Literature*. Ed. by Peter Conradi. London: Penguin, 1999 [1997].
Murphy, Richard. *Theorizing the Avant-Garde: Modernism, Expressionism, and the Problem of Postmodernity*. Cambridge and New York: Cambridge UP, 1998.
Parrinder, Patrick. *Nation & Novel*. London: Oxford UP, 2006.
Priest, Christopher. *Fugue for a Darkening Island*. London: New English Library, 1978 [1972].
———. *A Dream of Wessex*. London: Pan, 1978 [1977].
Quin, Ann. *Tripticks*. Illustrations Carol Annand. London: Calder & Boyars, 1972.
———. 'From *The Unmapped Country* an Unfinished Novel', in *Beyond the Words: Eleven Writers in Search of a New Fiction*. Ed. by Giles Gordon. London: Hutchison, 1975. 252–74.
Spicer, Andrew. 'Report: British Culture and Society in the 1970s', University of Portsmouth, 1–3 July 2008.' *Journal of British Cinema and Television*. 6 (1) May 2009: 134–40.
Stonehill, Brian. *The Self-Conscious Novel: Artifice in Fiction from Joyce to Pynchon*. Philadelphia: U of Pennsylvania P, 1988.
Tew, Philip. *The Contemporary British Novel*. 2nd ed. London: Continuum, 2007.
———. 'Otherness, Post-Coloniality and Pedagogy in B. S. Johnson's *Albert Angelo* (1964) and *See the Old Lady Decently* (1975)', in *Re-reading B.S. Johnson*. Ed. by Philip Tew and Glyn White. London: Palgrave Macmillan, 2007. 202–19.
Turner, Alwyn W. *Crisis? What Crisis? Britain in the 1970s*. London: Aurum, 2008.
Watts, Carol. '"The Mind Has Fuses": Detonating B. S. Johnson', in *Re-reading B. S. Johnson*. Ed. by Philip Tew and Glyn White. London: Palgrave Macmillan, 2007. 80–91.
Zola, Émile. *The Experimental Novel and Other Essays*. Trans. B. M. Sherman. New York: Cassell, 1893.

7

Fiction, Representation and the Contemporary British Novel: A Story of the American Reception of British Novels of the 1970s

Doryjane Birrer

Introduction: A metacritical preface to this chapter's story

Throughout the 1970s, many American literary-critical voices were embroiled in conversations about the relationship between fiction and representation, and so it seems fitting to begin the present essay with a self-reflexive assessment of its status as a realistic fiction. That is, the chapter will tell a story of the American reception of British novels of the 1970s, and that story will draw heavily on real, material documents (book reviews, interview transcripts and critical essays), which in turn are comprised of materially recorded statements by American writers, reviewers and critics. And yet the story is also in part a fictional construct. As an influential cadre of American writers and critics of the time would be swift to point out, the material sources underpinning my story's construction are comprised of immaterial language – language that represents select perceptions of British novels of this period rather than any single concrete reality. In the terminology coined at the end of the decade by postmodern French theorist Jean-François Lyotard, the story this chapter tells is a metanarrative comprised of myriad, at times competing, micronarratives.

To complicate the plot further, that even these micronarratives do not represent the whole story is clear via the most cursory attention to the institutional dimensions of the American literary scene at the time, particularly the publishing and reviewing establishments – not to mention the need in the present to be a selective storyteller given the space constraints of an academic book chapter. I also find myself in the unsettling position of being both an intra- and extradiagetic narrator. The scholarly choices I've made in crafting my story as if from its outside are paradoxically also the result of my own position within it as an American scholar whose interpretive lenses with regard to contemporary British fiction have been tinted by prior literary-critical stories about such fiction, which in turn have been shaped by prior such stories, and so on back to the stories produced during the 1970s themselves on which my own story draws. The present chapter is truly a *mise en abyme* in keeping with the myriad self-reflexive fictions produced in the decade in question. All this is not to say the story does not have its own significant truth-value despite its uneasy situation at a borderline between fiction and reality – another key seventies' literary-critical theme. Rather, I am highlighting complexities in order to make clear the importance of including some further metacommentary about the construction of this story, which may serve as a preface for the chapter's larger tale. In this sense, my chapter enacts what for American readers of the time was a central conundrum: In what ways and to what ends can we apprehend reality through fiction?

The stakes involved in teasing out responses to this question were high for American writers, reviewers and critics in the seventies, as my story will relate. For now, however, a few further thoughts about the realities this story purports to represent. For example, I have just used the adjective 'American' as a modifier for the significant literary-critical voices in the context of my story. But this adjective is not quite accurate: the story requires a larger cast of characters for its balance to tip further towards reality than fiction. In short, the American reception of British novels of the decade cannot be characterized as singularly 'American', and in fact, is paradoxically a transnational phenomenon. How so? To answer this question we must turn to how the American perception and reception of British novels was shaped. Already the story splits into two interconnected subplots: what I'll frame as tales of 'lay' and 'academic' reception. The former would have been circumscribed in the seventies primarily by reviews in major American literary and cultural periodicals such as the *New York Review of Books* and the *Atlantic Monthly*, as well as in popular magazines such as *Time* and *Life*. Readers in the 1970s hadn't recourse, for example, to the proliferation of electronic and social media central to the reception of fiction today, which presumably broaden that fiction's reach. And with regard to the novels themselves, both readers and reviewers would have had access largely, if not solely, to those British novels published within or imported into America in those days before the burgeoning transatlantic consumption later made available via the Web and conglomerates such as Amazon.

The academic reception of British novels in America during the 1970s was similarly imbricated in the vicissitudes of the publishing and reviewing establishments. Academic literary criticism of these novels was developing contemporaneously with the publication of the novels themselves, and with no significant body of prior criticism to draw on, academics turned to significant reviews to help establish and flesh out critical conversations about these texts. The bibliographies of academic articles, in fact, cite periodical reviews of novels and interviews with novelists as much or more than they cite 'academic' secondary sources. This is arguably also due to the time lag between a novel's publication and the growth of academic versus 'mainstream' criticism, given, for example, the publishing practices of academic journals and university presses, such as the time from submission/peer review/acceptance of an article or monograph to its eventual publication. Further, relatively few print venues focusing on the contemporary were even extant during this decade: the academic study of contemporary British literature in America was in a nascent state at best. This is not to say that the academic reception of contemporary British novels was not influenced by the discourses of book-length scholarly studies on particular novelists, as well as by articles in relevant academic journals (such as *Modern Fiction Studies* and *Contemporary Literature*). It was also certainly shaped by discussions at academic conferences and literary workshops and within university classrooms, about which we have access to few material documents. However, the influence of these academic venues notwithstanding, the critical contexts of academic reception would have been significantly shaped, at least in their initial stages, by discourses established within notable reviews, first within major American periodicals, and somewhat later within academic review quarterlies, before being more fully absorbed into the academic discourse communities comprised by scholarly journals and university presses.

The literary-critical power of periodical reviews begs the question of their authorship. Who was writing these influential texts for the consumption of the lay and academic public in America? Numerous American writers, certainly. But also – and here's where the story gets even trickier – by *British* writers, reviewers and critics who were tapped to write reviews of British novels, or whose seminal texts were published by American presses or widely catalogued in American library holdings. In this sense, the American reception of British fiction was being shaped in no small part by British voices alongside American ones. The case of Margaret Drabble's *The Ice Age* (1977) serves as one compelling example of the complexities involved in telling the tale of the American reception of even a single British novel of the 1970s.

Drabble's *The Ice Age*: A case study in transatlantic literary-critical stories

Drabble's *The Ice Age* was one of the most widely reviewed novels of the decade, and Drabble herself one of the most academically assessed writers.[1] No tightly woven story of the novel's reception, however, can be fabricated from the various strands of narratives about the novel published at the time, as an examination of three significant literary-critical discussions will make clear: two from major American periodicals, and one from a major academic journal. One of the two most substantive periodical reviews of *The Ice Age* appeared in the widely circulating and influential *New York Review of Books* in 1977. It was written not by an American, but by British poet, professor and critic Donald Davie, whose commentary on the novel is important to situating its 'American' reception. Davie takes up Drabble's direct engagement with the condition of England question, 1970s iteration, and assesses how she 'sounds every patriotic stop, and without any irony at all' (28). Davie uses Drabble's novel as a springboard to address a 'new patriotism' in contemporary British writing, a trend that he sees developing as a response not only to the economic and social 'freeze' of the mid-1970s that is Drabble's focus, but to a crisis of English national morale more broadly conceived (and I should note here that Davie deliberately uses the moniker 'English' rather than 'British'). Davie identifies this kind of risky patriotic move as both 'appropriate and necessary' given England's social climate. 'And yet,' he says, 'it *is* embarrassing' (28; emphasis in the original).

Davie's embarrassment and larger critique of Drabble's novel stems in large part from his sense that her focus is too narrow: her 'proletarian' voices are few (and her treatment of them 'offensive'), and she takes little account of 'English people of all age groups who have a longer historical perspective than any of [her] characters, and who accordingly do not see (as all her characters do) the 1960s as a great good time from which the Seventies are a striking and unaccountable falling away' (29). Davie continues:

> If indeed the present deep freeze is temporary, and Milton's eagle will someday soar out of it more splendid than ever – and Ms. Drabble fervently, not to say stridently, believes this – might not those eagle energies come from these English people whom she ignores, and may indeed be ignorant of, rather than from the well-meaning but muddle-headed and unproductive Englishmen that she deals with?

Davie's interesting literary-critical move in the review is not simply pointing out such misrepresentations and exclusions. Rather, it is highlighting the ways in which such egregious missteps in Drabble's novel are themselves representative of the blinkered responses of many English writers to an England in crisis as to its national identity. In short, for Davie, the book enacts English crisis better than it represents it. It is for this reason that Davie, rather than condemning Drabble's novel, dubs *The Ice Age* a 'brave and bold book, one that English men and women can be grateful for, and even, though awkwardly, proud of' because 'it betrays more than the author intended about the present state of England and the English'. Davie's review, then, is an interesting study of a British voice not only taking part in the reception of a British novel for an American readership, but also implicitly helping to shape American views of England and the English themselves.

Compare this micronarrative to the second significant review, this time published in one of America's premier popular cultural magazines: *Rolling Stone*. In this review, American author and cultural critic Greil Marcus opens with the following description of British culture:

> British society seems to have come to a dead end, to have turned back on itself, to be strangling on its own contradictions. Though they were more than that [...] the promises of the British Sixties now seem like naïve illusions [...] England seems a vacuum, and ugliness, physical and spiritual, is filling it. (99)

Marcus aligns Margaret Drabble with Johnny Rotten of the 1970s British punk band the Sex Pistols, characterizing both as 'deeply British', and both as 'responding to an overwhelming sense that their culture – political, economic, and aesthetic – has collapsed around them, leaving them stranded in a society that seems not only without prospects, but without meaning'. Unlike the British Davie, the American Marcus accepts Drabble's representations of England and the English at face value. And far from finding Drabble's characters unsympathetic, as Davie does, Marcus feels the richness of Drabble's personal engagement with the lives and socio-cultural situations of her characters in a manner that he identifies as largely absent in his experiences with American fiction of the time:

> Most novelists today, especially in America, where social bonds have always seemed looser than in England, write as if to disengage their characters, and by implication themselves, from the society in which they live. Margaret Drabble writes to connect her characters to a reality larger than her own, and to discover what can be made of that connection. (101)

Here and as the review concludes, Marcus pits Drabble (and the Sex Pistols) against 'disengaged' American writers as requiring their audiences to reflect on, rather than turn away from, the 'sordidness' and 'political disorder' of the 1970s, and posits this rhetorical stance as 'the only way to hang on to a sense of what it means to live without lying, without betraying yourself and everybody else'. Both Marcus's and Davie's reviews, then, proffer Drabble's novel as an important lens on the decade, but via different angles of vision: Marcus's from his sense of the 'honesty' (99) and unflinching accuracy of Drabble's portrait, and Davie's from his sense of its telling inaccuracies. Further, the American lay reception of Drabble's novel within different sectors of the population, as well as lay perceptions of the British 'crisis', might well be framed differently depending upon whether readers encountered one or the other review.

Add to these competing transatlantic perceptions the myriad angles of vision in close-to-contemporaneous academic criticism of the novel, and the picture becomes more complex still. To take a single representative example, consider American scholar Joan S. Korenman's article 'The "Liberation" of Margaret Drabble' published at the end of the decade in the respected journal *Critique: Studies in Modern Fiction* (more latterly subtitled *Studies in Contemporary Fiction*). Unlike Davie's and Marcus's reviews, Korenman's analysis attends almost not at all to the topics of England in deep freeze or national identity crisis, and instead turns to individual existential crisis. Korenman sees Drabble as shifting from her earlier more specifically feminist work to more abstract existential concerns faced by characters who have 'overcome the obstacles between [them]selves and success' and find themselves 'staring despondently into the void' and thinking 'is this it?' (70). Though her discussion of *The Ice Age* focuses on male protagonist Anthony Keating, Korenman's analysis is a vehicle for her larger point about finding individual purpose despite a sense of the 'meaninglessness of life' faced by women in the 1970s in the wake of some of the successes of the women's liberation movement. Korenman closes her discussion of the novel with considerations of how ironically to read (if ironically at all) Drabble's representations of characters' turning to religion in the face of such meaninglessness (71). The tenor and scope of Korenman's discussion – though citing a number of reviews of Drabble's fiction generally – is so significantly different from Davie's and Marcus's reviews as to be well nigh unrecognizable as a consideration of the same novel. Which view – if any – can or should be characterized as best representing the novel's American reception?

Even if the essences of literary-critical stories about Drabble's *The Ice Age* are distilled and taken together, they form a heterogeneous mixture rather than a solution. Juxtaposed, they also point up some of the transatlantic complications of my overarching reception tale's ostensibly 'American' setting. Perhaps, then, the most productive question to ask about the American reception of British fiction of the 1970s is less an ontological than an epistemological one: that is, not what the American reception somehow unequivocally 'was', but rather what the myriad stories comprising it can help contemporary readers apprehend about the cultural realities of the time, both as regards the institutional aspects of its reception, and that reception's broader literary-critical and socio-historical contexts – and, of course, their combined relevance to the questions of fiction and representation ubiquitous in the decade, and with which I began my tale. *The Ice Age* itself fictionally represents an England in social, cultural and political crisis as refracted through the lenses of its protagonists' angles of vision. Yet it is from within the literary-critical assessments of Drabble's novel that we can glean additional cues and clues about 1970s 'crisis' narratives more broadly conceived. The terms of each discussion of *The Ice Age* are substantially grounded in each critic's respective sense of the verisimilitude of Drabble's fictional story with regard to the British socio-historical realities that it purports to represent. In short, it is presumed, though not overtly stated, that a key duty of art is to reflect life. The value of this mimetic touchstone, however, did not in fact go without saying with regard to considerations of the decade's fiction as a whole. In fact, metacommentary about art/life and fiction/reality dyads was a hallmark of the American literary scene. Evaluations of the status of the novel as genre in relation to shifting conceptions of these dyads at the time therefore play a significant role in situating the reception of the British novels in an American setting. But an understanding of the permutations in the 1970s of such questions of literary representation requires a shifting of my narrative somewhat further back in time.

Analepsis and exposition: Stories of the novel's death

Consider the following titles of three substantial review essays about the British novel published during the opening years of the 1970s: 'Alive and Well: The Contemporary British Novel', 'Time of Plenty: Recent British Novels', and 'The British Novel Lives'. Such emphases on the life and health of the contemporary British novel beg the question of just when, how, and by whom it was declared ill or dead. Allan Massie, in his survey of the British novel from 1970–89 published under the auspices of the British Council, notes that by the 1970s, it had become 'fashionable to speculate about "the death of the novel"' (2), a literary-critical *topos* later examined by (British) critic Andrzej Gasiorek in his seminal revaluation of realism in the contemporary British novel, *Post-War British Fiction: Realism and After* (1995). In his introduction, Gasiorek delineates and historicizes writers' and critics' fears of the novel's continued viability in the wake of modernism, and later in light of the Second World War and new socio-historical realities. His origin story of crisis rhetoric in relation to the British novel begins with the heated debates about realist versus experimentalist fiction pervasive in mid-century state-of-the-novel symposiums in England. The story runs that explicitly stated concerns about the novel's future began in the forties with the 'end' of high modernism and its dedication to formal inventiveness, and in the fifties increasingly took up questions of how best to represent post-war realities, with polarities developing between experimental novelists characterizing traditional social realism as recidivist and realist writers decrying experimentalism as decadent – and each seeing the aesthetics of the other as heralding the 'death of the novel'.

To draw such a tidy binary between realist and experimentalist views (then or now) is overly simplistic, as Gasiorek makes clear, but an awareness of this demarcation resurfaces consistently in international considerations of the state of the British novel just prior to and throughout the 1970s. Representative British forays in this context at the decade's inception include Bernard Bergonzi's *The Situation of the Novel* (1970), David Lodge's *The Novelist at the Crossroads* (1971) and Malcolm Bradbury's *Possibilities: Essays on the State of the Novel* (1973), all of which were (re-)published by American presses. Most important to my present story of British fiction, however, is the by-now familiar American view epitomized by Rubin Rabinovitz's *The Reaction against Experiment in the English Novel 1950–1960* (1967). Rabinovtiz's story of the British novel in terminal decline through a retrenchment in social realism was seized upon and tarried over by American critics in the seventies with regard to perceptions of contemporary British fiction more broadly (that is, not just with regard to the immediately post-war fiction that was Rabinovitz's focus). Rabinovitz's realism/experimentalism and tradition/innovation binaries echo the tenor of roughly contemporaneous international discussions of the state of the novel stemming from Europe and Latin America as well. For example, the influential critical manifestos of French practitioners of the *nouveau roman* Alain Robbe-Grillet (*For a New Novel* [1965]) and Nathalie Sarraute (*The Age of Suspicion* [1963]) held realist fictional representation up for rigorous critique, and urged formal innovation as the necessary response to new social realities. Such polemics and related international discussions are inextricably connected with declarations of the death of the novel in America, and with what American experimental novelist John Barth, in the same vein, identified as the 'exhaustion' of particular literary forms and fictional possibilities (29). While prevalent perceptions of such 'used-upness' with regard to the novel were for many writers not 'a cause for despair' (29), they were a galvanizing factor in the American turn towards anti-realist fiction in the 1960s and 1970s, as well as in many American writers' and critics' devaluation of social realist fiction as part of a dying literary tradition.

Rumours of the contemporary British novel's terminal decline, then, are very much in line with literary-critical speculations of the times about fiction and representation generally, and about the roles of social realism and formal innovation in such representation more specifically. As my story will shortly relate, even when American voices challenged tales of the British novel's decline, they tended to do so on the basis of British writers' engagements with realist fictional modes, rather than instead, or also, directing readers' attention towards British experimental novels published in the 1970s by such established writers as Eva Figes, Rayner Heppenstall, Nicholas Mosely, Christine Brooke-Rose and B. S. Johnson, among many others. In fact, a subplot that my narrative leaves substantially to future literary-critical storytellers is the question of why reviews of experimental novels by British writers were so limited in number and in scope, and why comparatively little academic criticism of such novels was undertaken during the period. Only Anthony Burgess's *MF* at the beginning of the decade (1971) garnered the significant attention of reviewers on the American scene. This may have had to do in large part with what novels were being made available for review and American consumption. Experimental fiction placed a different kind of intellectual demand on a readership accustomed to social realism, and was likely perceived not only as less accessible to a lay audience, but also as a less lucrative commodity for American publishing houses – the latter a point that American experimentalists like Ronald Sukenick and Robert Coover noted with dismay with regard to the publishing difficulties faced by formally innovative American writers.[2] The relative neglect of experimental British novels may also have had to do with the fact that the novels of most of those British writers whose reputations were firmly established in the US at the inception of the 1970s had most often written in social realist modes. The work of Graham Greene would be a key case in point, as would that of Doris Lessing and William Golding, whose fiction, though increasingly turning towards the literary fantastic by the end of the 1960s, had prior to that point been perceived as less formally than thematically innovative.

The institutional politics of reviews aside, even American novelists of the time rarely evince interest in the fiction being produced in the 1970s by their fellow writers across the pond, experimental or otherwise. American writers in interview might make a passing reference to a particular British novelist as formally inventive (e.g., Robert Coover on Angela Carter), or mention an individual predilection (e.g., Rosellen Brown on Elizabeth Bowen and Margaret Drabble, and Tim O'Brien on John Fowles). Most often, however, when American writers refer to British fictional models during this decade, they refer to earlier work, such as the novels of Laurence Sterne, James Joyce and Virginia Woolf for the experimentalists, and Charles Dickens, George Eliot or Thomas Hardy for the social realists.[3] The eyes of experimental American writers in particular were turned elsewhere than Britain, especially to Latin America and the magic realist fiction of Gabriel García Márquez and his metafictional predecessor Jorge Luis Borges, but also to Europe and the French *nouveaux romans* of Robbe-Grillet and Sarraute, the metafiction of Italian writer Italo Calvino and the novels of German magic realist Günter Grass. It seems that American writers of anti-realist and self-conscious fiction perceived their experimental novels as more in line with formally innovative fiction in these international contexts than with contemporary British writing in any fictional mode. Many writers and critics also appear invested as viewing the work of American writers as 'deeply their own' (LeClair and McCaffrey 3), not just in a nationalistic sense, but in the sense that many saw themselves as writing in relatively isolated pockets throughout the United States rather than as part of any unified American fictional scene.[4] The review essays on the state of the British novel in the 1970s with which I began this stretch of analepsis and exposition, therefore, are significant in their status as what were then relatively rare correctives in America to reports of the British novel's death. They are also interestingly divergent as to their respective literary-critical tacks: exhaustively detailing the fecundity of the contemporary British fictional scene, complicating any unified vision of contemporary British novels' modes of realism, and calling to task reviewers who have not effectively attended to the ingenuity of contemporary British writers.

In 1974 in *American Libraries*, American poet and academic Sheridan Baker published 'Alive and Well: The Contemporary British Novel'. Baker's metaphor for the state of the British novel is that of a dead landscape slowly returning to life: The 'rolling downs' of English fiction are 'greening' (483), he announces. Baker's opening passage is worth quoting at length, reflecting, as it does, one determinedly optimistic American angle on the state of British fiction – and by extension, of Britain itself – purveyed by an established writer-critic at the time:

> The novel, like British life, goes on, and the quantity and quality are astonishing.
> The bleakness and anger, and the comedy that stood up to it, after the war, have

given way in the sixties and seventies to something like hope, creeping over the dark brown nihilism, now more than a century old, that deepened after the war. The search for identity, the abrasions of class, the assumption that God is dead, the brisk ironic scepticism, and cynicism, are all still there.... But things are looking up. The search seems to be reconsidering that God, though we can't manage to believe in Him, is, after all, in His heaven, wherever that could possibly be, and all's right with the world after all, if we could just live with it. (483)

Baker's cheerful description of a pervasive upturn on the British literary and social scene seems both overly simplistic and strikingly at odds with numerous British writers' representations of individual, social and national crises during even those early years of the 1970s. Nor does Baker's essay directly address visions of the death of the British novel that his title and opening scene seem designed to counter. He offers no commentary on the pervasive social realism of those novels he surveys, or on their relationship to broader literary-critical concerns about the continued viability of realism as a literary form.

To be fair, Baker's purpose is clearly not to undertake significant discussion of any particular novelist or critical trend, but rather to impress upon his audience an awareness of the sheer volume of novels published by British writers at the turn of the 1970s: he surveys the work of 63 novelists and 100 of their novels. After his exhaustive cataloguing of these texts, Baker is content to conclude (with a slight tone of surprise?), '[t]he British lion, with half a head gone, is certainly perky above the dubious green, and with an astonishingly able and productive group of novelists to prove it. The novel has never been more alive' (490). For Baker, the British novel's being 'alive and well' is a function of the prolific output of British novelists, rather than due to the nature of the relationship between British fiction and its representation of socio-cultural realities. Given the cursory nature of Baker's survey, his claims about the quantity of British novels are supported more effectively than those about their quality or unity of socio-historical outlook. And yet Baker's essay does serve as a reminder to his audience of the continued productivity in the 1970s of a number of British writers whose careers began prior to and just after the Second World War, and also draws attention to novels penned by emerging British writers with which the American scene will need to contend.[5] Further, Baker's reception of the British novel of the time is perhaps significant not only for its focused and extensive notice given to the British literary landscape – a relatively rare occurrence in American literary-critical discourse in the 1970s, as I've said – but also for its potential impact on American holdings of contemporary British novels in US libraries, given the publication of Baker's essay in the central periodical of the American Library Association.

More complex in its purview is American scholar Frederick McDowell's review article 'Time of Plenty: Recent British Novels', which appeared in 1972 in *Contemporary Literature*, one of the few academic journals then extant devoted to literature written after the Second World War.[6] Like Baker, McDowell tackles a swath of British writers (some 40-odd) and surveys those works of their fiction published during the opening years of the 1970s. Also like Baker, he includes a number of British writers whose reputations were solidified during the decade(s) previous, including Graham Greene, Iris Murdoch, Doris Lessing and Anthony Burgess, as well as Angry Young Men John Wain, Alan Sillitoe, John Braine and Kingsley Amis. However, unlike Baker, McDowell situates the novels of the early 1970s more overtly within the decade's burgeoning literary-critical conversations about fiction and representation. McDowell avers that, with few exceptions, 'tradition rather than innovation' (362) is the impetus behind these novels, and determines that in consequence, the trajectory of British fiction 'seems to be toward a modified realism rather than toward forthright experiment and the rejection of older conventions' (361). As with the assessments of Drabble's *Ice Age*, McDowell's brief discussions are more evaluative than analytical, and judge the effectiveness of different novels' realist social commentary in terms of the verisimilitude of their characters' lives and situations to 'real' human experience, as well as the ability of different plots and casts of characters to engage prospective readers' interests. As a whole, concludes McDowell, '[r]ecent British fiction perhaps instructs us as to what can be done within the confines of expected forms and how rich and various the modes of expression may yet be within them' (362–3).

An important phrase to note, however, in the context of McDowell's essay is 'modified realism'. Here McDowell presages what will later in the decade become an important consideration: the ways in which a more traditional social realism might be reimagined in light of modernist and postmodernist fictional experimentation and concomitant shift(s) in *zeitgeist*. As a brief prolepsis here to my more detailed narration of this literary-critical conversation below, a sketch of McDowell's examination of a number of novelists' quasi-fantastical, apocalyptic, and (for him, moderately) experimental departures from both historical realities and traditional forms is helpful.[7] 'As the writer's vision becomes increasingly urgent', asserts McDowell, 'there is ... a tendency to leave behind the social realities in which his [*sic*] art may be based and to voice instead a compulsive and compelling vision' (361). McDowell includes on a spectrum of such fictional departures the minor elements of fantasy inherent in Iris Murdoch's hallmark 'stylized formal patterns' and involuted plots in which 'the absurd and the unexpected entanglements which her people fall into provide in themselves instances of the strange and the unforeseen, the sometimes unbelievable, aspects of our personal lives in a fragmented age' (385). McDowell cites Murdoch's entire *oeuvre* in this context, and though he finds her two novels of the early decade – *A Fairly Honourable Defeat* (1970) and *An Accidental Man* (1971) – less intensely interesting than her earlier work, his sense of Murdoch's significance to the vitality of British fiction is borne out by her status as one of the writers garnering the most lay and academic interest during the 1970s.[8]

However, it is McDowell's discussion of British novels further along a spectrum of the literary fantastic that is most significant in the context of an emerging reimagined realism at the time. His analysis of Lessing's *Briefing for a Descent Into Hell* (1971) is particularly significant in that this novel, like Drabble's *Ice Age*, was one of the most widely and substantively reviewed novels of the decade, as well as being the subject of numerous academic essays. McDowell somewhat 'regret[s] that Lessing has given over the "realistic" novel as an untruthful and untrustworthy entity', given his concern that Lessing fails effectively to link the madness of her schizophrenic protagonist, an 'emissary from the gods', to 'our own mad age' (388). In other words, her 'apocalyptic mode' (389) compromises her social critique. Still, McDowell is intrigued by Lessing's 'deviation from traditional forms' in *Briefing*, especially her use of 'conventions of drama' (389), and he posits the novel as presaging a shift to a productive new fusing of multiple fictional modes. Productivity for McDowell might here be defined as both formally innovative and socially conscious: he makes clear in reference to British modified realism that its fantastical elements and formal innovations are consistently in the service of coming to terms with social reality rather than escaping it, a point to which my story will return. For now, suffice it to relate that McDowell closes by touting British novels of the early 1970s as indicative of the 'surprising vitality of the genre' (394) – surprising, presumably, given rumours of the novel's terminal decline.

Whereas Baker emphasizes the plenitude and optimism of the British fictional scene, and McDowell addresses its innovative realism, British scholar Frank Kermode turns to the roles and responsibilities of reviewers and critics in adequately critiquing contemporary British novels.[9] Kermode's 1972 review essay 'The British Novel Lives', commissioned by the editors of the nationally renowned American literary and cultural periodical *The Atlantic Monthly*, begins with a telling anecdote:

> An *Atlantic* editor, proposing this piece, asked half-jokingly whether the title of Muriel Spark's book, *Not to Disturb*, might be regarded as a fair indication of the

state of the British novel. It seems that word has got around that there's nothing much doing back home, where, before the British suffered what now looks like a permanent intellectual and imaginative power-cut, the modern novel got started. I think these reports are much exaggerated, but what can one do? (85)

What Kermode does, rather than attempting to name particular British writers who could 'go the distance' against innovative American novelists such as Pynchon and Vonnegut or 'our talented new competitors across the Channel', is to turn to institutional problems related to fiction and its reception. I cannot do justice in my own narrative to the interesting stories Kermode tells by way of supporting his assertion that 'a lot that seems to be wrong with the novel is wrong with other things, namely the trade, and the literary scene generally' in the UK versus the US. Kermode's tales of woe include the difficulty of British novels even getting into print; the paltry amount of pay British writers receive if finally published (unless their work is published in America); the slim chances that a given novel, if published, will be reviewed at all, let alone seriously; and the lack of public 'clamour' British writers attract in their home country in comparison to Americans in theirs.

Kermode proposes a series of remedies to these institutional ills, but more relevant to my story is his emphasis on the power of the literary review in shaping the reception of the British novel. He sees his own work in the remainder of the essay as placing a corrective lens on the state of British fiction through his positive valuation of a group of British novels published in America in 1971, including Muriel Spark's *Not to Disturb*, Iris Murdoch's *An Accidental Man*, William Golding's *The Scorpion God* and Kingsley Amis's *Girl, 20*. With regard to each novel, Kermode counters a prevailing criticism – Spark's triviality, Murdoch's repetitiveness and lack of closure, Golding's imaginative decline, Amis's shift to the political right – with a brief analysis that pinpoints just where reviewers have missed the mark, as with his discussion of Spark's 'intensely imaginative inquiries into the resources of fiction' (86). Kermode, in fact, makes overt statements throughout regarding the responsibility of reviewers to be more attentive and sophisticated readers (a critical discernment he presumably sees himself as modeling). This is 'the critic's job and a more useful one than that of lamenting the death of the novel in England' (87). He concludes that the 'remarkable' nature of the novels by Spark, et. al. 'justifies a measure of noisy celebration, not only in aid of these writers, but of all the others who deserve but rarely get the intelligent cooperation of readers and reviewers' (88).

Overall, I'm less interested in the details of Kermode's analyses than in his obviously strongly felt need to make them. His concern goes beyond shifting the terms of the reception of four British novels of the seventies to encompass the larger aim of enhancing his American audience's understanding of the British literary scene in response to perceptions of a moribund state of British fiction. Underlying Kermode's argument as well appears to be a fear that American readers and reviewers will take their cues from the poorly paid, overburdened, and insufficiently attentive British reviewing establishment that Kermode castigates early in his essay.[10] Here once again we see the voice of a British critic exerted strongly in the service of shaping the American reception of the British novel. More importantly still, that Kermode attends throughout to considerations of form in relation to social commentary points up once again the questions of fiction and representation central to the decade, and to which my story will now return.

Questions of fiction and literary representation: The case of John Fowles

The conclusion of American scholar Robert Alter's analysis of John Fowles's *Daniel Martin* (1977) at the end of the decade ties together a number of threads in my narrative so far as regards tradition and innovation, fiction and representation, and the status of the novel in the 1970s:

> Art is deep but human reality remains in part resistant to it, exposing many vivid facets to the light of representation, keeping others, perhaps some of the most essential, hidden in a penumbra of ambiguity, enigma, doubt. This double-awareness has often been richly suggested by the novel through its capaciousness, its narrative and meditative amplitude as an instrument of mimesis. That in the end is what *Daniel Martin* succeeds in doing, in being: it is at once a rather traditional novel and an acutely self-conscious one that bears witness to the undiminished vitality of the genre. (78)

Here, Alter's estimation of Fowles's novel rests both on what it *does* – it reflects and offers insight into the realities of human experience while simultaneously evoking the ineffability of that experience – and on what it *is*: its ontological status as both traditional and formally innovative literary artifact. The emphasis once again is on the idea of a reimagined realism that is intensely aware of the problematics of fictional representation underlying the decade's critique of realist modes, and that negotiates such complexities through a productive blend of formal tradition and innovation. Fowles's *Daniel Martin* struck a particular chord in this context not only with Alter, but also with regard to the American literary scene generally, and the reception of this novel is representative of key socio-aesthetic issues of the decade.

Like Drabble's *The Ice Age*, Fowles's *Daniel Martin* was one of the most widely read and reviewed British novels of the 1970s. Also as with *The Ice Age*, an analysis of the reception of Fowles's novel serves as an interesting case study in the American reception of the British novel – with both 'the' and 'American' again needing scare quotes – as well as a productive lens through which to view the relationship of the contemporary British novel to American discussions of fiction and literary representation during the decade. Fowles had already made a splash on the American scene with the publication of the metafictional novel *The French Lieutenant's Woman* in 1969, which garnered accolades almost everywhere it was reviewed. The reception of *Daniel Martin*, however, was more mixed, and highlights some of the same transnational reception intricacies noted with regard to *The Ice Age* in that a number of reviews in the most significant American periodicals – including *The New York Review of Books* and *The New York Times Book Review* – were penned by writers hailing from the UK.

Irish literary critic Denis Donoghue,[11] writing in the *New York Review of Books*, critiques the 'falsity' of Fowles's dialogue and representations of American and English characters' speech, and sees such falsity as compromising the effectiveness of Fowles's integration of 'recent lore about language' into the novel, such as references to 'narrative problems, plot as Destiny, alternative endings, and so forth' (45). For Donoghue, the 'naïveté' of Fowles's distinctions between American and English language usage undercuts the 'sophistication' of his theorizing about fiction. Further, as with Donald Davie on Drabble's *The Ice Age*, Donoghue is embarrassed by Fowles's apparently un-ironic patriotism with regard to 'We the English': this time as regards the author's comparisons between the speech of 'evil Hollywood' and that of 'pure, rural England'. Says Donoghue,

> If Fowles can hear enormous semantic subtleties in middle-class English intonation, no wonder his *Daniel Martin* endorses the values delivered in that intonation: a compound of Oxford, money, leisure, and mildly left politics. And this from a writer who finds his epigraphs in Marx and Gramsci. (46)

Here, too, the reviewer's class consciousness plays a role in his stance on the novel's representation of English social realities, pointing up the contradiction between Fowles's ostensibly leftist politics and the bourgeois values espoused via his fictional characters. While Donoghue doesn't quite dismiss Fowles's novel or his fiction more broadly, he does close by asserting that *Daniel Martin* 'puts in doubt the claim' (begun with the publication of *The French Lieutenant's Woman*) that Fowles is not just an 'interesting writer', but an 'artist'. Donoghue's challenge to Fowles's reputed artistry rests on the inability of Fowles's form and content to live up to the complexity and tenor of his apparent fictional aims. For Donoghue, if Fowles wants his readership to be receptive to his self-reflexive explorations of the realistic aspects of fiction and the fictional aspects of reality, as well as trusting of the discernment of his metafictional eye, Fowles's own representations of social realities need to be more accurately mimetic, right down to individual characters' speech at the sentence level.

American writer-critic Frederick Busch, in sharp contrast to Donoghue, lauds *Daniel Martin* as 'an awesome achievement, a necessary book' (21) in the inaugural year of *The American Book Review*. Important to note is this literary periodical's status as the brainchild of American experimental novelist Ronald Sukenick, who created it in 1977 as a independent venue for the reviewing of fiction and poetry slighted or neglected due to traditional reviewing agencies' 'insensitive, irrelevant, and incestuous methods' (LeClair and McCaffrey 280). Like Kermode on the British literary scene, Sukenick identified a need for a corrective to American institutional ills in order for the work of contemporary writers to be adequately and competently assessed. This difference in purview between the experimental sympathies of *The American Book Review* and the mainstream *New York Review of Books* suggests an important factor in the contrast between their published reviews of *Daniel Martin* beyond the issues of transnational reception. It is in this context of a periodical dedicated to promoting innovative fiction that we might usefully situate Busch's elevation not only of *Daniel Martin*, but of Fowles and his *oeuvre* tout court. Busch unequivocally asserts Fowles's status 'as a maker of extraordinary dimension, one of the most sizeable writers [...] we are graced with' (21).

The absence in Busch's review of any reference to the American/British speech comparisons highlighted by Donoghue is perhaps indicative of the reviewers' respective nationalities – though once again it is interestingly not the American reviewer who critiques the ostensible glorification of Englishness in the novel, but the (embarrassed) reviewer from the UK. But more interesting for my central storyline here is the significant difference with regard to the reviewers' considerations of form. Whereas Donoghue declares Fowles's form and subject matter at odds, for Busch (as with Alter) 'form and subject matter are one': Fowles 'writes an exciting narrative which is laden with ideas which are crucial, while he produces an artifact which is at the same time his subject matter'. Further, while Donoghue criticizes the falsity of Fowles's characters' dialogue and finds the novel 'laborious' and replete with vision-less 'odds and ends' (46), Busch finds in *Daniel Martin* the first 'novel of ideas' he has encountered 'in which argument and abstract considerations do not stand in the way of excitement' (21). Busch attributes this felicity of unified style and substance to Fowles's 'sheer narrative mastery', in short, his attention to '*story*' (emphasis in the original). It is easier to assert than to prove the idea that the marked difference in the two reviews' reception of Fowles's novel stems from the difference between a British critic reviewing *Daniel Martin* for a more traditional and commercial periodical versus an American critic reviewing it for the presumably more specialized audience of the independent *American Book Review*. But we can at least identify in the latter review important resonances with academic criticism of *Daniel Martin* in the context of the prevalent American considerations of the fiction/reality dyad.

Fowles's fiction was discussed extensively in American academic publications and Fowles himself consistently identified both as a major British talent and a significant figure to contend with as regards the relationship between art and life. Fowles's 1966 novel *The Magus*, for example, which was republished in a revised and extended version in 1977, was one of only three British novels to receive its own chapter in Robert Scholes's influential *Fabulation and Metafiction* (1979).[12] By the end of the 1970s, Fowles was also the only contemporary British writer to have been the subject of a special issue of the respected American *Journal of Modern Literature*, and one of only four to be the subject of a special issue of the similarly weighty *Modern Fiction Studies* in the following decade.[13] Fowles's *Daniel Martin* in particular generated a significant number of academic responses in the 1970s, of which Alter's analysis is representative. Alter's was an influential voice in American discussions of fiction and representation given his seminal work in *Partial Magic: The Novel as Self-Conscious Genre* (1975), and like the periodical reviews of *Daniel Martin*, Alter's critical essay situates the novel within these discussions. His arguments for Fowles's importance as a writer stem primarily from the fact that Fowles's fiction 'repeatedly points in interesting ways to the possibilities and problematics of the novel as an instrument for the apprehension of reality' (65). Alter takes pains early in the essay to delimit his praise of Fowles's achievement in *Daniel Martin*, making clear that the novel is no 'contemporary masterpiece', and rating Fowles as merely 'something of an exemplary novelist' within an 'age too artistically dispersed to have contemporary novels for emulation'. Alter does, however, declare Fowles 'the most instructive of living English novelists', which is about as far as any American voice goes in extolling a contemporary British writer. What Alter finds in Fowles's *Daniel Martin* is a well-crafted epistemological paradigm for exploring 'what the novel now is capable of doing', and why it 'continues to excite the imagination' at the close of the twentieth century. Alter's important role in the reception of Fowles's novel, then, is to see it as staging via its form and the 'large resonances' of its ideas one viable response to 1970s 'death of the novel' rhetoric, as well as to questions of fiction and representation.

In the course of his assessment of Fowles's exceptional 'mimetic effectiveness' (68), Alter alludes to recently imported French theorizing about *l'effet du réel/* fiction's 'reality effects' derived from French structuralist-cum-poststructuralist theorist Roland Barthes (the rise of theory being a subplot to which my story will shortly return). Primarily, however, Alter's analysis involves extensive and appreciative close reading, complete with neo-Augustan references to Fowles's sounds echoing his sense and formalist taxonomies of Fowles's aesthetic choices throughout the novel. In this sense, Alter enacts in his essay the kinds of literary-critical discernment with regard to contemporary fiction being demanded by his scholarly contemporaries Sukenick and Kermode. And Alter himself appears self-reflexively aware of this need to craft a new mode of criticism to suit the aesthetic shifts of the time. He reflects,

> [i]f a criticism directed toward the technical maneuvers of fiction can speak of an 'effect of the real,' a criticism that seeks to encompass the mimetic objects of fiction might speak also of a 'recovery of the real' as both the formal aim and the ultimate point of moral reference for novels like this one. (71)

Alter's implicit acknowledgement that there are in fact enough formally innovative realist novels like *Daniel Martin* to merit their own mode of criticism also testifies to what is becoming a motif in my literary-critical story: the sense of a developing trend in the seventies towards a reimagined realism. Alter, however, evokes the stock traditionalist view of the contemporary British novel as his essay closes. Though penned by an instructive English self-reflexive novelist of ideas, *Daniel Martin* is still more social realist than perhaps is quite proper in the 1970s given the significant shift in cultural and aesthetic paradigms: 'In this age after Structuralism, Fowles, however old-fashioned it may seem to some, remains true to a dominant generic assumption of the novel in his confidence that language with its formal properties can give us at least some of the handles we need to grasp the reality of psychology and relation' (76). And yet for Alter, it seems that herein lies the importance of *Daniel Martin* to the contemporary literary scene, and in particular to a belief in the novel's continued vitality as a genre.

The socio-cultural setting and the – political? ethical? moral? – status of fiction

The occasional deference to an innovator like John Fowles notwithstanding, the American story of British fiction as being hide-bound in an outmoded reflectionist aesthetic is so persistent that it might at first seem to imply that American literary-critical voices were unanimous in their devaluation of fictional realism. And certainly, as noted above, a particularly vocal cadre of American novelists was committed to writing under the banner of formal experimentation, just as numerous American critics were committed to expounding the significance of an anti-realist stance. However, despite this apparent aesthetic dominant, a significant number of well-known and respected American writers and their critical exegetes remained strongly devoted to the social realist fictional projects that they in their turn thought best suited to engaging the complexities of the time. As American critics Tom LeClair and Larry McCaffrey determine in their retrospective on the 1970s, 'Only "omni-" will do' as 'a prefix to fit the [American] fiction of decade' (2). Yet literary-critical attitudes about fiction and representation at the time seem more often polarized than merely eclectic. The urgency of competing viewpoints can best be understood as due not solely to questions of the novel's continued viability as a genre, but also with regard to the socio-historical realities of the decade.

Impassioned considerations of the status of fictional realism and anti-realism were fundamental in the 1970s, given the culturally radical and theoretically reflexive *Gestalt* shift developing apace in the late 1960s along what are by now familiar postmodern lines: conceiving of the human as a fluid, socially constructed subject rather than an autonomous, transcendent entity; assessing the nature of the social, itself, as a quasi-fictional construction; and evaluating the relevance of fiction and criticism to engaging and making sense of these shifting epistemological paradigms. Writers of metafiction in the seventies were formally experimental, yet still trying to get at something significant about the relationship between fictional representation and human experience within socio-cultural realities. John Barth teased out just such issues in his public discussion with fellow metafictional novelist John Hawkes at a landmark 1978 Fiction Festival at the University of Cincinnati. Drawing on Borges's fictional image of 'hronir', or 'objects that can imagine themselves into real existence' and 'displace prior reality', Barth asserts, 'there is no better example of a hron than a literary text […] a piece of imagined reality that you can hold in your hand. It can do work in the world […]' (19). American responses to the British novel must be read finally within the extra-literary contexts of such fiction/reality conundrums and of the shift in *zeitgeist* that stood in reciprocal relationship to contemporaneous aesthetic transformations. These contexts both implicitly and explicitly inflected Americans' discussions of British fiction – and once again, to characterize such contexts as singularly 'American' would be to misrepresent the story of what was, in fact, a transnational phenomenon.

Narrowing the lens, first, to socio-historical realities as experienced within the US at the time, it is unsurprising that conversations in literary aesthetics would turn increasingly to the relationship between fiction and reality, and, as we shall see, to the status of fiction as regards its political, ethical and moral obligations. American cultural and political sensibilities in the sixties and seventies were wildly unstable in the midst of one of the most volatile times in US history. In addition to the continuing Cold War and spectre of nuclear Mutual Assured Destruction (heightened in 1962 by the Cuban Missile Crisis), countercultural turbulence developed in the wake of post-War cultural conformity from an assemblage of events and movements: civil unrest and widespread campus protests over continued American involvement in Vietnam, leading to the shocking student deaths at Kent State and Jackson State Universities in 1970; national grief and disillusionment stemming from political tragedies and scandals, including the Kennedy assassinations and assassination of Martin Luther King, Jr., as well as the Watergate scandal leading to Republication President Richard Nixon's resignation in 1974; and the powerful and newly organized demands for legal and political rights of the Civil Rights and Women's and Gay Liberation movements. Culturally, as prominent American novelist Robert Coover speculated in 1979, American writers were also being influenced by 'the post-war appetite for change and newness'; the 'college boom' and 'all those new English professors ... needing something to write about'; and 'the resurgence of interest in the surrealists, ease of travel, [and] the explosion of all the new media, video especially' (qtd. in Cope and Green 48). Such dramatic historical shifts alongside seismic changes in the material and socio-cultural conditions of people's lives called for modes of fiction equal to the task of engaging the realities of the time – including feelings of their unsettling unreality.

In this vein, metafictionist John Barth's famous 1967 essay 'The Literature of Exhaustion' took up not merely questions of novelistic form, but questions of the 'fictitious aspect of our own existence' (33). Similarly, Robert Scholes in *Fabulation and Metafiction* addresses the ways in which 'the positivistic basis for realism has been eroded' (4), along with the lack of belief in an ultimate order to the world not created by one's own mind (56). Granted, the seeds of these flowerings in literary and cultural sensibilities had been germinating at least since high modernism, as Scholes is careful to note. However, their fruition during a time period increasingly perceiving itself as 'post'-modern was inflected in distinctive ways given an additional significant context: the rise of theory in the academy. Discussions of realism and representation in the 1970s were couched in a new argot in light of influential international and interdisciplinary academic contexts attending to the linguistic and social construction of reality, such as those stemming from theorists in the fields of linguistics, sociology and anthropology, and particularly as associated with French structuralism and post-structuralism. A narrative of the reciprocal interactions among fiction, criticism, theory and the academy is too intricate to embed even as a subplot here. However, their influence on American debates about fiction and representation, and by extension, on the American reception of the British novel, is clear via a brief sketch of Gerald Graff's important 1978 essay 'The Politics of Anti-Realism.'[14]

Published in *Salmagundi*, a highly respected American intellectual quarterly founded in the mid-1960s, Graff's essay surveys a wealth of prominent voices on the contemporary literary-critical scene and synthesizes key ideas relevant to the resonances among literature, criticism and theory as they had crystallized over the roughly ten years prior. Graff's discussion makes clear that such resonances are international in scope. He cites writers, critics and theorists ranging from J. Hillis Miller, Robert Scholes and Jonathan Culler from the US; to Frank Kermode and Terry Eagleton from the UK; to Alain Robbe-Grillet, Herbert Marcuse, Jacques Derrida and Roland Barthes from Europe. Positions taken up by these figures, and by the numerous other academic voices Graff cites, vary considerably. However, what their stances within the broader critical conversation overwhelmingly share is an interest in the social and political implications of different conceptions of the relationship between fiction and representation, along with the academic criticism that engages its complexities. In this important context, Graff highlights the prevalent view of his contemporaries of a 'parallelism ... between psychological, epistemological, esthetic, and political categories of experience' (5). For those aesthetic and cultural radicals (as Graff styles them) wanting to challenge the status quo with regard to such categories of experience, '[o]verthrowing the established form of society means overthrowing realism, or going "beyond realism"' (6).

Graff references Alain Robbe-Grillet's late 1960s view that 'academic criticism in the West [...] employs the word "realism" as if reality were already entirely constituted [...] when the writer comes on the scene. Thus it supposed that the latter's role is limited to "explaining" and to "expressing" the reality of his period' (qtd. in Graff 7). Robbe-Grillet's anti-realist stance in response to such criticism was echoed from the British side of the Channel by Frank Kermode in 1974. In the inaugural volume of the cutting edge academic journal *Critical Inquiry* Kermode argues, 'the whole movement toward "secretarial" realism' represents 'an anachronistic myth of common understanding and shared universes of meaning' (qtd. in Graff 6). The Marcusian 'radical perceptual disruption' (13) effected by anti-realist literary reflexivity was therefore perceived to be not just aesthetically but politically radical: 'by calling into question the referential adequacy of categories of understanding, it shakes us loose from our susceptibility to ideology' (Graff 14). Graff does acknowledge that some proponents of anti-realist aesthetic stances initially appear to be apolitical escapes into pure aesthetics and the primacy of reader response, such as American critic Susan Sontag's seminal *Against Interpretation* (1967). For Graff, however, such formalist 'disengagement from society and politics' still has a 'political animus' inherent in its rejection of repressive bourgeois over-intellectualization (17).

Beyond its useful synthesis of dominant theories of representation, Graff's assessment of the literary-critical landscape in the 1970s is interesting as a cultural artifact in and of itself. Most significant to the framing the British novel's reception in the decade is the conclusion to his intensive examination of the politics of anti-realism, which presages a significant shift in late-1970s America literary and cultural sensibilities to renewed questions of the moral status of fictional representation. I cannot do justice to the complexity of Graff's incisive challenges to anti-realist stances here, but in brief, he outlines the ways in which such stances may undermine their political impetus through their solipsistic alienation from society and complicity with the social confusion against which they rebel, and he questions the idea that radical aesthetics will necessarily lead to a more critically engaged readership. For Graff, 'there is no way of determining the critical character of a literary work unless we know its disposition to reality [...] its accountability to what is outside itself' (29). This idea of accountability to extra-literary reality became by the end of the seventies a matter of sustained public literary-critical debate.

Though voices and positions within such debates are best conceived of as situated along a spectrum, or perhaps within a web, of attitudes about fictional form and the representation of reality, one renowned event was seen at the time to epitomize competing literary-critical micronarratives in this context: the Gass–Gardner debate. This public debate between experimental American novelist William Gass and social realist John Gardner took place at the 1978 Fiction Festival mentioned above, and the transcript was printed in Tom LeClair and Larry McCaffrey's *Anything Can Happen* (1983), which collected interviews conducted at the end of the 1970s with American writers about the American literary scene during the decade. The Gass–Gardner debate was staged in order to address these two novelists' longstanding 'nature/art quarrel' (20) with regard to the status of fictional realism, as well as their respective stances on the social and moral responsibilities of fiction. The resulting two-hour exchange was perceived as encapsulating 'some of the most important issues in fiction today' (21).

Throughout the debate, Gass eschews the idea that novels should be in any way akin to moral philosophy, arguing instead that their 'aesthetic measure' be taken on the grounds of their formal artistic accomplishment and beauty (29). He draws on structuralist terminology to characterize his own experimental novels as objects 'full of signs', and hopes that they will be perceived as 'worthy of love' on an aesthetic plane that transcends 'mere' meaning. The closest he comes to ascribing a moral status to fictional aesthetic objects is to muse, 'Planting those objects is a moral activity, I suppose' (23). Gass also labels Gardner's valued moral realist fiction as 'promiscuous', as pandering to popular tastes (26–27). Gardner, in response, argues that anti-realist novels pander to academic tastes, with professors self-servingly choosing novels that 'students need help with', regardless of those novels' literary merit. Gardner also echoes Graff's concerns – albeit in more narrowly conservative moral aesthetic terms than explicitly political ones – about fiction's accountability to social reality, as well as its significance to ameliorating the complexities of human experience within that reality. 'You write the book to get control of in yourself things that you haven't been able to control and understand in the world', asserts Gardner. 'Maybe it's an illusory understanding, but I think it helps you live' (27). For Gardner, rather than 'academically popular' writing that creates 'beautiful or interesting or ornate or curious objects', fiction should be 'consciously moral' and attempt 'to understand important matters by means of the best tool human beings have': that is, language (21–22).[15] While the polarized views of Gass and Gardner during the debate represent the most extreme stances with regard to fiction and representation at the time, the importance of considering and declaring such literary-critical stances was both endemic and highly charged on the American scene by the end of the 1970s.

(Re-)enter the British novel. It is in this context of the renewed engagement with the moral, ethical, or political status of fiction that my story of the reception of British novels in America during the 1970s can perhaps finally best be understood. The reception of Drabble's *The Ice Age* and Fowles's *Daniel Martin*, as well as the more comprehensive American assessments of the British novel's continued vitality, are representative of reviewers' and critics' responses to British novels more broadly. Such responses explicitly or implicitly involved assessing the relationship between fiction and representation, with an eye towards what any particular British novel had to say about human experience within particular socio-cultural realities. And it is important to note that on the whole, those British novels of the 1970s receiving the most literary-critical attention were not perceived as naively reflectionist in their aesthetic. Rather, they were seen as actively engaging the complexities of their time, as with McDowell's commentary on their 'modified realism', above. It is to a few final brief narratives about the most widely and substantively reviewed novels in this context that my story will now turn.

The first of these involves the significant chords struck in America by the apocalyptic modes of Doris Lessing's *Briefing for a Descent Into Hell* (1971) and William Golding's *Darkness Visible* (1979), which were strongly resonant due to the innovative vision through which they explored alternative psychological realities. Lessing's novel is allied with the intelligent vision of social realist George Eliot, 'finger on the pulse of Everything' (Sale 14), but with the twist that her mad and alien protagonist 'experiences almost nothing offered by ordinary human life, yet his instance is touching and beautiful' (16). Though *Briefing* was not always judged a successful novel, reviewers consistently appreciated Lessing's commitment to exploring alternative social possibilities – what an unsigned review in the *Atlantic Monthly* characterized as Lessing's Laingian quasi-shamanistic attempt to 'melt old rigid patterns of thought, feeling, and behavior' and to forge 'new more satisfying and insightful approaches to life' (89).[16] Like *Briefing*, Golding's 'brilliantly spooky' *Darkness Visible* was read as twinning tradition and innovation: 'Thoroughly contemporary in its treatment of fanaticism, terrorism, and psychological destitution, this is nonetheless an old-fashioned story of the struggle between good and evil'; it has the 'aura of a Thomas Hardy novel' while also marked by a pervasive 'ambiguity' (*Atlantic Monthly* 92). Also like *Briefing*, *Darkness Visible* was not unequivocally celebrated, yet it was significant in the numerous substantive responses it garnered with regard to its gloomy and disturbing vision of contemporary social realities.[17] Both Lessing's and Golding's novels had a powerful effect on American readers through the kind of 'cognitive estrangement' celebrated by anti-realist writers (see Graff 13ff.), but here executed via a blend of the real and the strange, of tradition and innovation. Sale's closing statement on Lessing perhaps captures the response to both novelists as a whole: 'I do not see her scale or vision as being triumphantly right, yet no other writer in recent years […] has upset me as she has done' (17).

British writers' attentiveness to expanding the vision of social realities addressed in the contemporary novel similarly lay behind the high estimation in the 1970s of a number of what were then termed post-imperial novels, such as Ruth Prawer Jhabvala's *Heat and Dust* (1975), V. S. Naipaul's *In a Free State* (1971) and *A Bend in the River* (1979) and Nadine Gordimer's *The Conservationist* (1974) and *Burger's Daughter* (1979). American writer-critic Eugene Chesnick, in his discussion in the American leftist periodical *The Nation* of the influence of post-imperial fiction via Jhabvala's and Gordimer's work, comments that these writers' 'surroundings are exotic enough' without radical experimentation (149). He sees Jhabvala's task in particular as in line with English novelists who 'impose the novel's logic on an alien setting' in the Forster-esque tradition of presenting multiple points of view. 'How important these conventions have become to us!' cries Chesnick. 'How much we have come to rely on them to sort things out!' (150).

Though all the three writers were awarded Britain's prestigious Booker Prize during the 1970s, it was Naipaul and Gordimer who were most lauded in America as among the finest writers of the time. The reception of Gordimer's fiction in particular was marked by declarations of its moral and political importance as well as its 'strange angles of insight' (O'Brien 27) on the socio-historical realities of South Africa under apartheid. Here again too we see the issues of transnational reception addressed earlier in my story: the most substantive assessments of Gordimer's work in 1970s America were penned by writers from the UK, such as Irish politician and academic Conor Cruise O'Brien's review of *Burger's Daughter* in the *New York Review of Books*, and British journalist Anthony Sampson's front-page review of the same novel in *The New York Times Book Review*. Both writers were likely commissioned to review *Burger's Daughter* – which was banned in South Africa – due to their respective interests and involvements in South African politics, and their authoritative status in this respect led to their being strong voices in shaping the American reception of Gordimer's work. In the context of this final chapter of my literary-critical story, the commentary of these two reviewers is important in highlighting serious considerations in the 1970s of the political status of fiction, which go far beyond John Gardner's abstract and universalist moral formalism to address specific socio-historical circumstances in a way that presages the work of postcolonial critics beginning (at least) with the publication of Edward Said's groundbreaking *Orientalism* in 1978.

Both O'Brien and Sampson place Gordimer's work in the tradition of pre-revolutionary Russian social realist novelists – O'Brien cites Turgenev and

Tolstoy specifically (27) – through her moving and evocative blending of 'people, landscape, and politics' (Sampson 2). Significant to these reviewers is the power of Gordimer's verisimilitude in the service of the novel's politics as well as promotion of a universal readerly engagement with the novel's ideas and characters:

> It is the combination of political authenticity and sensuous awareness that makes this novel so powerful. Its account of black movements, against the historical background of real people, is harshly realistic; the intense argument in a house in Soweto has the sharp detail of a documentary.... Yet the political moments are always illuminated by the intense observation of people and places – tiny details precisely and lovingly described – that brings every incident to life, and that gives Miss Gordimer's writing such universality.[18] (Sampson 1–2)

O'Brien extends his commendation of the novel's realism to what might be termed the realism of Gordimer's own politics. He describes Gordimer as an 'artist who takes politics seriously', as opposed to one 'taking up political causes for the sake of relaxation, exercise, and display', as well as an artist not merely 'notionally opposed to the regime', but 'who rejects the system totally' and who 'is capable of entering into the minds of blacks who also reject it, but whose rejection takes the form of rejecting all whites' (31). O'Brien sees this double consciousness as cutting Gordimer off from both black and white society in a manner that will soon become a focus for such postcolonial writers and theorists of hybridity as Salman Rushdie and Homi Bhabha. It is just this idea of the unsettling hybrid 'stereoscopic vision' (27) of Gordimer's realism that perhaps best captures the nature of her re-imagination of traditional mimetic fiction in the face of disturbing new political realities, and that led to *Burger's Daughter* being declared 'the must-read fiction on South Africa for the 1970s' (*Kirkus* 753). The new angles of fictional insight and their moral and political relevance to social realities represented by Gordimer's work, as well as of those additional works of modified realism discussed above, lie at the heart of positive valuations of British novels of the seventies in America, and serve as bridges to continued developments along the lines of reimagined realism in British fiction from the 1970s on.

Epilogue: Reframing realism: On stories that represent realities

In the tradition of the highly self-conscious reflections on fiction and representation in the 1970s, I have tried to attend carefully in my own academic story to the ways in which it has been constructed and the resulting implications for a twenty-first century understanding of the American reception of British novels of the decade. I have tried to make clear that which British novels were most substantively reviewed and analysed in lay and academic venues, as well as the literary-critical terms in which they were discussed, helped to craft particular portraits of British fiction at the time and its significance in relation to the American literary scene, which then influenced successive portraits on up to the present day. And my own story has left numerous threads of narrative undeveloped and at times, untold. I am troubled, for example, by its neglect of the reception of feminist novels of the 1970s, and by the many ways in which my story fails to attend to the contexts of gender and ethnicity in relation to the literary-critical establishment as it evolved during the decade. From the vantage point of a new century in which the strong presence of the formerly marginalized voices of women and sexual and ethnic minorities is at times taken for granted, I was continually disturbed while gathering resources for my story at the material evidence of the dominance of bourgeois white male literary and academic voices in shaping the critical conversations of the time. Despite the growing importance of identity politics to literary criticism and theory in the 1970s, so comparatively few reviews, academic essays and reflections on the state of fiction were being published by the decade's cultural Others; so comparatively few interviews were being conducted with these writers. Along other lines, I have also had to set aside my own desires to reframe via a new reception tale the stories of 1970s novels whose significance I believe has been undervalued, such as the fiction of Muriel Spark. Such considerations are reminders once again of the provisional truth-value and limited scope of any literary-critical story.

This last idea brings my chapter full circle to the questions of fiction and representation with which I began, and that – though so endemic to contemporary English studies as nearly to go without saying – were the subject of such vociferous debate and controversy during the 1970s. And my nineteenth-century social realist urge to offer some semblance of closure to what is necessarily an open-ended story will take the form of a last bit of narrative on the state of the novel at the end of the decade in question. Robert Scholes speculated in 1979 with regard to narrative history that though some anticipated the imminent end of the novel as a viable literary form at hand, others (like himself) awaited the 'new dispensation' (211) of the fictional imagination conceived as an innovative blend of realism and fabulation. Such a re-imagination (a term Scholes invokes repeatedly) – a turn away from extreme poles of traditional realism and formal innovation – was emphasized consistently on the American literary scene at the decade's end. Along the lines of Frederick McDowell's discussion of a prevalent modified realism in British fiction, American writers and critics were coining terms like 'post-realistic fiction' and 'experimental realism' as they tried to capture the nature and status of mutating and hybrid fictional forms. 'Old assumptions about the effeteness of innovation and the simplicity of imitation are destroyed by our new experimental realists,' Tom LeClair and Larry McCaffrey assert with confidence as they reflect on the 1970s as a transitional decade. They continue,

> Whatever the causes – the insistence of the world, the writers' education and work outside the university, a lust for the new languages specialists have created, the natural progress of experiments from hypothesis to results – [the] engagement with large cultural themes is good news for the novel as a continuing form. It is also good news for the world, which is now so much a fiction – beyond verifiability and the ordinary imagination – that only fiction can adequately represent it. (6)

This description of American reimagined realism could just as easily be applied to the work of emerging British novelists at the turn of the decade, such as those heralded by the (reborn) British literary magazine *Granta*'s issues on 'The End of the English Novel' (1980) and 'The Best of Young British Novelists' (1983), including names now familiar in America like Martin Amis, Kazuo Ishiguro, Julian Barnes, Buchi Emecheta, Pat Barker and Ian McEwan. British novels of the 1970s were clearly significant, not only in their own right as negotiating in complex ways with questions of realism and experimentation, tradition and innovation, and fiction and representation, but also, as with the American novels of the time, in setting the stage for new fictional forms and literary-critical narratives to follow. And that these complex negotiations during the decade were both 'good for the novel' and 'good for the world' is a theme that I hope my story of the American reception of British fiction has persuasively figured forth.

Notes

1. My assessments throughout of particular British novelists/novels as 'among the most widely reviewed' or 'academically discussed' during the decade rest upon the number of review citations listed in the *Book Review Index Online Plus* database, which catalogues upwards of six million reviews from thousands of publications, and on the number of scholarly articles and monographs indexed in the *MLA International Bibliography*.
2. See, for example, McCaffrey's interview with Coover, as well as the introduction to his interview with Sukenick in *Anything Can Happen*; Jerome Klinkowitz's brief

overview in '8-1/2 Ronnies' (261ff.); and Sukenick's 1974 statement in *The New York Times Book Review* on his founding of the Fiction Collective.
3. The interviews collected in LeClair and Federman are representative in this context: the most referenced influences are Gabriel García Márquez, Italo Calvino and Günter Grass. See also the discussions in Cope and Green.
4. LeClair and McCaffrey identify this trend across American novelists. Robert Coover asserts that American writers have no 'communities' or 'natural center', aside from the 'loosely strung' academic circuit to which not all writers have access. American writers 'have no gathering places, no forum, no national magazines, no cafés, no boulevards' (65). For a similar view just prior to the 1970s, see Kostelanetz on the 'peculiarity of the American literary scene': 'the absence of a continuous cultural community, the diversity of writers' social and cultural backgrounds, [and] the general habit of residing outside established literary centers ... ' (41).
5. The then-newer generation of writers whose talent Baker emphasizes include Beryl Bainbridge, Richard Adams and, especially, Margaret Drabble, whom he dubs 'the brightest patch of new green' on the English literary landscape (483).
6. The journal was founded in 1960 and its website notes that it published the first interview with Margaret Drabble, as well as bringing to attention later contemporary British writers such as Kazuo Ishiguro and J. M. Coetzee.
7. These novels include Murdoch's *A Fairly Honourable Defeat* (1970) and *An Accidental Man* (1971), Muriel Spark's *The Driver's Seat* (1970), Lessing's *Briefing for a Descent into Hell* (1971), Paul Bailey's *Trespasses* (1970), Brigid Brophy's *In Transit* (1969; 1970 in US), Lawrence Durrell's *Numquam* (1970), Nicholas Mosley's *Natalie Natalia* (1971) and Anthony Burgess's *MF* (1971).
8. American reviewer Vivien Raynor, for example, assessing Murdoch's Booker Prize contender *The Black Prince* (1973) in the *Washington Post*'s review periodical *Book World*, highlights Murdoch's popularity: her books 'fly off the library shelves' (4).
9. Like a number of critics from the UK cited in my story (including Davie, Donoghue and O'Brien), Kermode was later to become a transplant to the American academic scene, but during the 1970s was spearheading the importation of French linguistic and literary theory as Lord Northcliffe chair at University College London during the more theoretically driven phase of his long and multifaceted academic career. According to the British periodical *The Guardian*, Kermode was '[w]idely acclaimed as Britain's foremost literary critic' (Flood np.), an assessment that further suggests the influence of his views within the US.
10. Kermode critiques the British reviewing establishment more so than the American, and cites as a key case in point the reviews of Anthony Burgess's *MF* (1970), a novel of which 'they made a complete mess'. He queries, 'What kind of critic do you have to be to miss the point that if you fail to see what so remarkable a writer is doing it may be your fault?' (86). See also similar comments made in the 1978 *New Review*

symposium on contemporary fiction about the 'hostility of the [British] reviewing establishment' to experimental fiction (qtd. in Bart 170). Kermode's description contrasts markedly with the American view of the British literary scene described by Kostelanetz.

11. Donoghue would later become New York University Henry James Professor in English and American letters.
12. The others were Durrell's tetralogy *The Alexandria Quartet* and Murdoch's *The Unicorn*, both published in the previous decades (1957–1960 and 1963, respectively). Nicholas Mosley's *Impossible Object* (1969) also receives a short section.
13. The others are Doris Lessing, Anthony Burgess and V. S. Naipaul.
14. Graff later set forth his ideas in this context more extensively in the oft-cited *Literature Against Itself* (1979).
15. For more extensive elaborations on the views represented by these two figures, see Gass, *Fiction and the Figures of Life* (1970) and Gardner, *On Moral Fiction* (1977).
16. The caricature accompanying this review features Doris Lessing alongside Norman Mailer, each in superhero costume, suggesting their attempts to 'save' the sick societies about which they wrote. Interestingly, two advertisements juxtaposed with the review are for John David Garcia's *The Moral Society: A Rational Alternative to Death* – in whose call for renewed moral engagement the 'historical significance is beyond questioning' (13) – and Michael W. Miles's *Radical Probe: The Logic of Student Rebellion*, which 'makes sense out of the events of the last decade, something not easy to do' (16).
17. A representative example is American critic John Leonard's 1979 review in *Books of the Times*.
18. Praise for Gordimer's having achieved 'universality' is a commonplace in reviews of her work: a reminder that postcolonial challenges to universality had not yet taken hold in this decade. See, for example, Johnson's assessment of *The Conservationist* as 'universal and timeless' (3).

Works cited

Alter, Robert. *Partial Magic: The Novel as Self-Conscious Genre*. Berkeley: U of California P, 1975.

———. '*Daniel Martin* and the Mimetic Task', in *Novel vs. Fiction: The Contemporary Reformation*. Ed. by I. Jackson Cope and Geoffrey Green. Norman: Pilgrim, 1981. 65–78.

Baker, Sheridan. 'Alive and Well: The Contemporary British Novel.' *American Libraries* 5.9, October 1974: 482–90. *JSTOR*. Web. 17 August 2011.

Barth, John. 'The Literature of Exhaustion.' *Atlantic Monthly* August 1967: 29–34.

—— and John Hawkes. 'A Dialogue', in *Anything Can Happen: Interviews with Contemporary American Novelists*. Ed. by Tom LeClair and Larry McCaffery. Urbana: U of Illinois P, 1983. 9–19.

Bergonzi, Bernard. *The Situation of the Novel*. Pittsburgh: U of Pittsburgh P, 1970.

Bradbury, Malcolm. *Possibilities: Essays on the State of the Novel*. London: Oxford UP, 1973.

Brown, Rosellen. 'Interview', in *Anything Can Happen: Interviews with Contemporary American Novelists*. Ed. by Tom LeClair and Larry McCaffery. Urbana: U of Illinois P, 1983. 45–62.

Busch, Frederick. Rev. of *Daniel Martin*, by John Fowles. *American Book Review* December 1977: 21.

Chesnick, Eugene. 'A Writer's Space', in *Rev. of Selected Stories*, by Nadine Gordimer, and *Heat and Dust*, by Ruth Prawer Jhabvala. *Nation* August 1976: 149–51.

Coover, Robert. 'Interview', in *Anything Can Happen: Interviews with Contemporary American Novelists*. Ed. by Tom LeClair and Larry McCaffery. Urbana: U of Illinois P, 1983. 63–78.

Davie, Donald. 'Fatal Attitudes.' Rev. of *The Consul's File*, by Paul Theroux, and *The Ice Age*, by Margaret Drabble. *New York Review of Books* November 1977: 28–9.

Donoghue, Denis. 'Only Disconnect.' Rev. of *Daniel Martin*, by John Fowles, and *The Sea and the Moon*, by Niccolò Tucci. *New York Review of Books*, December 1977: 45–6.

Flood, Allison. 'Celebrated Critic Frank Kermode Dies Aged 90.' *Guardian* August 2010: np. Web.

Gardner, John. *On Moral Fiction*. New York: Basic, 1977.

Gasiorek, Andrzej. *Post-War British Fiction: Realism and After*. London: Arnold, 1995.

Gass, William. *Fiction and the Figures of Life*. New York: Knopf, 1970.

—— and John Gardner. 'A Debate', in *Anything Can Happen: Interviews with Contemporary American Novelists*. Ed. by Tom LeClair and Larry McCaffery. Urbana: U of Illinois P, 1983. 20–31.

Graff, Gerald. 'The Politics of Anti-Realism.' *Salmagundi* 42, Summer-Fall 1978: 4–30. JSTOR. Web. 3 January 2012.

——. *Literature against Itself*. Chicago: U of Chicago P, 1979.

Johnson, Diane. 'Out of Africa.' Rev. of *The Conservationist*, by Nadine Gordimer. *Book World* April 1975: 3.

Kermode, Frank. 'The British Novel Lives.' *Atlantic Monthly* July 1972: 85–8.

Klinkowitz, Jerome. 'Experimental Realism', in *Post-Modern Fiction: A Bio-Bibliographical Guide*. Ed. by Larry McCaffery. New York: Greenwood, 1986. 63–78.

——. '8-1/2 Ronnies', in *Musing the Mosaic: Approaches to Ronald Sukenick*. Ed. by Matthew Roberson. New York: SUNY P, 2003. 251–70.

Korenman, Joan. 'The "Liberation" of Margaret Drabble.' *Critique* 21.3, March 1980: 61–72. EBSCO. Web. 18 August 2011.

Kostelanetz, Richard. 'The English Literary Scene: An American's View.' *Salmagundi* 1.3, 1966: 39–55. *JSTOR*. Web. 3 January 2012.

LeClair, Tom and Larry McCaffery. 'Introduction', in *Anything Can Happen: Interviews with Contemporary American Novelists*. Ed. by Tom LeClair and Larry McCaffery. Urbana: U of Illinois P, 1983. 1–8.

Leonard, John. Rev. of *Darkness Visible*, by William Golding. *Books of the Times*, November1979: 552–4.

Levine, David. 'Caricature.' *New York Review of Books* May 1971: 13.

Lodge, David. *The Novelist at the Crossroads, and Other Essays on Fiction and Criticism*. Ithaca: Cornell UP, 1971.

Marcus, Greil. 'Johnny Rotten's Soul Sister.' Rev. of *The Ice Age*, by Margaret Drabble. *Rolling Stone*, October 1977: 99–101.

Massie, Allan. *The Novel Today: A Critical Guide to the British Novel 1970–1989*. London: Longman and The British Council, 1990.

McDowell, Frederick. 'Time of Plenty: Recent British Novels.' *Contemporary Literature* 13.3, Summer 1972: 361–94. *JSTOR*. Web. 18 Jan. 2012.

Moore-Gilbert, Bart. 'Apocalypse Now? The Novel in the 1970s', in *The Arts in the 1970s: Cultural Closure?* Ed. by Bart Moore-Gilbert. London: Routledge, 2002. *EBSCO*. Web. 10 August 2011.

O'Brien, Conor Cruise. 'Waiting for Revolution.' Rev. of *Burger's Daughter*, by Nadine Gordimer. *New York Review of Books*, October 1979: 27–31.

O'Brien, Tim. 'Interview', in *Anything Can Happen: Interviews with Contemporary American Novelists*. Ed. by Tom LeClair and Larry McCaffery. Urbana: U of Illinois P, 1983. 262–78.

Rabinovitz, Rubin. *The Reaction against Experiment in the English Novel: 1950–1960*. New York: Columbia UP, 1967.

Radical Probe: The Logic of Student Rebellion. 'Advertisement.' *New York Review of Books* May 1971: 17.

Raynor, Vivien. 'Something Keeps One Reading.' Rev. of *The Black Prince*, by Iris Murdoch. *Book World*, June 1978: 4–5.

Rev. of *Briefing for a Descent Into Hell*, by Doris Lessing. *Atlantic Monthly* August 1971: 89–90.

Rev. of *Burgher's Daughter*, by Nadine Gordimer. *Kirkus* July 1979: 753.

Rev. of *Daniel Martin*, by John Fowles. *Choice* December 1977: 1359.

Rev. of *Darkness Visible*, by William Golding. *Atlantic Monthly* November 1979: 92.

Robbe-Grille, Alain. *For a New Novel: Essays on Fiction*. Trans. Richard Howard. New York: Grove, 1965.

Said, Edward. *Orientalism*. New York: Vintage, 1979 [1978].

Sale, Roger. 'Watchmen, What of the Night?' Rev. of *Of a Fire on the Moon*, by Norman Mailer, and *Briefing for a Descent Into Hell*, by Doris Lessing. *New York Review of Books* May 1971: 13–17.

Sampson, Anthony. 'Heroism in South Africa.' Rev. of *Burger's Daughter*, by Nadine Gordimer. *New York Times Book Review* August 1979: 1–2.

Sarraute, Nathalie. *The Age of Suspicion: Essays on the Novel*. Trans. Maria Jolas. New York: Braziller, 1963.

Scholes, Robert. *Fabulation and Metafiction*. Urbana: U of Illinois P, 1979.

Sukenick, Ronald. 'Guest Word', in *New York Times Book Review*. September1974.

———. 'Interview', in *Anything Can Happen: Interviews with Contemporary American Novelists*. Ed. by Tom LeClair and Larry McCaffery. Urbana: U of Illinois P, 1983. 279–97.

The Moral Society: A Rational Alternative to Death. 'Advertisement.' *New York Review of Books* May 1971: 16.

University of Wisconsin Press Journals Division. *Contemporary Literature*. Web. 13 Jan. 2012.http://uwpress.wisc.edu/journals/journals/cl.html

8

Melancholy Interest: J. G. Farrell's *Troubles* and the Politics of Perspective

Tamás Bényei

Troubles on the continent

This chapter offers a reading of J. G. Farrell's greatest novel, *Troubles* (1970) from a continental perspective, even though such a perspective is to a large extent something of a fiction. After the briefest of glances at Farrell's reception, or lack thereof, on the European continent, I shall suggest a feasible 'continental' theoretical perspective on *Troubles*, also emphasizing the way the novel stands in the continental as well as the English tradition.

As indicated by the Lost Man Booker prize awarded posthumously to *Troubles* in 2010, J. G. Farrell is by no means a forgotten writer, at least in Britain. His 1970s Empire trilogy, comprising *Troubles, The Siege of Krishnapur* (1973) and *The Singapore Grip* (1978), is constantly in print, and there is a modest but steady trickle of articles about his work as well as the odd monograph (and Farrell has been lucky with his monographers). Nevertheless, if asked about major figures of post-1945 British fiction, more particularly of the 1960s and the 1970s (two decades that are thought to lack strong period markers at least in terms of fiction), very few continental readers or even critics would think immediately of J. G. Farrell. They would be more likely to come up with some of the protagonists of the critical account of the period created mainly by Malcolm Bradbury, a narrative that gained considerable currency on the continent by the end of the 1970s, which centralized writers like William Golding, Iris Murdoch, Anthony Burgess or Muriel Spark.

The invisibility or extremely limited visibility of someone of the stature of Farrell on the continent is rather puzzling. None of his novels are available in German or Russian (let alone languages like Romanian, Norwegian, Swedish,

Finnish, Croat, Greek or Dutch). To date, French and Danish seem to be the only European languages in which the entire trilogy is available. *The Siege of Krishnapur* and *Troubles* have made it into Spanish, Italian, Portuguese and Czech; *Troubles* and *The Singapore Grip* have been translated into Polish; and *Troubles* is also available in Slovak. The surprising absence of German translations is particularly detrimental to Farrell's continental fame, given that German translations are frequently followed by translations into other Central European languages. In the case of Farrell, interestingly, the process seems to have been reversed, as *Troubles* is already available in Czech, Slovak and Polish, and is scheduled for publication in Hungarian more than 40 years after its original publication. This latter fact alerts us to a remarkable feature of Farrell's continental presence: most of the European translations are fairly recent, some of them surprisingly so. About a decade ago, the result of a similar survey would have been embarrassingly meagre: all translations were published after 1980, and the process took off only after 1990. In France, the trilogy appeared between 1990 and 2003, while the Italian renditions arrived in 2001 (*Krishnapur*) and 2003 (*Troubles/Tumulti*). In Spanish, *Krishnapur* was published in 1991, while *Troubles* appeared in 2011 (as *Disturbios*), during the same year as the Portuguese translations of *Troubles* and *Krishnapur*.

Although it would be mistaken to look for a general 'continental' pattern behind these random facts, and while it is clear that many of the translations are due exclusively to the efforts of enthusiastic individuals, the recent flurry of international interest in Farrell might be due to two phenomena: the rise of postcolonial criticism and the growing critical prestige of (postmodern) historical fiction, especially through the international critical currency of Linda Hutcheon's coinage 'historiographic metafiction', despite the fact that Farrell is a notable absence in Hutcheon's influential *The Poetics of Postmodernism* (1988).

It is clear that the degree and nature of the continental visibility of Farrell cannot be separated from his critical vicissitudes within the British scene. In this sense, it has to be noted that, for several decades, the critical establishment in Britain had not been able to come up with a discourse or, more significantly, a critical narrative that would have made Farrell an 'interesting' prospect for European scholars, translators or publishers. How significant this factor might be is indicated by the sudden upsurge of interest in *Troubles* (Hungarian, Portuguese and Spanish translations coming out in quick succession) many years after its publication, a development that is probably not unrelated to the posthumous Booker.

Although Farrell has not been forgotten by British readers and critics, he has not been construed as a figurehead of a period, decade or tendency, someone with whom a catchphrase could be associated. On the other hand, and this is a crucial factor in continental canonization, the British reception has not been especially concerned with the question of whether Farrell's work responds at all to recent international theoretical developments and discourses – barring postcolonial criticism, of course, but then postcolonial criticism is still largely restricted to English departments on the European continent.

While it is not the purpose of the present chapter to trace the critical reception of Farrell, a few major tendencies and directions need to be indicated in order to see how his reception has been unable to construct a Farrell that would have appealed to continental critics. In general terms, and as John McLeod discusses in his book *J. G. Farrell* (2007), the critical reception of Farrell's fiction has been often bogged down in the rather uninspiring context of the debates between the relative merits of realism as opposed to experimentalism. In my view, this dichotomy has defined and curtailed the critical discourse on post-war fiction in Britain, providing an almost exclusive context for the discussion and appraisal of recent fiction from the sixties, predominantly through the influence of Malcolm Bradbury's work. In his final summation of post-war British fiction in *The Modern British Novel* (1993), Bradbury devotes a page to Farrell, discussing him as a historical novelist concerned with the demise of the British Empire, claiming, rather non-committally, that these novels are 'works of contemporary consciousness as well a large-scale historical re-creation [...], works of elaborate form and complex metaphor as well as descriptive writing' (382). This reading has persisted even beyond the rise of 'historiographic metafiction'. Crane and Livett's otherwise insightful monograph *Troubled Pleasures: The Fiction of J. G. Farrell* (1997) claims that although Farrell does not write historiographic metafiction and is averse to taking those sorts of liberties, he is not old-fashioned either, showing at times 'an almost New Historicist awareness that history is a continual process of interchange between events, texts and the general culture of any period' (16–17), later going as far as to assert that Farrell 'engages in a metahistorical, metafictional project which is centrally postmodern' (18). In practically all these treatments, the realism/experimentalism dichotomy overrules all other aspects, and the mapping of the field allows a discussion of individual texts only either as pure types or as hybrids of fifties realism, the visionary and experimental extremes represented by the likes of Lowry, Beckett and B. S. Johnson, and the reassuring middle ground said to be occupied by Murdoch, Angus Wilson and others. For all its liberating effect, Bradbury's convenient construction was reductive inasmuch as the criteria or features that might make a novel or writer noticeable in the first place were chosen with exclusive concern for an aesthetics that is extremely uneasy about its own half-admitted implied politics. It was largely this critical mapping that defined what became visible on the continent, and the crippling effect of this discursive hegemony had an adverse effect on the (continental) fortunes not only of Farrell but also of more visible writers like Murdoch, Powell and Spark.

For a long time, the only alternative context for Farrell's fiction besides the realism/experimentalism dichotomy was the imperial theme, but – at least before the rise of postcolonial criticism – even this context remained rather uninspiring. One curious example of this approach (mostly ignoring the 'literary' qualities of the texts) is found in Randall Stevenson's *The British Novel since the Thirties* (1986), where Farrell and Paul Scott are lumped together with Ian Fleming as fundamentally realist investigators of the Empire, albeit equipped with a modern scepticism (note that *Troubles* is not even mentioned). In D. J. Taylor's *After the War* (1994), *Troubles* receives a non-commitally positive treatment as a representative of a chastened post-imperial interrogation of colonial ideologies along with Paul Scott's work and Murdoch's *The Red and the Green* (1965), although the more extensive treatment is reserved for John Masters's *Bhowani Junction* (1954). Over the past two decades, mainly as a result of the rise of a more exciting and theoretically informed postcolonial criticism that undertook the rereading of British imperial fiction, *The Siege of Krishnapur* has found for itself a niche within the critical reappraisal of the literature of the Raj, although this discourse, once again, has a fairly limited appeal for continental readers and scholars (Booker *passim*, Rubin 35–41, McLeod 55–73, Morey 109–33). The critical construction of 'Raj fiction', while making the texts contained therein look like an internal British affair for continental readers, has also tended to focus on the thematic and political/ideological aspects of this fiction, making the novels' innovative stylistic features invisible. It is this factor that is partly responsible for making two poetically innovative and original fictional ventures of the post-war decades that are 'major' by any international standard – Farrell's trilogy and Paul Scott's *Raj Quartet* (1966–75) – largely irrelevant from the perspective of the poetics of fiction, which is the perspective that tends to determine the intensity of a continental response that goes beyond the continental representatives of English studies. Also, even if *Krishnapur* has found for itself a niche, *Troubles* remains an elusive text, and the various contexts that had been established for it in British criticism point to several of the reasons why so much post-1945

British fiction has found it rather difficult to gain wide readership and elicit significant critical response on the continent.

A potentially more enabling perspective on Farrell's achievement has been opened up by a focus on genre – notably, the historical novel. Although this approach, initiated by Bernard Bergonzi in his 1979 essay 'Fictions of History', was a welcome index of the diversification of critical discourse on post-war fiction, the stakes of his discussion were not really different from those of the dominant discourse and dichotomy. Bergonzi's construal of Farrell as a 'cunning and self-conscious realist (61) within the mode of historical fiction is fundamentally a reiteration of Bradbury's argument in a more restricted field (no wonder that Bradbury, in turn, was to rely on Bergonzi in his brief assessment of Farrell). This emphasis was perpetuated by their followers, with most discussions hinging on the categorization of Farrell in terms of the same realism/experimentalism dichotomy, although in generic terms: Neil McEwan's major claim is that 'Farrell is a realist' (130), conceding that the point of the trilogy is philosophical rather than historical and arguing that it dramatizes the clash of ideas and hard reality (126-7). Bergonzi's approach was adopted in an unaltered form more than 20 years later by Dominic Head, who devotes a three-page, entirely content-based discussion to *Troubles* (129-31).

Even in surveys of the post-war historical novel, Farrell remains under-represented. Stuart Laing's chapter in Alan Sinfield's *Society and Literature 1945-1970* (1983) completely ignores him, even though it contains a discussion of two other Marxist writers of historical fiction (John Berger and David Caute). Farrell is absent from David Leon Higdon's *Shadows of the Past in Contemporary British Fiction* (1984), and, in Steven Connor's excellent *The English Novel in History, 1950-1995* (1996), only a single allegorical image is borrowed from *Krishnapur* (134-5). On the other hand, Farrell receives a separate chapter in Neil McEwan's *Perspective in British Historical Fiction Today* (1987), and, most significantly, *Troubles* is discussed extensively by Margaret Scanlan, who in *Traces of Another Time: History and Politics in Postwar British Fiction* (1990) provides an exciting new context for it alongside Elizabeth Bowen's *The Last September* (1929) and Iris Murdoch's *The Red and the Green*, two other novels concerned with the Irish Troubles of 1916-22. A telling detail might suggest at least one reason for the relative neglect of Farrell even in surveys of historical fiction. In A. S. Byatt's chapter in the 1979 volume edited by Bradbury and Palmer which also contains the Bergonzi essay, Farrell is mentioned briefly – together with John Berger's *G.* (1972) – as an example of a new kind of realist writing that had been made possible by a self-reflexive framework (30), but only after John Fowles's *The French Lieutenant's Woman* (1969) has already stolen the show in a three-page discussion. In general terms, as a major representative of a new kind of self-reflexive historical fiction *Troubles* was eclipsed by the more immediately innovative strategies of Fowles's near-contemporary novel which went on to feature in Hutcheon's work and in many other accounts as the figurehead of (British) historiographic metafiction, as a text that responds to certain current theoretical and critical concerns. In this context, Farrell's 'milder', more subtle questioning of the codes of realism, which (unlike Fowles) does not disrupt these codes openly, might have seemed less interesting for non-English readers. Bergonzi's essay is no exception: although Farrell is presented as a very significant figure, compared favourably with David Caute, the discussion of his work is preceded (in a way, pre-empted) by a section on *The French Lieutenant's Woman* (54–6).

While Fowles's novel has become a textbook case of historiographic metafiction, and *The Siege of Krishnapur* is now regarded as a major post-war reassessment of the Raj (and of Raj fiction), *Troubles*, although recognized as probably Farrell's masterpiece, remains an elusive text after four decades. It is the premise of this chapter that *Troubles* – like Farrell's other historical novels and like Paul Scott's quartet – is a major work by any international standard, and, moreover, that at the time of its publication it was very much in tune with international trends in historical fiction, although its 'place' is not easy to define.

Ronald Binns argues that Farrell's fiction 'forms part of an international trend among such writers as Gabriel García Márquez, William Styron and, more recently, E. L. Doctorow towards a vigorous, aesthetically self-aware historical fiction' (34), but this claim remains rather vague, primarily because the context created by the three writers mentioned is too broad to provide a meaningful starting point for a reading. In order to appreciate Farrell's achievement more fully, we might think of the European continent rather than the American context. It is enough to refer to some of the most enduring near-contemporary novels to see that the allegorical-fabulating strain in *Troubles* was very much of its time. Apart from *The French Lieutenant's Woman*, this period of European historical fiction produced novels like Michel Tournier's *The Erl King* (*Le Roi des Aulnes*, 1970), the third instalment of Günter Grass's Danzig trilogy, *Dog Years* (1963), Marguerite Yourcenar's *The Abyss* (*L'oeuvre au noir*, 1968), Claude Simon's *Histoire* (1967), and, at the other end of the continent, Aleksandr

Solzhenitsyn's *The First Circle* (1968), greatly admired by Farrell, and some of Bulat Okudzhava's great historical novels, including *Poor Avrosimov* (1969) and *The Adventures of Shipov* (1971), the latter of which, also available in English, has some interesting parallels with Farrell's work.

One reason for these parallels is the fact that Farrell, although his writing seems very English in many ways, very much stood in the European tradition of the novel, and *Troubles* can be read as a fictional rethinking especially of the *modernist* engagement with history and historical experience. Both John Spurling and Ronald Binns stress some of these links: besides Malcolm Lowry, Richard Hughes and Joseph Conrad, Spurling mentions Stendhal and Thomas Mann – there is not a little of the magic mountain in *Troubles* – and the great Russians while Binns refers to Farrell's admiration for Nabokov. To this list, I would certainly add Goncharov's *Oblomov* (1859) and Chekhov's short fiction and plays, going as far as to suggest that, if Ford Madox Ford's *The Good Soldier* (1915) is the best French novel written in English, then *Troubles* might be a candidate for the best Russian novel in the language.

In one of the most thoughtful comments on *Troubles*, Margaret Scanlan has described it as dramatizing a 'failure of awareness' (41). In the same vein, Brian Appleyard suggests with his characteristic acuteness that Farrell's trilogy provides the analysis of 'a culture hopelessly unaware of its place in history' (290), with this lack of awareness represented as a farce rather than a tragedy. Like many of Chekhov's stories, *Troubles* presents a community that is painfully and comically unaware of what we conveniently refer to as history and their own role in it, with their helplessness both a cause and a symptom of this unawareness. In *Troubles*, the 'Chekhovian' (non-)experience of what one could call missing history is given a unique inflection as Farrell links this gigantic unawareness and helplessness with a modernist poetics and politics. Thus, the Chekhovian–Goncharovian predicament is rendered through the inflections and refractions of Henry James and post-Jamesian writers like Elizabeth Bowen, or Henry Green (a name that is unaccountably absent from most discussions of Farrell), all this in a vaguely allegorical fashion. In this sense, as we shall see, the Major's 'private' unawareness of his surroundings is exemplary: several times, he finds himself an actor involved in affairs that he fails to understand. In what follows, I shall explore this lack of awareness, unpacking some of the implications of the allegorical features of *Troubles* and suggesting critical resources that might be able to bring out those aspects of Farrell's text that respond to certain continental theories.

Allegory and perspective

When *Troubles* is characterized as an allegorical text, allegory is usually meant as a narrative studded with objects and creatures with fixed meanings. Indeed, innumerable elements and episodes of the novel suggest some allegorical surplus: the scavenging women clad in black, the sheep's head that the Major finds in one of the drawers in his room and which remains unexplained throughout, the statues (Venus and Victoria) that make their repeated appearances in the narrative. There is Evans the tutor with his deathly pallor, and the many animals, like Edward Spencer's spaniel Rover, when it is punished by Edward for killing a chicken and when it is a decrepit dog with failing sight, the ubiquitous cats, including the great cat massacre in the Majestic, the dead rabbit, the toad and the dead mouse, both victims of Edward's grotesque experiments, the peacock that is killed by one of the Auxiliaries, and Edward's beloved pigs, slaughtered by the Sinn Fein. On the other hand, when we try to 'fix' the allegorical meaning of these elements, we run into difficulties. One of the most frequently cited examples is the marmalade cat with green eyes, usually taken to signify Irishness (Taylor 53-4). That Farrell's novel does not lend itself to such facile reading becomes clear if we actually look at some of the scenes featuring the marmalade cats.

The most memorable episode is probably the one in which the cat that habitually reclines in old Mrs Rappaport's lap unexpectedly attacks the plump stuffed pheasant decorating the hat of one of the old ladies residing in the hotel. It is undoubtedly inadequate to claim that the cat's assault is in some way reminiscent of the threat of violence represented by the Irish. First of all, the emotional key of the scene (what we might call its *Stimmung*) is defined by the major's lurking jealousy of Edward over Sarah Devlin. The Major 'coldly watched' the troubled expression on Edward's face, his gaze anticipating the cat's 'bitter green eyes [...] glued on the plump pheasant' (214). In fact, the cat's violent attack, rendered grotesque by its outlandish object, has something vaguely sexual about it, especially in the context of the Major's dormant fears and his crippling inhibitions that provide the emotional tone of the episode. By pouncing upon the object of its desire, the cat might be said to carry out what the Major is never able to bring himself to do. The 'political allegory' vaguely suggested by the animal's colouring is made ironical by what follows: the scene continues with the excessively violent retribution of Evans, the Irish tutor, who suddenly 'springs forward' (just like the cat before him) and deals it a heavy blow, eventually hurling the animal against the wall 'with terrible force', with 'fierce exultation' (215) in his face. Since the inner world of the tutor remains entirely self-enclosed throughout the text, no-one even guesses at the motivations for such a violent reprisal.

The other scene in which an identical cat plays a major role is when, towards the end, the Major is trying to persuade Mrs Rappaport to leave the Majestic and return to Britain. The old lady, who is blind and has an extremely tenuous grasp on the external world, believes that they want to force her to return to Calcutta where she had spent her youth, and protests violently, with the cat staring piercingly into the Major's eyes and crouching on her lap 'like a furry bulldog' (367). A bulldog, furry or not, is clearly not a very Irish symbol; if we insist on a symbolic reading, the cat may be said to 'represent' Mrs Rappaport's uncomprehending but stubborn militancy. When the cat relaxes, sensing that its mistress is no longer under pressure, it rubs its head against Mrs Rappaport's other constant accessory, the hard leather bolster she wears strapped round her waist at all times. Thus, instead of an all-too-obvious allegory of Ireland rising against the colonizers, the cat seems to stand for the unthinking, animal aspect of the colonial matriarch who is always ready to fight the mutinous natives.

The purpose of these micro-readings is to suggest that, if *Troubles* is an allegorical text, it is certainly not allegorical in the sense of various items in the fictional world 'standing for' some abstract notion ('cat' standing for 'Irishness'). The allegorical impulse, while clearly detectable in the text, manifests itself in more complex ways, and a brief comparison with the best known modernist allegory, Kafka's *The Castle* (1926), might go some way towards exploring the workings of this impulse in Farrell's text. Although there is at least one crucial difference between the Majestic Hotel and Kafka's castle – the former is obviously and obtrusively material, living its own life – the Majestic does resemble Kafka's castle and Mervyn Peake's Gormenghast (Bergonzi 60) to the extent that its interior space remains unmappable, rejecting the totalizing gaze as well as the attempts to chart its depths. Upon his arrival in the Majestic, the Major rings the bell that he finds on the reception desk:

> The sound echoed over the dusty tiled floor and down gloomy carpeted corridors and away through open double-leafed doors into lounges and bars and smoking-rooms and upwards into spiral after spiral of the broad staircase [...] until it reached the maids' quarters and rang in the vault high above his head (so high that he could hardly make out the elegant gilt tracery that webbed it); from this vault there was suspended on an immensely long chain, back down the middle of the many spirals from one floor to another to within a few inches of his head, a great glass chandelier studded with dead electric bulbs. One of the glass tassels

chimed faintly for a brief moment beside his ear. Then all was silent again except for the steady tick-tock of an ancient pendulum clock over the reception desk showing the wrong time. (16)

The long first sentence, the meandering syntax of which re-enacts the imagined progress of the sound, presents the Majestic as an emphatically self-enclosed space in which everything is endlessly replicated, multiplied: corridors, lounges, bars are so numerous that only this vague plural is able to suggest their numbers. The effect, evoking Piranesi's fantastic prison etchings, is one of an unmeasurable space (besides the ubiquitous plural referring to various architectural features, the chain is 'immensely long', the vault is so high that the gilt tracery is hardly visible from below) that, paradoxically, is also radically restricted. It is as if the restrictedness of the space generates the endless repetitions, like reverberating spatial-architectural echoes. This recalls Walter Benjamin's speculations in *The Arcades Project* (1999) about the Romantic 'infinite regress of reflection' that both expanded the space of life in ever-widening circles and reduced it within ever narrower frames' (348). No wonder, then, that the only movement in the passage is that of the sound spiralling upwards ('spiral' is repeated three times), suggesting, paradoxically, that the farther it gets, the more closed in it remains, its trajectory both tracing and palpating an ever increasing degree of inwardness in a kind of *schlechte Unendlichkeit*.

The passage can also be seen as a trailer, anticipating the Major's interminable exploration of the premises that is the rest of the novel. The trajectory of the sound that, reverberating all over the infinite space, returns to the Major as the attenuated chime of a glass tassel also indicates that the Majestic is not simply a spatial symbol of the Anglo-Irish Ascendancy (its unawareness and inability to relate to the outside world), but also a projection of the Major's mental condition. This is reinforced by the Major's second, more determined attempt to announce his arrival. He 'gives a clout' to the gong beside him, generating a 'thunderous boom' (16): the Major 'could feel it growing throughout the house like a hugely swelling fruit that would burst out of all the windows. He shuddered and thought of the first moments of heavy barrage before a "show"' (17). It is this quasi-equation of the Major's body (or body-consciousness) and the hotel's interior that concludes in the first of many unexpected evocations of the war, with the result that the text establishes the reverberating interiority of the hotel-cum-big house as an objective correlative for the Major's shell-shocked mind. The Major's strange inability to leave the Majestic even after the death of his fiancée is due to this affinity between the Major's mind and the place: whatever the space of the Majestic 'means', the allegorical signification is filtered through this correlation.

Allegory, like Flaubert's stupidity, is 'both a mode of perception and a quality of objects' (Culler 178). Thus, although the Majestic is clearly allegorical in many respects, it is difficult to decide exactly what the allegorical nature of the hotel is. The affinity between the crumbling place and the Major's mind suggests that the allegory is rooted not so much in the place itself as in the way it is represented, filtered through the mind of the Major, who at one point recalls the injunction of a Scottish doctor to the effect that, as a war survivor, he ought to do the living for all the others as well as himself. The doctor is 'trying to coax him back out of the cold areas of chagrin and indifference where his mind had chosen to stray. But of course that was easier said than done, particularly at the Majestic' (286). The Major's life is curiously like an afterlife; and, if it is through his gaze that the Majestic is transfigured, we can say that the allegory of *Troubles* is a version of the melancholic allegory theorized by Walter Benjamin.

In *Troubles*, allegory is inseparable from perspective, precisely because in Farrell's Benjaminian universe an object is 'drained of all immanent meaning, it lies as pure facticity under the manipulative hand of the allegorist' (Eagleton 6). One thing that *Troubles* does brilliantly is the overlaying of personal, communal and historical perspectives, making the politics of perspective inseparable from the aesthetics or poetics of representing both the Majestic and Ireland in general. The most obvious layer of this predicament is that, in a rethinking of the modernist poetics of history, *Troubles* emphasizes the fact that (historical) experience is available only through a particular perspective (as Scanlan says, 'history reaches the reader through refraction and indirection' (51)). In a sense, the very possibility of 'historical experience' as such is questioned: it seems to evaporate between the vaguely registered direct experiences of the characters and the newspaper articles that are already texts, interpretations rather than experiences. All these aspects are evident in the way the Ireland of the Troubles is consistently misread through a twofold filter of an inevitably politicized perspective, and these two overtly political perspectives are further filtered through the private (but in fact far from entirely private) distortions of the Major's point of view. In the novel Ireland is misread in two basic ways by those members of the Anglo-Irish community whose perspective becomes a structuring principle, and the Major occupies a key role in the way both of these readings take shape: he both embodies these misreadings and offers a particular slant or inflection that unwittingly questions their relevance.

First of all, Ireland is conceived by most characters as a non-European colonial space, and the Major is in this sense an imperial subject, a newcomer from the mother country arriving in a colonial environment. From this perspective, the Majestic is reimagined as a cantonment in the Raj, having only tenuous links with the native town of Kilnalough, and one's existence in the Majestic calls forth a repetition of the politicized geography of colonial life. We have the Imperial Bar in the Hotel itself, the club outside Kilnalough with its reminiscences of Chittagong and its 'colonials' (355), and the whole environment is filtered through Edward Spencer's and Mrs Rappaport's Indian reminiscences (indeed, in Mrs Rappaport's mind, Ireland and India tend to merge). Evans is referred to as the 'appalling tutor-wallah' (81), and Spencer insists on calling a local pub 'ghusl-khana' (78). The colonial parallel is also suggested in many of the inserted newspaper cuttings, where the conflation of the Irish troubles with colonial unrest in more distant parts of the empire clearly obeys a political agenda. Upon his arrival, the Major, observing the natives, is full of colonial clichés, repeatedly marvelling at the 'typically Irish' (24) nature of much that he sees, even though as often as not, what the Major calls 'incredibly' or 'typically' Irish behaviour characterizes the inhabitants of the Majestic rather than the local population. The early scene of the game-like hunt for mutinous natives in the grounds of the Majestic also suggests a thoroughly, even obtrusively colonial context: the weapons are mixed in with various kinds of sporting equipment, and the expedition is accompanied by constant references to the Victorian ethics of war, the importance of 'the game' (23) itself rather than of victory. The colonial refashioning of Ireland runs into the problem that, unlike in more exotic climes, the natives are not immediately different from their rulers. In India or Africa, 'one knew instantly which side everyone was on' (103), with 'people using their skins like uniforms' (103). In Ireland, skin colour (that is, race) does not help in distinguishing the warring parties; the tokens of religion (which replaces race in the Irish context), if at all visible, are obviously cultural. The result is that, lacking more obvious marks of difference, the paraphernalia of Catholicism – 'One of those frightfully gruesome Sacred Hearts' (78) – are likened to pagan idols in an effort to recreate the absolute and visible difference between the natives and the colonists.

The opening mock-battle, the Major's first experience of colonial life, is also related to the second type of politicized understanding of the Troubles. If the Irish are degraded by being implicitly dehumanized and likened to Indian natives, their resistance is also denied dignity because it does not deserve the appellation of 'war'. The role of the Major's perspective as somehow both representing the accepted Majestic view and being at an angle to it is particularly ironical, as he is the only member of the Anglo-Indian community to have seen combat (he is a war veteran in what is a war zone). The Major is rapidly getting tired 'trying to comprehend a situation which defies comprehension, a war without battles or trenches' (154). What is confusion for the Major becomes the basis of value-laden dichotomies for others, as in Lloyd George's address quoted in one of the newspaper cuttings:

> If it is necessary to have further powers we shall seek them (Hear, hear), for civilization cannot permit a defiance of this kind of the elementary rules of its existence (Hear, hear). These men who indulge in these murders say it is war. If it is war, they, at any rate, cannot complain if we apply some of the rules of war [...] If it is war, the rules of war apply. (256)

In this approach, war appears as a prerequisite of civilization (contrasted to the barbarity of the natives) because it has certain rules that have to be observed during atrocities – one rule being that war is fought exclusively by male individuals in easily distinguishable uniforms.

Thus, war is brought up as a perspective for reading the Troubles only to be dismissed as irrelevant, at least for the official Anglo-Irish view and for the residents of the Majestic. It is here that the individual perspective of the Major becomes crucial. Unlike Lloyd George or the militant old ladies, the Major knows war, and he knows that war, contrary to what Lloyd George says, is where rules do *not* apply. 'In wartime innocent old people were killed', he thinks, referring to a scene he witnessed in Dublin, and goes on to add, 'but Ireland was a peaceful country' (92). The novel presents the Troubles rather like what Clausewitz calls 'real war' as opposed to 'absolute war' (368–9): real war is what actually happens, defined by contingencies and accidents, defying the rules of warfare, yet creating a zone where there is 'no neutral space' (371), a zone where violence erupts in unpredictable moments and places, as in the scene of the cat and the tutor. In such a zone, the meaning attributed to individuals, places and objects becomes provisional and shifting; once again, the Major's problems of making sense of the situation have broader reverberations.

Since, as I have suggested, Ireland and the Majestic appear throughout the novel as an objective correlative of the shell-shocked Major's mental condition, the relationship that is established in his mind between the Troubles and the Great War is not one of a tidy set of correlations. The Major deliberately avoids both Edward's war memorial in the dining room and participation in the morning memorial services officiated by his host. He also feels alienated from the pageant of the Peace Day parade in Dublin. In these solemn and over-choreographed ceremonies, and in other scenes in the novel too, the Major is a spectral figure. He is always referred to (even by the narrator) as the Major, with each of these references becoming an evocation of the war. He materializes as an all-too-real actual fragment or residue of the war, embodying direct continuity (the war is still going on in his shell-shocked mind) in opposition to the reassuring pastness of the heroes' names inscribed in the memorial book. The monument is preferred to the returning soldier. In this sense, the Major is not simply someone whose access to 'history' is hindered by several factors but someone who, without knowing what it is, comes allegorically to embody 'history'.

Rather than being consciously remembered by the Major, in *Troubles* the war intrudes in unpredictable flashes – 'the cold and constant surprise' (42) – that fail to create any meaningful pattern: 'the war, which he thought he had escaped, had pursued and caught him after all' (265). It is not only that smudged photographs seen in the papers haunt him and that his sleep is 'punctuated by nightmares which continually returned him to the trenches' (266), but there are more unlikely reminders even within the Majestic, like the dish that reminds him of a Boche helmet or the cook's kitchen knife that is 'as big as a bayonet' (48). Sometimes the parallels are more abstract, like when the guests of the Majestic retire for the night 'like a platoon under fire' (38); returning to his own room, the Major has to fight 'a squadron of fat brown moths' (38). The unexpected flashes include the vision of the naked maid seen when he wanders into one of the rooms, reminding him of the 'democratic' (364) effects of nakedness experienced during the war, or, in a different way, his bloodstained field-glasses, removed during the war from the 'massive punctured chest of an apoplectic Prussian officer' (172). It is this object that indicates the presence of the war as a perspective (introduced through the placid Major). When the Major, at the time of the clandestine harvesting of Spencer's fields of corn, is scanning the landscape through his field-glasses, he unwittingly transforms the place into a war zone: war is that which is seen through the perspective provided by field-glasses. The Major fails to make sense of Ireland as a place of proper war, yet it is he who – through his field-glasses, through his spectral presence – transfigures the place into a war zone.

Ireland, then, is seen variously as a war zone and as a colonial space – two frames or perspectives in which emotional colouring is inextricably entangled with politics, as in what is a veritable *mise-en-scene* of 'perspective' when the Major and Captain Bolton are watching the crowd through the binoculars after the alleged miracle of the bleeding statue. The Major is contemplating the huge waves that seem to be on the verge of engulfing the young Irishman who is speaking to the crowd, but then realizes that the wave is in fact much farther out: 'it was, after all, only the lack of perspective that made it seem as if he would be swept away' (248).

What the Major calls a lack of perspective is simply the lack of a larger perspective, the creaturely impossibility to step out of one's restricted point of view. *Troubles* is a novel that is almost obsessively concerned with perspective, exploring the perspectival, anamorphotic and conditioned nature of all perception and knowledge, and replete with allusions to the limitations of perspective. Shell-shocked and somewhat dazed, the Major is a self-consciously Jamesian reflector whose distorted view implies a politics of which he himself is entirely unaware, and the narrative, apart from a few brief sections, is filtered through and inflected by his clearly 'inadequate' perspective. As a somewhat incoherent bundle of received imperial opinions, perceptual, mental and emotional limitations, and a vague, universal but inefficient compassion, the Major might even be read as a walking allegory of 'point of view'. Throughout the novel, the incessant process of the 'worlding' and 'unworlding' of his environment embeds and colours all the happenings: the episode when he enters a room full of cats, with 'the room abruptly dissolved in a shattering percussion of sneezes' (135) is just a local example of a general strategy. The text stresses the various kinds of limitations of the Major's perception to such an extent that there is practically no episode in which we are not forced to become aware of the intrusive – restricting, distorting – presence of a 'perspective'.

In Farrell, melancholy is not unlike the Renaissance melancholy that comes from the ineluctable contingency of the individual perspective; the realization that, lacking a transcendentally guaranteed perspective – this is the 'lack of perspective' the Major complains of – the individual has to bear the terrible burden of assigning meaning to all that s/he sees from a contingent perspective, knowing that all meanings assigned in this way are bound to be provisional and arbitrary. Such awareness paralyses the observer and results in an inability to act (including the mental act of assigning meaning to the things of the world). The refusal of the objects of the world to solidify into a fixed meaning is the correlative of the melancholic ailment called acedia or accidie. It is enough to consider the Major's doomed love for Sarah to understand that he suffers from 'the perversion of a will that wants the object, but not the way that leads to it, and which simultaneously desires and bars the path to his or her own desire' (Agamben 6). The most energetic activity of which he seems capable is the vivid daydreaming in his nest in the linen room, supine and naked in the tropical heat of the place, as if the extent of his physical passivity were in proportion to the intensity of his mental life.

Afflicted with what Walter Benjamin calls a 'dullness of the heart' (*Origin* 155), the Major, when he is not wandering restlessly about the Majestic, is most typically seen 'slumped in an armchair' (197), contemplating the world 'with melancholy interest' (149) or 'transfixed with sadness' (197). If the Major is the idle, contemplative melancholic, Edward is the manic one, always embarking enthusiastically on projects that remain unfinished (recalling Dürer's allegory of *Melencolia* (1514), full of discarded instruments of various abandoned pursuits). The clearest examples are his aborted 'economy drive' (161) and his absurd scientific experiments, as when he wants to get the exact measurement of the thirst induced by fear. Interruption is also present as a larger structuring – or destructuring – principle: the novel is studded with dozens of interrupted or just broken sentences, including Ripon's explanations, Edward's unfinished confessions, the conversations between Mr Devlin and the Major, Miss Porteous's unfinished sentence, or the Major's many similar flounderings, instances when he is 'unable to broach the subject' (199), or his marriage proposal to Sarah. These local instances of aposiopesis indicate a more general narrative aposiopesis, a world where things planned by characters are not brought to their conclusion.

Doomed to passivity, the Major is basically defined by his gaze. He watches the others in a variety of moods, from his military surveillance of the fields through the field-glasses through 'lurking' and 'spying' (196) to voyeurism. Most of the time, gazing replaces acting: the Major is excluded from life, which is invariably the life of others, as emblematized in the scene when he is left standing outside the room in which Ripon is probably deceiving his wife. When something actually happens to the Major, even the syntax suggests that he suffers the action rather than initiating it, as in the scene when he 'suddenly found himself being kissed by Sarah' (226). His most typical mood is a puzzled fascination, a mixture of bewilderment and admiration especially for practically anything that involves vivacity and passion. From his perspective, any activity that requires energy is admirable, independently of its intention, including Edward's antics or Captain Bolton's devouring of a rose, thorns and all. This is what we see in the scene – framed by images of the Major's scanning of the landscape for the clandestine harvesters – where he watches the twins dancing, both admiring their youthful vivacity and relishing the 'enjoyable display' (174). However, even outright voyeurism seems to be beyond his powers: it is delegated to old Mr Norton, the Major's double in this scene. The Major thinks even Mr Norton 'truly amazing' (175): 'one almost had to admire him for the tenacity with which he held on to the remnants of his youth' (175).

The paradoxical nature of the Major's filtering role is inseparable from the originality of the novel's narrative technique that involves more than those passages that follow the Major's rambling thoughts. Such sections, in which free indirect discourse, direct quotation and narrative diegesis modulate into each other with imperceptible ease and smoothness, recall post-Jamesian writers like Elizabeth Bowen, Henry Green and Richard Hughes. But it is in the rendering of dialogue where Farrell works out a unique way of indicating both the necessary inflectedness of all the information that reaches the reader and the Major's vagueness. In terms of perspective and narrative, the novel's most conspicuous feature is the vagueness, blandness and softness of its centre, and the Major's consciousness is clearly the centre that does not hold. John Spurling claims that the Major is 'a perfect sounding-board for everything that happens' (163). His metaphor is perhaps more apt than the Jamesian 'reflector', for the latter evokes an optical metaphorics of straight lines of light and angles and the hardness of glass, while what we have is an amorphous, soft interiority that reflects (upon) whatever it receives only to absorb it in its shapeless centre. This is most evident, as I have suggested, in the way the Major's conversations (oral and written) are rendered. Most of what is communicated to the Major reaches us in a form of reported speech that is filtered through him without being transformed. One of the most sustained examples is the rendering of Sarah's letter to London:

> She had no reason for sending him a letter (she wrote) and he didn't have to read it if he didn't want to. But she was in bed again with 'an unmentionable illness' and bored to tears, literally ('I sometimes burst into tears for no reason at all') and, besides, her face was so covered in spots that she looked 'like a leopard' and she had become so ugly that little children fled wailing if they saw her at the window and nobody ever came to see her these days and she had no friends now that Angela had died and (that reminded her) why had he not come over to say hello on the day of Angela's funeral... after all, she (Sarah) didn't bite, but then she supposed that he was too high and mighty to be seen talking to the likes of her and he, probably, anyway, couldn't read her writing because she was scribbling away in bed, her fingers 'half frozen off' and surrounded by stone hot-water jars against which she kept cracking her 'poor toes' and which were practically freezing anyway. (104)

The text proceeds like this for almost six pages. The effect is twofold. On the one hand, this is Sarah's letter as it is *being read* by the Major, that is, the Major is present throughout not only as the reader but also as the addressee, the cause, the person without whom the words would not have existed in the first place. On the other hand, however, the Major's position as reader is also hollowed out, as the indirect discourse follows the rhythm of Sarah's sentences rather than of his mind, and the Major is simply a semi-transparent medium that does not seem to modify the message – or not quite. It is the internal quotations that introduce a note of ambiguity. As the text seems to follow the wording of Sarah's letter very closely, they look gratuitous: there seems to be no point in putting certain bits of the letter in inverted commas if, apart from the grammatical markers of indirect speech, it all seems to be unchanged. It is precisely the smoothness and faithfulness of this transfer that the inverted commas or inserted quotations seem to question. Their presence suggests that the rendering of the letter (or of the spoken communications in other parts of the novel) is perhaps, after all, not complete; the dazed and unreliable perspective of the Major, whose mind the narrative follows, might have filtered the contents. Thus, the strategy, which is ubiquitous in the novel, asserts the necessary presence of the filtering or screening perspective that is the condition of meaning, while at the same time it cancels or erases the Major's perspective, indicating his vast inability to bear the burden of giving meaning. The Major, whose contributions are usually either deduced from the indirectly reported replies or left out entirely, is, as it were, constantly (re)defined, (re)shaped by his interlocutors – as it happens in Sarah's letter quoted above – and not only by central characters like Sarah or Edward, but also by minor figures like Sarah's father, the Dublin architect and Ripon. The emblematic scene in this respect is when the Major is first introduced to blind Mrs Rappaport, who traces his face with her fingers, but then shrieks 'That's not him! That's someone else!' (36).

It is to this figure that the burden falls of making sense of experience, of assembling and arranging the many details around him into meaningful signifying patterns. The Major's melancholy gaze is responsible for the unity of this world. This general strategy of rendering dialogue reinforces the fundamental paradox at the heart of Farrell's novel. The perspective that is always interposed between the world and the reader, that is supposed to endow with meaning the objects and inhabitants of the world, is in fact hollow, unable to shape the world. Instead of filling the objects of the world with meaning, the Major's melancholic and uncertain gaze, his 'contemplative paralysis' (Benjamin, *Origin* 140) sucks the possibility of meaning out of things, unable to transfigure them. The Major is in some ways like Benjamin's brooder whose melancholy interest ranges over a heap of rubble, a dead lore. For his melancholic gaze, things 'stand for' the loss of meaning in their very signifying function (Pensky 26–8). A shell-shocked soldier, the Major can only see the world under the sign of a memory that is largely inaccessible to him:

> If the object becomes allegorical under the gaze of melancholy, if melancholy causes life to flow out of it and it remains behind dead, but eternally secure, then it is exposed to the allegorist, it is unconditionally in his power. That is to say it is

now quite incapable of emanating any meaning or significance of its own. Such significance as it has, it acquires from the allegorist. (Benjamin *Origin* 183–4)

In Farrell's novel, as in Benjamin's modern allegory, the point is not primarily a gap that opens between social existence and some essential being, but rather a 'diffraction of selfhood through the infinity of its objects' (Pensky 170). In this sense, the Major becomes emblematic in his self-effacement and inability to endow things with meaning. As Ross Chambers put it in his account of early modern melancholy, the identity of the melancholic 'has become the truth of modernism' (208). Although in *Troubles* 'everybody is touched by' melancholy (197), it is precisely his blandness, his inability to make sense of the world that makes the Major stand out as an adequate observer, his shell-shock an adequate means of worlding in its very inadequacy. The Major is melancholic also in the Freudian sense of unsuccessful mourning. Shell-shock is at the same time the inability to mourn: 'the Major was once again trying to delve into the past with the paralysed fingers of his memory, hoping to grasp some warmth or emotion, the name perhaps of a dead friend that might mean the beginning of grief, the beginning of an end to grief' (42). The Scottish doctor's injunction that he must 'do the living for all the others as well as yourself' (286) proves an enormous, unbearable burden for this grossly inadequate and unbelieving Christ-figure.

In what is perhaps his most emotional moment, the Major complains of his metaphysical displacement: 'In all the aching void of the world where should he go? Why should he choose one place rather than another?' (225) When he is not slumped in an armchair, he is 'wandering aimlessly' (183), like the melancholic Andreas Tscherning quoted by Benjamin: 'Nowhere do I find rest, I must even quarrel with myself, I sit, I lie, I stand, but am always in thought' (*Origin* 138). Without a place he could belong to, the Major adopts 'the nomadic existence of moving from room to room' (261), obeying a compulsion that is, again, not unrelated to his shell shock. Persecuted by his unwelcome memories,

> he felt himself compelled to keep moving from room to room, corridor to corridor, upstairs and down. Only now did he consider that this compulsion might stem from the irrational fear that a trench-mortar shell was about to land in the spot where he had been standing a moment before, invisible explosions that tracked him from the lounge to the dining-room to the library to the billiard room, on and on, perpetually allowing him to escape by a fraction of a second. (266)

The non-hierarchical space of the Majestic is the objective correlative of his internal predicament and his consequent nomadism also in this sense. In such entropic space, everybody keeps changing rooms whenever something goes wrong, and characters become increasingly accustomed to this permanent displacement. As a figure who carries this nomadity in himself, the Major becomes the spirit of the house, the genius loci, while also remaining a ghostly presence; in the course of the novel, the Majestic ceases to belong to the Spencers and becomes more and more relevant for the Major, who takes over from Edward.

The aesthetics and politics of detail

In one of the most haunting scenes of the novel, the Major, upon his return to Ireland, comes across the forgotten letter of his fiancée, written some time before her death. Instead of a revelation that would perhaps tell the Major why he has returned to the Majestic, the letter is full of the customary insipid observations and details. The Major finds himself unable to read the letter, because, as he thinks, 'the detail in it is intolerable' (143). We never learn why he thinks so, but presumably not because he is mourning Angela, whom he hardly knew. The unbearable details are not those of a shared intimacy. It is more likely that the details are intolerable because they go on interminably but fail to add up; because, instead of building up a whole, they are in the way of the whole.

The motif of details getting in the way of seeing the whole is present on several levels of the narrative. The infinite vastness of the Majestic is impossible to control and survey: instead of surrendering to a totalizing perspective, it breaks down into details that because of the impossibility of panoramic vision fail to cohere. Both in terms of its internal politics and in terms of its readability and chartability, the place is made up of separate, independently functioning domains and zones, like that of the tutor's, who is 'forgotten in this remote part of the house and lived his own life' (254). The proprietor Edward Spencer, obsessed with keeping Sinn Feiners away from the estate, does not seem to be preoccupied with the internal politics of the hotel, letting the parallel zones exist in their own ways.

The focus on details, the 'allegorical dismembering' (Benjamin, *Arcades* 365), is frequently a correlative of the Major's fragmented perspective, as, for instance, in the scene in which he is confronted with the world of sexual passion and violence from which he is forever excluded. This episode is dominated by close-ups of details that lend a slightly fetishistic colouring to the Major's perspective: The metonymic detail of 'an iron bed and a tangle of dirty sheets' (342) which evidences the affair between Sarah and Edward is the closest the Major ever gets to sex in the book. In this 'bizarre scene of destruction' (341), there is even a *par excellence* fetishistic object that is, however, also grotesque by its incongruity and gender ambiguity: an odd man's shoe smouldering in the embers of the fire, suggesting an intensity of passion (of whatever kind) unknown for the Major. Contemplating the bed and a discarded dress, the Major just stands there, 'painfully absorbing every detail' so that 'when he turned his head away every tiniest thread was stitched into his memory' (343). At the same time, he notices another telltale detail, 'the blue mark of the bruise left by Captain Bolton's fingers' (343) disfiguring Sarah's arm, another intimation of the world of violent passion inaccessible for him. The evening concludes, with great appropriateness, with the Major asexually sharing his bed with the twins who had nearly been raped by British soldiers a few minutes ago, 'lying in the middle of this chaste, warm, heavenly sandwich' (345). If the fetish, as Jean-Joseph Goux says, entails 'the erasure of a genesis, the obliteration of a history' (33), then the non-epiphanic (or anti-epiphanic) details in *Troubles* are fetishistic inasmuch as they do not suggest either a transcendental level where they would make sense or a continuous process (history) that would endow them with meaning.

In her book on the aesthetics of detail, Naomi Schor talks about the 'classical equation of the Ideal with the absence of particularity' (3). This idea is very relevant to the Benjaminian, melancholic allegoricity of Farrell's novel where details keep getting in the way both of purposeful action and of making sense of the narrated world, dismantling the arc of narrated events or processes. The more details are amassed in recounting an episode, the more likely it is that the continuity of the action suffers. Schor argues that allegory is '*the* modern art of detail' (60), adding that the allegorical detail is 'disembodied and destabilized' (61), a disproportionately enlarged ornamental detail that, bearing the seal of transcendence, testifies to the loss of all transcendental signifieds in the modern period (61). 'This close attention to detail', writes John Spurling about Farrell, 'which starting soberly in fact can later be made to yield episodes of pure surrealism, is brought to a fine art in the three historical novels' (159). I suggest that Farrell's technique in *Troubles* is that of the melancholic allegorist. As Benjamin claims, that 'which the allegorical intention has fixed upon is sundered from the customary contexts of life' (*Arcades* 329), adding that 'allegory views existence, as it does art, under the sign of fragmentation and ruins' (330).

The effect of the allegorical detail in *Troubles* is mostly comic, but usually in a gruesome or grotesque manner that fails to bring relief. For instance, in the scene of the attempted double rape of the twins, the very practical problem of undressing the drunk and unconscious Charity diverts the attention of rapist and reader alike from the grim ulterior purpose. When the Major is giving a decent funeral to the old spaniel called Rover after a mercy killing by Edward, he chooses to bury Rover too close to a tree, and the roots prevent him from laying out the dog, which is thus buried in a rather grotesque stance, standing on his hind legs. A similar strategy is used in the scene when the Major is performing the obsequies for the unknown Sinn Feiner shot by Edward who simply dumped the corpse in a potting-shed. It is because he looks at the body in too much detail that the Major notices the jaw of the corpse hanging open and decides to do something about it. He closes the mouth which, however, falls open once again.

> He tried again and the same thing happened. The position of the head was wrong, that was the trouble. On the shelf below the silver he found a copy of Wisden's Almanac for 1911 which he judged to have the right thickness. He blew the dust from it and slipped it under the boy's head. This time the mouth stayed closed. (382)

While the Major is striving to reinstate the corpse into the symbolic system by going through the motions of a wake, the sheer materiality of the body gets in the way, also infecting the rest of the scene. The redundant details of the book distract from the action: it is Wisden's Cricketers' Almanac, a book of incongruous yet also apposite imperial associations, and also a book that is dated, 'dead' like the corpse, a compendium of ten-year-old information. The proximity of the corpse, this Benjaminian emblem of Baroque melancholy, means that the Almanac is used not for its contents but for its thickness and materiality.

The contagiousness of the materiality of the corpse does not end here. After these uncharacteristically energetic exertions, the Major slumps down into an armchair, sitting motionlessly for five minutes (382), and when Edward joins him, 'with his tilted head and mouth open', he 'strangely resembles the corpse's attitude of a few minutes earlier' (382). After this spell of infectious rigor mortis, the Major proceeds to imagine the way Edward must have disposed of the dead body, dragging it to the potting-shed. The more details the Major evokes, the more gruesome the scene becomes in his imagination: he next recalls how he had made sure that the Sinn Feiner was in fact dead, the fatal round-shaped wound that was found only after a careful search. The section obsessed with the dead body concludes with the Major's visit to the Catholic priest. The Major's eyes follow the priest's gaze, and when they rest on the crucifix on the wall, the text returns to the image of the corpse, which is fragmented into details, some of them, like the parted lips, evoke the dead Sinn Feiner: 'The yellowish naked body, the straining ribs, the rolling eyes and parted lips, the langurously draped arms and long trailing fingers, the feet crossed to econimize on nails, the cherry splash of blood from the side' (387). The catalogue of details does not lead to any conclusion, yet, despite the debunking and sacrilegious references to economizing and cherry splashes, the passage that links the dead Sinn Feiner to the body of Christ through the melancholic gaze of the Major suggests the key to melancholic allegory: the inability of the spirit to transfigure matter, 'the profound gulf between materiality and matter' (Eagleton 4). At some point, the allegorical vision of the novel has to be confronted with the Christian image of the dead body as a site of the transcendence and transfiguration of materiality. But in *Troubles*, it is not the vision of the body of Christ that redeems the former vision of the corpse that has transmogrified its environment in a kind of anti-allegory: instead, it is the body of Christ that is swallowed up by the logic of the allegorical, unredeemed and anti-epiphanic detail. On the other hand, the Major, the possessor of the gaze that turns away from the vision and hope of redemption, is himself a kind of Christ figure, a holy idiot, the hollowed-out, melancholic transmuter of this allegorical world. 'Melancholy' says Benjamin, 'emerges from the depth of the creaturely realm' (*Origin* 146): the morbidity residing in objects is revealed for the subjective eye precisely because the subject himself is an object, a thing.

In *Troubles*, as in the Baroque allegory of Benjamin, the world of things overcomes man in his creatureliness, just as 'the house asserts itself against its remaining occupants' (McEwan 133). People, as old Dr Ryan is never tired of repeating, are 'insubstantial' (*Troubles* 407), while the physical world is present in its sheer, indomitable materiality, with the sheer reality of things always undermining and defying ideas in ways that range from the tragic to the grotesque and farcical. The ideas and the things that fleetingly contain them are cut loose from each other, creating a volatile and dysfunctional dialectic.

While modernist literature – at least as Julia Kristeva and Max Pensky conceive of it – sublimates melancholia, with meaning translated into the frustrated fascination with the rifts that remain in the proliferation of signs, a 'melancholy jouissance' (Pensky 38) of the allegorical, there is no such aesthetic sublimation in Farrell. It is here that the politics which resides in the poetics of allegory becomes visible. The impossibility of modernist sublimation is due to the link between allegory and history. 'Melancholy itself, however' suggests Adorno, 'is the historical spirit in its natural depth' (qtd. in Düttmann 49). The absence of transcendence means that all meaning is immanent, coming from the series of events themselves. There is only history. As Benjamin proposes, 'In the final analysis the image of petrified unrest called up by allegory is a historical image' (*Arcades* 366); or, one might add, the image of history. In *Troubles*, however, history, the succession of events is unable to provide the details with meaning. On the one hand, the newspaper cuttings are clearly unable to provide a framework in which the individual events become meaningful: 'What could one learn from the details of chaos?' (154) muses the Major. On the other hand, the action of the novel is fragmented into self-enclosed units, as indicated by the ubiquity of temporal adverbs like 'on the following day' (195), 'one morning' (197) and dozens of other examples like these. Just as the adverbs fail to create connections, there is no overarching plot structure. In melancholic allegory, the successive segments of the plot are simply items in a string or 'rubbish heap of partial, inauthentic actions' (Benjamin, *Origin* 139), with no inherent connection between the allegorical items that are laid out in what looks like temporal sequence.

Ronald Binns is perfectly right when he claims that history 'is represented as a dimly understood force which moves sluggishly towards the incomprehending and indifferent inhabitants of the Majestic, only at the end engulfing their world, dispossessing them and driving them out' (52). In this historical novel, history is not a horizon of meaning, a teleological process (for instance the events leading to Irish independence), but a relentless attrition that has no purpose, unredeemed by any transcendental telos or meaning. In Benjaminian allegory, the non-dialectical relationship between nature and history is profoundly ambiguous. On the one hand, as Carol Jacobs puts it, 'nature in Trauerspiel is that which has already become history – as written signs that mark the mortality of that which they ostensibly name' (6). On the other hand, Benjamin claims that the basis of allegory is 'the movement from history to nature' (*Origin* 182); creation 'absorbs history back into itself' (91), the materiality of the world triumphing over symbolic meaning. For Benjamin, the key of this process is the ruin: 'In the ruin, history has physically merged into the setting' (177–178). *Troubles* is set in what is a vast and rambling ruin, and there is a further irony in the fact that the only 'majestic' or magnificent phenomenon in the novel is the declining Majestic Hotel that, as Bergonzi says, 'diminishes the human characters. It is not just a static symbol, but is malignly active in decay' (61). The only uninterrupted 'story' chronicled by the text is that of the crumbling of the building, absorbing into its decay all meaning and all effort at meaning-making. In the course of the novel, the hotel grows – or deteriorates – to fit the shell-shocked Major's melancholy, allegorical temper. The final assault against the Major and his subsequent ordeal also dramatize this melancholic process.

The attack takes place in the apple-house, among piles of 'bruised and rotting' apples, in 'a pungent smell of rotting fruit' (400), and the Major is buried under an avalanche of this putrescence. When he is taken down to the seashore, the text becomes almost stilted in its efforts to cancel the possibility of agency through a proliferation of passive structures, as if the extinguishing of his consciousness entailed the end of human agency as such: 'Then the Major's limp body was conveyed lower still, on to the rocks, and from there with considerable difficulty was handed to the beach' (400). The kind of death that is intended for the Major amounts to an allegory of the relentless triumph of weighty creatureliness, the slow crumbling of the human body under the weight of matter into amorphous materiality. Just like the Black and Tan soldier ahead of him, he is 'buried up to his neck in the sand, ready for the incoming tide' (400) and arranged in a kneeling position so as to be able to bear the weight of creatureliness: 'a heavy rock was then laid on the back of his calves' (401). After his re-emergence from this sandy-watery grave – his unlikely rescuers are three returning old ladies – the deterioration of the Majestic is accelerated and concluded by a fire, ignited and presided over by the butler Murphy, 'a hideous, cadaverous figure' (408), yet another memento mori. The aftermath of the cataclysm is heralded by two miracles: the inexplicable pregnancy of Viola O'Neill and the survival of the statue of Venus (also evoking the earlier miracle of the bleeding statue of Mary) among the charred ruins of the Majestic, spotted by the Major on his last 'melancholy visit' (410) to the place. While in Ireland an ironic immaculate conception signals regeneration (Viola insists that she has not been with men), the Major, like a melancholic Pygmalion, prefers the statue of Venus, and makes arrangements to have it sent to him, intending to live his life with it.

The novel, thus, ends with the Major's choice of an allegorical figure over the life that seems to have eluded him forever. The final gesture encapsulates the strategy of Farrell's novel, where the melancholic, disabused trope of allegory is 'chosen' against the romantic ideology of the symbol and the concomitant devaluation of allegory (cf. Culler 226, Benjamin, *Arcades* 374). The stake of Farrell's very modern Baroque allegory is the possibility of the 'salvation of phenomena by means of ideas' (Benjamin, *Origin* 34), and the melancholic gaze of the brooder which assigns admittedly temporary and arbitrary meanings to the things of the world is like the negative of the transfiguration of the objects of the world by the spirit.

The purpose of this chapter was to re-read J. G. Farrell's *Troubles* from the vantage point provided by a hypothetical 'continental' (that is, 'European') perspective, and thereby to dislodge the novel from the relatively unrewarding critical contexts in which his work has been read in Britain. As the chapter has shown, seeing the novel as related to Kafka's *The Castle* as much as to postcolonial fiction, and interpreting the unique point of view technique, narrative strategies and major motifs of *Troubles* from the perspective supplied by Walter Benjamin's theory of melancholic allegory enable us to see many features of the novel in a fresh light, including the strange and bland passivity of the main reflecting consciousness, the obsessive interest in perspective, the treatment of history, the ubiquitous phenomenon of broken sentences and narrative lines, the nomadic existence of the residents of the Majestic Hotel, as well as the strategy of indicating, through the proliferation of physical details, the inability of human imagination to transfigure the intransigent materiality of objects. From a Benjaminian perspective, Farrell's novel offers an unrelenting view of what Terry Eagleton, in his book on Benjamin, calls 'the profound gulf between materiality and matter' (4).

Works cited

Agamben, Giorgio. *Stanzas: Word and Phantasm in Western Culture*. Trans. Ronald L. Martinez. Minneapolis: U of Minnesota P, 1993.
Appleyard, Brian. *The Pleasures of Peace*. London: Faber, 1990.
Benjamin, Walter. *The Origin of German Tragic Drama*. Trans. John Osborne. London: Verso, 1998.
———. *The Arcades Project*. Trans. Howard Eiland and Kevin McLaughlin. Cambridge, MA: The Belknap Press of Harvard UP, 1999.
Bergonzi, Bernard. 'Fictions of History', in *The Contemporary English Novel*. Ed. by Malcolm Bradbury and David Palmer. NY: Holmes and Meier, 1979. 41–65.
Binns, Ronald. *J. G. Farrell*. London: Methuen, 1986.
Booker, M. Keith. *Colonial Power, Colonial Texts: India in the Modern British Novel*. Ann Arbor: U of Michigan P, 1997.
Bradbury, Malcolm. *The Modern British Novel*. London: Secker and Warburg, 1993.
Byatt, A. S. 'People in Paper Houses: Attitudes to "Realism" and "Experiment" in English Postwar Fiction', in *The Contemporary English Novel*. Ed. by Malcolm Bradbury and David Palmer. NY: Holmes and Meier, 1979. 19–42.
Chambers, Ross. *The Writing of Melancholy: Modes of Opposition in Early French Modernism*. Chicago: U of Chicago P, 1993.
Connor, Steven. *The English Novel in History 1950–1995*. London: Routledge, 1996.
Crane, Ralph J. and Jennifer Livett. *Troubled Pleasures: The Fiction of J. G. Farrell*. Dublin: Four Courts Press, 1997.
Culler, Jonathan. *Flaubert: The Uses of Uncertainty*. London: Paul Elek, 1974.

Drabble, Margaret. 'Things Fall Apart', in J. G Farell: *The Hill Station*, Ed. by John Spurling. London: Flamingo, 1989 [1981]. 178-91.

Düttmann, Alexaner García. *The Gift of Language*. Trans. Arline Lyons. London: Athlone, 2000.

Eagleton, Terry. *Walter Benjamin or Towards a Revolutionary Criticism*. London: Verso, 2009[1981].

Farrell, J. G. *The Singapore Grip*. London: Weidenfeld and Nicolson, 1978.

———. *Troubles*. Harmondsworth: Penguin, 1981[1970].

———. *The Siege of Krishnapur*. London: Flamingo, 1989 [1973].

———. *The Hill Station*. Ed. by John Spurling. London: Flamingo, 1989 [1981].

Goux, Jean-Joseph. *Symbolic Economies: After Marx and Freud*. Trans. Jennifer Curtiss Cage. Ithaca: Cornell UP, 1990.

Hartveit, Lars. 'The Carnivalistic Impulse in J. G. Farrell's *Troubles*'. English Studies 73.5, 1992: 445-457.

Head, Dominic. *The Cambridge Introduction to Modern British Fiction*. Cambridge: Cambridge UP, 2001.

Higdon, David Leon. *Shadows of the Past in Contemporary British Fiction*. London: Macmillan, 1984.

Jacobs, Carol. *In the Language of Walter Benjamin*. Baltimore: Johns Hopkins UP, 1999.

Laing, Stuart. 'Novels and the Novel', in *Society and Literature 1945-1970*. Ed. by Alan Sinfield. London: Methuen, 1978. 235-259.

McEwan, Neil. *Perspective in British Historical Fiction Today*. Basingstoke: Macmillan, 1987.

McLeod, John. *J. G. Farrell*. Tavistock: Northcote House, 2007.

Morey, Peter. *Fictions of India: Narrative and Power*. Edinburgh: Edinburgh UP, 2000.

Pensky, Max. *Melancholy Dialectics: Walter Benjamin and the Play of Mourning*. Amherst: U of Massachusetts P, 2001.

Rignall, J. M. and J. G. Walter Scott. 'Farrell, and Fictions of Empire'. *Essays in Criticism* 41.1, 1991: 11-27.

Rubin, David. *After the Raj: British Novels of India since 1947*. Hanover: UP of New England, 1986.

Scanlan, Margaret. *Traces of Another Time: History and Politics in Postwar British Fiction*. Princeton: Princeton UP, 1990.

Schor, Naomi. *Reading in Detail: Aesthetics and the Feminine*. London: Routledge, 1989.

Spurling, John. 'As Does the Bishop', in J. G. Farell: *The Hill Station*. Ed. by John Spurling. London: Flamingo, 1989 [1981]. 155-77.

Stevenson, Randall. *The British Novel since the Thirties*. Athens: U of Georgia P, 1986.

Taylor, D. J. *After the War: The Novel and England since 1945*. London: Flamingo, 1994.

Von Clausewitz, Carl. *On War*. Harmondsworth: Penguin, 1988.

Timeline of Works

1970

Richard Allen *Skinheads*
J. G. Ballard *The Atrocity Exhibition*
J. G. Farrell *Troubles*
David Lodge *Out of the Shelter*
George MacDonald Fraser *Royal Flash*
Iris Murdoch *A Fairly Honourable Defeat*
Christopher Priest *Indoctrinaire*
Muriel Spark *The Driver's Seat*

1971

Richard Allen *Suedehead*
Angela Carter *Love*
Frederick Forsyth *The Day of the Jackal*
William Golding *The Scorpion God*
M. John Harrison *The Committed Men*
M. John Harrison *The Pastel City*
B. S. Johnson *House Mother Normal*
John le Carré *The Naive and Sentimental Lover*
Doris Lessing *Briefing for a Descent into Hell*
George MacDonald Fraser *Flash for Freedom!*
Michael Moorcock *A Cure for Cancer*
Iris Murdoch *An Accidental Man*
V. S. Naipaul *In a Free State*
Muriel Spark *Not to Disturb*
Fay Weldon *Down among the Women*

1972

Richard Allen *Skinhead Escapes*
John Berger *G.*
E. R. Braithwaite *Reluctant Strangers*
Alan Burns *Dreamerika! A Surrealist Fantasy*

Angela Carter *The Internal Desire Machines of Doctor Hoffman*
Margaret Drabble *The Needle's Eye*
Margaret Drabble and B. S. Johnson (eds) *London Consequences*
Buchi Emecheta *In the Ditch*
Eva Figes *B*
Frederick Forsyth *The Odessa File*
Wilson Harris *Black Marsden*
Jennifer Johnston *The Captains and the Kings*
Kamala Markandaya *The Nowhere Man*
Michael Moorcock *The English Assassin*
Ann Quin *Tripticks*
Christopher Priest *Fugue for a Darkening Island*

1973

Richard Allen *Skinhead Girls*
Martin Amis *The Rachel Papers*
J. G. Ballard *Crash*
Alan Burns *The Angry Brigade: A Documentary Novel*
Ramsey Campbell *Demons by Daylight*
J. G. Farrell *The Siege of Krishnapur*
B. S. Johnson *Christie Malry's Own Double-Entry*
Jennifer Johnston *The Gates*
Doris Lessing *The Summer before the Dark*
George MacDonald Fraser *Flashman at the Charge*
Iris Murdoch *The Black Prince*
Muriel Spark *The Hothouse by the East River*

1974

J. G. Ballard *Concrete Island*
Buchi Emecheta *Second-Class Citizen*
Eva Figes *Days*
Frederick Forsyth *The Dogs of War*
John Fowles *The Ebony Tower*
Nadine Gordimer *The Conservationist*
Jennifer Johnston *How Many Miles to Babylon?*
John le Carré *Tinker Tailor Soldier Spy*
Doris Lessing, *The Memoirs of a Survivor*
Iris Murdoch *The Sacred and Profane Love Machine*
Muriel Spark *The Abbess of Crewe*
Christopher Priest *Inverted World*

1975

Martin Amis *Dead Babies*
J. G. Ballard *High-Rise*
Malcolm Bradbury *The History Man*
Christine Brooke-Rose *Thru*
Margaret Drabble *The Realms of Gold*
George MacDonald Fraser *Flashman in the Great Game*
M. John Harrison *The Centauri Device*
Jack Higgins *The Eagle Has Landed*
Ruth Prawer Jhabvala *Heat and Dust*
B. S. Johnson *See the Old Lady Decently*
Gabriel Josipovici *The Present*
David Lodge *Changing Places*
Ian McEwan *First Love, Last Rites*
William McIlvanney *Docherty*
Iris Murdoch *A Word Child*
V. S. Naipaul *Guerillas*
Salman Rushdie *Grimus*
Sam Selvon *Moses Ascending*
Fay Weldon *Female Friends*

1976

Ramsey Campbell *The Doll Who Ate His Mother*
Ramsey Campbell *The Height of the Scream*
Buchi Emecheta *The Bride Price*
Beryl Gilroy *Black Teacher*
Iris Murdoch *Henry and Cato*
Christopher Priest *The Space Machine*
Muriel Spark *The Takeover*
Emma Tennant *Hotel de Dream*
Fay Weldon *Remember Me*

1977

Paul Abelman *Tornado Pratt*
Angela Carter *The Passion of New Eve*
Margaret Drabble *The Ice Age*
Buchi Emecheta *The Slave Girl*
Eva Figes *Nelly's Version*
John Fowles *Daniel Martin*

Rayner Heppenstall *Two Moons*
Jennifer Johnston *Shadows on Our Skin*
John le Carré *The Honourable Schoolboy*
Doris Lessing *Memoirs of a Survivor*
George MacDonald Fraser *Flashman's Lady*
William McIlvanney *Laidlaw*
Michael Moorcock *The Condition of Muzak*
Christopher Priest *A Dream of Wessex*
Fay Weldon *Little Sisters*

1978

Martin Amis *Success*
Zoë Fairbairns, Sara Maitland, Valerie Miner, Michèle Roberts and Michelene Wandor, *Tales I Tell My Mother: A Collection of Feminist Short Stories*
J. G. Farrell *The Singapore Grip*
Wilson Harris *The Tree of the Sun*
Ian McEwan *The Cement Garden*
Ian McEwan *In Between the Sheets*
Timothy Mo *The Monkey King*
Iris Murdoch *The Sea, the Sea*
Michèle Roberts *A Piece of the Night*
Michèle Roberts *The Visitation*
Emma Tennant *The Bad Sister*
Fay Weldon *Praxis*
Raymond Williams *The Volunteers*

1979

J. G. Ballard *The Unlimited Dream Company*
Angela Carter *The Bloody Chamber*
Buchi Emecheta *The Joys of Motherhood*
Zoë Fairbairns *Benefits*
William Golding *Darkness Visible*
Nadine Gordimer *Burger's Daughter*
Jennifer Johnston *The Old Jest*
John le Carré *Smiley's People*
Doris Lessing *Shikasta*
V. S. Naipaul *A Bend in the River*
Muriel Spark *Territorial Rights*
Emma Tennant *Wild Nights*
Raymond Williams *The Fight for Manod*

Timeline of National Events

1970

Thames barrier construction begun, completed in 1981.
British Caledonian Airways is founded.
Ted Heath becomes Conservative prime minister after narrowly defeating Harold Wilson.
Many strikes protesting the Industrial Relations Bill.

1971

Rolls Royce is nationalized in Britain after bankruptcy.
Britain switches to decimal currency.
British postal workers strike.
British troops in Northern Ireland increased in number to 12,500.
Habeas corpus later suspended as British authorities detain nationalists without trial.
British spacecraft Black Arrow is decommissioned, eliminating Britain from the space race. Britain does, however, launch a satellite later that year.
House of Commons votes 356–244 in favour of EEC membership.
London's Post Office Tower bombed by IRA.
British military bases in Malta are closed.

1972

Bloody Sunday in Derry as British paratroopers kill 13, ostensibly in reaction to threat of nail-bomb attack; Widgery Report published soon after exonerates British military forces. Saville Report published in June 2010 revised this verdict, stating that British troops fired without due provocation.
Anti-British riots take place throughout Ireland. British embassy in Dublin is burnt down.
The IRA becomes active on mainland Britain with the Aldershot bombing in which seven soldiers die.
Direct Rule of Northern Ireland begins in March.
Operation Motorman commences in July, designed to reclaim "no go" areas of Belfast and Derry.
State of emergency declared over the British Miner's strike.
Second Cod War is militarized with the deployment of Royal Navy vessels.

1973

United Kingdom enters the EEC.
IRA bombs explode at the Old Bailey and in Whitehall.
The Miners go on strike and the Three Day Week begins in Britain due to coal shortages affecting electricity supply.
Ann Quin commits suicide in Brighton at the age of 37.
J. R. R. Tolkien dies in September at the age of 81.
B. S. Johnson commits suicide on 13 November at the age of 40.

1974

Labour and Conservative parties reach almost dead-heat in February general election; Harold Wilson becomes prime minister again.
Thirty-three people die and over 300 are wounded in the Dublin and Monaghan bombings in the Republic of Ireland. Members of the loyalist Ulster Volunteer Force are behind the attacks, allegedly in collusion with members of the British intelligence service.
Houses of Parliament and the White Tower at the Tower of London are bombed by IRA.
Prevention of Terrorism Act passed in the United Kingdom.

1975

Margaret Thatcher becomes leader of the Conservative Party, succeeding Ted Heath.
UK votes to stay in the EEC in the first ever national referendum.
Inflation rate in Britain reaches 25%.
British Leyland comes under government control.
Third Cod War, 1975–76 – Icelandic sovereignty upheld.
The Equal Opportunities Commission is established to combat sex discrimination.

1976

Race Relations Act established by parliament.
First commercial Concorde flight leaves London.
IRA bombing campaign in mainland Britain escalates to include 12 separate explosions in January alone.
Harold Wilson resigns as prime minister to be succeeded by Jim Callaghan.
Britain successfully applies for $5.3 million loan from the IMF.
100 Club Punk Festival held in London, helping to launch the careers of The Clash, the Sex Pistols, the Buzzcocks and the Damned.

1977

Labour government lose working majority due to by-election losses.
Queen Elizabeth II celebrates Silver Jubilee with a tour of the Antipodes and Canada followed by celebrations across Britain.
Aircraft and shipbuilding industries are nationalized.
Punk movement gathers momentum with release of debut albums by The Clash and the Sex Pistols.
Strike at Grunwick film-processing plant begins.
Feminist publishing house Virago publishes first title.

1978

European Court of Human Rights finds British government guilty of mistreatment of prisoners in Northern Ireland but not guilty of torture.
The world's first test-tube baby, Louise Brown, is born.
So-called Winter of Discontent begins in the United Kingdom with trade union strikes and freezing weather.

1979

In the devolution referendum of 1 March 1979, Scotland voted in favour of devolution by 52% to 48% – but only 32.9% of the electorate had joined the majority and thus the requirement that 40% of the electorate support the measure was not met. In Wales the vote was against devolution, by 80% to 20%.
Jim Callaghan's Labour government loses a vote of no confidence forcing the general election to be held in May; Margaret Thatcher's Conservative Party achieves a majority of 43 seats. Conservatives remain in power until 1997.
IRA bombings kill high-profile figures Airey Neave, MP and Lord Louis Mountbatten.
J. G. Farrell drowns in an accident off Bantry Bay, Ireland.

Timeline of International Events

1970

Biafran rebels surrender to Federal Nigerian Government; end of Civil War.
US planes bomb Cambodia.
Student protestors in anti-Vietnam War protest shot at Kent State University, Ohio, US.
Ulrike Meinhof assists Andreas Baader's escape from prison; the group continues their activities including the robbery of three banks later that year.
Fiji gains independence from Britain.
Egypt, Libya and Sudan reveal intentions to form a federation.

1971

Idi Amin seizes power in former British protectorate of Uganda.
East Pakistan declares itself to be the republic of Bangladesh.
Seabed Treaty signed by Britain, US and USSR outlawing undersea deployment of nuclear weapons.
Sierra Leone becomes a republic.
British military bases in Malta are closed.

1972

President Amin of Uganda expels Asians from country.
SALT I signed by US and USSR.
East and West Germany formally recognize each other.
US president Nixon visits China.

1973

Paris Peace Accords signal end of active American involvement in Vietnam.
Watergate scandal breaks in the US.
Yom Kippur war in the Middle East leads to worldwide cuts in the supply of oil.

1974

Turkey invades Cyprus.
Nixon resigns as US president following Watergate.

1975

Saigon falls to North Vietnamese forces in April.
Civil war begins in Lebanon.
Death of General Franco in Spain.
Civil war begins in Angola.
The Australian prime minister Gough Whitlam is sacked by the British Governor General, sparking a constitutional crisis.

1976

Nationalist guerrillas intensify attacks on Ian Snith's administration in Rhodesia.
Trinidad & Tobago along with the Seychelles achieve independence from Britain.
Israeli commandos rescue plane hijack hostages at Entebbe in Uganda.
Jimmy Carter elected US president.

1977

Zia Ul-Haq overthrows Zulfiqar Ali Bhutto in Pakistan.
Elvis Presley dies in Gracelands, Memphis.

1978

Rioters attack British embassy in Tehran. Shah of Iran imposes martial law.
President Carter organizes the Camp David summit between Israel and Egypt.
The Afghan Army launch a coup backed by the Soviet Union.
Italian politician Aldo Moro is kidnapped and then murdered by the Red Brigade.

1979

Overthrow of Shah of Iran; US embassy staff in Teheran taken hostage.
USSR invades Afghanistan.
The Sandinista movement overthrow President Somosa in Nicaragua.
Lancaster House agreement in Rhodesia leads to independence and elections.
Israel and Egypt sign peace treaty.

Biographies of Writers

Martin Amis

Born in 1949 in Swansea, south Wales, Martin Amis is the son of the novelist Kingsley Amis. After graduating from Oxford in 1971, where he studied English, Martin Amis worked as a literary journalist until 1979. During this time he worked on his first four novels: *The Rachel Papers* (1973), *Dead Babies* (1975), *Success* (1978), and *Other People: A Mystery Story* (1981). In 1984, he published his most acclaimed novel, *Money: A Suicide Note*. After publishing a collection of essays, *The Moronic Inferno and Other Visits to America* (1986) and a collection of stories, *Einstein's Monsters* (1987), he published the second of an informal trilogy of novels, *London Fields* (1989) (the first being *Money*). His other works include: *Time's Arrow* (1991), *The Information* (1995) (the third novel of his trilogy), *Night Train*, a pseudo-detective story (1997), *Yellow Dog* (2003), *House of Meetings* (2006), and *The Pregnant Widow* (2010). His other published work includes a collection of stories, *Heavy Weather and Other Stories* (1998); a highly original memoir, *Experience* (2000); a collection of his journalism, *The War against Cliché: Essays and Reviews, 1971–2000* (2001); and a political essay about Stalin's years of terror, *Koba the Dread: Laughter and the Twenty Million* (2002).

J. G. Ballard

J.G. Ballard was born in 1932 into a wealthy expatriate family in Shanghai. His early exposure to death and violence while interned by the Japanese in Lunghua Camp from 1943 to 1945 inevitably shaped the apocalyptic tone of much of his fiction, even though he admitted being 'largely happy' in this environment. These experiences are documented in his autobiography, *Miracles of Life* (2008), but were earlier fictionalized in the semi-autobiographical novel, *Empire of the Sun* (1984), which won Ballard the *Guardian* fiction prize and the James Tate Black Memorial Prize, and was also shortlisted for the Booker Prize, establishing him as a successful mainstream author. After the war, Ballard arrived in Britain in 1946 and completed his schooling before joining the RAF and being posted to Canada, where he was introduced to American science fiction magazines. Ballard's first stories appeared in 1956, instigating a relationship with *New Worlds* magazine. His work helped transform science fiction by turning towards the 'inner space' of psychological trauma and urban psychosis. In 1960, he moved to the London suburb of Shepperton, where he was to remain in residence for the rest of his life. Following the death of his wife, Mary, in 1964 he was left to bring up their three children as a single parent, eventually settling into a pattern of writing during the day while the children were at school. After a series of novels including *The Drowned World* (1962), he produced his 'condensed novel' experiment, *The Atrocity Exhibition* (1970), which unveiled the hidden relationships between sex, consumerism and the death drive that underpinned the liberalization of social attitudes at the time. Publishers' readers doubted his sanity and questions were asked in Parliament about his work, but Ballard went on to produce a series of novels *Crash* (1973), *Concrete Island* (1974) and *High-Rise* (1975), that established 'Ballardian' as a synonym for bleak, entropic urbanity. Later works include *Cocaine Nights* (1996), *Millennium People* (2003) and *Kingdom Come* (2006). He died in 2009.

John Berger

John Berger, born in 1926, is an English novelist who is also well known for his art criticism, sociological studies and journalism. At 16 he left school and enrolled at the Central School of Art. In 1944 he was conscripted into the army but returned to art school afterwards and eventually became a painter and teacher. In the mid-1950s, however, he decided to give up painting and concentrate on his writing. His first novel, *A Painter of Our Times*, appeared in 1958 and was followed by *The Foot of Clive* (1962) and *Corker's Freedom* (1964). He was a controversial figure in his early career, often as a result of his essays published in the *New Statesman* which criticized nuclear proliferation. He has since said that he was never comfortable with the social and political climate of Britain and in 1962 he left to live in France. He won the Booker Prize in 1972 for his historical novel *G.*, infamously donating half his prize money to the Black Panther Party in Britain. In the same year he also wrote *Ways of Seeing*, a Marxist-inspired study of how people process the images that surround them, which was both a BBC television series and a book. Later novels include *To the Wedding* (1995), *King: A Street Story* (1999) and *From A to X* (2008).

Malcolm Bradbury

Malcolm Bradbury was born in Sheffield in 1932. He was an English author and academic renowned for his work on modern literature. He is also known for his association with the University of East Anglia where he helped launch the MA in Creative Writing and whose students have included Ian McEwan and Kazuo Ishiguro. His first novel, *Eating People is Wrong*, was published in 1959. This was followed by *Stepping Westward* in 1965. *The History Man*, the novel for which he is best known, appeared in 1975. His later novels were *Rates of Exchange* (1983), *Doctor Criminale* (1992) and *To the Hermitage* (2000). Bradbury has been compared to David Lodge, with whom he worked in the English Department at the University of Birmingham during the early 1960s, because of both authors' work on the campus novel. Bradbury was made a CBE in 1991 and later knighted shortly before his death in 2000.

Angela Carter

Angela Carter was born in 1940. She spent the war years in Yorkshire, and after the war moved with her family to Balham in South London. Her father apprenticed her to the Croydon Advertiser, where she first acquired her journalistic skills. In 1960, she married Paul Carter, an industrial chemist, and followed him to Bristol University the next year. While studying for a degree in English, specializing in the medieval period, she wrote her first novel, *Shadow Dance* (1966) – called *Honeybuzzard* in the US – a gothic detective novel. Her second novel, *The Magic Toyshop* (1967), won the John Llewellyn Rhys Prize, and her third novel, *Several Perceptions* (1968), won the Somerset Maugham Prize. Using the money from the prize to leave her husband, Carter spent two years in Japan. She wrote about her Japanese experiences in articles for *New Society* and in the stories collected in *Fireworks* (1974). She published two more novels, *Heroes and Villains* (1969), a post-apocalyptic novel, and *Love* (1971). Her newfound feminism found expression in *The Infernal Desire Machines of Doctor Hoffman* (1972). This highly anti-realist novel marked a turning point in Carter's career, receiving a lukewarm reception but gaining a cult readership. After returning to London, she published *The Passion of New Eve* (1977). Her distinctive brand of feminism attracted criticism from some feminists when she brought out *The Sadeian Woman* (1978), a polemical essay defending the Marquis de Sade. In 1979, she published *The Bloody Chamber and Other Stories*, the book that made her well known in the US and resulted in several visiting professorships at universities there. The collection retells a number of European fairy stories from a feminist point of view, restoring the sexual content that had been removed by earlier writers. Her last two novels were *Nights at the Circus* (1984), which won the James Tait Black Memorial Prize, and *Wise Children* (1991). Carter died in 1992.

Margaret Drabble

Margaret Drabble was born in 1939 in Sheffield. She was the daughter of a barrister and her elder sister is the novelist, A. S. Byatt. Drabble read English at Newham College, Cambridge, and graduated with a starred first. After a period working as an actor, Drabble turned to writing. Her first novel, *A Summer Bird Cage*, was published in 1963. Other novels include *The Needle's Eye* (1972), *The Realms of Gold* (1975), *The Ice Age* (1977), *The Middle Ground* (1980), *The Radiant Way* (1987), *A Natural Curiosity* (1989), *The Gates of Ivory* (1991), *The Witch of Exmoor* (1996), *The Peppered Moth* (2001), *The Seven Sisters* (2002), *The Red Queen* (2004) and *The Sea Lady* (2006). In 1972 she co-edited the experimental collective novel *London Consequences* with B. S. Johnson. Drabble, who lives in London with her second husband, the biographer Michael Holroyd, has also published two major biographies herself, *Arnold Bennett* (1974) and *Angus Wilson* (1995). She was awarded a CBE in 1980 and made a Dame in 2008.

Buchi Emecheta

Buchi Emecheta was born in Lagos, Nigeria, in 1944. She was orphaned when only nine years old, and went on the following year to be educated at the Methodist Girls' School, where she stayed until she was 16. The same year she married a student, Sylvester Onwordi, to whom she had been engaged since she was 11. In 1962, she followed him to London, where he was studying. Emecheta and her husband had five children together, but separated in 1966. As recounted in her early novels, the marriage was an unhappy and sometimes violent one. Following the end of her marriage, Emecheta began studying at the University of London, graduating with a BSc in sociology in 1972. During this time, she also worked as a library officer at the British Museum, and raised her children on her own. She went on to work as a youth worker and sociologist with the Inner London Education Authority. Emecheta's first two novels, *In the Ditch* (1972) and *Second Class Citizen* (1974) are semi-autobiographical works, based on her childhood, her marriage, her move to London and her struggles as a single mother. She published her autobiography, *Head above Water* in 1986, and has published 11 more novels, as well as plays for television, works for children and young adults, and non-fiction on women's experiences in Nigeria. In 1983 she was one of Granta's 'Best of Young British Novelists'. Emecheta's success led to numerous lectureships in the 1980s in universities in Nigeria, the US and the UK. From 1982 to 1983 Buchi Emecheta, together with her son Sylvester, ran the Ogwugwu Afor Publishing Company. She was awarded an OBE (Order of the British Empire) in 2005.

J. G. Farrell

J. G. Farrell was born in Liverpool in 1935 and spent the remainder of his childhood after the Second World War in Dublin as his family returned to their maternal Irish roots. He contracted polio while studying at Oxford in the late 1950s, which resulted in some physical disability. After graduating, he taught in France, where his first novel, *A Man from Elsewhere* (1963), is set. Subsequently, he published *The Lung* (1965) and *A Girl in the Head* (1967). He is most famous for his Empire Trilogy, which consists of the three completed novels, *Troubles* (1970), *The Siege of Krishnapur* (1973), which won the Booker Prize, and *The Singapore Grip* (1978). Farrell drowned in Ireland in 1979 after being swept away to his death by a storm in Bantry Bay. His unfinished novel *The Hill Station*, which would have turned the Empire Trilogy into a quartet, was posthumously published in 1981. In 2010, *Troubles* was awarded the 'Lost Booker' for 1970.

Eva Figes

Eva Figes was born in 1932 in Berlin to prosperous secular Jewish parents, who managed to escape with her and her brother to Britain during the following year. In 1953 she graduated from Queen Mary College, University of London, with a BA honours degree in English. She left determined to become a writer and subsequently became part of the experimental writing scene in London alongside figures such as Alan Burns, Ann Quin and B. S. Johnson. Her first novel, *Equinox*, was published in 1966 and her second, *Winter Journey* (1967), won the *Guardian* fiction prize. She came to even greater public prominence with the publication of her feminist polemic *Patriarchal Attitudes* in 1970. Subsequent novels include *Days* (1976), *Light* (1983), *The Seven Ages* (1986), *The Tree of Knowledge* (1990), and *The Knot* (1996). Figes died in 2012. Her archive at the British Library includes correspondence with Johnson and with John Berger.

John Fowles

John Fowles was born in 1926 in Leigh-on-Sea in Essex. After completing his military service in 1947, he studied French at Oxford, where he first read Jean-Paul Sartre and Albert Camus, who were to be considerable influences on his work. He then spent a year teaching at the University of Poitiers, and then taught English in Greece until 1953. On his return to the UK, he spent the next ten years teaching English as a foreign language in London. Having already completed much of *The Magus* (1966), the first of Fowles's novels to be published was *The Collector* (1963), for which he received one of the highest advances to date for a first novel. The novel was a critical and commercial success, and Fowles stopped teaching in order to concentrate on writing. He published *The Aristos*, a collection of his writings on philosophy, in 1964, and then *The Magus*, which he revised and republished 11 years later. Fowles went on to publish five more fictional works: *The French Lieutenant's Woman* (1969), *The Ebony Tower* (1974), *Daniel Martin* (1977), *Mantissa* (1982), and *A Maggot* (1985). His two volumes of journals were published in 2003 and 2004. Fowles died in 2005.

George MacDonald Fraser

George MacDonald Fraser was born in Carlisle in 1925 to a Scottish family. He fought in Burma during the Second World War and on his return from eventual demobilization in 1947, trained as a newspaper reporter on the *Carlisle Journal*. His career as a journalist took him to Glasgow, where he eventually became deputy editor of the *Glasgow Herald* in the late 1960s. However, his life changed with the publication of his first novel *Flashman* in 1969, based on the ingenious idea of turning the bully of that name from Thomas Hughes's *Tom Brown's Schooldays* (1857) into a national hero in order to satirize the traditional perception of Victorian imperialism. The book was an immediate success and was quickly followed by *Royal Flash* (1970), a pastiche of Anthony Hope's *The Prisoner of Zenda* (1894), and *Flash for Freedom!* (1971). Parodic in style, the *Flashman* novels turned into a series stretching on until 2005, although the rate of publication dramatically slowed as Fraser turned to writing scripts for films such as *The Three Musketeers* (1973) and *Octopussy* (1983). Fraser also wrote a number of lesser-known historical novels and a memoir of his experiences fighting in Burma, *Quartered Safe Out Here* (1992). Fraser died in 2008.

Beryl Gilroy

Beryl Gilroy was born in Guyana, then British Guiana, in 1924. She did not receive a formal education until she was 12. Between 1943 and 1945 she attended teacher training college in Georgetown. She moved to Britain in 1951 to take up a place at the University of London to study for a Diploma in Child Development. She spent a number of years in other kinds of employment, while bringing up her family, unable to find work as a teacher because of racism. In 1968 she returned to teaching, and progressed to be the first black headteacher in London, writing about these experiences in her *Black Teacher* (1976). She went to work as a researcher at the University of London, and worked as a psychotherapist, mainly with black women and children. Gilroy gained a PhD in Counselling Psychology in 1987. In 2000 she was also awarded an honorary doctorate from the Institute of Education. Gilroy's creative writing began in childhood, as a teacher for children and then in the 1960s when she began writing what was later published by Peepal Tree Press as *In Praise of Love and Children* (1991). Between 1970 and 1975 she wrote the pioneering children's series *Nippers*. Her first novel was published in 1986, *Frangipani House*. *Boy-Sandwich* was published in 1989, followed by *Stedman and Joanna: A Love in Bondage* (1991). Her poetry collections include *Echoes and Voices* (1991). Her last novel, *The Green Grass Tango*, was published posthumously in 2001.

B. S. Johnson

B. S. Johnson was born in 1933 in London to a working-class family. As he describes in his 1966 novel *Trawl*, he was evacuated during the Second World War and also failed his eleven plus examination so that he could not go to a Grammar school. However, he did eventually make it to university. Following his graduation from Kings College, London, with a 2.2 in English Literature, Johnson decided to visit Dublin in honour of his favourite writers James Joyce and Samuel Beckett. During the process of hitchhiking to Holyhead in order to catch the ferry, he was picked up on the A5 by the owner of a country club on the Llŷn peninsula in North Wales and subsequently worked as a barman there for the summers of 1958 and 1959. This experience informs his first novel, *Travelling People* (1963). Subsequent novels included *Albert Angelo* (1964) and *The Unfortunates* (1969), which was famously published as 21 sections in a box that could be read in any order. *House Mother Normal* (1971) was written while Johnson had a position as writer in residence at Gregynog in West Wales. Johnson was also a poet, dramatist and film-maker. In 1973, at the age of 40, he committed suicide. His last novel *See the Old Lady Decently* was posthumously published in 1975.

Jennifer Johnston

Jennifer Johnston was born in Dublin in 1930 but has lived much of her life in Northern Ireland. A graduate of Trinity College Dublin, she published her first novel, *The Captains and the Kings*, in 1972 at the age of 42. This was followed by *The Gates* (1973) and *How Many Miles to Babylon?* (1974). *Shadows on Our Skin* (1977) marked a departure with its contemporary setting amongst the troubles in Derry and was shortlisted for the Booker Prize. In 1979, she won the Whitbread Book Award for *The Old Jest*, which was subsequently filmed as *The Dawning* (1988). Later novels include *The Invisible Worm* (1991), *This Is Not a Novel* (2002), *Grace and Truth* (2005), and *Foolish Mortals* (2007).

John le Carré

John le Carré is the pen name of David Cornwell, born in 1931. From 1950 to 1964, he worked first in army intelligence, then for MI5 and finally for MI6. Le Carré is known for his espionage fiction including *The Spy Who Came in from the Cold* (1963), *A Perfect Spy* (1986) and *The Russia House* (1989). *Tinker, Tailor, Soldier, Spy* (1974) is loosely based on the hunt for the real-life British double agent Kim Philby and was made into an acclaimed BBC television series starring Alec Guinness before being re-made as a film in 2011. Le Carré has published over 20 novels and continues to write at his home in Falmouth, Cornwall, where he has lived for over 40 years. He is known to have refused a Knighthood.

Doris Lessing

Doris Lessing was born in Persia (now Iran) in 1919 to British parents but grew up in Rhodesia (now Zimbabwe) after her parents moved there to run a farm. She left her convent school at the age of 14 and her home soon after to become a nursemaid. In 1937, she moved to Salisbury (now Harare) to become a telephone operator and subsequently married and had two children. After her first marriage ended in divorce in 1943, she became involved with the communist politics of the Left Book Club and there met her second husband Gottfried Lessing. When that marriage ended in 1949, she moved to Britain. Lessing's first novel, *The Grass Is Singing* (1950), dealt with racial politics in Rhodesia and had an immediate impact. *The Golden Notebook* (1962) marked an important moment in the post-war rise of feminist consciousness. In the 1970s, similarly to J. G. Ballard, but probably more influenced by R. D. Laing's critique of conventional psychiatry, she chose to focus on 'inner space' in novels such as *Briefing for a Descent into Hell* (1971) and *The Memoirs of a Survivor* (1974). *Shikasta* (1979) was the first of five books in the overtly science-fictional *Canopus of Argos* series (1979–1983), which was a major factor in Lessing's award of the Nobel Prize for Literature in 2007. While novels such as *The Good Terrorist* (1985) were seen by some as evidence of a 'return to realism', more recent work such as *The Cleft* (2007) and *Alfred and Emily* (2008) demonstrate speculative and fantastical elements. Lessing died in 2013.

David Lodge

David Lodge was born in Brockley in 1935. His first novel, *The Picturegoers*, was published in 1960 shortly before he moved to Birmingham in order to complete his PhD and lecture for the English Department, in which he worked for 27 years before retiring to concentrate fully on writing. Subsequent novels included *The British Museum Is Falling Down* (1965) and *Out of the Shelter* (1970). *Changing Places* (1975) is the first of the three campus novels for which he is perhaps best known. The other two, *Small World* (1984) and *Nice Work* (1988), were both shortlisted for the Booker Prize. Lodge has also written a number of significant academic publications, including the influential edited collection *Modern Criticism and Theory: A Reader* (1992). He is a fellow of the Royal Society of Literature. His later novels include *Thinks…* (2001), *Deaf Sentence* (2008) and *A Man of Parts* (2011).

Ian McEwan

Ian McEwan was born in Aldershot, Hampshire, into an army family in 1948. He spent much of his childhood abroad until he was 12. He graduated from the University of Sussex in English Literature in 1970, and went on to be one of the first students to graduate from the MA in Creative Writing at the University of East Anglia. His first collection of short stories, *First Love, Last Rites* was published in 1975, followed by another, *In Between the Sheets*, in 1978. His first two novels, *The Cement Garden* (1978) and *The Comfort of Strangers* (1981), were both short and concerned with dark psychological states, perverse relations and violence. His next novel, *The Child in Time* (1987), marked a change in his work, the novel combining political satire with the possibility of redemption, and won the Whitbread Novel Award. McEwan's nine subsequent novels have generally alternated between historical fiction and narratives dealing with very contemporary concerns and situations. They are: *The Innocent* (1990), *Black Dogs* (1992), *Enduring Love* (1997), *Amsterdam* (1998), *Atonement* (2001), *Saturday* (2005), *On Chesil Beach* (2007), *Solar* (2010), and *Sweet Tooth* (2012). McEwan has been shortlisted for the Booker Prize six times, winning in 1998 with *Amsterdam*. He has also won many other prizes and awards, has written screenplays including adaptations of his own work, an oratorio and children's fiction. He was awarded a CBE in 2000.

William McIlvanney

William McIlvanney was born in Kilmarnock in 1936. He is the youngest child of an ex-Miner and his older brother Hugh is a well-known sportswriter. McIlvanney was the first in his family to go to university, graduating from Glasgow in 1960 and pursuing a career in teaching until 1975. His first novel, *Remedy Is None* (1967), won the Geoffrey Faber Memorial Prize and *Docherty* (1975) won the Whitbread Award for Fiction. This latter novel fulfilled one of McIlvanney's aims since his student days of finding working-class experience expressed in literature. Characters from this novel, or their descendants, appear in some of his later novels such as *The Kiln* (1991). *Laidlaw* (1978) and *The Papers of Tony Veitch* (1983) both gained Silver Daggers from the Crime Writers' Association. *Strange Loyalties* (1991), the third in the Laidlaw trilogy, won the *Glasgow Herald*'s People's Prize. It has become apparent over the years that McIlvanney's fictional universe has begun to link up as parts of the extended Docherty saga intersect with the Laidlaw novels. Since April 2013, McIlvanney has launched a twice-weekly blog.

Michael Moorcock

Michael Moorcock was born in London in 1939. At age 17 he became the editor of *Tarzan Adventures*. He was subsequently the editor of the controversial science fiction magazine *New Worlds*, between 1964 and 1971 and again between 1976 and 1996. The magazine was responsible during the 1960s for developing the 'new wave' in science fiction in the UK; the magazine published writers such as J. G. Ballard and Brian Aldiss. Moorcock's first novel, *The Stealer of Souls*, the first novel in his Elric Saga series, was published in 1961. He has gone on to produce a huge number of stories and novels, publishing nearly 100 works of fiction and non-fiction. While best known in the US for his science fiction and fantasy, in the UK he came to prominence for non-genre work, winning the Guardian Fiction Prize in 1977 for *The Condition of Muzak*, the final book in his Jerry Cornelius Quartet. In the 1980s in particular he concentrated on such non-genre writing, completing *Mother London* (1988) which was shortlisted for the Whitbread Award. A number of his novels, such as *Behold the Man* (1966) and *The Final Programme* (1969), have been read as non-genre work. All Moorcock's work expresses his political commitment, and he has been particularly critical of the misogynistic and escapist elements in science fiction and fantasy fiction. In the 1990s, Moorcock moved to the US. In 2002, he was inducted into the Science Fiction Hall of Fame. He has been the recipient of a great many awards and prizes.

Iris Murdoch

Iris Murdoch was born in Dublin in 1919. Her parents moved to London while she was still a baby. She studied Classics at Oxford, and between 1944 and 1946 she worked for the United Nations Relief and Rehabilitation Administration in Europe. She went on to study philosophy as a postgraduate student at Oxford, and eventually became a fellow of St Anne's College, Oxford. She published essays on philosophy and a monograph on

Jean-Paul Sartre. Her first novel, *Under the Net*, was published in 1954. She went on to publish over 20 more novels, including *The Black Prince* (1973) and *The Book and the Brotherhood* (1987), and several more works of philosophy. Her novel *The Sea, the Sea* (1978) won the Booker Prize, and she won numerous other awards for her fiction. She was made a Dame Commander of the Order of the British Empire in 1987. Murdoch developed Alzheimer's disease in the mid-1990s, and the account of her husband, John Bayley, of her illness was adapted as a film, *Iris* (dir. Richard Eyre, 2001). She died in 1999.

Christopher Priest

Christopher Priest was born in 1943 and grew up in Cheshire, leaving school at 16 when his family relocated to Essex. For the next seven years, he worked unhappily with a firm of chartered accountants in Central London, but found consolation when a colleague introduced him to science fiction. Priest began writing his own stories from the mid-1960s and published his first novel *Indoctrinaire* in 1970. *Fugue for a Darkening Island* (1972), *Inverted World* (1974), *The Space Machine* (1976), *A Dream of Wessex* (1977) and *The Affirmation* (1981) followed before his inclusion among 'The Best of Young British Novelists 1983'. Priest's characteristically acerbic memoir of the photo-shoot and launch party marking the announcement of this list, 'Where Am I Now?' (2008), mercilessly condemns the whole process as a charade and is scathing about the behaviour of some of his peers. Priest's ninth novel *The Prestige* (1995), winner of both the James Tait Black Memorial Prize and the World Fantasy Award, was filmed by Christopher Nolan in 2006. *The Separation* (2002) won the Arthur C. Clarke Award. His most recent work includes *The Islanders* (2011) and *The Adjacent* (2013).

Michèle Roberts

Michèle Roberts was born in Hertfordshire in 1949. Her mother was French and Roberts has dual nationality. After graduating in English from Somerville College, Oxford, Roberts studied as a librarian and then spent a year working for the British Council in South-East Asia before quitting in order to go travelling. After returning to Britain, she became involved in the women's movement. Her first novel, *A Piece of the Night*, was published in 1978. During this period, Roberts was poetry editor for *Spare Rib*, a role she subsequently took at *City Limits* in the early 1980s. Her other novels include *The Visitation* (1978), *Daughters of the House* (1992), *Flesh & Blood* (1994), *Fair Exchange* (1999), *The Mistressclass* (2002), *Reader, I Married Him* (2006) and *Ignorance* (2012).

Emma Tennant

Emma Tennant was born in London in 1937, the daughter of Charles Tennant, 2nd Baron Glenconner, and Elizabeth, Lady Glenconner. She spent the war years in her family's house in Scotland, The Glen. She later worked as a travel writer for *Queen* magazine, and for *Vogue*. She published her first novel, *The Colour of Rain*, under the pseudonym Catherine Aydy in 1964. She became a full-time novelist in 1973, and between 1975 and 1979 she edited the literary magazine *Bananas*. Tennant has written many novels, biographies and autobiography. A number of her novels, such as *Two Women of London: The Strange Case of Ms Jekyll and Mrs Hyde* (1989), *Tess* (1993), *Pemberley: Or Pride and Prejudice Continued* (1993) and *Adele: Jane Eyre's Hidden Story* (2000), rewrite or continue the stories of well-known novels by other writers. Other novels, such as *Heathcliff's Tale* (2005), entwine the biographies of writers into new narratives.

Raymond Williams

Raymond Williams, the son of a railway worker, was born in 1921 in a village near Abergavenny in 1921. He attended the local grammar school and went to Cambridge at the outbreak of Second World War. Military duties interrupted his studies and Williams went on to serve as a tank commander in Normandy. After the war, he completed his degree and worked in adult education, while writing the cultural criticism that made him famous such as *Culture and Society* (1958) and *The Long Revolution* (1961). His first novel, *Border Country* (1960), was followed by a sequel, *Second Generation* (1964). By now, Williams had moved on to lecture at Cambridge, and was associated with the 'New Left', becoming one of the chief contributors to the *May Day Manifesto* (1968). For the rest of his career, he interspersed critical works such as *The Country and the City* (1971) and *Marxism and Literature* (1977), with novels such as *The Volunteers* (1978), *The Fight for Manod* (1979), and *Loyalties* (1985). Williams died in 1988 and his last unfinished novel, *People of the Black Mountains*, was published posthumously in two volumes in 1989 and 1990.

Index

Note: The letter 'n' following locators refers to notes.

Abelman, Paul 11, 171, 174, 175, 176
An Accidental Man (1971) 193, 194
adolescence 24–5
After the War (1994) 218
Against Interpretation (1967) 203
Agamben, Giorgio 229
The Age of Suspicion (1963) 188
Alexander, Sally 71
Ali, Monica 89
Alibhai-Brown, Yasmin 5
'Alive and Well: The Contemporary British Novel' 187, 190–1
Allen, Richard 9, 27, 28
Alone of All Her Sex (1976) 73
Alter, Robert 195–6, 198–9
alternative lifestyles 61
The American Book Review 197
American culture, in Britain 171–5
American Libraries 190–1
American literary scene 181
    anti-realist fiction 189
    'death of the novel' 188–9
    feminist writing 73–4, 79–80
    reviews of *Daniel Martin* (1977) 195–9, 204–5
    reviews of *The Ice Age* (1977) 184–7, 196, 204–5
American perception of British novels
    'academic' 182–3, 186–7
    'death of the novel' 188–9
    Denis Donoghue 196–7
    Frank Kermode 193–5
    Frederick Busch 197–8
    Frederick McDowell 192–3
    lack of interest of American novelists in British writers 189–90
    'lay' 182–6
    neglect of feminist novels 208
    Robert Alter 195–6, 198–9
    Sheridan Baker 190–1

Amis, Kingsley 132, 194
Amis, Martin 11, 12, 38, 120, 131–2, 143n. 19, 209, 251
Andermahr, Sonya 69, 109
Angry Brigade 1, 151, 165
The Angry Brigade: A Documentary Novel (1973) 37, 163–5
anti-fantasy fictions 37
Anti-Nazi League (ANL) 6
anti-realism 83, 200–3
anxiety of influence 16
Anything Can Happen (1983) 204
apartheid 206–7
'Apocalypse Now?: The Novel in the 1970s' (1994) 60
Appleyard, Brian 221
Aren't You Rather Young To Be Writing Your Memoirs? (1973) 145
The Arts in the 1970s (1994) 17
Atlantic Monthly 182, 205
The Atrocity Exhibition (1970) 26, 29, 34, 162–3, 171
authorial intrusions 27–8
avant-garde prose 26–7, 145–6, 158, 167
    horror 32

The Bad Sister (1978) 79
Baker, Sheridan 190, 191, 192, 193, 210n. 5
Bakewell, Michael 175
balance of payment deficit 2
Ballard, J. G. 8, 9, 11, 12, 25–6, 27, 29, 30, 31, 38, 47, 159–61, 162, 163, 171, 251–2
Barker, Pat 10, 69, 89, 209
Barritt, Brian 37
Barth, John 189, 200, 201
BBC 3
    and black writing 95
    television comedy 107

Beatles 120
Beckett, Andy 1, 2, 6, 17, 45, 61, 62, 74, 83, 93, 94, 99
A Bend in the River (1979) 95, 206
Benefits (1979) 81, 86–8
Benjamin, Walter 224, 225, 229, 232, 233, 234, 235, 236, 237, 238, 239, 240
Bényei, Tamás 215
Berger, John 17, 18, 85, 119, 136, 141n. 3, 145, 168, 169, 170, 176, 219, 252
Bergonzi, Bernard 137, 148, 188, 219, 220, 223, 238
Berry, James 100
Berry, Mark 36
'Best of Young British Novelists' 96, 209, 254, 260
Bhowani Junction (1954) 218
bildungsroman 76, 78, 131
Binns, Ronald 220, 221, 238
Birch, Sarah 170–1
Birmingham Six 120
Birrer, Doryjane 181
black community 4–5
black feminism 73, 79–80, 109–11
Black Marsden (1972) 96
Black Panther movement 136
Black, Pauline 97
The Black Prince (1973) 77–8, 155–6
Black Teacher (1976) 96, 101, 111–14
black writing
    Caribbean 94–6
    domestic servitude 105–6
    and feminism 73, 79–80
    mockery of political integrity 106–7
    poetry 100
    and racism 97, 99–100, 112
    racist chauvinism 107
    separatism within black community 104–5, 113
    sexist chauvinism 107–9
    women's writing 79, 98, 101, 109–11
    writers outside Britain 95
Blatty, William Peter 32
The Bloody Chamber (1979) 138, 139
'Bloody Sunday' 6, 151
Bloom, Harold 16
Bluefoot Traveller: Poetry by Westindians in Britain (1976) 100
Bond, James 30

Booker Prize 96, 119, 136, 206
    Lost Man Booker prize 215–16
bookkeeping double-entry system 165–7
Books of Blood (1984) 33
Border Country (1960) 51
Bowers, Maggie Ann 140
Boycott, Rosie 73
Bradbury, Malcolm 11, 18, 19, 20, 21, 22, 60, 120, 124, 127, 128, 129, 130, 131, 132, 135, 136, 137, 188, 215, 217, 219, 252
Braithwaite, E. R. 10, 94, 96, 97, 101, 102, 103, 104, 111, 114
    black pride 103
    overcoming prejudicial contempt 102–3
Brathwaite, Edward Kamau 95
The Break-Up of Britain (1977) 45, 51
Briefing for a Descent Into Hell (1971) 193, 205
'Bristol Trilogy' 21
Britain: A Future that Works (1978) 61
British Council 187
British Culture and Society in the 1970s: The Lost Decade (2010) 17
British Industrial Welfare State 44
British Low Culture: From Safari Suits to Sexploitation (1998) 27
'The British Novel Lives' 187, 193–4
The British Novel since the Thirties (1986) 218
Britton, David 37, 38
Brixton Black Women's Group 109
Brixton Riots 4
Brontë, Charlotte 74
'The Brood' (1976) 33
Brooke-Rose, Christine 11, 146, 147, 148, 149, 167, 168, 170–1, 189
Brown, Rosellen 190
Buckell, G. J. 154, 155
Burger's Daughter (1979) 206–7
Burgess, Anthony 146, 165, 189, 192, 210nn. 7, 10, 211n. 13, 215
Burk, Kathleen 2
Burns, Alan 11, 37, 145, 153, 163, 164, 165, 171–2
Busch, Frederick 197, 198
Butor, Michel 19, 147
'Butterflies' 34
Butterworth, Michael 26, 37, 38
Byatt, A. S. 148, 149, 219

Cabal (1988) 33
Cactus (1980) 80
Cadwalladr, Carole 71
Cairncross, Alec 2
Calder, Angus 122–3, 141n. 2
Callaghan, James 7–8
Campbell, Ramsey 9, 30, 33
campus fictions 21
Canopus in Argos series 48–9
capitalism, resistance to 44–5
Caribbean Voices radio programmes 95
Carol Watts 166
Carrie (1974) 32
Carter, Angela 9, 10, 12, 21, 22, 23, 25, 28, 29, 30, 31, 36, 38, 69, 70, 77, 78, 80, 137, 138, 139, 190
The Castle (1926) 223, 240
Castle, Barbara 154
'Cautious Feminism' 77–8
Celtic Fringe of Scotland and Wales 7
The Cement Garden (1978) 31
Centre for Contemporary Cultural Studies 98
Chambers, Ross 233
Changing Places (1975) 21–2
Chesnick, Eugene 206
child abuse 31–2
Child Benefit 71–2
The Child in Time (1987) 32–3
Childs, Peter 19, 25
Christie Malry's Own Double-Entry (1973) 18, 165
Christine Brooke-Rose and Contemporary Fiction (1994) 170–1
Churchill, Winston 122
Cixous, Hélène 81, 85
class mobility 26
Coe, Jonathan 167
Cold War 120–1
Colditz 3
'collective autobiography' 37
'Colonial Wales' 7
colonialism 7, 49–50
comedy 78, 93
 dark 151, 156
 television 107, 120
Commando comics 122
Commission for Racial Equality 5
'Common Market' *see* European Union
Concrete Island (1974) 161–2

The Condition of Muzak (1979) 26
confessionalism, literary 76–7
Connor, Steven 219
'consciousness-raising' 70
The Conservationist (1974) 206
Conservative government 2, 8, 44, 114, 117
consumer culture 43
contemporaneity 20
The Contemporary British Novel (2007) 3
Contemporary Literature 183, 192
Coover, Robert 189, 190, 201, 209n. 2, 210n. 4
Cornelius, Jerry 25–6, 43
counter-culture 36–7
 of sixties 21, 24
Courtman, Sandra 112
Craig, Cairns 56
Crane, Ralph J. 143n. 22, 217
Crash (1973) 26–7, 162–3
Creation Books 32
Crews, Brian 164, 165
crises, social 1–2, 44–6, 151, 166
 and feudalism 50
Crisis? What Crisis? Britain in the 1970s (2008) 151
Critique: Studies in Modern Fiction
 review of *The Ice Age* (1977) 186–7
Crockford, Sue 72
'Crossroads: The Sixties to the Eighties' 18
Culler, Jonathan 202, 205, 239
cults 29
'Cultural Turn' 121
culture, levels of 16
'Culture is Ordinary' (1958) 51
Culture and Society (1958) 51
Cwmardy (1937) 51

Daly, Claire 69, 73
A Dance to the Music of Time (1951–75) 21
Daniel Martin (1977) 195–9, 204–5
 review of Denis Donoghue 196–7
 review of Frederick Busch 197–8
 review of Robert Alter 195–6, 198–9
Darkness Visible (1979) 205
Davie, Donald 184
 review of *The Ice Age* (1977) 183–5, 185
Davies, R. R. 7
Days (1974) 81–3, 85, 86
de Beauvoir, Simone 82

Dead Babies (1975) 21, 22, 23, 24, 139
decolonization 1, 3–4, 128, 130–1
  see also Empire, the
democratization 50
Devolution Referendum (1979) 57
Dhondy, Farrukh 96
disintegration of Britain 45–8, 59–60
Docherty (1975) 56
Domestic Violence Act (1976) 72
Donnell, Alison 99
Donoghue, Denis 196, 197, 210n. 9, 211n. 11
Down Among the Women (1971) 18, 78
Drabble, Margaret 12, 77–8, 145, 146, 152, 153, 183, 184, 185–211, 253
The Dragonlance Chronicles (1984 onwards) 35
Dread, Beat an' Blood 100
A Dream of Wessex (1977) 54, 62–4, 159–61
Dreamerika: A Surrealist Fantasy (1972) 171–2
The Driver's Seat (1970) 77–8
Dungeons & Dragons (1974) 35
Düttmann, Alexaner García 237

The Eagle Has Landed (1975) 138–9
Eagleton, Terry 52, 202, 225, 237, 240
Earls Court 100–1, 104
East End at Your Feet (1976) 96
Ehrenberg, Felipe 158
Eliot, T. S. 126
Emecheta, Buchi 10, 12, 79, 96, 97, 101, 109, 110, 111, 112, 114, 209, 254
The Emigrants (1954) 95
Empire, the
  and paternalism 128, 130, 132
  see also decolonization
'The End of the English Novel' (1980) 209
The Enigma of Arrival (1987) 95
Equal Pay Act (1970) 72
European Economic Community (EEC), British entry into 117–18, 131
European Union 45
Evenson, Brian 173, 174
exhaustion, use of 27
existentialism 147–50, 154
  see also experimentalism
Existentialists and Mystics: Writings on Philosophy and Literature (1997) 154
The Exorcist (1973) 32

The Experimental Novel and Other Essays (1893) 146
'experimental realism' 209
experimentalism 145–7, 158, 167, 175–7, 188–9
  versus realism 188, 217–18
  see also existentialism

Fabulation and Metafiction (1979) 198, 201–2
Fairbairns, Zoë 10, 69, 72, 79, 81, 84, 86, 87, 88
A Fairly Honourable Defeat (1970) 77–8, 193
Falklands 46, 140
fantasy fiction 25, 28, 30, 35–8, 78–9, 192–3
Farrell, J. G. 12, 58, 119, 132, 133, 134, 135, 136, 137, 139, 141n. 4, 143n. 22, 254
  Bernard Bergonzi's construal of 219
  critical reception in Europe 215–17
  imperial theme context 218
  Lost Man Booker prize 215
  recent interest in 216
  under-representation of 218–20
Fat Is a Feminist Issue (1978) 73
Fawlty Towers 120
Felski, Rita 70, 72, 75, 76, 77, 83, 88
  self-discovery in feminist literature 72, 76–7
The Female Eunuch (1970) 73
Female Friends (1975) 78
feminism 18
  discourse 72–3
  and Marxism 73–4
  second-wave 70
  and US feminism 74
  see also feminist writing
Feminist Review 72
feminist writing 18
  in America 73–4, 79–80
  black writing 73, 79–80, 109–11
  discourse 72–3
  and domesticity 87–8
  lesbian writing 80, 84–5
  literary anti-confessionalism 81–3
  literary confessionalism 76–7
  and Marxism 73–4
  and mother-daughter relationships 83–6

and myths of feminity 78–9
self-reflection in writing 77–8
and traditional women's writing 75
and US feminism 74
younger women's writing 79
see also feminism
feudalism 45, 50
Fiction and the Northern Ireland Troubles since 1969 (2003) 57–8
'Fictions of History' 219
Figes, Eva 10, 73, 77, 78, 81, 83, 85, 87, 189, 254–5
The Fight for Manod (1979) 52–4, 65
The Final Programme (1969) 43
Finding a Voice: Asian Women in Britain (1978) 73, 109
First International Women's Day March 71
First Love, Last Rites (1975) 31
Flashman series 136–7
Fleming, Ian 134, 218
Flood, Allison 210n. 9
For a New Novel (1965) 188
Forster, Laurel 17
Forsyth, Frederick 138–9
Four Quartets (1943) 126
Fowles, John 11, 148, 149, 150, 151, 190, 195–9, 200, 255
Fraser, George MacDonald 136–7, 255–6
French feminism 81
The French Lieutenant's Woman (1969) 148–50, 196, 220
Fugue for A Darkening Island (1972) 156–8

G. A Novel (1972) 17, 18, 168–70
Gardiner, Michael 8
Gardner, John 203, 204, 206
Gasiorek, Andrzej 187–8
Gass, William 203–4
Gass–Gardner debate 203–4
Gee, Maggie 89
gentrification 120
Ghose, Zulfikar 145, 165
Gifford, Douglas 56
Gilbert, Sandra M. 85
Gilbert, Zanna 158
Gilroy, Beryl 11, 96, 111–14, 256
Gilroy, Paul 3
Gindin, James 148
Girl, 20 194
GLC funding 80

Golding, William 189, 194, 205, 215
Goodbye, Great Britain: The 1976 IMF Crisis 2
Goodman, Sam 117
Gor novels 36
Gordimer, Nadine 206, 207, 211n. 18
Goux, Jean-Joseph 235
Graff, Gerald 202, 203, 204, 205, 211n. 14
Greene, Gayle 89
Greene, Graham 189
Greenland, Colin 26
Greer, Germaine 73
Grimus (1975) 96, 139
Grunwick strike 93, 109
Gubar, Susan 85
Guerrillas (1975) 95

Habermas, Jurgen 72
Half a Life (2001) 95
Hall, Stuart 98
Harper, Sue 17
Harris, Wilson 96, 145
Harrison, M. John 26
Harvie, Christopher 126
Hawkes, John 200
Head, Bessie 79
Head, Dominic 219
Heat and Dust (1975) 79, 206
Heath, Edward 1–2, 157, 166
Heath, Ted 117
The Hellbound Heart (1986, 1988) 33
Hellraiser (1987) 33
Henry V (1944) 126
Heppenstall, Rayner 11, 145, 148, 153, 154, 155, 163, 165, 189
Hickman, Tracy 35
Higdon, David Leon 219
Higgins, Jack 138, 139
High Rise (1975) 26, 162
hippie subculture 29
'historiographic metafiction' 216
history
    defined 118–19
    'history from below' 121–2
    as instructive to contemporary identity 124–7, 129–30
    rejection of 127–30
The History Man (1975) 21–2, 60–1, 120, 127–30

Home, Stewart 27, 28
horror fiction 31–4
    avant-garde 32
    history of 32
    and sexuality 32
Hotel de Dream (1976) 79
The Hothouse by the East River (1973) 77–8
House Mother Normal (1971) 18
House of Lords 50
Howard, Joanna 173
Hubble, Nick 1–11, 43–66, 64
Huggan, Graham 96
Hunt, Leon 27
Hutcheon, Linda 140, 216, 220

The Ice Age (1977), review of
    Critique: Studies in Modern Fiction 186–7
    New York Review of Books 183–5
    Rolling Stone 185
identity crisis 3, 11–12, 76–7, 119–20, 124–31, 159, 184–6
IMF 2
immigration 93
Immigration Act (1971) 96
imperial decline 1, 3–4
'The Importance of Community' (1989) 51
In A Free State (1971) 95, 206
In Between the Sheets (1978) 31
In The Ditch (1972) 79, 96, 101, 110–11
incest 31–2
India: A Wounded Civilisation (1977) 95
individualism 48–9
    right-wing 2, 8, 55, 164–5
Industrial Relations Act 166
inequality, material 50
The Infernal Desire Machines of Dr Hoffman (1972) 30, 78, 137
Inglis, Fred 52, 53
INLA 1
'Introduction to *Aren't You Rather Young to be Writing Your Memoirs?*' (1973) 19
IRA struggle 1, 6–7, 120, 151
    see also Ireland
Ireland 6–7, 57–9
    see also IRA struggle; Northern Ireland
Irish fiction 57–8
irreverence 136

J. G. Farrell (2007) 217
Jackson, Steve 35
Jacobs, Carol 238
Jameson, Fredric 54, 61, 142n. 11
Jane Eyre (1847) 74
Jhabvala, Ruth Prawer 79, 206
John, Harrison, M. 9, 26, 37, 38
Johnathan Livingston Seagull (1970) 35–6
Johnson, B. S. 9, 11, 25, 145, 152–3, 163, 165, 166, 168, 175–7, 189, 217, 256
Johnson, Diane 211n. 18
Johnson, Linton Kwesi 93, 97, 100, 103
Johnston, Jennifer 10, 57, 58, 59, 64, 65, 66, 257
    and break-up of Britain 57–8
Jonathan, Coe 167
Josipovici, Gabriel 145–6, 159–60
Journal of Modern Literature 198
The Joys of Motherhood (1979) 79

Kafka 223, 240
Kaveney, Roz 30
Keneally, Thomas 119
Kennedy, A. L. 89
Kennedy, John F. 171–2
Kennedy-Andrews, Elmer 57–8, 59
Kermode, Frank 193, 194, 195, 197, 199, 202, 203, 210n. 9, 210n. 10
King, John 28
King, Stephen 32
Klinkowitz, Jerome 209n. 2
Knuckle Girls (1977) 27
Korenman, Joan S. 186
Kostelanetz, Richard 210n. 4, 211n. 10
Kristeva, Julia 81, 82, 170, 237
Kureishi, Hanif 94–5
Kynaston, David 117

Labour Party 2, 7–8, 50, 55, 59, 118, 154, 166
Laidlaw (1978) 56–7
Laing, Stuart 219
Lamming, George 94, 95, 102
La Poubelle: It's a Kind of Disease 158
Larkin, Philip 127
La Rose, John 95
le Carré, John 30, 31, 134–5, 257
LeClair, Tom 190, 197, 200, 203, 209, 210n. 3, 210n. 4

Lend-Lease Act 118
Leonard, John 211n. 17
lesbian writing 80, 84–5
Lessing, Doris 9, 10, 11, 12, 46, 47, 48, 49, 50, 54, 55, 60, 61, 65, 69, 77, 78, 158, 159, 189, 192, 193, 205, 210n. 7, 211n. 13, 257–8
   and challenges to masculinity 158–9
   and condemnation of civilization 47–8
   cultural conservatism 60
   indictment of individualism 48–9
   and marginalization of public authority 46–7
   Nobel Prize for Literature (2007) 48
   and patriarchy 48–9
   social crisis and feudalism 50
Levy, Benn 117–18
liberalism 23
'The "Liberation" of Margaret Drabble' 186
liberationary politics 18, 22
Life 182
Life on Mars (2006–2007) 17, 120
Like a Fiery Elephant (2004) 167
Literary Women (1978) 74
'The Literature of Exhaustion' 201
The Literature of Terror (1996) 38
A Literature of their Own (1977) 74
Livett, Jennifer 217
Livingston, Ian 35
Lodge, David 11, 18, 19, 21, 120, 124, 125, 128, 129, 130, 131, 135, 136, 139, 140, 188
   'composure' 126
London Consequences (1972) 145, 152–3
The Lonely Londoners (1956) 104
'the long eighties' 18
The Long Revolution (1961) 15, 51
'the long sixties' 18
Lost Man Booker prize 215
Love (1971) 22–3
'The Love Affair(s) of Ann Quin' 173–4

MacDonald Fraser, George 136
The Magic Toyshop (1967) 21
The Magus (1977) 198
Maitland, Sara 69, 81
The Making of the English Working Class 121–2
'Mangrove 9' 93
Manson, Charles 29, 172

Marcus, Greil 185
   review of *The Ice Age* (1977) 185–6
Markandaya, Kamala 96
The Marriages Between Zones Three, Four and Five 48–9
Mars-Jones, Adam 31
Marwick, Arthur 50
Marxism
   and feminism 73–4
   philosophies 121, 123–4
Marxist Feminist Literary Collective 74–5, 81
masculinity 24–5, 156, 158–9
Massie, Allan 21, 31, 187–8
Masters, John 218
McDowell, Frederick 192, 193, 205, 208
McEwan, Ian 8, 12, 30, 31, 38, 59, 209, 258–9
McEwan, Neil 219
McIlvanney, William 10, 56, 57, 59, 64, 65, 66
McLeod, John 1–12, 80, 93–114, 133, 137, 143n. 22, 217, 218
McWhirter, Ross 7
The Memoirs of a Survivor (1974) 46–8, 49, 60–1, 78, 158–9
memorial culture 121–3
Mid Pennine Association for the Arts (MPA) 17
Midnight's Children (1981) 139–40
'"The Mind Has Fuses": Detonating B. S. Johnson' 166
Mind Your Language 5
Miners' Strike 120, 151
'minimal impact' thesis 3
Miss World Competition 71
Mitchell, David M. 26, 38
Mitchell, Juliet 71
Mo, Timothy 37, 94–5, 96, 99, 125, 129, 136
mobile privatization 43–4, 64
The Modern British Novel (1993) 217
Modern Fiction Studies 183, 198
Mod Rule (1980) 27
modernism 18–20
'modified realism' 192
Moers, Ellen 74
Moffat, James 27
'The Moment of British Nationalism 1939–70' 126
Monarchy 50

Money (1984) 59–60
The Monkey King (1978) 96
Monty Python's Flying Circus 120
Moorcock, Michael 9, 21, 25, 26, 28, 30, 36, 43, 259
Moore-Gilbert, Bart 17, 55, 60, 61
morality tales 22
Morey, Peter 218
Morley, Lorraine 173
Moses Ascending (1975) 96, 104–9, 110
multiculturalism 5–6
Munich massacre 154
murder 31–2
Murdoch, Iris 77, 78, 93, 154, 155, 156, 192, 193, 194, 210nn. 7, 8, 211n. 12, 215, 217, 218, 219, 259–60
music 97
   and racism 97
The Myth of the Blitz (1991) 122–3
mythologizing of Britain 100, 122–3, 124, 131–2, 138

Naipaul, V. S. 94, 95, 100–1, 104, 206
Nairn, Tom 7, 8, 9, 60, 117, 120
   disintegration of Britain 45–6
   feudalism 50–1
Nathaniel, Hawthorne 156
The Nation 206
Nation & Novel (2006) 147
National Front 6, 120
National Women's Liberation 71
nationalism 51
Natives of My Person (1972)
Neave, Airey 1, 7
neoliberalism 49, 62
Neville, Richard 37
New English Library 27
'New New World Dreams' (1994) 30
'New Wave' of science fiction 25–30
New Worlds 25–30, 37
New York Review of Books 182, 196, 197, 206
   review of *Daniel Martin* (1977) 196–7
   review of *The Ice Age* (1977) 183–5
The New York Times Book Review 206
Nicholson, John 32
Nightbreed (1990) 33
Nights At the Circus (1984) 138
Nineteen Eighty-Four (1949) 49, 87, 88
Nobel Prize for Literature (2007) 48
Nora, Pierre 117

Norman, John 36
Northern Ireland 6–7, 57–8, 65–6
Not to Disturb (1971) 77–8, 194
Notting Hill Carnival 4–5, 93–4
nouveau roman 147–9, 188
novel 146–7
   'death of' 187–9, 194
'The Novel as Research' (1968–1970) 19, 147
The Novelist at the Crossroads (1971) 188
The Nowhere Man (1972) 96

Oakley, Ann 73
O'Brien, Conor Cruise 206–7
O'Brien, Tim 190
O'Day, Marc 21
The Odessa File (1972) 138–9
Okri, Ben 96
The Old Jest (1979) 58
Olivier, Laurence 126
'On Sex and Horror' (1998) 32
Only Fools and Horses 107
Onlywomen Press 72
Oranges Are Not the Only Fruit 84
Orbach, Susie 71, 73
Organisation of Women of Asian and African Descent (OWAAD) 109
Orientalism 206
Orwell, George 49, 87, 88
Other People (1981) 139
Out of the Shelter (1970) 120, 124–7, 129–30, 136, 139
Owusu, Kwesi 99
Oz 37

Paid Servant (1962) 101–3
Palmer, Paulina 81, 82, 83, 84, 85, 88
parody 137, 148–9
Parrinder, Patrick 147
The Passion of New Eve (1977) 28–9, 138
The Pastel City (1971) 37–8
Patriarchal Attitudes (1970) 73
patriarchy 74–5, 86
'patrician hegemony' 50
Peace, David 17
Peach, Blair 94
The People's War (1969) 122–3
Pensky, Max 237
Pentonville Five 151
Perks, Robert 126

personal experience 46
Phillips, Caryl 94–5, 96
A Piece of the Night 84–6
Pinkney, Tony 56
　analysis of Raymond Williams' work 53–4
Play Power (1971) 37
'pluri-culture' 95
The Poetics of Postmodernism (1988) 216
Policing the Crisis: Mugging, the State, and Law and Order 99
'The Politics of Anti-Realism'(1977) 202
pornographic writing 26–7
Possibilities: Essays on the State of the Novel (1971) 18–19, 188
post-experimental works 26
'post-realistic fiction' 209
Postwar British Fiction: New Accents and Attitudes (1962) 148
Post-War British Fiction: Realism and After (1995) 188
Powell, Anthony 21, 218
Powell, Enoch 4, 94, 151, 157
The Present (1975) 159–60
Priest, Christopher 10, 11, 12, 54, 62, 64, 65, 156, 157, 158, 159, 160, 161, 260
'Printing Liberation: The Women's Movement and Magazines in the 1970s' 17
Procter, James 95, 99
public schools 50
Public Sector Borrowing Requirement (PSBR) 2
pulp fiction 27–8
　impact on literary fiction 28
Punk Rock (1977) 27
Punter, David 38

A Question of Silence (1974) 79
Quin, Ann 11, 145, 163, 165, 171, 173, 174

Rabinovitz, Rubin 188
Race and Class 98
Race Relations Act 5, 93
Race Today 93
The Rachel Papers (1973) 21, 22, 23–4, 120, 131–2, 139

racial oppression 4–5, 97
　and police 4–6
racism *see* racial oppression
Raynor, Vivien 210n. 8
Rayner Heppenstall (2007) 154
The Reaction against Experiment in the English Novel 1950-1960 (1967) 188
A Reader's Guide to the Twentieth-Century Novel in Britain (1993) 18
Re: Colonised Planet 5: Shikasta (1979) 48–9, 54–5
Reagan, Ronald 49
realism 188, 191, 200–3
　versus experimentalism 188, 217–18
　'modified' 192
　reframing 207–9
recapitulation 18
The Red and the Green (1965) 218
Red Hedz (1990) 32
Red Riding Quartet (1999–2002) 17
Red Stains (1991) 32
Reluctant Neighbours 101, 103, 104
Rennison, Nick 22
revelation 18
Rhondda Roundabout (1934) 51
Rice, Philip 74
Rich, Adrienne 84
right-wing individualism 2, 8, 55, 164–5
Riley, Joan 94–5
'Rivers of Blood' 4
Robbe-Grille, Alain 148, 150, 188, 190, 202, 203
Roberts, Michèle 10, 69, 77, 79, 81, 84, 85, 86
Rock Against Racism (RAR) 5–6
Role Play Games 35
Rolling Stone, review of *The Ice Age* (1977) 185
A Room of One's Own (1929) 73
Rotten, Johnny 185
Rowbotham, Sheila 71, 73, 81
Rowe, Marsha 73
Rubin, David 218
Rubin, Jerry 37
Rushdie, Salman 5, 94, 96, 139, 140, 207

The Sadeian Woman (1979) 36
Said, Edward 206
Sale, Roger 205
Salkey, Andrew 94, 95

Salmagundi 202
Sampson, Anthony 206, 207
Samuel, Raphael 51, 123, 141nn. 2, 9
Sandbrook, Dominic 3, 5, 141nn. 6, 10, 142n. 12
Sarraute, Nathalie 188, 190
Satan's Slaves 29
satire 26, 97, 100, 104, 106, 108, 128, 130
Saturday (2005) 59-60
The Savoy Book (1978) 37
Scanlan, Margaret 219, 221, 225
Scholes, Robert 198, 201, 202, 208
Schor, Naomi 235
Schwarz, Bill 3
science fiction
 impact on literary fiction 28
 'New Wave' of 25-30
The Scorpion God 194
Scott, Paul 119, 136, 218
Scottish fiction 56-7, 65
Scottish nationalism 7-8, 45-6, 56-7
Second Generation (1964) 52
Second World War, relevance of 50, 118-19, 121-4
 generation gap 123
 versus present dynamism 127-30
Second-Class Citizen (1974) 79, 96, 101, 110-11
See the Old Lady Decently (1975) 168, 175-7
Segal, Lynne 71, 73
selective tradition 9
The Self-Conscious Novel: Artifice in Fiction from Joyce to Pynchon (1988) 146
Selvon, Sam 10, 94, 96, 97, 102, 104, 105, 106, 107, 108, 109, 110, 114
Seventies: the Sights, Sounds and Ideas of a Brilliant Decade (2006) 93
Several Perceptions (1968) 21
Sex Discrimination Act (1975) 72
Sex Pistols 185
sexual equality 36
sexuality 11, 22, 23-4
 and horror fiction 32
 and technology 26-7
 and teenage sex 47-8
 Victorian 148-50
 and women 72-3, 107-9
Shadow Dance (1966) 21

Shadows on Our Skin (1977) 57-8
Shame (1983) 140
Showalter, Elaine 73, 74
Shrew 70-1
The Siege of Babylon (1978) 96
The Siege of Krishnapur (1973) 119, 132-4, 215-16, 218
Simmons, Rochelle 17
simulacra 33-4
The Singapore Grip (1978) 119, 134, 136, 215-16
The Situation of the Novel (1970) 188
Sivanandan, A. 98, 99, 100
sixties, counter-culture of 21, 24
 end of 21-5
Skinhead Escapes (1972) 27
Skinhead Girls (1972) 27
Skinheads (1970) 27
Skinheads (2008) 28
Smith, Zadie 12, 89
social mobility 26
'The Social Significance of 1926' (1977) 51
Sontag, Susan 203
Sounes, Howard 93
South Africa 206-7
Spare Rib 72-3
Spark, Muriel 77, 193, 194, 208, 210n. 7, 215, 218
'speculative fiction' 28
Spicer, Andrew 154
Spinrad, Norman 26
Spurling, John 221, 231, 235
spy fiction 30-1, 134-5
Stein, Mark 98
Stevenson, Randall 18, 57, 95, 218
Stoke Newington Eight trial 163-4
Stonehill, Brian 146
Stories, theories and things (1991) 148-9, 167, 170-1
Studies in Contemporary Fiction, review of *The Ice Age* (1977) 186-7
stylization 23-4
suburban bohemia 21
Success (1978) 21, 22
Suedehead (1971) 27
Suez Canal 1, 128
Sukenick, Ronald 189, 197, 199, 209n. 2
The Summer before the Dark (1973) 78
'sus' laws 5

Tales I Tell My Mother (1978) 81, 84
Tate, Sharon 172
Taylor, D. J. 218
teenage sex 47–8
television 3, 5, 107, 120
   commercial 43
   consumer 43–4
Tennant, Emma 10, 69, 77, 79, 80, 260–1
Tew, Philip 1–12, 145–77
Thatcher, Margaret 1–3, 8, 44, 99, 114, 135–6, 140
   neoliberal policies 49, 62
Themerson, Stefan 145
Thompson, E. P. 51, 60, 122, 123, 126, 127
Three Day Week 120
Thru (1975) 170–1
Time 182
'Time of Plenty: Recent British Novels' 187, 192
Tinker, Tailor, Soldier, Spy (1974) 134
Todd, Selina 70, 73
Tolkien, J. R. R. 35, 36
Tornado Pratt (1977) 171, 174–5
To Sir, With Love (1959) 101–3
totalitarianism 49
Towards 2000 (1983) 44
trades unions 1, 2, 8, 18, 45, 55, 62, 103, 154
tradition, concept of 15–16
Transport and General Workers' Union 62
The Tree of the Sun (1978) 96
Tremain, Rose 69, 89
Tripticks (1972) 171, 173–4
Troubled Pleasures: The Fiction of J. G. Farrell (1997) 217
Troubles (1970) 58, 119, 132–4, 218
   aesthetics of detail 234–40
   allegory and perspective 222–34
   colonial parallel 226
   comments on 221
   concept of Ireland 225–6, 228
   Lost Man Booker prize 215–16
   melancholy 229–33
Turner, Alwyn W. 151
'Twentieth Century War' 49
Two Moons (1977) 154–5, 163, 165

Ulster Volunteers Force 6
unemployment, *see* crises, social
United States, *see* American literary scene; American perception of British novels
The Unlimited Dream Company (1979) 159–61
The Unmapped Country (1975) 173

Victorian era 11, 136, 148–50
Vietnam 118
violence 22–3, 31–2, 151–3, 155
Virago Press 72
Viriconium novel 38
'The Voice of the Beach' 34
Voices of the Living and the Dead 100
The Volunteers (1978) 54–5, 65
Von Clausewitz, Carl 227

Wages for Housework Campaign 71, 87–8
Walmsley, Ann 96
Wandor, Michelene 81
The Warlock of Firetop Mountain (1981) 35
Warner, Marina 73
The Wasp Factory (1984) 32
Waters, Sarah 89
Watership Down (1972) 35–6
Watson, Ben 36
Watts, Carol 166
Waugh, Patricia 74, 76, 77, 78, 79, 80, 86, 88
We Are Everywhere (1971) 37
Weis, Margaret 35
Weldon, Fay 10, 18, 69, 71, 77, 78, 80
Welfare State International 17
We Live (1939) 51
Wells, Steven 27
'Welsh Culture' (1975) 51
'The Welsh Industrial Novel' (1979) 51
Welsh nationalism 7–8, 46
Welshness in fiction 51–4
When the Lights Went Out: What Really Happened to Britain in the Seventies (2009) 17, 45, 93
Whisper: A Time Script (1971) 37
White, Tony 27
Whiteley, Gillian 17
Williams, Mark P. 15
Williams, Raymond 9, 10, 12, 15, 50, 261
   consumerism 43–4

exclusion from working-class communities 51–2
'mobile privatisation' 44
persistence of agency 55–6
science fiction elements 54
Wilson, Amrit 73, 109
Wilson, Anna 79, 80
Wilson, Elizabeth 73
Wilson, Harold 2, 118
winter of discontent 2, 62, 120
Winterson, Jeanette 10, 69, 80, 89
Wise Children (1991) 138, 139
Women's Aid Federation 71
Women's Liberation Movement 69, 70
basic demands 71, 72, 76

Women's Liberation Workshop 70
Women's Press 72, 84
Woolf, Virginia 73
working-class culture 25, 26, 28
The World and the Book: A Study of Modern Fiction (1971) 145
World at War (1973) 122
Writing Black Britain (2000) 95

xenophobia 122–3

'youth exploitation' novels 27–8

zeitgeist 200–1
Zola, Émile 146

www.ingramcontent.com/pod-product-compliance
Ingram Content Group UK Ltd.
Pitfield, Milton Keynes, MK11 3LW, UK
UKHW021905220326
469204UK00008B/197